Intimate Lies and the Law

Intimate Lies
and the Law

JILL ELAINE HASDAY

OXFORD
UNIVERSITY PRESS

OXFORD
UNIVERSITY PRESS

Oxford University Press is a department of the University of Oxford. It furthers the University's objective of excellence in research, scholarship, and education by publishing worldwide. Oxford is a registered trade mark of Oxford University Press in the UK and certain other countries.

Published in the United States of America by Oxford University Press
198 Madison Avenue, New York, NY 10016, United States of America.

Library of Congress Cataloging-in-Publication Data
Names: Hasday, Jill Elaine, author.
Title: Intimate lies and the law / Jill Elaine Hasday.
Description: New York, NY : Oxford University Press, 2019. |
Includes bibliographical references and index.
Identifiers: LCCN 2019002682 | ISBN 9780190905941 (hardback)
Subjects: LCSH: Fraud—Social aspects—United States. |
Domestic relations—United States.
Classification: LCC KF1271 .H37 2019 | DDC 346.7301/5—dc23
LC record available at https://lccn.loc.gov/2019002682

1 3 5 7 9 8 6 4 2

Printed by Sheridan Books, Inc., United States of America

To my loved ones. You did not inspire me to write this book.

CONTENTS

Introduction

So Much Deception, So Little Time

Suppose you discovered one day that the foundations of your life were shakier than you ever imagined. An intimate relationship that you thought was grounded in trust actually depended on deception. The betrayal could take many forms. You could discover that your husband secretly sold the family business away from you.[1] You could learn that your wife surreptitiously siphoned money from the marital coffers to fund her affairs.[2] You could find out that your boyfriend, who knew you wanted to have a child, lured you into a sexual relationship by deceiving you to conceal his vasectomy.[3] You could learn that your ex-girlfriend spent months falsely claiming to be pregnant, even after her deceit helped trigger your wife's suicide.[4] You could discover that your fiancé duped you into resigning by falsely claiming that your employer would not permit engaged couples to work together.[5] You could find out that your father tricked you into giving away your share of the family home by lying about the paperwork he demanded you sign.[6]

After the initial shock and sadness, you might wonder whether the law will help you secure redress for the harms you have suffered. But these people, like most deceived intimates, got no help from the courts. The law's interest in condemning, deterring, and remediating deceit did not extend to deception within an intimate relationship. Why not?

This book uncovers a legal field that has been hidden in plain sight, revealing an enormous body of law that has not been systematically examined. People often assume that deception within intimate relationships is a quintessentially private phenomenon that courts and legislatures leave untouched. But the law pervasively regulates intimate deception. Inside courtrooms and beyond them, legal rules, practices, and presumptions create incentives to deceive, make deception easier to accomplish, and protect deceptive intimates while routinely denying remedies to the people they duped.

Intimacy and deception are often entangled. Many sexual, marital, and familial relationships pivot on deception about matters that one or both parties consider vitally important. People turn to deceit to lure someone into intimacy or to keep her there, to drain an intimate's bank account or to use her to secure government benefits, to dominate an intimate or to resist an intimate's domination, and for myriad other purposes. No subject is immune from deception. Intimates lie or otherwise intentionally mislead each other about anything and everything.

Deceit can rob someone of control over his own life, limiting choices, distorting decisionmaking, and destroying plans. Deceived intimates have experienced severe—even life-altering—injuries, including financial losses, illnesses and infections, physical endangerment and abuse, violations of sexual autonomy and bodily integrity, unexpected vulnerability to criminal prosecution, lost time, missed opportunities, and emotional distress.

Examining the regulation of intimate deception across legal doctrines and subjects makes clear that the law has shielded this persistent and pervasive source of injury. The legal system treats deception within intimacy differently than deception outside of it, regularly blocking deceived intimates from accessing the remedies that are available for deception in other contexts. Courts tend to blame deceived intimates for having been fooled and to overlook how difficult detecting an intimate's deceit can be, in part because the law wisely prohibits some forms of investigation in order to safeguard privacy, liberty, and security.

I argue that the law has placed too much emphasis on protecting intimate deceivers and too little importance on helping the people they deceive. Judges and legislators should not begin with an unexamined assumption that deception within intimacy is different in kind from deception outside it. Legal authorities can and should do more to recognize, prevent, and redress the injuries that intimate deceivers inflict, giving deceived intimates access to the same causes of action they would have if equivalently deceived outside of intimacy, countering incentives to deceive, and thwarting duplicitous intimates from accomplishing their plans. The law should not refuse to help just because the deception took place between intimates. Entering an intimate relationship—or being duped into one—should not mean losing legal protection from deceit.

Intimate deception and its governance have attracted remarkably little critical scrutiny, but the field is illuminating and important. Legal decisionmakers regulating deceit within intimacy make judgments that extend beyond any specific case to reflect, configure, and enforce societal norms. Courts and legislatures classify relationships as intimate or not, establish the legal consequences of forming intimate ties, announce what counts as acceptable conduct within intimacy, and decide which harms deserve legal redress. They respond to existing practices and standards of behavior and simultaneously help mold those practices and standards by officially classifying conduct as either normal and expected or deviant and blameworthy. Judges and lawmakers have also used their regulation of intimate deception as a powerful platform for expressing and enacting their views on gender, race, class, national origin, and other divides.

When I started work on this book, I suspected that courts denying remedies to deceived intimates might be operating on the assumption that intimate deception is not important enough to merit judicial attention. Instead, however, courts routinely take their intimate deception decisions to be crucially important opportunities to define what counts as ordinary behavior in intimate relationships and to enforce that vision of normalcy by shielding what judges understand to be commonplace intimate deception from legal redress and legal condemnation. We are living in an era when odes to marriage and intimacy abound. But rather than valorize intimate life, judges reasoning about intimate deception commonly accept and protect a much gloomier vision that presumes the ubiquity—even naturalness and inevitability—of significant deceit in intimate relationships.

American popular culture has long shared the judiciary's intense interest in intimate deception. The topic endlessly inspires discussion, gossip, news reporting, and (most recently) reality television.[7] Countless works of fiction, drama, and song revolve around deceit within intimacy. This fascination simultaneously reflects the prevalence of intimate deception, the curiosity it sparks when it has happened to someone else, and the disruption and harm it can inflict. Intimate deception can implicate virtually every human emotion, from love and triumph to greed, envy, shame, and rage.

There are several potential explanations for the paucity of sustained critical analysis. First, the regulation of intimate deception cuts across traditional categories within and outside the law. It overlaps and intersects with the regulation of families, torts, contracts, property, public health, privacy, and even crime. At the same time, understanding the law's treatment of intimate deception requires an interdisciplinary investigation that reaches beyond conventional legal materials like judicial opinions and statutes to also include historical sources, psychological findings, anthropological studies, sociological research, philosophical treatises, medical literature, popular commentary, and first-person accounts by people who have deceived their intimates or been deceived.

Recognizing and tracking phenomena that extend through many arenas can become more difficult as scholarship becomes increasingly specialized. Looking across doctrinal and disciplinary boundaries allows us to appreciate and assess the full scope of the law's regulation of intimate deception, revealing recurring themes and choices as well as some conspicuous inconsistencies and disjunctions.

A second potential explanation for the scarcity of critical attention is that the law often regulates intimate deception by denying deceived intimates remedies. In fact, the available legal relief has contracted significantly since the early twentieth century. As intended, the limited likelihood of success dissuades many deceived intimates from filing suit—although a steady stream of litigation persists nonetheless. Judicial opinions frequently drive the agendas of legal scholars, who as a group tend to focus on the law's most visible manifestations. The law governing intimate deception is less likely to attract notice to the extent that it operates by discouraging rather than producing lawsuits.

However, the legal system is regulating intimate deception whether the law sides more frequently with plaintiffs or defendants. Whether courts and legislatures choose to provide deceived intimates with remedies or not, they are determining the legal rules, rights, and obligations that govern deception within intimate relationships. Either way, the law is distributing entitlements, structuring incentives, enforcing normative judgments, and setting baselines. The question is not *whether* the law will govern intimate deception; the law already pervades this arena and will continue to do so. The relevant questions are about *how* the law will govern, when, why, where, and in whose interests.

A third possible explanation for the comparative paucity of critical attention is that deceit within intimate relationships is often associated with women's injuries and women's claims. The underexamination of intimate deception parallels and reinforces deeply rooted presumptions within and outside the law discounting harms that women disproportionately experience.

Popular culture routinely assumes that men are more likely to deceive their intimates and women are more likely to be deceived. The self-help literature features titles like *101 Lies Men Tell Women*,[8] *Why Men Must Lie*,[9] and *Romantic Deception: The Six Signs He's Lying*.[10] Women's magazines focus on how women are deceived within intimate relationships. *Glamour* published *Should the Law Punish Lovers Who Lie?*, an article reporting that 64% of the respondents to the magazine's survey said that someone had induced them to have sex by lying to them and 84% agreed that legal remedies should be available to people who have suffered physical injuries stemming from a sexual partner's lies.[11] A men's magazine like *Maxim*, in turn, starts from the premise that its readers have deceived their intimates, plan on remaining deceitful, and would like tips for improving their techniques to reduce the chances they will get caught. *Maxim*'s articles include *Fake Your Way into Her Bed* and *Perfect Your Poker Face: Card Champs Mike Caro and Chris Ferguson Show How Bluffing Can Help You Get Lucky*.[12]

This conventional wisdom notwithstanding, the available evidence cannot establish whether women are more likely to be deceived within intimacy and men are more likely to deceive. Although a few studies have reported findings along those lines, the social science research on this topic remains extremely underdeveloped. For example, a survey of 196 male and 226 female sexually active college students in southern California,[13] a survey of 169 University of Minnesota undergraduates,[14] and a survey of 153 sexually active high school students in San Francisco found that men were more likely to report having told a lie in order to have sex, while women were more likely to report having been lied to so they would have sex.[15] A study of 239 men and 240 women attending a university in the southwestern United States found that more women than men reported that a past partner had deceptively overstated his income.[16]

However, the existing research has been confined to small-scale investigations that asked limited numbers of respondents a narrow range of questions. This research has also relied on self-reports, and determining the extent to which the findings reflect actual differences in rates of deception is not possible. Perhaps men are simply more willing to report deceit they have committed and women are more willing to report deceit they have experienced. To my knowledge, there are no broad, representative studies available that would support general conclusions about whether men or women are more likely to deceive their intimates. But assumptions nonetheless persist that the typical intimate deceiver is male and the typical deceived intimate is female. Those assumptions have probably contributed to the lack of critical attention devoted to this arena.

A final explanation for the scarcity of sustained critical analysis is that thinking too much or too long about intimate deception can be disquieting. Readers may find that the stories in this book alternate between comedy and tragedy, hilarity and heartbreak, and sometimes embody both extremes at once.

The stories can seem amusing because they are not about us, we can tell ourselves that we would not have been fooled, and we know how the stories end. Discovering that an intimate has deceived you is often a bitter shock, but deception tends to seem more obvious and detectable to third parties considering the matter in hindsight after the deceit has already been revealed. Here, moreover, readers have the advantage of knowing at the outset that any example in these pages is likely to involve intimate deception.

Nonetheless, many of the stories in this book are sad and discomforting—even when read about rather than lived. People generally expect and believe that their closest companions are trustworthy. They rely on that foundation in structuring their lives. Deception betrays that, and deceived intimates frequently suffer serious harms whose sting may be all the sharper when legal redress is unavailable.

Moreover, the unsettling reality is that deception is prevalent in intimate relationships. Most of us would like to think that intimacy shields us from deceit and that any deception that does occur is an anomaly confined to a few relationships—not involving us or anyone like us. But intimacy and deception are often intertwined, and intimate deception can harm people in all walks of life. The unease associated with acknowledging the frequency of intimate deception helps explain the paucity of critical attention.

Some people may also be uncomfortable examining intimate deception as a social practice and subject of legal regulation because the evidence features deceived intimates who have not quietly forgiven their deceivers. Instead, they have sought legal remedies or otherwise disclosed their experiences to people outside their inner circles. They have challenged how their intimates treated them, insisted that they deserved better than to be injured through deception, and asked for recognition that their intimates wronged them. Just as there is a widespread expectation that intimates will be trustworthy, some people expect deceived intimates—especially if they are women—to forgive their deceivers and stay silent about the deceit. The cases and stories in this book reveal the voices of deceived intimates who do not want to forgive and who are not quiet.

An Abundance of Intimate Deception

Deception within intimate relationships and the body of law governing the field are enormous topics. The title of this introduction—*So Much Deception, So Little Time*—is meant to both highlight the relative scarcity of previous scholarly interest and acknowledge that one book cannot cover every aspect of the law and phenomenon of intimate deception.

My working definition of intimates includes dates, sexual and/or romantic partners, and family members such as spouses, parents, and children. I do not think that this is a perfect definition, or the only possible one, or necessarily the best one. In fact, I doubt whether an ideal and unassailable definition of intimacy exists. However, this book focuses on how ideas about intimacy are deployed in law. My working definition of intimacy reflects how judges think about intimacy (whether or not they use that term), tracking the law's tendency to distinguish between deception in sexual, marital, and familial relationships and deception in other contexts. Accordingly, my definition of intimacy does not include everyone a person might feel close to or confide in, such as a friend, clergy member, therapist, or accountant. At the same time, some of the people who come within my working definition of intimacy may never have known each other well—much less loved each other. Some people who deceive an intimate exploit their intense familiarity with each other, and some people who deceive an intimate exploit their unfamiliarity with each other. People who dated briefly or had sex once fall within my definition of intimacy because courts treat them as intimates. One remarkable aspect of the law governing deception within supposedly intimate relationships is that this body of law extends to regulate many abbreviated and superficial interactions. Courts tend to define intimacy broadly when considering deception in romantic and/or sexual relationships. In contrast, courts tend to define intimacy narrowly when considering deception in familial relationships, excluding family members not connected by marriage or parenthood—such as siblings, aunts, uncles, nieces, and nephews.

I also follow courts in focusing on relationships as they existed when the deceit took place. By the time litigation begins, the parties often do not consider themselves to be intimates any longer and they are likely to be divorced or divorcing if they were once married to each other. But judges deciding lawsuits emphasize whether the parties shared an intimate relationship at the time of the deception—even if that relationship has since ended, perhaps because the plaintiff discovered the defendant's deceit.

I define deception as intentional acts or omissions—including statements, deeds, and silence—designed to make another person believe something that the deceiver himself does not believe to be true. I derived this definition from the large philosophical and social science literature discussing the definition of deception.[17] I wanted to use a definition of deception that was independent from what courts recognize as wrongful behavior. Adopting a consistent definition of deception that does not turn on whether a court has reached a legal judgment that the defendant deceived the plaintiff allows me to capture a fuller picture of how the law regulates intimate deception, including by denying claims.

To conclude that an intimate was deceived does not necessarily mean that the intimate had a right to the truth, that the deceiver had a duty—legal, moral, or otherwise—to disclose the truth, or that the deceiver has no redeeming qualities and nothing to say in his own defense. Deeming an act or omission deceptive means only that the deceiver deliberately sought to mislead his intimate. For example, a person may have no obligation to reveal how much money he has, how he has been spending his time, what he has done in the past, or the state of his health. He may even reasonably think that he is morally justified in lying about or obfuscating those facts. But he is nonetheless being deceptive if he intentionally misleads someone into thinking that he is wealthy, or attending school, or never married, or healthy when he knows all that is untrue.

I will insert an explanation about pronouns here. I used "his" and "he" in the preceding paragraph because the English language sometimes forces sex-specificity where none is intended—a remarkably persistent weakness in the language. Similarly, I sometimes use "her" or "she" because there are no sex-neutral alternatives. I considered using either masculine or feminine pronouns exclusively throughout the book, but was concerned that such an approach would lead readers to lose sight of the reality that both intimate deceivers and the people they deceive can be male or female. Ultimately, I decided that I would sometimes use male pronouns and sometimes use female pronouns when no sex-neutral pronoun is available. I will note when a particular type of deception—or litigation about a particular type of deception—appears to have a sex imbalance, with men or women more prominent as deceivers or deceived.

Lies may be the type of deception that springs first to mind. When someone deceives by lying, she intentionally makes a statement—verbally or in writing—that she believes is untrue, but wants her target to think is true.

However, lies are hardly the sole form of deception. Deliberate omissions with intent to mislead can perform the same functions as lies and may be a much more prevalent type of deception. Here, a person refrains from revealing information because he wants his intimate to believe something that the deceiver thinks is false. For every adulterer who has lied by falsely denying infidelity, there are probably many more people who have intentionally misled their spouses by not disclosing unfaithfulness. Mark Twain, an astute observer of deception, estimated only half-jokingly in 1899 "that the proportion of the spoken lie to the other varieties is as 1 to 22,894."[18]

Intentional omissions designed to mislead may be such a popular form of deception because they can offer deceivers many advantages over lies. Some deceivers may be more comfortable rationalizing their behavior to themselves when they deliberately mislead through omissions rather than lies. At the same time, deliberate concealment can be both easier to accomplish and more useful than lying. Intentionally concealing information can be less taxing than constructing a convincing lie. Similarly, a deceiver may find it easier to remember that she purposely withheld information than to recall the details of a lie she told. In addition, deceivers may believe that their target is more likely to discover evidence that unmasks a lie than to discover evidence that reveals a deliberate omission meant to mislead. If an intentional omission is uncovered, moreover, the deceiver may be able to pretend—in or out of court—that his failure to reveal information was inadvertent, whereas pretending that a false statement was accidental may be harder.

Deception can also take myriad other forms, including half-truths, exaggerations, distortions, and misdirections. Indeed, the potential manifestations of deception may be innumerable given the ingenuity of some deceivers. Even literally true statements can be deceptive if the speaker makes the true statement for the purpose of leading the listener to a false conclusion. A politician once expressed this point by asking: "What *is* the use of lying, when truth, well distributed, serves the same purpose?"[19] Focusing on lies alone would miss much of the deception within intimate relationships.

Recognizing what does not constitute deception is equally important. Consider an intimate who makes a promise or announces a plan intending to fulfill it, but then changes his mind. Such reversals can inflict significant injury—and there are many intriguing questions about how the law does and should respond to this kind of injury that I could explore in another book. But if a person meant to carry out his promise or plan when he declared his intentions and then did not mislead his intimate about his change of mind, the injury does not stem from deception because there was no intent to deceive. Instead, the injury stems from the change of mind itself. Determining whether a person has been deceptive or has just reconsidered may sometimes be difficult, but a person's behavior and statements over time often provide strong evidence about his initial intentions.

Similarly, the simple fact that a person has remained silent about something does not necessarily mean that she has been deceptive. A person might not reveal information to an intimate for many reasons. For example, the person may have forgotten about it, assumed the intimate was not interested, mistakenly thought she had already revealed the information, or wanted to keep certain subjects private and not discuss them. It is impossible to tell someone else everything that one thought and did every day. Moreover, people who are determined to avoid deceitfulness do not need to reveal everything they possibly can to their intimates. Failing to convey information is deceptive only when the person stays silent because she wants her intimate to believe something that the deceiver herself believes to be false.

Accordingly, a person is not deceptive when he makes a false statement or conveys a false impression because he believes the statement or impression to be correct. A mistaken or deluded person may be objectively wrong and his error may harm others. Yet there is no intent to mislead if the mistaken or deluded person believes the same propositions that he is trying to convince the listener to believe are true. Some people who are mistaken or deluded about the truth might be engaged in self-deception—probably the most common and the most intimate kind of deception of them all. And again, considering self-deception and how the law does and should respond to that phenomenon could fill another book. Deceiving others, however, requires an intent to mislead.

An abundance of intimate deception remains, even after recognizing these definitional boundaries. While working on this project, I have been asked about which kinds of intimate deception I find most surprising. No example surprises me anymore. Any topic that anyone might imagine—anything that might matter to one or both people in a relationship—has been the subject of intimate deception. The list is endless.

This book examines both the social practice of intimate deception and its legal regulation, so I have focused the bulk of my attention on types of deceit that intimates have been most likely to bring to legal forums. There tend to be patterns to the sort of deception that leads deceived intimates to come forward despite the obstacles, expense, and public exposure involved.

For this reason, I am concentrating on instances of deception that succeeded in duping an intimate—meaning that the person subject to the deception was convinced by it, at least for a while, and thought that the messages the deceiver was conveying through his words, actions, or inactions were true. A lie is a lie whether or not the listener ever believes it, and the same holds for other forms of deception. Moreover, deceit can wound someone even when she recognizes right away that her intimate is trying to dupe her. But intimate deception usually causes less injury when it is uncovered immediately, and intimates who were told a lie that never fooled them have been much less likely to seek legal redress.

I am not focusing on deception that was in the deceived intimate's best interests—according to the deceived intimate herself. Essentially by definition, these instances of intimate deception do not produce lawsuits or other calls for legal relief or reform because the deceived person concludes after learning about the deception that the deceit did not harm him and/or was justified.

For example, both the deceived intimate and her deceiver may appreciate and benefit from some quotidian examples of deception, such as insincere compliments on appearance or accomplishments. False reassurances along the lines of "you look wonderful tonight" or—my personal favorite—"I really enjoyed reading your book" may sometimes be important to the daily contentment of listener and speaker alike. Similarly, remaining silent so an intimate does not realize that his behavior is momentarily annoying, or pretending to be interested in the details of an intimate's day, may sometimes leave everyone happier and calmer. Indeed, interacting with an intimate who refused to offer insincere compliments, hide temporary annoyance, or feign interest in your daily activities could be harsh and unpleasant for all concerned. Here too, Mark Twain made the point well. "None of us," he observed in 1882, "could *live* with an habitual truth-teller; but thank goodness none of us has to."[20] A hundred and ten years later, 72% of the more than three thousand readers who took *McCall's* "marriage-ethics survey" reported that it was ethical to tell one's husband that he looks "'fantastic' even though he's starting to look old."[21] There is no reason to expect that deceit along these lines would be brought to the attention of legal authorities, and it is not.

Yet intimate deception is often not mutually satisfactory. Deceivers routinely tell themselves that they are acting in everyone's best interests because the intimates they are deceiving are better off not knowing the truth, even about vital issues with high stakes. It is hardly surprising that such rationalizations appeal to people deceiving their intimates. But intimates who discover that they have been duped often do not think that the deception benefited them and frequently conclude that the deceiver's purported concern for them was a facade covering the deceiver's determination to advance his own interests at his intimate's expense.[22]

In short, there is a tremendous amount of deception within intimate relationships to consider. Little research has directly targeted this subject. But empirical investigations conducted for other purposes—along with evidence revealed within legal cases and first-person accounts such as memoirs or interviews—can provide a sense of the range and frequency of intimate deception when the material is examined with that issue in mind.

What Do People Deceive Their Intimates About?

One obvious topic of deception within intimate relationships is infidelity. Surveys find robust rates of sexual unfaithfulness—even when the surveys are limited to studying people's behavior during marriage, which might be expected to be more monogamous. For example, four studies examining large, nationally representative samples all found substantial percentages of respondents who admitted to having committed adultery during their marriages, with the figures ranging from 13.3% of the respondents in one study,[23] to 11.6% of the women and 22.7% of the men in another study,[24] to 15.0% of the women and 24.5% of the men in a third study,[25] to 31% of the respondents in a fourth study.[26]

The existing research focuses on infidelity itself, rather than deception about infidelity, so these large-scale studies do not ask respondents whether they have been deceitful to conceal their infidelity from their primary sexual partner. But it is probably safe to assume that such deception is common, although not universal, among the sexually unfaithful. The many first-person accounts and lawsuits describing a sexual partner's infidelity and its aftermath almost always discuss the unfaithful partner's deceit to hide the infidelity.[27] One small-scale study asking 173 people about "the most serious lie they ever told" and/or "the most serious lie ever told to them" found that concealing sexual unfaithfulness was the most commonly cited motivation for these lies.[28]

However, infidelity is hardly the only subject that people deceive their intimates about. We can start by considering other issues linked to sexuality that are recurring topics for intimate deceivers.

Considerable intimate deception appears to revolve around children's biological parenthood, especially paternity. Many first-person accounts and cases discuss women who deceived their husbands, boyfriends, or other sexual partners to conceal who their child's biological father was or might be.[29] No large-scale empirical studies have focused on this deceit itself, but researchers have attempted to measure how often a child's supposed biological father is not the actual biological father. A review consolidating the findings of sixty-seven studies from across the globe found that typically 1.7% to 3.3% of "men with high paternity confidence" were not the biological father of a child they thought was their offspring. In addition, over a quarter (29.8%) of the men with "low paternity confidence," who had sought laboratory testing to dispute their paternity, were not the biological father of the child at issue.[30]

Researchers have been less interested in situations where women do not know the truth about the biological paternity of a child born to someone else. But numerous first-person accounts and lawsuits feature men who deceived their intimates by denying or concealing that they had fathered a child. Former presidential candidate John Edwards, who reportedly lied to his wife about having fathered a child with his girlfriend, provides a prominent example of a man denying paternity of a child his wife knew had been born.[31] Other men who fathered a child either as part of an infidelity or in a prior relationship have concealed the child's entire existence from their wives, fiancées, girlfriends, and/or other children.[32]

Likewise, many first-person accounts and lawsuits feature parents who intentionally misled a child about the identity of her biological father—or the identities of her biological father and mother—by concealing from the child that she was adopted,[33] or conceived through assisted insemination by donor,[34] or conceived in an affair,[35] or conceived in a prior relationship.[36] In addition, some parents have hidden from their children that the children have full or half-siblings who were adopted away into other families.[37]

Birth control, fertility, and/or the desire for children are also persistent subjects of intimate deception. First-person accounts and lawsuits discuss a range of variations, including sexual partners who lied in claiming they had been sterilized,[38] sexual partners who lied in claiming they were using birth control,[39] sexual partners who hid that they had poked holes in the couple's condoms,[40] sexual partners who concealed their use of contraception in order to convey the impression that they were not using it,[41] sexual partners who lied about whether they were pregnant,[42] and fiancés who lied about their desire to have children or their intent not to have them.[43] Here again, empirical researchers have not systematically focused on this kind of deception, but investigations directed at other topics sometimes reveal its presence. Scholars interviewing women for small-scale studies of domestic violence have found that a notable proportion of the women report deceiving their abusive partners about their use of birth control.[44]

In addition, intimate deception about sexual orientation persists. Recall that deception requires intentional action or inaction designed to make someone else believe something that the deceiver believes to be false. So a person who thinks—or has convinced himself—that he is straight is not being deceptive when he conveys that information to others, even if he later realizes that he is not heterosexual. However, some people have written or spoken about deliberately misleading their intimates to conceal their homosexuality or bisexuality,[45] and several lawsuits have focused on such deceit.[46] Many of the intimates who have publicly discussed their experiences as the target of this type of deception are heterosexual women who were married to homosexual or bisexual men who lied about their sexual orientation or deliberately concealed it from their wives with the intent to mislead.[47]

No large-scale empirical investigations have focused on measuring the prevalence of intimate deception about sexual orientation. But empirical research on related subjects reveals a significant number of women questioning their husband's sexual orientation. A 2013 study found that the word "gay" was the most common ending for Google searches in the United States that began "Is my husband . . . ." These searches were 10% more common than searches asking whether a husband was "cheating," eight times more common than searches asking whether a husband was "an alcoholic," and ten times more common than searches asking whether a husband was "depressed." Twenty-one of the twenty-five states where searches about whether a husband was gay were most frequent had below-average support for same-sex marriage, suggesting that marriages that lead women to question their husband's sexual orientation are concentrated in states with less support for gay rights.[48]

The available evidence, although very incomplete, similarly suggests that sexual history is a persistent subject of intimate deception. In one study of 322 sexually active college students, 23.7% of the students reported that they had lied to a potential sexual partner about their sexual history and 17.7% reported that they had lied to a family member about their sexual history.[49] Two other studies of college students utilized nonfunctioning polygraph machines to measure deception about sexual history—albeit not deception directed at intimates specifically. The first study of 105 female and 96 male unmarried, heterosexual college students connected a subset of the participants to a machine that could supposedly detect dishonest answers and found that the average number of sexual partners the women reported was higher than the men's average reported number. In contrast, when another subset of the participants was not connected to any purported lie detecting machine and was led to believe that a peer might see their responses, the men reported more sexual partners than the women.[50] A second study of 160 female and 133 male unmarried college students who did not identify themselves as bisexual or homosexual similarly found that women reported more sexual partners than men when they were connected to a purported lie detecting machine, while men reported more sexual partners than women when they were not connected to any supposed lie detecting machine.[51]

Intimate deception about marital history and marital status are also recurring topics within first-person accounts and lawsuits. Some divorced people present themselves to new mates as never married or widowed.[52] Some people lie about their number of previous spouses. One husband told his wife that their marriage was his third, when it actually was his fourth.[53] Other people have made more dramatic alterations in discussing their marital history with their fiancés, claiming two previous husbands when the real number was seven,[54] or three ex-husbands when the true number was eight.[55]

Some people deceive their intimates about whether they are currently married or not. Probably the most common scenarios involve married people falsely presenting themselves to dates and sexual partners as unmarried. Numerous lawsuits and first-person accounts focus on such deceit,[56] and many people in the dating world think it is widespread.[57] Yet there is a dearth of carefully controlled studies attempting to measure the prevalence of this type of deception. That said, one study surveyed a self-selected group of 6581 people who completed a questionnaire on the websites of "Canada's main online dating service" and found that 11% of the male respondents and 8% of the female respondents reported having misrepresented their marital status in online personal ads.[58] True. com, an online dating service in the United States that sought to exclude married people by verifying the marital status of all users, claimed in 2007 that it rejected 3% of its applicants and in 2005 that it rejected 4% because the applicants were married and had lied about it.[59]

Other types of intimate deception about marital status are less common, but still visible. Some people have staged fake marriage ceremonies to dupe their partners into thinking that they have been legally married.[60] Some people have secretly obtained divorces while concealing their conduct from their spouses or falsely denying it.[61] Some have not only falsely presented themselves as unmarried, but have committed bigamy by marrying again without first obtaining a divorce. Crime reports, news accounts, and lawsuits periodically feature men with two or more wives who did not know about each other.[62] One man married four women without any woman learning about the others and found that his web of deceit was so elaborate that he needed written notes to help him remember all his lies. When his deceit was unmasked and police officers searched his home, they reportedly discovered that one of his note cards was entitled "Who to Marry." It listed several additional women's names.[63]

Intimate deception also frequently revolves around health issues. Perhaps most prominently, many first-person accounts and lawsuits discuss people who concealed their sexually transmitted diseases from their intimates through lies or deliberate omissions with intent to mislead.[64] In addition, public health researchers studying whether people with sexually transmitted diseases reveal their infections to their sexual partners have repeatedly found significant rates of nondisclosure. The existing public health research tends not to explore whether the respondents have been deceptive,[65] and it is possible that many people remained silent about their sexually transmitted diseases because they thought that their sexual partners already knew or assumed they were infected. But it seems likely that at least some people who remained silent were being deceptive, meaning they wanted their sexual partners to draw the incorrect conclusion that they were uninfected.

Much of the public health research on nondisclosure has focused on people infected with human immunodeficiency virus (HIV). Studies have consistently found that some HIV-positive people do not disclose their infection to their primary sexual partner, and more people do not disclose their HIV infection to short-term or casual sexual partners. One study of a nationally representative sample of HIV-positive people found that 42% of the gay or bisexual men, 19% of the heterosexual men, and 17% of the women reported having had sex without disclosing that they were HIV-positive. The sex without disclosure occurred predominantly in nonexclusive relationships, but 5% of the women and 1% to 2% of the men reported that they had not revealed their HIV infection to an exclusive sexual partner whose HIV status was negative or unknown. Most of the people who reported having sex without disclosure denied engaging in unprotected anal or vaginal sex. That said, the HIV-positive respondents reported that they had unprotected anal or vaginal sex without disclosure in 13% of their sexual relationships with partners whose HIV status was negative or unknown.[66] Another review consolidated the results from sixteen studies of HIV-positive men and found that just 67% to 88% of the men reported disclosing their HIV infection to their primary sex partner, and just 25% to 58% of the men reported disclosing their HIV infection to all sex partners.[67] Research focused on people with other sexually transmitted diseases has similarly uncovered considerable nondisclosure.[68]

Other health issues also appear to be common subjects of intimate deception. Many first-person accounts and lawsuits feature people who lied or otherwise intentionally misled their intimates to conceal their addictions, such as alcoholism,[69] drug addiction,[70] compulsive gambling,[71] or smoking.[72] Similarly, numerous first-person accounts and lawsuits discuss people who deceived their intimates about whether they had other serious diseases, such as amyotrophic lateral sclerosis,[73] polycystic kidney disease,[74] or myelodysplastic syndrome.[75] People usually deceive their intimates by pretending to be healthier than they are. However, sometimes people take advantage of their intimates by pretending to be less healthy. One man convinced his ex-wife to remarry him by falsely telling her that he was terminally ill.[76] A woman persuaded her husband to move out of their home by falsely claiming to have cancer and convincing him that "she needed complete rest and quiet because of alleged chemotherapy treatments."[77]

In addition, there are multiple accounts of parents deceiving their children to keep the children from learning the truth about their own health or bodily condition, even when they reach adulthood. Such parental deceit appears to be more common when the child has a diagnosis that the child's parents and doctors consider stigmatic, such as being born intersex.[78]

Intimate deception is hardly limited to deceit about sexuality and/or health. People frequently deceive their intimates about many other topics as well. For example, surveys designed to track people's financial behavior and understand their financial planning strategies often uncover significant intimate deception about finances. A 2012 survey of 2213 women with household incomes of at least $30,000 found that 16% of the married women and 8% of the women in same-sex relationships—partially overlapping groups—reported having "a secret stash of money [their] partner doesn't know about."[79] A 2014 study by the National Endowment for Financial Education surveyed more than two thousand adults and found that one-third of the respondents who combined finances with their partner reported lying to their partner about money.[80] First-person accounts and lawsuits about intimate deception over finances are abundant, describing a husband who concealed that he owed millions of dollars in unpaid taxes,[81] an engaged woman who hid that she was forging checks and intercepting mail in order to siphon money out of her fiancé's bank accounts,[82] a boyfriend who falsely claimed to own a million-dollar home,[83] a husband who concealed that he had charged tens of thousands of dollars to credit card accounts that he had opened without his wife's knowledge,[84] a wife who hid that she had won the lottery,[85] a brother who concealed that he had taken out five fraudulent mortgages in his sibling's name,[86] and myriad other variations.

Deception about finances is sometimes interwoven with deception about professional or educational achievements. To my knowledge, no empirical studies have investigated the frequency of intimate deception about professional attainments or schooling. The existing research focuses on deceit directed at employers and makes clear that such deception is widespread. Firms that assist or screen job applicants routinely observe that significant misrepresentations on resumes are common, with reported figures ranging from under 10% of resumes to over 40%.[87] Of course, not everyone who deceives an employer similarly dupes his intimates, but some people surely do because it can be risky to tell an employer about accomplishments that the liar's intimates know are fabricated. Many first-person accounts and lawsuits describe intimate deception over educational or professional achievements, recounting conduct that extends from the more mundane to the more outlandish. For instance, intimates have written, spoken, and/or testified about a son who claimed to have graduated from college when he had actually dropped out and pocketed the money his parents sent for tuition,[88] a fiancée who falsely claimed to have a college degree,[89] a father who falsely maintained that he had graduated from the Sorbonne and Yale,[90] and boyfriends or husbands who falsely claimed to be a pilot,[91] doctor,[92] astronaut,[93] or CIA agent.[94] Notably, those glamorous fake professions also provide ready explanations for irregular schedules and long absences, which can help duplicitous intimates conceal how they spend their time.

There is good evidence that many people have deceived their intimates about their achievements in the military. In 2008, the *Chicago Tribune* examined 273 obituaries published in the prior decade and found that over 80% of the decorations for bravery discussed in the obituaries did not appear in official military records. The newspaper—understandably—did not contact next-of-kin to ascertain whether the deceased people had lied to their intimates about their military service. But misrepresentations in obituaries are notable because the deceased person's relatives often provided biographical details to the newspaper or drafted the obituary. The *Tribune* also discovered that 103 of the 333 people (30.93%) who claimed in *Who's Who* to have been awarded one of the nation's top military medals had no official military records to support their claims. Some of the men who had submitted unsubstantiated information to *Who's Who* confessed in interviews with the *Tribune* that they had fabricated military achievements so they could tell their wives, children, or other intimates about them.[95] Beyond the *Tribune's* investigations, many first-person accounts and lawsuits discuss people who lied to their intimates about their military service. For example, one husband falsely claimed to be a Medal of Honor winner, a war hero who had served in combat in the Korean War, and a retired Air Force pilot,[96] a father falsely claimed to have been awarded a Medal of Honor that he had actually purchased from a dealer,[97] a Navy aviation ordnanceman lied and told his mother and three younger brothers that he was an elite Navy SEAL who had experienced combat in Afghanistan,[98] and an insurance adjuster falsely told dates that he was a Navy SEAL.[99] One husband told his wife that he was beating and strangling her in the middle of the night because his combat service in Vietnam had left him with horrible nightmares that he acted out in his sleep. In reality, the man had never seen combat or gone to Vietnam.[100]

First-person accounts and lawsuits also feature people deceiving their intimates about their criminal records and/or criminal behavior. The exact deceptions vary, from the fiancé and then husband who hid that he had been convicted of a criminal misdemeanor,[101] to the father who hid from his children that he was a career pickpocket,[102] to the fiancée who hid that she had committed a felony under federal immigration law and escaped detection,[103] to the fiancé and then husband who hid that he had a felony conviction for theft,[104] to the boyfriend who hid that he had been convicted of murder and insurance fraud,[105] to the husband and father who hid from his wife and children that he had killed two people while drunk driving and then fled from authorities before he could be sentenced,[106] to the husband who hid from his new wife that he had murdered his previous wife, their three children, and his mother.[107] To my knowledge, no systematic empirical research attempts to measure the prevalence of intimate deception about criminality. However, True.com, the online dating service that conducted some screening, claimed in 2007 that it rejected

2% of its applicants because they were convicted felons who had falsely denied their felony convictions and claimed in 2005 that it rejected 5% of its applicants for that reason.[108]

This brief survey has explored some of the most common subjects that people deceive their intimates about, but by necessity it cannot be exhaustive. Lawsuits and first-person accounts reveal innumerable other topics for intimate deception. For example, some people have deceived their intimates about their age,[109] their religion,[110] or their racial background.[111] Some people have deceived their intimates about their entire life history. In one notorious case, a serial imposter named Christian Karl Gerhartsreiter posed for years as Clark Rockefeller, supposedly a member of the prominent and wealthy family. He married a successful businesswoman who believed he was a Rockefeller and the couple had a daughter together as part of a relationship that lasted for over a decade before his deceit was exposed.[112] In short, intimate deception is a recurring feature of life and the forms it takes can range from the everyday to the extraordinary.

An Overview of the Book

This book is organized into three parts. The first part investigates the phenomenon of deceit within intimate relationships. The second part considers how the law currently governs intimate deception in the United States and examines how that regulation has changed since the early twentieth century. The third part explores how courts and legislatures should reform the law's treatment of intimate deception.

Part I—*The Practice of Intimate Deception*—asks why some people deceive their intimates, why intimate deception often works, and what harms intimate deceivers can inflict. Beginning the book by exploring the social practice of deception within intimate relationships can help us better understand and assess the law's treatment of the subject. This part reveals how the law shapes intimate deception even before a deceived intimate brings a lawsuit seeking redress. Moreover, it reveals how a distorted vision of social practice shapes the law. Courts and legislatures routinely rely on explicit and implicit theories about how intimate deception operates and what its consequences can be. But examining the actual practice of intimate deception makes clear that those theories frequently reflect unfounded assumptions more than reality.

Chapter 1—*Why Do People Deceive Their Intimates?*—focuses on what motivates intimate deception. I start by examining deceivers because legal and popular scrutiny of intimate deception too often begins with the people who have been deceived, faulting them for having been fooled. Where the introductory chapter reviewed some of the topics that are frequent subjects of intimate deception, Chapter 1 presents a taxonomy of common motivations for deceiving intimates. Although there can be substantial variations between individual cases, these motivations tend to reflect recurring themes. Psychological factors can make some people more likely to deceive their intimates. In addition, there can be tremendous concrete and practical incentives to deceive intimates or to deceive people into intimacy—and the law itself has created or exacerbated some of those incentives. Courts denying remedies sometimes minimize or discount the role that deception played in an intimate relationship. But exploring why people deceive their intimates reveals that deceit can be crucial to relationships and can produce enormous benefits for deceivers.

Chapter 2—*Why Does Intimate Deception Work?*—considers why deceivers often succeed in duping their intimates. Judges frequently blame deceived intimates for not discovering the deceit sooner. A court will commonly explain in denying redress for intimate deception that the plaintiff should have been suspicious of the deceiver's claims and promptly sought to verify everything the deceiver said and did. Moreover, judges assume that such an investigation would have rapidly revealed the deception. These arguments typically ignore the obstacles to detecting an intimate's deceit and discovering the truth, even for a person of ordinary or above-average shrewdness and sophistication. First, almost all of us have much less ability to spot deception than we may like to imagine. We tend to be no better at detecting deception from an intimate and may actually be especially unlikely to spot an intimate's deceit. Second, powerful social norms discourage the investigation of intimates. These norms urging and expecting us to have faith in our intimates help relationships, caregiving, and society flourish, but the trust they promote is sometimes misplaced. Third, even if a person would like to disregard social norms against investigating intimates, it is often difficult or impossible to mount an investigation without the investigation itself jeopardizing or ending the relationship because the investigated person finds out about it. Practical realities often preclude reconnaissance without the subject's knowledge. Moreover, the law prohibits—for legitimate and important reasons—many forms of research into someone else's life without the subject's consent. It is deeply ironic for courts to fault plaintiffs for not swiftly uncovering intimate deception when laws protecting the privacy and security of people's homes, computers, emails, postal mail, phones, cars, tax returns, credit reports, medical records, and the like make investigating a potentially deceptive intimate without that intimate's consent much more difficult.

Chapter 3—*What Injuries Can Intimate Deceivers Inflict?*—draws on lawsuits, first-person accounts, and social science research in exploring the sometimes life-changing injuries that intimate deceivers can inflict on the intimates they target as well as on third parties and even society at large. Courts denying remedies for intimate deception frequently devote little, if any, attention to the harm that plaintiffs have experienced. This judicial disregard tracks the perspective of deceivers, who routinely underestimate the damage their deceit has caused. But considering these injuries in detail helps us better understand the consequences that intimate deception can have. At the start, it is important to recognize that intimate deception can cause financial and bodily injuries—the sorts of harms that the law is usually most willing to redress. Intimate deception can also create unexpected vulnerability to criminal prosecution and other legal harms. Deceit frequently costs deceived intimates wasted time and lost opportunities. And of course, people often suffer psychologically and emotionally when their intimates deceive them. Indeed, some deceived intimates report that what hurt most was that their trust had been betrayed. Others emphasize that the most damaging aspect of being duped was that the experience undermined their confidence in their ability to judge people. To be sure, the law cannot fully remedy all the injuries that intimate deception can cause. Here as elsewhere, monetary compensation for a personal injury does not erase the injury. The law cannot restore health that has been permanently damaged, cannot give back time that has been lost, and cannot recreate trust that has been destroyed. However, money damages can provide some compensation, deterrence, and recognition that the plaintiff has suffered significant harm and the defendant should be held accountable for his conduct.

Part II—*The Law of Intimate Deception*—examines the law's treatment of intimate deception over time and to the present day, exploring the norms, standards, and presumptions that distinguish this vast and understudied body of law. While the volume of law governing intimate deception is enormous, courts routinely return to a set of dominant themes.

Chapter 4—*A Legal History of Intimate Deception*—places modern law in historical context. Exploring the legal regulation of intimate deception since the early twentieth century reveals that the present reluctance of courts and legislatures to offer remedies to deceived intimates is not a constant, unchanging, and unchangeable aspect of the legal system. To the contrary, legal authorities in the early twentieth century were often markedly more willing than their modern-day counterparts to provide deceived intimates with redress. Some legal remedies for deception within intimate relationships disappeared over the course of the twentieth century or became much less valuable. There now appears to be proportionately less litigation over intimate deception than there once was and that decline helps explain why modern scholars have tended to overlook this legal arena. At least three factors contributed to the contraction. First, starting in 1935 a wave of state "anti-heart balm" laws abolished causes of action for seduction and breach of promise to marry that some women had been using to sue intimates who deceived them. Courts then interpreted anti-heart balm statutes expansively, relying on the laws to block a wide array of claims against deceptive intimates. Second, changing norms about race and gender left judges unwilling to grant redress for some types of intimate deception that they had once been willing to remediate. Third—and most significant in diminishing the volume of litigation—the advent and swift spread of no-fault divorce starting in 1970 meant that securing an annulment or fault-based divorce because of intimate deception became a much less valuable remedy than when courts permitted divorce only for cause. Deceit still ends many marriages, but it is less likely to be litigated because a person does not need to prove spousal wrongdoing to secure a no-fault divorce. Meanwhile, some courts have cited the advent of no-fault divorce as a reason to rule against plaintiffs seeking remedies for injuries a deceitful spouse has inflicted.

Chapter 5—*Modern Law's Sharp Divide Between Deception Within and Outside Intimacy*—turns to contemporary legal treatment of intimate deception. The chapter explores an overriding theme in this regulatory regime: the judiciary's routine refusal to allow deceived intimates to access remedies that are available to redress, deter, and repudiate deception in other contexts. The persistently differentiated treatment of intimate deception has heightened consequences because courts often define intimacy broadly to include relationships that were not especially developed or long-lasting, where the deceit was facilitated by the reality that the parties did not know each other well. One woman had no face-to-face interactions with the person who targeted her for a relentless campaign of deceit and abuse until close to the time when her deceiver was unmasked, but nonetheless lost her suit for redress because the court concluded that she was deceived within a "personal relationship."[113] Judges frequently stress their overarching commitment to shielding intimate deceivers even when ruling for the occasional plaintiff. For example, a court will make clear that it is allowing a particular deceived intimate to pursue her suit only because the litigation advances other public policy goals, such as the public health interest in deterring the spread of sexually transmitted disease.

Chapter 6—*The Legal Protection of Ordinary Deception in Courtship, Sex, and Marriage*—explores the law's commitment to preserving the existing norms and practices that shape these areas of life. Judges denying deceived intimates legal relief commonly emphasize that deceit is widespread within courtship, sexual relationships, and marriage. Moreover, they assume and insist that courts should protect such ordinary deception from legal redress. One result is that judicial intuitions about what constitutes normal behavior within intimacy have considerable practical import. Judges are much less likely to provide remedies for examples of intimate deception that they believe are commonplace and more likely to give remedies in cases they think are deviant and unusual. When judges assume that many forms of deceit are typical in courtship, sex, and marriage, they help make that so—normalizing the deception by protecting it from legal disapproval and redress. This dedication to safeguarding ordinary deception in intimate relationships has also functioned to protect extraordinary deceit. Courts have sometimes denied remedies for admittedly egregious intimate deception out of concern that providing redress might create a slippery slope that would ultimately jeopardize more ordinary deceivers. Indeed, the judicial commitment to shielding commonplace intimate deception has even helped defendants who deceived business competitors or government officials. Judges have cited this commitment as a reason to narrow or reject statutes whose impact reaches far beyond intimacy, such as a law against computer fraud and abuse and a statute penalizing false claims about military awards.

Chapter 7—*Intimate Deception Outside of Romantic, Sexual, or Marital Relationships*—considers some of the least examined parts of an understudied field, exploring deceit between family members who are not connected to each other as spouses, sexual partners, or romantic interests. The premise that the law should protect intimate deceivers and shield them from redress still appears in this context, but is almost exclusively confined to cases considering parents who have deceived their children—including their adult children. Judges are often unwilling to impose legal penalties on deceptive parents and quick to blame children for having been duped. Indeed, courts sometimes write as if parents have a legal prerogative to deceive their children, one that extends into the children's adulthood. When the parties are reversed, however, courts are frequently eager to grant remedies to parents suing deceitful adult children and willing to empower parents to inflict their own penalties on deceptive children below the age of majority. Moreover, when courts move beyond marital and parental relationships to consider deception by other relatives, they routinely treat these family members—deceitful siblings, aunts, uncles, nieces, nephews, and the like—as if they were unrelated to the people they deceived and give plaintiffs access to remedies available for nonintimate deception. Family law tends to focus narrowly on marriage, parenthood, and (sometimes) their functional equivalents and to spare little attention for other family ties. The case law on intimate deception reflects and reinforces this circumscribed perspective, with courts assuming that family relationships beyond marriage and parenthood fall outside the boundaries of legally recognized intimacy.

Part III—*Reforming the Law of Intimate Deception*—turns from the present and the past to the future, exploring how judges and legislators can improve their treatment of intimate deception. With too little discussion and deliberation, the law has placed too much value on shielding people who deceive their intimates and not enough weight on protecting intimates who have been deceived. The last part of the book examines an array of strategies that courts and legislatures could usefully pursue in reorienting this body of law.

Chapter 8—*Work to Be Done*—focuses on law reform both within and outside of courtrooms. The law's power to govern intimate deception is particularly visible when courts adjudicate disputes between deceived people and the intimates who duped them. Whether judges side with plaintiffs or defendants, their decisions set legal ground rules for intimacy, establish rights and responsibilities, and enforce normative judgments. But the legal regulation of intimate deception also operates before litigation begins, structuring incentives to deceive and the ease with which deceivers can carry out their schemes. Law reform will be most transformative and effective if it reaches the multiple ways that the legal system shapes intimate deception.

Chapter 8's first proposal is meant to expand the remedies available to deceived intimates who sue for redress. I argue that courts are more likely to reach wise decisions if they begin with a rebuttable presumption that a plaintiff suing a deceptive intimate will have the same causes of action available to her that she would have when suing an equivalently deceptive nonintimate. This reorientation would have numerous advantages over the judiciary's present practice of assuming that intimate deception is fundamentally unlike deceit outside of intimacy and should be governed by a different legal regime. A judiciary that starts with a rebuttable presumption that the law's response to intimate deception should track its response to deception between strangers would be more likely to recognize that deception within intimate relationships can inflict severe and unwarranted injuries, more able to provide compensation to intimates who have been duped, and better situated to deter at least some people from harming their intimates through deceit. Moreover, enfolding intimate deception within the legal doctrines that ordinarily govern deceit would place intimate deception claims securely at the heart of the legal system rather than leaving those claims at the more vulnerable peripheries. Treating intimate deception like deception in other contexts would allow courts and litigants to draw on well-established and developed bodies of law. It would mean that much less would pivot on how judges define the boundaries of legally recognized intimacy, boundaries that are always contestable and contested.

That said, I do not contend that courts should provide remedies for every instance of deception within an intimate relationship that inflicts harm, even severe harm. Chapter 8 highlights two exceptional contexts where granting redress would be inappropriate and compelling arguments for additional exceptions may emerge over time. Courts should not provide deceived intimates with remedies when doing so would inflict significant injury on a blameless third party, such as a child. For example, judges should turn away plaintiffs seeking tort remedies for deception about a child's biological paternity—or tort remedies for a sexual partner's deceit about using contraception or being infertile that led to the birth of a child—if providing such remedies would cause the child in question significant injury. Courts should also not provide redress when telling the truth would have placed the deceiver or a third party in imminent physical danger. For instance, legal remedies for harms stemming from deception would be inappropriate when an abused woman deceived her violent intimate because she believed based on her experiences with him that he would respond to the truth with brutality against her or her children.

After proposing a transformation in the judiciary's approach to intimate deception cases, Chapter 8 explores how to improve the legal regulation of intimate deception before plaintiffs file suit. The law now adds to the tremendous incentives that can exist to deceive an intimate, but legislatures and courts should instead work to counter such incentives. The law often helps people succeed in duping their intimates and taking advantage of them, but legislators and judges should instead look for opportunities to thwart deceivers. The law should make it easier for deceived intimates to discover that they are being duped when such facilitation can be accomplished without threatening privacy, liberty, or security. At the same time, the law should make it more difficult for a duplicitous person to harm his intimate without the intimate's knowledge when such safeguards can be imposed without unduly burdening everyday transactions. In short, legal reforms that better recognize, prevent, and remediate harms inflicted through intimate deception should reorient the judicial response to litigation and also extend beyond courtrooms.

Intimate deception and its legal regulation have an enormous impact. They shape people's lives, decisions, opportunities, and challenges in ways that can be simultaneously far-reaching and so taken for granted that work is required to render them visible. But the law and practice of intimate deception have remained vastly understudied, operating in the assumed background rather than examined in the light. Intimate deception is a persistent part of life and a consistent issue for the law. It deserves much more sustained attention, both to understand present realities and to uncover possibilities for legal reform. This book is for and about judges, legislators, and anyone who interacts with, influences, and/or lives under the law. In other words, it is for all of us.

PART I

THE PRACTICE OF
INTIMATE DECEPTION

Deception is common within intimacy, but frequently shielded from view. Uncovering this hidden phenomenon reveals disturbing aspects of intimate relationships, exposes understudied consequences of inequality, and illuminates how people's intimate experiences can affect and reflect other parts of their lives. Examining intimate deception can show us people's most intense desires, fundamental expectations, and stinging injuries.

Investigating the social reality of intimate deception also helps us better understand and evaluate its legal regulation. Adequately assessing the law requires knowing what exactly it is governing.

Moreover, the law and social practice of intimate deception have informed and influenced each other. The legal system shapes intimate deception before any plaintiff files suit. The law can add to the incentives to deceive, help deceivers escape detection, and intensify the injuries that intimate deception causes. At the same time, legal regulation builds on social practice—or how legal authorities understand or misunderstand that practice. Courts and legislatures commonly rely on entrenched assumptions about intimate deception and its consequences. But studying intimate deceivers and the people they deceive makes clear that many of these assumptions are based on misperceptions rather than facts.

This part investigates the social practice of intimate deception by focusing on three overarching questions. Chapter 1 examines what motivates people to deceive their intimates. Chapter 2 considers why intimate deception often works. Chapter 3 explores what injuries intimate deceivers can inflict.

1

Why Do People Deceive
Their Intimates?

Legal and popular discussions of intimate deception often focus most of their critical attention on the person who was duped. Judges, journalists, and community members routinely scrutinize deceived intimates for shortcomings, interrogate their reasoning, suggest that they did not act as ordinarily sensible individuals would, and tacitly or openly fault them for having trusted their intimates and fallen for deceit.[1] But deception is intentional conduct that begins with the decision to deceive. With that in mind, this book starts by considering what drives people to deceive their intimates.

The motivations behind intimate deception can sometimes be as varied as each specific deceiver and each particular intimate relationship. On occasion, these motivations may be unknowable—even to the deceiver himself. Yet examining what spurs people to deceive their intimates also reveals recurring themes and patterns.

Most of this chapter explores motivations for intimate deception that cannot be attributed simply to the vagaries of individual psychology. But of course, psychological factors help explain why some people are more likely to deceive their intimates in some situations. For example, low self-esteem can prompt deceitfulness.[2] People may deceive their intimates to make themselves feel better, to present themselves as they wish they were, or to conceal aspects of themselves that they wish were not true.

In addition, deceivers tend to be adept at rationalizing their deceitfulness. They assure themselves that their deception will not cause undue injury, is directed at people who do not deserve better treatment, and is unlikely to be discovered. Social science studies have found that deceivers are prone to underestimate the harm their deceit causes, compared to the harm that deceived people report experiencing.[3] This tendency is frequently visible in first-person accounts. James McGreevey—New Jersey's governor from 2002 to 2004—deceived his wife, Dina, to hide that he was gay. After his deceit was revealed, the former governor recalled how he had convinced himself that the deception was not "unfair to Dina." In his words, he chose to keep "overlooking" his wife's desire for "honesty, intimacy, true romantic love" and told himself that he "was offering her some things she truly coveted: the stability of marriage, the prospect of a loving family, a chance to share a life of public service, political excitement in spades."[4]

Social science studies have also found that deceivers tend to defend their conduct to themselves by denigrating the people they are deceiving. After someone is deceptive, he is more likely to perceive the person he deceived as less honest—perhaps even less honest than the deceiver himself.[5] Along similar lines, some research has found that deceivers tend to convince themselves that they are skilled at escaping detection for deceit within romantic relationships and that their romantic partners are less adept at avoiding detection for deceit.[6]

Social science research on the psychology of deception can be illuminating. However, this work has been tightly focused on how people's internal thoughts, feelings, and tendencies help explain why, when, and whether they deceive. While those are crucial issues, there are also other, more external, factors that prompt people to deceive their intimates.

Focusing on the material conditions of people's lives, the incentives they confront, and the legal rules they face reveals a basic, yet fundamental trigger for intimate deception: People can capture tremendous concrete and practical advantages by deceiving their intimates—advantages that the law itself has sometimes created or exacerbated. Courts sometimes discount the significance of intimate deception about wealth,[7] alcohol abuse,[8] criminal history,[9] marital history,[10] children from a previous relationship,[11] and more.[12] But exploring the motivations behind intimate deception quickly establishes that deceit can be central to intimate relationships and can secure crucial benefits for deceivers.

This chapter presents a taxonomy of why people deceive their intimates. It draws on myriad first-person accounts of intimate deception as well as a multitude of judicial opinions that report such deceit, whether or not the courts provide or even contemplate the possibility of redress. By necessity, the taxonomy cannot include every possible motivation and cannot consider every possible way of thinking about those motivations. Some instances of intimate deception fall into none of the categories I discuss and some occupy multiple categories simultaneously. However, the taxonomy provides a useful way to organize and explore some prominent and recurring motivations.

Linchpin Deception

Sometimes people deceive in order to begin or maintain an intimate relationship. Someone practices what I call *linchpin deception* when he believes or fears that if he is not deceptive he will be unable to have his desired relationship with the person he is deceiving. Even intimates who are not otherwise deceptive—whether because they value truthfulness or find honesty easier or safer—may deceive when they conclude that deception is a linchpin. Another term for linchpin deception could be *but for deception* because the deceiver thinks that but for his deceit the relationship he wants will be unattainable.

Linchpin deceptions are central to the relationships in which they occur. A person practicing linchpin deception thinks that this deceit is a necessary condition for the relationship—a piece that holds the relationship together and makes it possible. The available evidence in first-person accounts and lawsuits suggests that deceivers often accurately identify relational linchpins. The deceived person frequently agrees after the deception is uncovered that but for the deception she never would have begun or continued her intimacy with the deceiver.

What constitutes a linchpin varies by person, relationship, and culture. Something that is crucial to one person in a specific relationship in a certain culture could be much less important or even irrelevant to another. However, three distinct, although sometimes overlapping, types of linchpin deceptions dominate the available evidence.

With *mirroring linchpins*, the deceiver falsely claims to have the same characteristics, goals, or attitudes as the person he is deceiving because the deceiver thinks he will otherwise be rejected. Michael Dolitsky falsely told Anne Bilowit that he shared her devotion to Orthodox Judaism because he loved Bilowit, wanted to marry her, and knew she would only marry a man with the same religious commitments and practices.[13] M.J.B. falsely told V.J.S. before their marriage that he shared her desire to remain childless because he knew she would not marry a man who wanted children.[14] Similarly, mirroring linchpin deceptions can revolve around sexual orientation, such as when a person falsely claims to share the heterosexuality of his sexual partner because he thinks his intimate will end the relationship if she learns the truth.[15] Mirroring linchpins can also revolve around gender identity, such as when someone deceives to conceal that she is transgender because she fears rejection by a cisgender intimate whose gender identity aligns with the sex he was assigned at birth.[16]

With *aspirational linchpins*, the deceiver falsely claims to have achievements, status, resources, or plans because he thinks that his intimate relationship depends on those markers of success and ambition. One recent dating guide counsels men to "get a raise" in order to improve their prospects.[17] With this genre of advice and cultural value system in mind, someone might falsely claim to have a well-paying job, a thriving business, or an advanced degree because he thinks that the person he is deceiving would be unwilling to be involved with him if she knew his true situation.

With *defensive linchpins*, the deceiver intentionally misleads by concealing or denying what he thinks is a black mark making him undesirable. Anything that a deceiver's intimate cares about can become the subject of defensive linchpin deception. For example, people might conceal or falsely deny that they are already married, have been divorced multiple times, have committed infidelity, are pregnant by another man, have impregnated another woman, have a sexually transmitted disease, are addicted to drugs or alcohol, have a criminal record, or have significant debts, because they think that telling the truth would cause their desired person to avoid, terminate, or curtail their relationship.

Initiating or maintaining a relationship through deceit carries the risk that the deceived intimate may end the relationship once the truth emerges. But using linchpin deceptions can nonetheless appeal to people for many reasons.

Linchpin deceptions can be attractive to people seeking only short-term intimacy. Once their immediate goals are met, these deceivers may not care if their deceit comes to light and the relationship ends. Indeed, some deceivers may appreciate how revealing their deceit is likely to push intimates away. Rosemary Counter wrote about a man who showered her with affection, attention, and gifts during a whirlwind romance. They met after she responded to a "missed connections" advertisement that he had posted indicating that he had seen a woman dancing with her friends "at the Drake Hotel, slim with red hair in a black satin top," regretted not approaching her, and wanted a second chance to connect. The relationship ended ten days after it began when the man revealed that he was married and that his wife was pregnant with their second child. He also confessed that he had never been in the Drake Hotel, but had posted the ad hoping to lure someone into responding. It was probably no coincidence that the man went on his first date with Counter right after he dropped his wife and child at the airport and then revealed his deceit shortly before his family was scheduled to come home. As Counter observed, the man's announcement of the truth was "timed almost to the day of his wife's return."[18]

Richard McNutt allegedly deceived his fiancée, Dorothy Zauhar, to conceal that he did not intend to marry her and was romancing another woman. McNutt reportedly wanted to maintain his relationship with Zauhar for the short term because he needed a new kidney, hoped to get one from Zauhar's brother, and knew this donation would not take place if the brother learned that McNutt did not plan to marry Zauhar.[19] McNutt received the brother's kidney and announced two days after leaving the hospital that he was indefinitely postponing his wedding to Zauhar.[20] He married another woman less than a year later.[21]

Sometimes a person wants a longer-term relationship with the intimate he is deceiving, but hopes or expects that his deceit will never be discovered. This expectation can be more or less plausible depending on the circumstances. The frequency of undetected deception is necessarily difficult to measure, but some instances of intimate deception are clearly never unmasked. Consider a divorced person who lies about her marital history because she wants to marry someone who for religious reasons will not knowingly wed a partner with a living former spouse. Some people deceived in this way have learned about the deception and filed suit to end their marriages.[22] But some of the cases reveal that years passed before the deceived spouse discovered that he had been duped.[23] This long lag before detection suggests that there are probably many other marriages in which the deceiver's true marital history has never come to light.

Sometimes a person may anticipate that the intimate he is deceiving will eventually feel stuck in their relationship and find it difficult to extricate herself, even if she realizes that she has been deceived. Indeed, some people have reported feeling unable to leave a relationship even after they conclude or suspect that they were duped into beginning it.[24] By the time the deceit is fully or partially revealed, the deceived intimate may have structured her life around her deceiver, become economically dependent on him, had children with him, or developed other reasons for maintaining the relationship.

Selina Volz married Robert David Madrid, who told her during their courtship that he was a millionaire with a glittering resume that included a medical degree. As Volz recalled, "[h]e was very appealing to a single mother with three young children." After Volz and Madrid wed, the family moved to Alabama and Madrid began lucrative work as a forensics expert and investigator. The couple also had a baby together, so the family included four children.

Volz eventually began to suspect that something was wrong. Madrid would tell her stories about his past and then tell other people different versions of those stories. But "[h]e always had an explanation," and she felt unable to end the relationship. As Volz explained later: "I knew there was a problem, but you try to make it work. I was trapped. I didn't want another failed marriage." Madrid was ultimately arrested on perjury charges for lying about his educational credentials when testifying as an expert witness. Once law enforcement authorities began investigating, they could find no evidence that Madrid had even graduated from college.[25] The investigation concluded with Madrid pleading guilty to perjury and going to prison.[26]

Alternatively or in addition, someone may tell himself that the person he is deceiving into an intimate relationship will not mind having been intentionally misled once she gets to know her deceiver better and realizes how appealing he is. Paul Oyer, an economics professor at Stanford's business school, wrote a book recounting his experiences with online dating. Oyer reported that he falsely presented himself as a nonsmoker because he realized that some women "would never agree to meet" him for a date if they knew he smoked.[27] Indeed, Oyer suggested elsewhere in his book that he himself screened out smokers in choosing which women to ask for dates.[28] Oyer acknowledged that lying about

his smoking was a linchpin deception, but contended—quite conveniently—
that the lie nonetheless advanced the interests of the deceived women and Oyer
alike. He cloaked his explanation in the language of economic theory: "I ra-
tionalize that, even if a woman eventually finds these things out after we're in a
deeper relationship, she'll accept these small negative traits as part of the whole
package. And I justify my minor deception by arguing I'm doing myself *and* the
woman a favor. It's cooperative game theory. Our interests are aligned, and I've
simply removed some minor hurdles."[29]

Gateway Deception

While someone practicing linchpin deception often wants an intimate relationship for its own sake, sometimes people seek an intimate relationship
as a means to an end. For example, people practice what I call *gateway deception* when duping someone into intimacy is a route to legal rights or privileges
that are otherwise unavailable or difficult to obtain, such as legal immigration,
spousal benefits from the Social Security program, or government benefits for
the spouses of veterans. Legal rules conditioning rights or privileges on intimate
ties—most commonly, marriage—can create powerful incentives to deceive in
order to establish or maintain the favored intimate relationship. In short, the law
can help produce the conditions that make deceiving an intimate appealing and
can shape the sorts of deceit that people pursue.

Consider immigration law, which creates enormous incentives for noncitizens
to marry American citizens if they would like legal authorization to live and
work in the United States. Federal statutes generally impose tight restrictions on
immigration. But the law facilitates the immigration of people married to United
States citizens and exempts those spouses from numerical limitations on immigration.[30] A noncitizen who has been married to an American citizen for at least
two years is immediately eligible to become a lawful permanent resident, which
allows the noncitizen to live and work in the United States indefinitely and to
pursue naturalization.[31] A noncitizen who has been married to an American
citizen for less than two years is immediately eligible to become a conditional
lawful permanent resident,[32] and she can become a lawful permanent resident
after a two-year waiting period if the immigrant and her citizen spouse file a joint
petition toward the end of the two years and agree to be interviewed by immigration officials.[33]

The opportunity to become a lawful permanent resident and then a citizen of
the United States is both extremely valuable and difficult to acquire. Marrying
a citizen offers the only realistic route to legal immigration for many people
who want authorization to live and work in the United States. Approximately

one-quarter (26.0%) of the people (292,909 out of 1,127,167) who became lawful permanent residents in 2017 were the spouses of United States citizens. Moreover, at least 66.4% of the people who became lawful permanent residents in 2017 were the close relatives—spouses, parents, children, or siblings—of citizens or alien residents. This means that just 33.6% of the spots went to everyone else in the world seeking to become a lawful permanent resident of the United States.[34]

Once someone becomes a lawful permanent resident, she keeps that status even if she later divorces her citizen spouse—so long as immigration officials do not conclude that the marriage was a sham, meaning a marriage "entered into for the purpose of evading the immigration laws."[35] Millions of people have become lawful permanent residents through their marriages to United States citizens, but they do not need to stay in those marriages forever to maintain that immigration benefit.

This legal framework has spurred two basic types of marriage-related immigration fraud. In the first scenario, a citizen and noncitizen who would not otherwise marry and who are not interested in sharing their lives together choose to marry so the noncitizen can become a lawful permanent resident of the United States. The noncitizen often pays the citizen for her cooperation.[36] Immigration law provides that this is a fraud against the United States.[37] But this is not an example of deceit within an intimate relationship because both spouses know the truth.

The second basic type of marriage-related immigration fraud does constitute intimate deception. Here, a noncitizen dupes a citizen into marriage by concealing that he sees their marriage as a scheme to evade immigration requirements, would not otherwise marry the citizen, and perhaps plans to divorce once he has obtained lawful permanent residency. Although presently subject to the same legal penalties as sham marriages where both spouses were in cahoots,[38] sham marriages based on intimate deception inflict much more injury because these marriages ensnare individual victims in addition to undercutting United States immigration policy. Part III of this book argues that the federal government should recognize that added harm and do more to dissuade people from inflicting it. Before we get there, let's explore how deceiving a citizen into a sham marriage can benefit the deceiver while harming the duped spouse.

Dozens of cases have revolved around gateway intimate deception for immigration benefits, and presumably many more examples have never led to publicly available judicial opinions. Some of these cases have centered on federal efforts to prosecute or deport immigrants for entering into sham marriages.[39] Duped citizens have also initiated litigation, seeking to end their marriages—and sometimes also seeking to secure damages—on the ground that their noncitizen spouses deceitfully concealed that they were marrying for immigration purposes and not interested in building lives with the citizens.[40]

Kashif Ur-Rehman, whose visa to stay in the United States was about to ex-pire, met Annila Qamar, a United States citizen, through a matchmaker.[41] Qamar wanted to marry a man who shared her desire to have children right away, and Ur-Rehman said that he did.[42] But after their wedding, Ur-Rehman refused to have sex without contraception. He also would not permit Qamar to have a key to their mailbox and did not tell her when he received his lawful permanent res-ident card. Soon after acquiring permanent residency, Ur-Rehman secretly ap-plied to a professional school in another state. A few months later, he moved out with no advance warning and filed for divorce.[43]

Duping a citizen into marriage can offer the unscrupulous some advantages over entering into a marriage that both spouses know is for immigration purposes only. First, the deceiver does not need to compensate the citizen for her coop-eration in the immigration fraud because the deceived spouse is unaware of the fraud. Second, it may sometimes be easier to find a citizen who wants to marry you for your own sake than to identify a citizen who is willing to violate fed-eral immigration laws for money. Third, if immigration authorities interview the couple to determine whether their marriage is bona fide,[44] the marriage may be more likely to appear genuine because one spouse believes it is and has organ-ized her life on that basis. Fourth, the duped spouse may provide the deceiver with other benefits in addition to legal immigration, including financial support, domestic services, a place to live, and contacts for finding work.

Miguel Montenegro, who lived in Colombia, and Yamel Avila, who lived in Texas, met through an internet dating site and eventually married. Immediately after the wedding, Montenegro went to a lawyer to begin the process of applying for conditional lawful permanent residency based on his marriage to a United States citizen. He also relied on Avila financially as he did not have a job for the first year of the marriage. Indeed, Montenegro persuaded Avila to add his name to her bank accounts and he made regular withdrawals. Montenegro left Avila approximately two months after he secured lawful per-manent residency. He then promptly opened a bank account in his own name and deposited $4000—money that Avila suspected he had accumulated by siphoning funds from her.[45]

The Social Security system also makes marriage a gateway to important legal benefits and accordingly creates powerful incentives for people to marry someone who is entitled to receive larger Social Security benefits than they are. The Social Security program provides old-age insurance benefits to qual-ified workers and also pays spousal insurance benefits to some of the current, divorced, and surviving spouses of primary beneficiaries.[46] Social Security benefits for primary beneficiaries are set based on the length of time the bene-ficiary worked in the market and the wages he earned.[47] Spousal benefits are set based on the primary beneficiary's entitlement. A current or divorced spouse of a primary beneficiary is eligible to receive a spousal benefit that is up to 50% as large as the payment the primary beneficiary receives.[48] A surviving spouse is eligible to receive a spousal benefit that is up to 100% as large as the payment that the primary beneficiary would have received.[49]

A person who has reached the end of her working life cannot go back in time and augment her Social Security benefits by working or earning more. Beyond delaying retirement, marrying a primary beneficiary is one of the only steps someone can take to increase her Social Security benefits or to become eligible for Social Security if not already eligible.

Many women are eligible for larger Social Security benefits through their intimate relationships than through their own working histories because the combination of disproportionate domestic responsibilities and persistent employment discrimination frequently leaves women with shorter and more poorly compensated records of market employment. Almost half (46.8%) of the women aged sixty-two or older who received Social Security in 2016 collected as a wife, widow, or mother—whether because their own working histories did not entitle them to any Social Security benefits (21.4%) or because they were entitled to larger benefits as a family member than as a worker (25.4%).[50]

Social Security law—like immigration law—allows people to obtain benefits by marrying and often permits people to keep those benefits even after their marriage ends. A primary beneficiary's death or divorce does not stop his surviving or divorced spouse from collecting Social Security benefits so long as she was married to the primary beneficiary for the requisite amount of time and does not remarry (or does not remarry before a certain age).[51] In fact, spousal benefits under the Social Security program frequently increase after the primary beneficiary dies.[52]

As with immigration law, this legal framework creates powerful incentives for two basic types of marriage-related fraud. In the first, both parties to the marriage are in cahoots and agree to take advantage of the Social Security system by marrying simply so that one spouse will be able to collect Social Security spousal benefits based on the other spouse's working history. In the second scenario— where there is intimate deception—one spouse dupes the other into marriage by deliberately concealing that she is marrying in order to secure spousal benefits from the Social Security program.

Congress has structured the provision of Social Security benefits in ways designed to discourage both types of marriage-related fraud. In general, no spousal benefits are available until a spouse has been married to a primary beneficiary for at least one year or has a child with the primary beneficiary.[53] Similarly, benefits for surviving spouses are generally unavailable unless the widow has not remarried before turning sixty and was married to the primary beneficiary for at least nine months before he died or has a child with him.[54] Benefits for divorced spouses are generally unavailable unless the ex-spouse was married to the primary beneficiary for at least ten years before they divorced and has not remarried.[55] These rules strive to diminish the appeal of duping someone into marriage in order to collect Social Security benefits by extending the time a deceiver needs to remain married to the person she is deceiving and restricting the deceiver's ability to remarry and still collect Social Security benefits based on her earlier marriage.

Concetta Salfi, a widow whose husband died less than six months after their wedding, sued to challenge the constitutionality of the legal provision denying her eligibility to collect Social Security benefits as a surviving spouse.[56] There was no evidence that deception tainted Salfi's decision to marry her husband or his decision to marry her. But the Supreme Court's opinion upholding the law stressed that the rule served Congress's interest in deterring fraud, even if some of the people whom the law touched had not themselves been deceitful.[57] As the Court reasoned, it was "undoubtedly true that the duration-of-relationship requirement operates to lessen the likelihood of abuse through sham relationships entered in contemplation of imminent death."[58] The Court also emphasized that "[t]he danger of persons entering a marriage relationship not to enjoy its traditional benefits, but instead to enable one spouse to claim benefits upon the anticipated early death of the wage earner, has been recognized from the very beginning of the Social Security program."[59]

Gateway intimate deception is similarly possible anywhere else intimacy is a pathway to legal rights or privileges that are otherwise unavailable or difficult to obtain. For example, many people do not have access to affordable health insurance. The federal government's provision of health care benefits to veterans and their spouses can spur people to dupe veterans into marriage in order to acquire insurance coverage. Margaret McClay Garnett wanted fertility treatment, but apparently had no health insurance to pay for it. She married J. Sistrunk, a mentally ill veteran, allegedly in a scheme to secure health care benefits through the federal government's Civilian Health and Medical Program of the Uniformed Services. Even after Sistrunk's conservator had the marriage annulled, law enforcement authorities believe that Garnett identified herself as the veteran's wife on insurance forms she completed for her fertility clinic and authorized the clinic to bill the Civilian Health and Medical Program for her treatment. She used the health care benefits that she had supposedly acquired through marriage to undergo in vitro fertilization—not using Sistrunk's sperm—that led to her giving birth to premature quadruplets. By the time federal prosecutors indicted Garnett for defrauding the United States, the federal government had paid $303,000 for her fertility treatment and maternity care.[60]

Con Artistry

Con artistry is another form of deceit where the deceiver seeks an intimate relationship as a means to an end. A con artist lures someone into intimacy with deception so he can extract money or other resources from the person he is deceiving. While I have had to coin new names to describe other types of intimate deception, the term con artist is already in widespread circulation. This fascinating phrase suggests that deception is an art, or can be when performed by a master.

As we will see, the law often seeks to differentiate con artistry from other varieties of intimate deception. When judges punish con artists, they frequently justify their decisions by emphasizing that the deceitfulness of these ne'er-do-wells falls outside the boundaries of ordinary intimacy.[61] But in fact, distinguishing con artists, who tell lies for a living, from ordinary serial deceivers, who live by telling lies, can sometimes be difficult. For example, both con artists and ordinary serial deceivers can utilize linchpin deceptions. One basic dividing line is that ordinary serial deceivers seek to establish and maintain intimate relationships for reasons that extend beyond material rewards. In contrast, con artists focus on material rewards above all else and induce people into relationships in order to strip them of their assets and drain their bank accounts. A typical con artist is not otherwise interested in a relationship with the person he is deceiving and does not plan to maintain intimacy after the con is completed.

Someone can practice gateway deception and con artistry simultaneously, or pursue one type of deceit without the other. Where gateway deception is focused on duping an intimate in order to acquire legal rights or privileges from a government, con artistry is focused on duping an intimate in order to acquire resources from the deceived person herself.

Crime reports, news accounts, and lawsuits regularly feature con artists who established and then exploited intimate relationships.[62] For instance, law enforcement authorities believe that William Barber married perhaps as many as twelve women under a multitude of aliases.[63] The women reported that Barber told them endless lies, while hiding his other marriages and his criminal record. He posed variously as a pediatric cardiovascular surgeon, a war hero, a former professional football player,[64] and a leukemia patient.[65] Barber was none of those things. Indeed, one of his stints in jail had been for deserting the Army.[66]

The women also recounted that they were much poorer by the time Barber was through with them. Barber reportedly siphoned $400,000 from one woman, left another woman with more than $60,000 in credit card bills, and took out an $18,000 loan in yet another woman's name.[67]

Similarly, law enforcement authorities believe that Leslie Joseph Gall lured at least a dozen older women into romantic relationships in order to strip them of their assets. Gall utilized many aliases, concealed his long criminal history, and charmed the women with flowers, constant phone calls, and romantic dates. He reportedly stole $54,000 in stock certificates from one woman, swindled $42,000 from another, and convinced another to buy him a $28,000 motor home.[68]

Once his con artistry came to light, the aptly named Gall had a lot to say for himself—much of it suggesting misogyny. Gall emphasized that he had targeted women exclusively because he did not want to fleece other men, telling a reporter in a jailhouse interview: "Put yourself in my position—if you were going to rip somebody off, you'd go opposite sex."[69] Gall also embodied the tendency of deceivers to underestimate the damage their deceit has caused, betraying an inability or unwillingness to understand the financial and emotional harm he had inflicted on the women he duped. "Sure I took their money, but they got their money's worth out of me," Gall boasted in another jailhouse interview. "I made them very happy. They had the time of their lives with me." "I fulfilled their needs. They got attention, affection, companionship, and, in some cases, they got love."[70]

Barber and Gall exemplify how con artists use deceit to strip their intimates of their assets. Their stories also illustrate how intimate deception that happens to someone else can seem both tragic and comedic to people who learn about it later. More than that, observers often make clear that they find the skillfulness of con artists impressive—even if they do not want others to emulate these masterful deceivers. Barber inflicted enormous injuries on his victims, who were robbed and betrayed by a man they thought was their husband. Yet newspapers delighted in recounting Barber's many misdeeds. The New York Post called him the "Don Juan of con."[71]

Gall preyed on lonely women, taking advantage of their desire for love, affection, and companionship. But newspapers seem to have found Gall's con artistry—along with the whole subject of late-in-life romance—even more amusing than Barber's exploits. Journalists embraced age-related stereotypes and gave Gall a series of nicknames they apparently took to be hilarious, including "the balding Lothario," "the portly playboy," "the bespectacled Romeo," the "Sweetheart Swindler, the Blue-Rinse Romeo and the Geritol Bandit."[72]

Deception for Mastery and Control

Even if they are not con artists, people sometimes deceive in order to exert power over an intimate and manipulate her. What I call *deception for mastery and control* can appear in numerous, sometimes overlapping guises.

With *deception for thrills*, the deceiver seeks control over an intimate largely for its own sake. Someone might engage in deception for thrills because he enjoys feeling that he is more intelligent, knowledgeable, accomplished, and powerful than the people he is duping and can shape their decisions, actions, beliefs, and emotions at will.

Deceivers do not appear eager to discuss deception for thrills. But some deceived intimates believe they have experienced it. One woman wrote that before she learned of her boyfriend's many deceptions it had not occurred to her "that somebody might just lie, that there are people who lie for pleasure, for the feeling of superiority and power."[73]

Psychologists have similarly observed that some people delight in being deceptive, although the subject remains underexplored.[74] It is also interesting to note that several small-scale experiments focused on unethical behavior in contexts where there was no obvious victim have found that, on average, people who cheat on problem-solving tasks report feeling better afterward than people who have not cheated—with the cheaters believing that they have gotten away with something.[75]

Deception for thrills can be intertwined with domestic violence, further magnifying the power a batterer wields over the person he is abusing.[76] A woman who was emotionally and physically abused during her marriage recalled that her husband "lied about everything. He lied about stupid insignificant things, such as his high school prom date, who did the grocery shopping during his first marriage, and whether he had been a member of the PTO. He would tell different versions of events in an apparent attempt to make me crazy. This is a frequent technique utilized by emotional abusers in order to make their victims think they are crazy, instilling doubt and confusion in order to sustain control."[77]

Where deception for thrills revels in control for its own sake, other forms of deception for mastery and control are more focused on steering the deceived intimate in the deceiver's preferred direction. *Greedy deception* (deception for financial gain or material goods), *lustful deception* (deception for sex), and *paternalistic deception* (deception to guide the deceived intimate away from actions or feelings that the deceiver believes will harm the deceived) can be forms of deception for mastery and control.

A married person might practice greedy deception by concealing from her spouse that she has had sex with someone else so her spouse will agree to a more financially favorable divorce settlement.[78] Consider Paige Von Hoffman, who concealed her infidelity from her fiancé and then husband, Gordon Ball. A few weeks before Von Hoffman and Ball were scheduled to marry, Ball became suspicious that Von Hoffman might have been unfaithful with a former boyfriend who had spent the weekend with her and her children. But Von Hoffman repeatedly denied the accusation and the couple wed. After a little over a year of marriage, both spouses agreed that they had irreconcilable differences and should divorce. According to Ball, Von Hoffman told him that she would consent to an uncontested divorce only if he assumed her $350,914.67 mortgage debt, gave her $240,000, and paid the private school tuition for her two children until the children finished high school. Ball agreed, and the couple divorced after signing a marital dissolution agreement that included those terms. About six months later, Von Hoffman told Ball that she had been unfaithful before and during their marriage.[79] Von Hoffman probably had multiple reasons for lying about and hiding her infidelity for as long as she did. For example, she presumably knew that Ball considered her sexual monogamy a linchpin of their relationship, without which he would be unwilling to continue it. But one plausible reason why Von Hoffman concealed her infidelity—even after the couple decided to divorce—is that she thought Ball would press for a harsher divorce settlement if he knew about her unfaithfulness.

Although con artistry and greedy deception sometimes overlap, the two forms of deceit can also be distinct. There was no evidence or accusation that Von Hoffman was a con artist who had married in order to extract financial resources from her husband. She did not dupe her intimates for a living. But she did live by practicing deception, possibly in part for financial gain.

While greedy deception focuses on money and material goods, lustful deception focuses on sex. A man might practice lustful deception by falsely claiming to have had a vasectomy so a woman will agree that he does not need to use condoms.[80] Lustful deceptions and linchpin deceptions can overlap in many cases, but they can also diverge. A man may falsely claim to be sterile knowing that he does not need to lie in order to have an intimate relationship with the woman he is deceiving. The woman may have already made clear that she does not consider sterility a necessary condition for forming an intimate relationship or for having sex, so long as condoms are used.[81] In such cases, the deceit is not deployed to establish or maintain a relationship; it is used to access a certain kind of sex within the relationship.

With greedy deception and lustful deception, the deceiver is patently attempting to manipulate someone else in his own self-interest. With paternalistic deception, the deceiver believes he is deceiving his intimate for the intimate's own good. For example, a parent practicing paternalistic deception might never tell his child that she was adopted because the parent wants "to protect the child from feeling different."[82] Similarly, some parents plan to keep secret that they used assisted insemination with an anonymous donor's sperm because the parents fear that their children—even as adults—would feel stigmatized and bereft if they knew the circumstances of their conception and realized they did not know their biological father's identity. One of these parents explained: "I feel that it could be traumatic to a child to know that it was conceived in that way. . . . To imagine [the child's biological father] was somebody who nobody *knew* I think could have a disturbing effect on a child."[83] Another reported: "I don't see the need to tell her. It would just confuse her. There's no way you could ever find the father. . . . It would just, I would think, make her unhappy."[84]

Sometimes both deceiver and deceived agree after paternalistic deception is revealed that the deceit was in the deceived person's best interests. Essentially by definition, intimate deception that ends in mutual satisfaction does not generate litigation or calls for legal relief or reform. I am accordingly not focusing on it here.

Often, however, the person subject to paternalistic deception does not agree that the deceit served her interests—no matter how confident and sincere the deceiver was in the belief he was helping. I think the law should be concerned about paternalistic deception in those cases. For instance, Part III explores how the law might help adult children who have been deceived about the identities of their biological parents, sometimes for paternalistic reasons. For now, we can consider some examples where paternalistic deception backfired, leaving the deceived intimate convinced that the deceit left her worse off. Suzanne Ariel did not learn that she had been conceived with donor sperm until she was thirty-two years old. Thirteen years later, she explained how she felt about her parents' deceit: "We were all lied to as children by parents who were trying to protect us . . . . In my mind there is no justification for keeping it a secret. It does a lot of psychological damage to be kept in the dark about something this essential."[85] Judith also learned as an adult that she had been conceived with donor sperm. She reported that she "felt anger at both my mother and my father for having lied to me for so many years so unnecessarily. I felt betrayed by those lies."[86] Deceived intimates sometimes conclude—rightly or wrongly—that their deceivers' supposed paternalism was a rationalization masking self-interest.[87] Judith observed that the adults involved in her conception "made it a point to never keep records" of the assisted insemination and the biological father's identity because "[e]verybody was scared of the truth."[88]

Deception from Subordination

While deceit can help people control their intimates, it can also help people resist the power that intimates or others wield over them. People practice what I call *deception from subordination* when they are disempowered and think deception will enable them to mitigate that condition.

The disadvantages that spur people to deceive their intimates can be legal, economic, social, all of these, or otherwise. Just as the law can create incentives for intimate deception by attaching important rights and privileges to marriage, the law can tilt people toward deceit by placing them or leaving them in situations where they believe they have no better alternative than duping their intimates. Exploring deception from subordination reveals a frequently overlooked consequence of legalized inequality and one more reason for reform to promote equal rights and opportunities: Inequality—paired with violence or standing alone— can lead the disempowered to deceive the people who are closest to them.

The existing evidence cannot reveal the full range and extent of deception from subordination. But virtually by definition, members of relatively disadvantaged groups in our society may be more likely to resort to this form of intimate deception.

Deception from subordination and deception for mastery and control can focus on the same topics. Where one person might deceive about money in order to dominate her intimate, another person might deceive about money to resist her intimate's domination.

Indeed, some illuminating examples of deception from subordination involve stay-at-home wives whose husbands refuse to provide them with cash or strictly limit the cash they provide. These women do not have cash of their own because they do not perform market work, earn a salary, or have their own savings or investments. The law provides that a married person with the means to support his spouse cannot leave her without the basic necessities of life, such as food, housing, and clothing. But despite the many other changes in marriage law since the nineteenth century, courts still overwhelmingly hold that a person in a legally intact marriage has no obligation to give his spouse cash if he prefers to offer her only goods and services. While a wife could divorce or legally separate from a husband who denies her access to cash, she may find those options unappealing for financial, personal, religious, cultural, or other reasons. For example, she may recognize that divorce law tends to operate to the systematic economic detriment of wives who have prioritized domestic responsibilities over market work.[89]

One might think that the problem of husbands dramatically restricting their wives' access to cash has been left behind in the distant past.[90] But even today, some husbands with resources give their wives little or no cash. The men typically withhold cash as a way to wield more power over their wives. A husband might provide his wife with credit cards but little or no cash because he can track his wife's credit card purchases and thus more easily control what she buys and how much she spends. Similarly, a husband might limit his wife's access to cash in order to make leaving him more difficult. A woman with no cash reserves can be very vulnerable financially after leaving her husband, at least in the short term, while she is negotiating or litigating the economic consequences of her divorce.

The legal regime that makes this possible is objectionable on many grounds, and Part III of this book discusses potential legal reforms to encourage and facilitate more egalitarian marital relationships in which both spouses have adequate access to cash. For the moment, we can note that one reason to criticize the present legal regime is that it can leave some wives in situations where they believe they have no better alternative than deceit.

Now, as in times past,[91] some women subject to their husbands' strict financial control have responded by deceiving their husbands in order to acquire access to money and the autonomy cash can bring.[92] A *Wall Street Journal* reporter actually wrote a handbook for married women seeking to accumulate a secret stash of cash that their husbands do not know about. The book is called *How to Hide Money from Your Husband . . . and Other Time-Honored Ways to Build a Nest Egg*.[93] This title is not satirical. The book—published by Simon & Schuster in 1999—is a how-to guide, brimming with tips for siphoning money from husbands by lying about how much goods and services cost, taking cash from unattended pockets, covertly selling items to keep the proceeds, opening secret bank accounts, and employing related deceptive tactics.[94] The author promises that "by the time you finish this book, you'll be running to put your hands in [your husband's] pants—or wherever he keeps his wallet."[95]

One of the women interviewed for this book called herself "a maid with a Jaguar—meaning that I have everything in life but it's only good as long as we are married." Holly was a stay-at-home wife and mother of two. Her husband, Rick, insisted on "the first and last word when it comes to money." Rick controlled spending decisions in the marriage, and he limited Holly's freedom to make spending decisions to a weekly $300 allowance. The two times that Holly and Rick separated, her life of material abundance disappeared "and the Jaguar was traded in for a Hyundai."

Holly responded to her husband's domineering by falsifying the couple's checkbook register. Rick allowed her to use this account to pay utilities bills, so Holly would report in the checkbook register that she wrote three checks a month to the same utilities company when she actually wrote two of the checks to herself. She ended this recurring deception only when Rick computerized their bill paying "to get more control over our checkbook."[96]

Liz, a homemaker also interviewed in *How to Hide Money from Your Husband*, was married to Bob, the chief executive officer for a *Fortune* 500 company. Bob paid Liz's credit card bills from shopping at some of the most luxurious stores in New York, but kept "her on a short cash leash as a form of control." Liz responded by using her credit cards to buy expensive clothing, jewelry, and accessories and then covertly selling the merchandise to her friends, offering them a 50% discount off the retail price in exchange for cash payments. She kept the money she accumulated in a secret Swiss bank account.[97] Liz's behavior provides a vivid illustration of deception from subordination—perhaps an unexpected one because it features luxury goods and money laundering strategies most commonly associated with having abundant cash stockpiles rather than little access to cash. This example simultaneously shows how inequality within a relationship and deceit in response to that inequality can produce enormous waste. Bob refused to provide her with cash, so Liz used credit cards to spend two dollars for every one she pocketed.

Holly and Liz did not report physical violence in their marriages. But unsurprisingly, the threat, fear, or experience of violence can also prompt deception from subordination. Domestic violence is a crime in every state, yet those legal prohibitions remain dramatically and disproportionately underenforced. Many observers agree that the legal system still leaves people in violent relationships with too few options and too little protection.[98] Moreover, even the United States Supreme Court has noted that "[m]ere notification of pregnancy is frequently a flashpoint for battering and violence within the family. The number of battering incidents is high during the pregnancy and often the worst abuse can be associated with pregnancy.... The battering husband may deny parentage and use the pregnancy as an excuse for abuse."[99]

Under these circumstances, some women partnered with violent men have used deception to conceal their pregnancies because they feared that revealing the pregnancies would enrage their partners and escalate abuse—whether because the men would not want to father additional or any children, because the men would suspect infidelity, or for additional or alternative reasons. Carrie Godwin's relationship with Herbert Wiley Sigmon, IV, "was punctuated by chronic episodes of domestic violence, substance abuse, and out of relationship affairs." Godwin became pregnant, thought Sigmon might not be the father, and believed that Sigmon was "likely" to commit violence against her if he learned that she was pregnant with another man's child. Godwin decided to hide the pregnancy from Sigmon—even though she lived with him—and to place the baby for adoption. Godwin repeatedly denied her pregnancy to Sigmon, his mother, and others, first pretending "that she was just gaining weight" and then reporting that she was undergoing treatment for a tumor that had caused her to put on weight. Remarkably, Sigmon did not discover that Godwin had been pregnant until a little over a month after she gave birth when he searched Godwin's car and found baby photos and signed adoption paperwork. Genetic testing later revealed that Sigmon was the child's biological father.[100] He was eventually able to stop the adoption.[101]

Along similar lines, several small-scale studies of domestic violence have found that some battered women deceive their abusers about their use of birth control. One group of researchers interviewed fifty-three women in domestic violence shelters. The researchers found that the partners of twenty-one of the women had told them to forgo birth control. In response, eleven of the women managed to deceive their partners by successfully concealing their use of contraception.[102] One woman interviewed for this study reported that her partner finally agreed that she could have an intrauterine contraception (IUC) device inserted, but then changed his mind after they arrived at the clinic. She knew that her partner did not understand what the clinic doctor was telling her in English, so she lied and told her partner in Spanish that the doctor had warned her that they would have to pay a hundred dollar fine if they did not go forward as planned. Her partner did not want to pay the fine, so he permitted her to have the device inserted.[103] A second small-scale study of young women in relationships with abusive partners who were actively seeking to impregnate them found that four out of fourteen women had been deceitful to hide their use of contraception.[104]

Inequalities that many readers would find unjust, even outrageous, can spur deception from subordination. But inequalities that most readers would take to be both justified and frequently unavoidable can also spur such deceit. For example, parents often have enormous power over their children. Some of this power flows from the law itself, which grants parents far-reaching control over their minor children's custody, education, employment, punishment, and safety.[105] Parents do not have those same legal prerogatives over their competent adult children. However, the law generally gives parents the right to provide or deny financial support to their adult children as the parents see fit,[106] and this can be a source of significant control. Parents' power over their children also comes from sources outside the law, such as the emotional influence that parents tend to exercise over children they raised.

Some children, including some adult children, deceive their parents as a way of countering the emotional, financial, and legal power that their parents wield over them. One study of 229 high school students and 261 college students found that 82% of the students reported that at least once in the past year they had lied to their parents about friends, alcohol, drugs, parties, money, dating, and/or sex. The students believed that one of the most acceptable reasons for lying to parents was that the child "[f]elt she had the right to make her own decisions."[107]

Another study asked 120 high school students how they dealt with issues where they thought their parents disagreed with them. The students reported that for 68% of those issues they chose to deceive their parents by lying or deliberately omitting information with the intent to mislead. Almost half (47%) of the time this deceit took the form of the students not revealing key information they thought their parents would want to know, while 25% of the time the students completely avoided mentioning the issue and 27% of the time the students lied.[108] Two of the most common reasons the students cited for deceiving their parents were that they feared the consequences of disclosure and believed that "the issue was not in their parents' jurisdiction."[109]

In the examples of deception from subordination that we have considered so far, the deceiver's relative powerlessness was importantly grounded in the specifics of her intimate relationship. But sometimes people deceive not so much because of how their intimate has acted or will act and more in response to their disadvantaged position in wider society.

Some parents have deceived their children about their religious, racial, or ethnic background to shield the children—and themselves—from discrimination. Geoffrey Wolff's father, Arthur, was Jewish, but both of Geoffrey's parents lied to hide that from him.[110] When Geoffrey was twenty-six, he successfully prodded his mother to reveal the truth, which Geoffrey suspected by then. She explained that the lie was "maybe to spare [Geoffrey] the pain [Arthur] felt" from antisemitism.[111]

Brando Skyhorse's Mexican-American mother lied and told her son that they were both Native American and that his father was an imprisoned Native-American activist. She changed his name from Brando Ulloa to Brando Skyhorse with this deception in mind, never mentioned Brando's actual biological father (who had immigrated from Mexico), and changed her own name from Maria Teresa to Running Deer Skyhorse.[112] One apparent motivation for the deceit was her conviction that Native Americans experienced less discrimination and better treatment than Mexican Americans. Even after Brando discovered the truth when he was approximately twelve or thirteen,[113] his mother continued to deceive her romantic partners about her background. Brando later recalled one of those episodes: "Pat was kept oblivious about us being Mexicans so that we could benefit from what my mother called 'white man's guilt.' That made no sense, I told my mother. Wouldn't whites feel guilty about how Mexicans are treated too? 'Are you fucking serious?' my mother asked."[114]

Deception to Maintain a Preexisting Facade

While many people deceiving an intimate consider the intimate to be the primary focus of their deceptive schemes, sometimes people deceive an intimate as part of a plot to dupe another target. Deceivers practice what I call *deception to maintain a preexisting facade* when they have already committed themselves to deceiving someone—or many people or everyone—and want to convince an intimate or intimates of the same falsehood(s) in order to bolster the story's credibility or otherwise keep their deceit from being discovered. Courts routinely differentiate between intimate deception and deception outside of intimacy, but sometimes people pursue the same deceit in both contexts.

For example, a person who lies to his employer, clients, or professional contacts about his educational achievements, professional experience, or military service may tell his intimates the same lies so the intimates do not knowingly or unwittingly reveal inconsistent information. Geoffrey Wolff's father, Arthur, did not limit his deceit to lying about his religious background. Arthur told his employers that he had graduated from prestigious universities and was qualified to work as an aeronautical engineer. Telling the same lies to his wife and son helped Arthur maintain those deceptions.[115]

Much like Arthur Wolff, people who deceive to maintain a preexisting facade about their professional training or employment frequently pretend to have more glamorous, interesting, and remunerative jobs or credentials than they actually possess. Sometimes, however, an intimate deceiving to maintain a preexisting facade makes his life and credentials appear more humdrum than they really are. Pretending to work for the CIA is a popular choice for people lying to their intimates about their employment. Fake CIA agents appear all too eager to talk about their exploits.[116] In contrast, Jack Devine actually worked for the CIA, but told his children that he had another career. Devine deceived his children about his occupation because he feared they were not "old enough to handle it responsibly" and might reveal the truth to their friends or acquaintances, compromising or destroying the professional cover Devine had established in the foreign communities where he was operating. Devine did not "break cover and tell [his] children that [he was] a CIA officer" until his children were in their teens and the family was back in the United States.[117]

Devine was proud of his CIA career and wanted his children to know where he worked once they were old enough to keep the secret. But intimates deceiving to maintain a preexisting facade are often concealing activities that they know their intimates and many other people would find deeply unappealing.

Robert P. Hanssen worked for the FBI, but also had a secret life as a double agent who spied for the Soviet Union and then Russia from 1979 to 1980 and from 1985 to 2001. Hanssen gave the Soviets the names of Soviet officers who were spying for the United States. At least three of the people he betrayed were executed.

After Hanssen was arrested in 2001, his wife, Bonnie, admitted that Robert had told her around 1980 that he was having unauthorized contacts with Soviet agents and had received approximately $30,000 from them. However, Bonnie contended that Robert had insisted that "he was just tricking the Russians and feeding them false information." Bonnie reported that Robert agreed to donate the money to charity and vowed that he would never be involved with the Soviets again. Over the following years, he repeatedly assured her that he was abiding by these promises.

On her account, Bonnie never knew the true nature of Robert's interactions with the Soviets between 1979 and 1980 and had no idea that he resumed dealing with the Soviets in 1985. Assuming that Bonnie was telling the truth—and the federal government agreed to a plea bargain for Robert in which Bonnie received the survivor's portion of Robert's FBI pension and kept the house the couple owned—this appears to be another example of intimate deception to maintain a preexisting facade. Robert kept Bonnie in the dark and that helped him keep everyone else (but the Soviets/Russians) in the dark.[118]

Steven H. Dickman was unable to practice law in his own name because he had been convicted of grand larceny and disbarred. Undeterred, he appropriated the identity and attorney registration number of a retired lawyer named Stephen G. Dickerman. Between 2009 and 2014, Dickman presented himself to clients, attorneys, and judges as Dickerman. He also falsified Dickerman's resume to include a master's degree in law from New York University.[119] FBI agents were investigating Dickman by the summer of 2014. When he was arrested, he was carrying a driver's license in his real name.[120]

The federal case against Dickman focused on his work life, rather than his intimate one.[121] But at Dickman's arraignment, the prosecutor indicated that Dickman's fiancée, a retired schoolteacher, apparently believed that he was a lawyer named Stephen G. Dickerman.[122] This woman reportedly attended the arraignment, said she was engaged to Dickerman, and declared that her betrothed was "honorable and very knowledgeable about the law."[123]

Unsurprisingly, Dickman did not tell the court why he deceived his fiancée. Indeed, Dickman's lawyer was still insisting at the arraignment that Dickman's name actually was Stephen G. Dickerman.[124] Presumably, however, Dickman deceived his fiancée about his real name and professional status because he wanted to seem like a more attractive mate and because he feared that revealing his scheme might prompt her to share the information with law enforcement authorities and/or the clients who had hired Dickman-as-Dickerman. Dickman eventually dropped the pretense that he was Dickerman and pled guilty.[125]

In short, one answer to the question of why people deceive their intimates is that deception can generate immense rewards and shield deceivers from terrible trouble. People use intimate deception to induce someone into an intimate relationship or to keep her there, to secure government benefits or to strip an intimate of her assets, to control an intimate or to resist his power, and to help maintain deceptive schemes the deceiver already has in place. This chapter does not exhaust all the reasons a person might have for deceiving an intimate. But exploring some of the most prominent and recurring motivations behind intimate deception helps reveal the significant roles that deception can play within intimate relationships, the advantages that intimates can derive from their deceit, and the ways that the law itself sometimes creates or exacerbates the incentives to deceive.

2

Why Does
Intimate Deception Work?

While intimate deception can benefit deceivers enormously, deceivers usually cannot obtain those benefits unless they manage to dupe their targets. One likely explanation for the prevalence of deception within intimate relationships is that would-be deceivers recognize that intimate deception often succeeds. The frequent efficacy of intimate deception also helps explain why it can be so harmful. Deception typically causes more injury when the person subject to it is actually fooled, at least for a while. Most, if not almost all, of the deceived intimates who have sought legal remedies did not instantly detect the deceit directed at them. This chapter explores why intimate deception often works.

Examining the recurring success of intimate deception can enhance our understanding of both the phenomenon of intimate deception and its legal regulation. Courts considering deceit within intimacy frequently fault plaintiffs for not promptly suspecting that their intimates were deceiving them and not mounting an immediate investigation to unearth the truth. Courts denying remedies to deceived intimates routinely declare or imply that the plaintiffs were unreasonably credulous, and judges presume that these plaintiffs would have readily uncovered the deceit had they become suspicious earlier.[1]

In some ways, it is unsurprising that courts are inclined to blame deceived intimates for having been duped. Indeed, this pattern is also visible in many popular discussions of intimate deception, which commonly contend that deceived intimates should have known that deceit was likely and should have investigated and protected themselves.[2] Faulting deceived intimates for their supposed failures of suspicion and investigation helps observers assure themselves that they are sharper, shrewder, and smarter than the pitiful person who was fooled. Thinking that a deceitful intimate might dupe you is unsettling. How comforting to believe that only the particularly gullible are vulnerable to that experience. Even apart from our desire to reassure ourselves, courts and other third-party observers may also be prone to blame deceived intimates for their plight because events tend to look more predictable and less surprising when we are assessing them in retrospect, aware of what actually occurred.[3] This suggests that when judges or other commentators know that an intimate's words and actions proved to be deceptive, they are likely to overestimate—with 20/20 hindsight—how likely it was that the intimate would be deceitful and how easy it would have been to uncover the deception at the time.

My point is not that people should believe everything their intimates try to convince them is true. Reading this book should make clear that in some cases a healthy dose of skepticism about an intimate's trustworthiness would be well-advised. Attempting to protect oneself by investigating whether an intimate is being deceitful may be prudent—especially given how little help the law offers to people suing for redress after a deceptive intimate has injured them. In Part III of the book, I discuss how the law might facilitate this sort of investigation while still respecting privacy, liberty, and security concerns. For our purposes now, however, the most relevant question is not whether suspicion and investigation are sometimes wise. Instead, the key question is whether the fact that a person was duped because she did not investigate her intimate, or did not investigate immediately or successfully, should be used as a reason to blame her for her own injuries and a rationale for denying legal redress.

One cause for wariness about legal arguments faulting deceived intimates for being overly trusting is that the law governing deception outside of intimacy is often more protective of the credulous—recognizing that such people are more likely to be duped, essentially by definition. When fraudsters use subterfuge to learn the bank account or credit card numbers of the unwitting people who answer their phone calls or emails, the legal system does not excuse this deceitfulness if the deceivers targeted overly trusting people who did not thoroughly interrogate and investigate the fraudsters' claims. To the contrary, judges and legislators frequently cite evidence that some victims were especially trusting as grounds for harshly penalizing the fraudsters for taking advantage of people who were more vulnerable to being fooled.[4] The law often views the fact that a deceiver preyed on a trusting person as a strike against the deceiver, not his exoneration.

Still more fundamentally, courts that are inclined to blame deceived intimates for having been duped routinely underestimate the difficulty of detecting an intimate's deceit and uncovering the truth—even for a person of ordinary or above-average shrewdness, intelligence, and common sense. While the obstacles to unmasking a deceptive intimate can vary, they frequently take three basic forms. First, almost everyone is much less able to spot deception than we may like to think. We are usually no better at detecting an intimate's deceit. Indeed, detecting an intimate's deception may be harder than spotting deceit from a stranger. Second, even if a person wonders whether or suspects that an intimate is being deceptive, strong social norms discourage us from investigating to verify the truthfulness of an intimate's claims. These norms promoting trust within intimacy can help foster individual fulfillment, productive cooperation, committed caregiving, and satisfying community life, but they can also leave people more vulnerable to deceitful intimates. Third, even if a person does not feel bound by social norms against investigating intimates or is willing to override those norms, it can be much harder than courts typically assume to verify an intimate's truthfulness without the investigation itself endangering or ending the relationship because the intimate learns about it. Practical realities often make researching an intimate without the intimate's knowledge difficult or impossible. Moreover, laws designed to protect people's privacy, liberty, and security frequently prohibit conducting reconnaissance on someone without the person's consent. There is a striking irony in courts faulting plaintiffs for not uncovering intimate deception sooner when the law itself—for good and important reasons—often makes investigation much more difficult by imposing strict civil or criminal penalties on people who search or monitor an intimate's home, computers, emails, postal mail, phones, cars, tax returns, credit reports, medical records, and the like without the intimate's consent.

The Difficulties of Detecting Deception, Especially by Intimates

Imagine how useful it would be if you always knew when someone was lying or otherwise deceiving you. The consistent ability to detect deception would help you at work, at home, on dates, and in any other social interaction. You would be better equipped to decide which relationships to pursue or avoid. You would be better able to protect yourself without having to rely on assistance from the legal system, which in the case of intimate deception is generally unavailable in any event.

The protagonists in detective fiction are often masters at detecting deception, which helps them solve mysteries others cannot crack. Stories as old as Arthur Conan Doyle's tales about Sherlock Holmes and as new as J.K. Rowling's novels about Cormoran Strike feature private investigators who can tell whether someone is being deceptive just by observing him.[5] Indeed, this conceit appears to be one of the core conventions of the genre.

Many people, well-known or otherwise, have implied or contended through the years that detecting deception is relatively easy. Friedrich Nietzsche declared as early as 1886 that "[l]ies come through our mouths – but the face that accompanies them tells the truth."[6] Sigmund Freud wrote in 1905 that "[h]e that has eyes to see and ears to hear may convince himself that no mortal can keep a secret. If his lips are silent, he chatters with his finger-tips; betrayal oozes out of him at every pore."[7] Today, a thriving commercial literature promises that anyone can learn how to "become a human lie detector"[8] who knows "how to spot a liar"[9] and "spy the lie,"[10] who knows "when people are lying, how they are feeling, what they are thinking,"[11] and who can "get the truth in 5 minutes or less in any conversation or situation."[12]

Such claims notwithstanding, an enormous body of empirical evidence suggests that detecting deception is very difficult. Volumes of social science research spanning decades find that the odds that a person will accurately assess whether a speaker is being honest or lying hover only slightly above chance. One review synthesized the results from 206 studies dating from the 1940s to the 2000s that asked participants to evaluate speakers and report whether they thought each speaker was telling the truth or lying. A total of 24,483 subjects participated in all the studies taken together and they assessed a total of 4435 speakers. On average, people correctly distinguished between true statements and lies just 53.98% of the time, where flipping a coin would have produced a 50% success rate. Moreover, the participants found it especially difficult to identify which statements were lies. While participants correctly identified 61% of the truthful statements as truthful, they correctly classified only 47% of the lies—a success rate worse than what random guessing would have achieved.[13]

These findings are particularly striking because the researchers explicitly instructed participants to distinguish truthful statements from lies. Such overt reminders about the possibility of deceit are typically absent from ordinary life. But participants had difficulty detecting deception even with such prompting.[14]

The available empirical evidence also suggests that our lack of skill in detecting deception does not vary much from individual to individual. A subsequent review consolidated the results from 247 studies that asked participants to assess whether speakers were telling the truth or lying. This review sought to determine whether some people were better able to detect deception. It found that people's ability to identify lies "range[d] no more widely than would be expected by chance."[15]

Some social scientists have reported finding a few individuals who are unusually adept at detecting deception—meaning that they managed to achieve at least 80% accuracy in three separate, ten-question tests asking whether speakers were lying or telling the truth. The psychologists who announced discovering these "'wizards' of deception detection" estimated that they represent less than 1% or 2% of the population.[16] Even if these wizards do live among us, their talents appear to be exceptional and rare.

Several common heuristics help explain why most people are not skilled deception detectors. Heuristics is the term that social scientists use to describe cognitive shortcuts that people unconsciously depend on to answer complex questions in ways that are adequate, even if often not entirely accurate. Heuristics help us function in a world of otherwise overwhelming information and complexity. They are ubiquitous and frequently very useful. Without realizing it, we rely on multiple heuristics every day to simplify our decisionmaking so we do not need to review every possible consideration and piece of data. However, heuristics can sometimes lead people to systematic biases, repeated errors in judgment, and mistaken conclusions.[17]

Our reliance on heuristics can make it more difficult to discern when someone is attempting to dupe us. For instance, most of us have a truth bias, meaning that we unconsciously begin with the default assumption that what people are telling us through their words, actions, or inactions is true. Many social science studies have examined truth biases by having people assess some speakers who were telling the truth and an equal number of speakers who were lying. These studies have repeatedly found that most observers believed that most of the speakers were being honest.[18]

Harboring a truth bias can have many advantages. This heuristic can promote trust and intimacy in relationships. It can protect our social interactions from the corrosiveness of suspicion and steer us away from erroneously accusing people of deceitfulness when they are being honest. A truth bias also spares us the psychological burden and emotional drain of constantly thinking about the possibility of being deceived. But at the same time, a truth bias makes detecting deception more difficult.

Many of us also have a confirmation bias, meaning that once we have formed a belief or expectation we will unconsciously look for evidence that supports what we already think, interpret the evidence we have in ways consistent with our current views, and overlook or undervalue contradictory evidence.[19] This heuristic spares us from spending our days constantly rethinking all our conclusions. But a confirmation bias can make spotting deception more difficult because once we have decided that someone is behaving honestly or expect him to do so—and a truth bias steers us to that starting place—we are likely to seek out evidence that confirms our assessment and dismiss evidence that undercuts it, without even realizing what we are doing.

One might think, and some have speculated,[20] that people would be better at detecting deception within intimate relationships. Intimates are often (although not always) intensely familiar with each other. Moreover, people might be more motivated to uncover deceit from an intimate compared to a stranger or acquaintance.

However, the available social science evidence suggests that most people are no better at detecting deception from an intimate.[21] In fact, people may be especially poor deception detectors in this context. The social science research on deception by intimates is exponentially less extensive than the research on deception outside of intimacy, but the existing small-scale studies highlight several factors that can make it difficult to spot an intimate's deceit. As an initial matter, the studies find (unsurprisingly) that people tend to trust their intimates when they think they know their intimates well and feel close to them. Phrased differently, our truth bias—our initial, unconscious, default presumption that someone is not being deceptive—tends to be even stronger when communications from an intimate are at issue and the bias may grow increasingly powerful the more developed the relationship becomes. In deciding whether an intimate is behaving deceptively, we tend to rely heavily on our starting assumption that he is not.[22]

Related small-scale studies focused on married and dating couples have found that people tend to hold "positive illusions" about their romantic partners. For example, the studies found that people were likely to assess a partner's attributes more favorably than the partner himself did, often presenting a positive spin on a partner's shortcomings.[23] This research was not focused on deceit within intimate relationships, but it seems likely that viewing an intimate through rose-tinted lenses can also lead people away from thinking that an intimate might be behaving deceptively.

At the same time, some small-scale studies have found that people tend to have an inflated sense of their ability to spot a romantic partner's deceit. They think their intimate is trustworthy, but also believe that they would know if their intimate strayed into deception. This overconfidence can lead people to assume that their intimate is not being deceptive, perhaps because the intimate's behavior is not triggering the alarms they think they would hear.[24]

These thought patterns often have tremendous upsides. Many people would find their lives and relationships less fulfilling if they were unable to have faith in their intimates, believe their intimates would not deceive them, and think that they know and understand their intimates very well. Intimacy requires trust to flourish. Indeed, some social science research suggests that having a view of one's romantic partner that is more favorable than the most objective evidence would support may make people happier and their relationships more satisfying, less conflictual, and longer lasting.[25] In other words, embracing a perception of one's intimate that is not wholly based in reality may sometimes change reality for the better. Yet these same patterns can also make people more vulnerable to being duped because they lead people away from thinking that an intimate might be deceitful.

In addition, intimate deception may sometimes be more difficult to discern because of the types of deceit that intimates tend to pursue. Both common experience and the existing social science evidence suggest that people are more likely to believe deception that flatters them, deception that is designed to ingratiate, and/or deception that they want to believe is true.[26] These characteristics describe much of the deceit within intimate relationships.

In short, the first reason why intimate deceivers often succeed in duping people is that detecting deception can be very difficult, perhaps especially when the deceiver is an intimate. We routinely presume that ordinary people are much more skilled at spotting an intimate's deceit than they actually appear to be. People often never suspect that an intimate is deceiving them.

Social Norms Against Investigating Intimates

A second major obstacle to unmasking intimate deceivers is that powerful social norms discourage us from conducting reconnaissance on our intimates and seeking to verify their honesty. Even if a person does suspect that an intimate is being deceptive, these social norms can make pursuing that suspicion and learning the truth more difficult than courts typically assume.

Social norms urging and expecting us to trust our intimates can promote closeness and security in relationships, which in turn can foster individual satisfaction, devoted caregiving, and rewarding social community. But norms that discourage people from investigating their intimates—or even from considering such a possibility—can also help intimate deceivers succeed.

Of course, social norms against investigating intimates do not inhibit everyone or make everyone feel constrained at all times, in all contexts, and with the same intensity. Moreover, the strength of these norms is likely to vary between subcultures and by life experience.[27] Learning about the prevalence of deception in intimacy may lead some readers of this book to conclude that they are no longer going to respect norms against investigation. Nonetheless, the social understanding that investigating intimates is inappropriate appears in myriad places in American culture—ranging from scholarly work, to popular writing, to the words of deceived intimates themselves.

Academics have not systematically studied social norms against investigating intimates, a subject that is ripe for research by social scientists. But scholars have sometimes noted these norms in the course of other projects. One psychologist observed in discussing the difficulties of detecting deception that "social conversation rules dictate credulity."[28] As he explained, "[c]onversational rules in daily life prevent the observer from showing suspicion." A person who violated those rules by declaring "I would like to check what you are saying,"[29] "I don't believe you," "That cannot be true," or "Could you prove that?" would expect the challenged person to "become quickly irritated"[30] and the conversation to "become awkward," to say the least. This psychologist was not focused on intimate deceivers, but mentioned that "[e]xpressing doubt is particularly difficult if the speaker is someone to whom the observer feels emotionally close, such as a friend or partner."[31]

Along similar lines, an economics professor wrote a dating guide that considered the social dilemma confronting a man who has included his "healthy income" in his online dating profile, but "wants to make sure [his date] believes he actually has a lot of money." As the professor observed, the rich man could "show her his recent tax returns as evidence of his wealth. But that would be rather weird behavior, thereby signaling something less positive than he is aiming for."[32] The professor did not raise the possibility of the man's date asking to inspect his tax returns so she could verify his income. Presumably such a request would be even more socially transgressive.

It is unclear whether the economics professor endorsed the social norms he discussed, but some scholars have explicitly argued that at least some ways of investigating intimates are socially inappropriate, even if legal. Jonathan Zittrain, a law and computer science professor at Harvard, told the *New York Times* that he opposed the covert use of Global Positioning System (GPS) devices to track an intimate's movements, even assuming such conduct is legal. "To have this as a routine tool strikes me as pretty chilling," he said. "We are talking about partners and spouses, not pets."[33]

Popular authors and readers also frequently stress in newspapers and magazines that investigating dates or potential dates is socially incorrect. Indeed, even something as seemingly innocuous and presumably common as a basic internet search on a date or potential date has sparked remarkable disagreement in popular media about its wisdom and appropriateness.

Some critics of internet investigation explicitly urge people to believe what their dates tell them. Aaron Silverberg, a "dating and life coach," advised readers of a Seattle newspaper not to run internet searches on dates or potential dates. He analogized conducting computer research on a date to acting less than fully human and alive, insisting: "You have to ask in person. You have to trust that person to tell you something is real. We're not just corporations. We're human beings with heart."[34]

Other critics warn in popular newspapers that using the internet to learn more about a date—even with no thought of unearthing deceit—will make subsequent conversations with that person less enjoyable and undermine the relationship's chances of success. One woman contended that internet research "sort of takes the spontaneity out of a date."[35] Another recounted how she had "ruined [her] chances with" a man by researching him on the internet. She stated flatly, "my advice to friends is: never Google a date. No Facebook, MySpace or Technorati, either. There's something to be said for the spontaneity and authentic facial expressions of utter ignorance."[36]

Still other critics characterize internet research as an invasion of the date's privacy. One reader wrote to a *Washington Post* advice columnist to report that she had searched the internet for the name of a man she was dating and discovered an article discussing the trial of the man's father for murdering the man's mother. Her note to the advice columnist, signed "Wish I Never Googled," sought to minimize her transgression of social norms by stressing how unsystematic and unpremeditated her investigation had been. She emphasized that: "One night I was casually Googling his name. Very innocently – I swear – I just thought I could see his work projects or something like that." Even so, she wrote, "I feel like I invaded his privacy, and now he doesn't have a chance to tell me on his own time."

The advice columnist, Carolyn Hax, reassured the letter writer, responding: "No no no, it's good that you Googled. It's there, it's public information, it's practically reflex for bored Web surfers, and it's just common sense to use this basic tool on someone new."[37] But Hax also assumed there would be debate and disagreement among her readership about the ethics of running an internet search on a date's name. She invited her readers to comment on the issue. Readers responded with an array of views, including the argument that even such rudimentary research was inappropriate. One reader wrote: "Wow, it's that accepted to Google someone? If a guy I was dating told me he did it, I'd think he was a crazy, paranoid creep. If I were this guy, I'd feel like my privacy had been massively invaded and I'd never call her again."[38] Just the minimal investigation represented by "Googling a date" can be socially controversial.

More extensive investigations can trigger still harsher social criticism. Even some commentators who have defended the permissibility of basic internet searches on a date or potential date have simultaneously insisted that going beyond internet searching to conduct additional research on an intimate is socially inappropriate. Randy Cohen drew that line when he was "the Ethicist" columnist for the *New York Times*. Shana Novak, a reader from New York, wrote to Cohen to discuss the behavior of a friend who had searched the internet for information about a doctor she had gone out with and discovered her date's repeated involvement in malpractice litigation. Novak wanted to know what Cohen thought "about using Google to check up on another person." Cohen reported that he was "for it," while explaining that he felt compelled to take that position because he had already done such searching himself. However, Cohen stressed that if someone "labored all afternoon at the courthouse checking equally public information on her date, she'd have crossed the border between casual curiosity and stalking." Describing the search of public records as "stalking" is remarkable. Cohen was apparently willing to apply that label to situations where the searcher did not intend to follow the investigated person, create fear, inflict injury, or harass. Cohen's language suggested the intensity of his determination to draw a sharp normative distinction between internet searching and more time-consuming methods of investigation. On Cohen's view, Novak's friend had acted acceptably because "[h]er Googling . . . was akin to asking her friends about this

fellow — offhand, sociable and benign." As Cohen phrased it, "laziness, or limiting yourself to insouciant Googling, is more honorable than perseverance, as in
hauling yourself down to the municipal archives."[39]

Other defenders of internet searches on intimates or would-be intimates have
likewise insisted on the inappropriateness of alternate or additional forms of
investigation. One of the readers who participated in the *Washington Post* discussion about conducting internet research on a date reported that he routinely
Googled people, but stressed that he was not "digging through [someone's]
trash."[40] Along the same lines, Jessica Bennett—executive editor at Tumblr, a
social networking website—disagreed with the title of the *Glamour* article em-
phatically advising readers to "Stop Googling Your Dates!" Bennett reasoned
that internet research on a potential date saved time, explaining "[y]ou can basi-
cally skip the first couple of dates and go straight to Google to see whether you're
compatible." But Bennett simultaneously stressed to *Glamour*'s readers that
some other means of gathering information would be socially inappropriate.
As she phrased the conundrum, "[y]ou definitely want to know the things you
could find out on a résumé. Except that it would be weird to ask for someone's
résumé."[41]

The self-help literature for people deceived within intimate relationships similarly recognizes the strength of social norms against investigating intimates. As
one self-help book asked rhetorically, "how many of us are willing to turn into a
private detective in the early stages of a relationship, especially when we've been
given no reason to be suspicious? Love and suspicion seem so contradictory."[42]
Another book noted that "challenging someone's story or perception might feel
wrong—especially if you're used to believing most of what people tell you."[43]
This book counseled readers to work on transforming their social role expectations by thinking of themselves as a "private eye" or "newspaper reporter" fact-
checking someone's claims by "ask[ing] who, what, why, where, when, and how
questions at every juncture, not because you're a difficult person, but because
you want to get the facts of your story right."[44] The author advised each reader to
"[s]ee yourself as curious, not rude."[45]

Some people duped within intimacy have also reported that they thought
investigating their intimates or seeking more information from them was inappropriate. One woman explained that she did not probe her husband for more
facts about his life and history because she felt that such questioning—even by a
spouse—would invade his "privacy." As she recounted, "[I did not ask] questions
I would have considered intrusive if anyone had asked them of me." After finally
learning of her husband's deceit, she concluded that her "tendency toward privacy" along with her "steadfast loyalty" had enabled her husband to dupe her.[46]
If questioning an intimate is seen as invasive and potentially disloyal, intimate
deceivers are well-positioned to keep their deceit from being discovered.

In short, even if a person worries or suspects that an intimate is less than honest, strong social norms can discourage us from investigating an intimate's veracity. These norms tell us not to dig too deeply in researching an intimate or not to dig at all.

Practical and Legal Obstacles to Investigating Intimates

A third major obstacle to unmasking intimate deceivers and discovering the truth is that it can be much harder than courts typically assume to investigate an intimate without the investigation endangering or ending the relationship because the intimate finds out about the sleuthing. As would-be detectives often recognize, many intimates will feel offended, appalled, and/or betrayed if they learn they have been investigated, including when—or especially when—the investigation uncovers no deceit. Yet practical realities make conducting many forms of reconnaissance without the intimate's knowledge challenging or impossible. Moreover, laws meant to safeguard important values of privacy, liberty, and security frequently impose civil or criminal prohibitions on searching or monitoring an intimate's home, computers, emails, postal mail, phones, cars, tax returns, credit reports, medical records, and the like without the intimate's consent. One profound irony in courts' eagerness to fault deceived intimates for not uncovering deception sooner is that the legal system itself can make investigating an intimate much more difficult.

Practical Impediments to Covert Investigation

While some types of investigations can be conducted without alerting the subject, those methods of covert reconnaissance often have practical limitations and drawbacks. Many other strategies for researching an intimate are difficult to employ without the intimate discovering them. This section explores some practical obstacles to investigation, starting with methods that are easier to use surreptitiously and moving to methods that are difficult or impossible to pursue in secret.

Internet research can sometimes provide a covert way to uncover information useful in assessing whether an intimate is being deceptive—especially if the intimate has a relatively unique name rather than a common one. However, many of the more advanced and complex strategies for searching the internet are probably less well-known to the average internet user. The average person may not know about or know how to use social media aggregators that consolidate information from multiple social media sites,[47] reverse image searches that scour the internet for an image and report where it appears,[48] or reverse directories that provide the name and/or address associated with a phone number, or the name and/or phone number associated with an address.[49] The average internet user may not know that email messages include IP (Internet Protocol) addresses that email programs hide by default. These addresses, when uncovered and entered into IP address directories, often indicate the approximate location from which an email was sent.[50] Similarly, an ordinary internet user may be unaware that the subject of an internet search will sometimes be able to discover who has viewed webpages about him, unless the searcher overrides default features of the websites she is using or takes other affirmative steps to hide her search.[51]

When I began researching this book, I knew relatively little about how to use the internet to investigate someone. Having undertaken this research, I can now report that a wary intimate who is highly motivated and computer savvy can seek out instructions from experts who have identified a range of techniques for personal investigation via the internet. It also helps to have financial resources, as some of these strategies—such as using reverse directories—can require payment.[52]

In addition, government authorities make a significant amount of public information available to those suspicious enough to look and resourceful enough and/or well-financed enough to find the data. To learn more about researching public records, I read manuals written by and for private investigators, professional background checkers, skip tracers, or other experts in locating and utilizing public documents.[53] This material explains how with time, effort, savvy, expertise, luck, and sometimes money—all resources unevenly distributed in the population—public records can potentially disclose information that casts light on whether someone is being deceptive. For example, public records can sometimes reveal marriages,[54] divorces,[55] birth records,[56] death notices,[57] military records,[58] criminal records,[59] civil court proceedings,[60] bankruptcies,[61] federal tax liens,[62] property ownership,[63] business ownership,[64] business and professional licenses,[65] professional disciplinary actions,[66] patents, copyrights, and trademarks,[67] and information about publicly traded companies, not-for-profit corporations, charities, and their officers.[68]

However, there are many caveats associated with relying on public records as a source of information. The types of records considered public can vary substantially between jurisdictions, so data that is public in one jurisdiction may be kept confidential in another.[69] Even when records are officially public, they are not always complete and accurate.[70] Moreover, nominally public records can sometimes be difficult to access in practice, including by professional investigators.[71] Many public records are not available online.[72] Locating and accessing public records can sometimes require payment.[73]

In fact, public record searches sometimes cannot be completed—as a practical matter—without the knowledge of the person being investigated. Governments refuse to release some public records unless the researcher already has multiple forms of identifying information about the subject of the search, such as his birth date and Social Security number.[74] A would-be detective will probably have to ask her intimate for those details if she does not already know them and cannot unearth them in other public records. Casual conversation might reveal a birth date, but would not uncover a Social Security number. Consider Kimberly Hall's experience as she recounted it in a *Washington Post* interview. Hall had previously dated married men who falsely presented themselves as single. Having encountered multiple intimate deceivers already, Hall wanted to conduct a background check on a new man she was dating, who had become her fiancé by the time of the *Post* interview. However, Hall apparently realized that she needed the man's Social Security number to complete the comprehensive search she desired. Hall did not have that number—so a covert, yet thorough public records search was not an available option for her. Hall decided to ask her intimate for his Social Security number and he ultimately disclosed it. But she obtained that information at the cost of her intimate knowing she was investigating him and potentially feeling hurt and/or offended. Indeed, Hall told the *Post* that her fiancé "wasn't happy" about providing his Social Security number for a background check, even though the check does not seem to have uncovered deceit.[75]

More generally, much of the information needed to assess an intimate's veracity cannot be acquired without significant risk that the intimate will discover the investigation. Sometimes what a person most wants to know about her intimate is whether he is honestly reporting his current beliefs and present intentions. Public records and/or internet searches might sometimes shed light on that question. But evaluating whether an intimate is being deceptive can often be difficult without questioning him directly to explore his beliefs and intentions and unearth any inconsistencies in his statements. While a particularly adept and subtle questioner might be able to extract the desired information without arousing suspicion, this type of direct inquiry necessarily creates a substantial risk that the questioned intimate will realize he is being probed for signs of deceitfulness and will be offended—whether or not he is actually being deceptive.

Attempting to assess an intimate's veracity by speaking with the person's relatives, friends, and colleagues can carry the same likelihood of discovery. Roberta Beier, an accountant in Oakland, once dated a man who lied about his name, job, and marital status, presenting himself as a widower when he was married. Beier told the *Chicago Tribune* that she now informs new dates in "the first week" of their budding relationship: "I want to meet your family, your friends, the people you work with. If that doesn't happen, I'm not wasting my time."[76] Beier's approach should help her identify and avoid men who are misrepresenting basic aspects of their lives. But it is difficult to see how someone could query the relatives, friends, and colleagues of an intimate or would-be intimate without either asking the intimate's permission first or proceeding without permission and risking the overwhelming probability of discovery. Either way, the investigation is apt to come to light and its subject may feel annoyed, betrayed, and/or smothered.

Along the same lines, following an intimate as he proceeds through his day or stationing oneself outside an intimate's home can also create a significant risk of discovery. Blanche, whose boyfriend had broken several dates, "went to his apartment and sat outside until two in the morning." By then, she "realized he was out all night." Blanche learned information that could help her determine whether her boyfriend was deceiving her.[77] But if her boyfriend had seen her, he might have soured on continuing their relationship—even or especially if he had no deceit to hide.

Similarly, a person could try to monitor her intimate's movements by calling to verify that he answers his work phone when he is supposed to be at work, his home phone when he is supposed to be home, and his mobile phone when he is supposed to be available. This method could potentially be an effective means of uncovering deceit—at least if the investigated person still uses landlines, is not forwarding his calls between phone numbers, and also enjoys good phone reception throughout the day. But a person who receives such calls may realize that he is being monitored, especially if the calls are frequent or deviate from previous routines. Dee began phoning her husband at work and home to check his whereabouts and then disconnecting when her husband answered. Dee reported that her husband sometimes asked her later if she had called, and she was "not sure" whether he believed her denials. In Dee's words, "things started to get quite uncomfortable."[78]

An intimate wholly committed to learning what she can from the investigative techniques of police officers, private investigators, and professional skip tracers might follow their lead by rummaging through the garbage of the person she is investigating.[79] Richard Deubel searched his ex-wife's trash in the hopes of finding evidence that she had deceived him about her financial situation at the time of their divorce in order to negotiate a more favorable divorce settlement.[80] Digging through refuse could help uncover deception. But the investigated intimate might spot the search or learn about it, and such socially deviant behavior is likely to provoke anger and disgust.

Even some of the most sophisticated and modern investigative techniques can be hard to pursue covertly because the techniques require access to the investigated person's body or bodily materials. For example, noninvasive procedures are now available to determine paternity as early as eight weeks into a pregnancy. But these procedures require blood samples from both the mother and the man whose genetic connection to the fetus is being tested.[81] Obtaining those samples without alerting the mother and potential father would be very difficult.

Once a child is born, testing paternity requires access to genetic material—such as cheek swabs—from the potential father and the child. Some men may be able to gather this material without alerting the child or the child's mother. A man might have free access to a baby, who will not remember being swabbed. If so, he can purchase a paternity testing kit at a drugstore, collect the necessary cheek swabs in secret, and mail the swabs to a lab for testing.[82]

But some men will be unable to pursue paternity testing without alerting the child and/or the mother. Covertly collecting a DNA sample may be difficult or impossible if the child is old enough to realize his cheek is being swabbed and to report that information to his mother. Chadwick Craig, who suspected he might not be the biological father of his fourteen-year-old son, resorted to collecting a sample of the boy's DNA while the child slept. Craig managed to complete the task without waking the boy, but that outcome was hardly guaranteed in advance and Craig exposed himself to considerable risk of discovery.[83] Richard W., who wanted a DNA sample from his nineteen-year-old son to test paternity, obtained the sample by telling his son that he was verifying the son's abstinence from drugs and alcohol.[84]

A man who recognizes or fears that he will be unable to pursue paternity testing covertly might be reluctant to ask for a paternity test and take the risk that his expression of doubt could destabilize his relationships with the mother and child—even if the test establishes that he is the child's biological father. Part III explores whether states should institute routine DNA testing at birth, in part to overcome that obstacle to discovering deception about paternity.

Testing someone for a sexually transmitted disease likewise requires access to biological material, typically a blood sample, urine sample, vaginal swab, or oral swab.[85] Acquiring that surreptitiously can be hard, if not impossible.

Just as maintaining secrecy while investigating an intimate can be difficult, covertly protecting oneself from a possibly deceptive intimate can be similarly hard. Deception about sexually transmitted diseases provides an illuminating example here as well. Suppose a man tells a woman he is courting that he has had a vasectomy, just tested negative for sexually transmitted diseases, has been abstinent for the past several months, and will be monogamous with her. A woman who hears that, but suspects or worries that her would-be sexual partner may be lying about something—or everything—could insist on condoms to reduce the risk of pregnancy and sexually transmitted infection. But then her partner would know she doubted his veracity and that knowledge might undermine his commitment to their relationship. With this in mind, it is unsurprising that several small-scale public health studies have found that some people believe that a willingness to forgo condoms is a powerful way to demonstrate trust in a sexual partner's honesty and fidelity. One husband explained that using condoms would be "an insult" to his wife and marriage. As he elaborated, "[i]t wouldn't do that relationship any good at all if some sort of doubt was injected into it by suggesting that possibly one of us could be having an affair and to be absolutely certain we must use a condom."[86]

In short, practical realities can present much more of an obstacle than courts commonly assume when faulting deceived intimates for having been duped. Investigating whether an intimate is being deceptive often creates a significant risk that the investigation itself will threaten or end the relationship because the intimate will discover the sleuthing and feel betrayed, whether or not he has actually been deceitful. Covertly protecting yourself against the possibility that an intimate is being deceptive can sometimes be equally difficult.

Legal Restrictions on Investigating an Intimate Without Permission

The legal limitations on investigating intimates are still more striking. The same legal system that frequently faults deceived intimates for their failures of detection has established a vast array of civil and even criminal laws prohibiting many forms of reconnaissance without the subject's consent. These laws have surely dissuaded some intimates from investigating. People who are not deterred—whether because they do not understand the law or think they can keep their investigation hidden—can pay a steep price. Not everyone who breaks the law by investigating without consent is sued or prosecuted, of course. But violators place themselves in legal jeopardy and can face serious legal consequences. Some people who attempted to discover whether an intimate was deceiving them have had to pay civil damages because of their snooping, some have had to pay criminal fines, some have lost their jobs, and a few have been incarcerated or placed on probation.[87]

Moreover, those legal penalties are not the unintended consequences of laws designed to restrict other sorts of investigations. One remarkable feature of the web of legal regulation that bars various types of reconnaissance without consent is that the legislators who enacted these prohibitions repeatedly recognized and appreciated that a substantial proportion of the investigations they were impeding would involve intimates. Restricting people's ability to spy on their intimates was not an unanticipated result or a peripheral effect of this body of law. Instead, controlling inquiring intimates was an explicit policy goal. The law commonly evinces little interest in deterring or remediating intimate deception, but it is a different story when someone deceives his intimate to conceal surveillance without consent.[88]

For example, Congress in 1968 prohibited private parties from intentionally intercepting wire or oral communications (such as phone calls or in-person conversations) without the prior consent of at least one of the participants.[89] Congressmen championing this law—known as Title III of the Omnibus Crime Control and Safe Streets Act of 1968—frequently emphasized that the statute would make it harder for people to investigate their spouses. Senator Edward Long explained at a subcommittee hearing he was chairing in 1966 that "[t]he three large areas of snooping in this field are (1) industrial, (2) divorce cases, and (3) politics." He declared that "[s]o far we have heard no real justification for continuance of snooping in these three areas."[90]

Professor G. Robert Blakey—"the acknowledged author of Title III"[91] according to many subsequent federal court decisions—appeared before Long's subcommittee in 1967. Blakey testified that "private bugging in this country can be divided into two broad categories, commercial espionage and marital litigation." He argued that seeking "to use electronic equipment in the invasion of privacy of the home and, particularly, the marital relationship" might be "a far more fundamental and objectionable invasion of privacy" than commercial snooping. Blakey urged Congress to prohibit such "domestic espionage."[92]

By 1968, Senator Karl Mundt was declaring on the Senate floor that "[e]veryone agrees that private wiretapping or eavesdropping should be prohibited. It is repugnant to our way of life." Mundt observed that "[d]omestic relations, industrial espionage, and counterespionage, information obtained for civil litigation are all fertile fields for those who traffic in other people's privacy." He explained that "Title III takes care of this by making it a crime to intercept communications without the consent of one of the participants."[93] Senator Joseph Tydings similarly emphasized that without Title III "snoopers" could "tap with impunity anybody's wire, on any action from a domestic relations case to a real estate operator or a major manufacturing concern." Tydings praised Title III for "correct[ing] this situation" by making "illegal the indiscriminate tapping of wires and the electronic surveillance now going on throughout this nation."[94]

The Senate report explaining the need for Title III also stressed that the law would protect the privacy of intimate life. The report warned that without the statute it was "[n]o longer . . . possible . . . for each man to retreat into his home and be left alone. Every spoken word relating to each man's personal, marital, religious, political, or commercial concerns can be intercepted by an unseen auditor and turned against the speaker to the auditor's advantage."[95] Senators Everett Dirksen, Roman Hruska, Hugh Scott, and Strom Thurmond declared in their contribution to the same report that Title III would impose "[a] broad prohibition ... on private use of electronic surveillance, particularly in domestic relations and industrial espionage situations."[96]

My point here is not to criticize statutes like Title III for hampering intimate investigations undertaken without the subject's permission. Although the legal prohibitions and restrictions on covert surveillance could no doubt benefit from some fine-tuning,[97] this body of law promotes and protects important values.

Let's pause to consider the benefits of banning some forms of surveillance without consent before exploring how these rules can make investigating a potentially deceptive intimate much more difficult. Spying on someone without her knowledge or permission can undermine privacy, autonomy, and serenity by revealing a person's beliefs, speech, associations, activities, habits, movements, resources, and more. Carol Fischer's ex-husband surreptitiously recorded her phone conversations without her permission. She reported that after learning about this covert surveillance "she felt shocked, upset, invaded upon, wronged, violated, cheated, angry, distressed, and deceived."[98]

The harm inflicted can extend from the investigated intimate to all of her associates. Michele Mathias's husband, Danny Lee Hormann, monitored her cellphone and computer use and also tracked her car with a GPS device. She described the scope of injury this way: "It wasn't just invasion of my privacy. It was an invasion of the privacy of everyone who ever texted me or anyone who was ever on my computer." When Mathias became suspicious that her husband was spying on her, she and her children rearranged their lives in an attempt to thwart the surveillance. For example, Mathias feared that Hormann had bugged her home so she and her children curtailed the conversations they had there, whispering to each other on the lawn instead.[99]

Surveillance without consent can also undermine security. While banning some forms of reconnaissance can make getting away with deception easier, permitting unimpeded investigations into someone else's life would itself facilitate deceit and fraud. For instance, laws protecting the confidentiality of federal income tax returns (described in more detail below) help some deceivers keep their intimates in the dark.[100] But making everyone's tax returns available for public inspection would expose taxpayers to con artists and identity thieves.

Indeed, permitting investigations without the subject's permission can potentially jeopardize the safety of both investigators and the people being investigated. Not every surveillance operation that begins in secret stays under wraps, and some people might turn to violence after learning that they have been investigated. An intimate's brutality toward his investigator could reflect the fury of an unmasked deceiver or the rage of an intimate offended that he has been spied upon, even if the surveillance has not found anything (yet). Such violence would be reprehensible, of course, but self-control is not a universal trait.

Similarly, some people who investigate their intimates without permission also take remedies into their own hands if they discover deception. Criminal cases, news stories, and the self-help literature contain numerous accounts of amateur sleuths who uncovered an intimate's deceit and then physically harmed their deceiver. Many of the reported examples involve violence directed at intimates who allegedly were deceitful to conceal infidelity. Ronald Thomas had recently separated from his wife and suspected she was deceiving him to hide a sexual relationship with another man. He made an unauthorized key to his wife's apartment, entered while she was away, and installed "spyware" on her computer that allowed him to monitor her computer use remotely and without her knowledge. Thomas wanted proof that his wife was having an affair. When he thought he had obtained that proof through the spyware, he went to his wife's home to confront her, forced his way into her apartment, seized her, pushed her, "struck her on the arm and choked her until she almost passed out."[101]

Lankford Carroll secretly recorded his wife's phone calls and discovered that she had been deceiving him to hide her sexual relationship with her former boss. Carroll responded to the revelation by beating his wife and sending death threats to her lover.[102]

Brian Clancy reportedly read his wife's email and concluded that she was having a sexual or sexually charged relationship with a married man who worked as a gym teacher and football coach in Newburyport, Massachusetts. Clancy allegedly went to the gym teacher's home to confront him, threatened to tell everyone about the emails, punched the teacher twice, and pushed him into a mailbox. The story attracted considerable attention because Clancy's wife, Mary Anne, was Newburyport's mayor at the time.[103] She subsequently decided against running for reelection.[104]

Christine Gallagher, who had been deceived by an unfaithful boyfriend, wrote a how-to guide and created a website, RevengeLady.com, in order to advise people intent on vengeance.[105] The book—entitled *The Woman's Book of Revenge: Tips on Getting Even When "Mr. Right" Turns Out to Be All Wrong*—informs readers that "[w]hen lies and betrayal are involved, retaliation is always justified. Even the Old Testament sanctions the returning of evil for evil and blood for blood."[106] Gallagher describes a variety of vengeful acts that people have purportedly committed after learning about an intimate's deceit, including pointing a realistic fake gun at the deceiver and ordering him to strip at work,[107] placing lice eggs on the deceivers' pillows,[108] and hiding food inside a deceiver's mattress so the food would rot and the smell would become unbearable.[109] The book also includes recipes for "Homemade Stink Bombs" and "Itching Powder."[110]

As this material suggests, one powerful argument in favor of providing more legal redress for intimate deception is that improving plaintiffs' prospects could persuade some deceived intimates to sue rather than resort to private violence, destruction, or mayhem. Civil litigation is never a perfect forum for seeking justice, but should be calmer and safer than many of the extralegal alternatives. The hazards associated with covert investigation also provide good reasons for lawmakers to be concerned.

In short, I agree that the law should limit the types of investigations that can be pursued without consent. The point I want to stress, however, is that this body of law can make assessing an intimate's trustworthiness much more difficult. Courts and commentators routinely fault deceived intimates for not uncovering deceit sooner. Yet the law itself is often an obstacle to unmasking intimate deceivers and learning the truth. The legal barriers to investigation are so numerous that they cannot all be reviewed here, but we can consider some of the most interesting and important examples.

One might imagine that technological means of surveillance would be a boon for people seeking to investigate their intimates surreptitiously, at least where the suspicious have the money, expertise, and time for this sort of spying. Indeed, many people have reported using technology to uncover an intimate's deceit without the intimate's knowledge.[111] The president of one spyware company reported in 2002 that 40% of his customers were married people who wanted to monitor their spouses. Spying spouses even outnumbered spying parents, a group that constituted under a third of the company's customers. The chief executive of another spyware company estimated in 2002 that approximately a third of the company's customers were investigating a spouse and approximately another third were investigating their children.[112] In more recent years, many spyware industry entrepreneurs have become savvy enough to avoid explicitly discussing how people can use their products in potentially illegal ways. But spyware companies appear to have long known that at least some of their customers are monitoring people without their knowledge or consent. In fact, some companies have emphasized in their promotional materials that their spyware can be deployed covertly—which makes noteworthy discoveries more likely. One advertisement lured buyers by offering them a way to "[s]ecretly record everything your spouse, children & employees do online."[113] That said, spyware companies typically advise their customers—at least as a formal matter—that they should notify the people they are monitoring and get their permission for the surveillance.[114]

The reason for these official disclaimers is that federal and state laws restrict the legal use of technological surveillance without the subject's permission. The Electronic Communications Privacy Act of 1986 (ECPA)[115] updated Title III so that federal law now prohibits private parties from intentionally intercepting electronic communications, as well as wire or oral communications, without the prior consent of at least one of the participants.[116] The ECPA makes this conduct a federal crime, punishable with up to five years in prison, a fine, or both.[117] The ECPA also creates a private right of action,[118] empowering victims to sue the people who spied on them for damages, punitive damages, a reasonable attorney's fee, and other reasonable litigation costs.[119] Courts calculating damages may award either the sum of the plaintiff's actual damages and any profits the defendant made from the violation, or $100 for each day of violation, or $10,000—whichever is the largest amount.[120]

Another portion of the ECPA prohibits people from intentionally accessing an electronically stored communication without authorization.[121] Violating this part of the ECPA—which is sometimes called the Stored Communications Act to distinguish it from the rest of the statute—is a federal crime that depending on the circumstances is punishable with up to ten years in prison, a fine, or both.[122] The Stored Communications Act also gives victims the right to sue for damages, punitive damages, a reasonable attorney's fee, and other reasonable litigation costs.[123] Courts calculating damages may award either the sum of the plaintiff's actual damages and any profits the defendant made from the violation, or $1000—whichever is greater.[124]

Such federal provisions, and state statutes supplementing and extending them, have enabled prosecutions and lawsuits against people who conducted unauthorized technological surveillance during or at the end of intimate relationships.[125] Some people have been criminally convicted or held civilly liable because they investigated whether an intimate was deceiving them by tracking an intimate's car, installing spyware on an intimate's computer, reading an intimate's email and instant messages, planting concealed video cameras or recording devices in an intimate's home, and/or wiretapping an intimate's phone. Consider just a few of the many striking examples, starting with criminal law and then turning to civil suits.

Danny Lee Hormann was convicted of stalking in Minnesota and spent thirty days in jail for secretly placing a GPS device on his wife's car and using it to track and follow her. Hormann wanted to monitor his wife's movements in order to investigate whether she was deceiving him to hide an affair. His wife, Michele Mathias—whose reaction to her husband's surveillance was quoted earlier—became suspicious that Hormann was monitoring her car because he always seemed to know where she had driven. Mathias had a mechanic search the car, which uncovered a tracking device Hormann had hidden on the vehicle's underside.[126]

Roy Klumb successfully sued Crystal Goan for $20,000—plus reasonable attorney's fees and costs—after she put spyware on his computers during their marriage so she could monitor him without his knowledge or consent.[127] The litigation revealed that Goan had suspected Klumb of deceiving her to hide infidelity.[128] Although Goan was a newly minted lawyer who should have known better, she secretly installed the eBlaster spyware program on Klumb's work computers soon after marrying him.[129] Goan used eBlaster to monitor internet activity on those computers and to obtain copies of emails and instant messages that Klumb received and accessed on the computers.[130] She also intercepted and altered at least three emails sent to Klumb in order to plant fabricated evidence that Klumb was committing adultery, as part of a scheme to trick a court into awarding her more assets in a divorce.[131] Klumb's colleagues eventually found clues suggesting the presence of spyware, and Klumb hired a computer forensics expert who uncovered what Goan had done.[132] A federal district court in Tennessee held that Goan had violated the ECPA and a Tennessee wiretap law.[133] The court's $20,000 award included $10,000 in punitive damages.[134] Discovering the covert surveillance apparently helped enrage Klumb. The court observed that Klumb's behavior toward Goan during and after their divorce constituted "harassment" and "bordered on stalking."[135] Klumb also reported Goan's unprofessional conduct as an attorney to the Tennessee Supreme Court's Board of Professional Responsibility, and the court censured Goan publicly.[136]

Duke Lewton won damages from his ex-wife, Dianna Divingnzzo, because she secretly recorded his conversations by placing a recording device inside their daughter Ellenna's teddy bear. Divingnzzo and Lewton were embroiled in a custody dispute, and Divingnzzo planted the recording device to monitor Lewton after he won the right to unsupervised time with Ellenna.[137] Divingnzzo schemed to keep the teddy bear close to Ellenna by telling Lewton that the child was deeply attached to the bear and needed it wherever she went.[138] For about four and a half months, the device inside the bear recorded what took place in the stuffed animal's presence—including many conversations that did not include Ellenna.[139] The surveillance apparently remained secret until Divingnzzo gave her lawyer the recordings as evidence in the custody dispute, and her lawyer provided copies to Lewton's attorney.[140] After the state court adjudicating the custody dispute held that the recordings were inadmissible and had been obtained illegally, Lewton filed a federal suit against Divingnzzo and her father, Sam, who had assisted her.[141] The federal district court in Nebraska agreed that Divingnzzo and her father had violated Title III as amended by the ECPA, infringing on the rights of Lewton plus five other plaintiffs whose conversations the recording device also captured.[142] Divingnzzo and her father each had to pay $10,000 in damages to each of the six plaintiffs, plus a reasonable attorney's fee and other reasonable litigation costs.[143]

Since sex and lies feature prominently in this book, some readers have perhaps been awaiting the appearance of videotape, to complete the trilogy in the title of the 1989 movie.[144] That moment has arrived. Several people have had success in suing intimates who secretly videotaped them without their consent.[145] Jeffrey Tigges and his wife, Cathy Tigges, had what the Iowa Supreme Court described as "trust issues." Jeffrey decided to monitor Cathy covertly by installing surveillance equipment in the bedroom Cathy regularly used in their home. His setup included a video camera hidden in an alarm clock, a motion detector installed in the bed's headboard, and a video cassette recorder placed above a ceiling. Cathy discovered the surveillance when she saw her husband removing a cassette from his recorder.[146] It was unclear from the evidence presented in court whether Jeffrey had recorded Cathy while he was still living in the house or after the couple had separated and he had moved out. But the unanimous Iowa Supreme Court held that even if Jeffrey was living with Cathy when he secretly recorded her, he had nonetheless wrongfully invaded Cathy's privacy because she had a reasonable expectation that her activities would be private when she was alone in the bedroom.[147] Jeffrey had to pay Cathy $22,500 in damages.[148]

Wiretapping telephones without prior consent has been prohibited since before video cameras, personal computers, or GPS devices were common consumer items, so it is not surprising that many people have been successfully sued or prosecuted under federal or state law for surreptitiously recording their intimate's phone calls. The vast majority of courts to consider the issue have held that a married person violates federal wiretapping law when he intentionally records his spouse's phone calls without permission, even if the wiretapping takes place in the marital home.[149] Tom Heggy, who was then director of the Oklahoma Bureau of Narcotics and Dangerous Drugs, had a colleague install a wiretap on the home phone Tom shared with his wife, Catherine Heggy. Tom did not tell Catherine about the wiretap and secretly recorded her phone calls for almost three months. After Catherine discovered Tom's surveillance, she sued him for violating her rights under federal wiretap law. The jury awarded Catherine $75,000 in compensatory damages and $140,000 in punitive damages, and the United States Court of Appeals for the Tenth Circuit unanimously affirmed the award.[150] Tom resigned from directing the drug bureau a month after Catherine filed her lawsuit.[151] He filed for bankruptcy soon after the jury made its award.[152]

Of course, the federal prohibition on wiretapping phone calls without prior consent also applies to intimates who are not married to each other.[153] David Schrimsher was sentenced to up to three years in prison for violating federal wiretapping law by secretly recording his ex-lover's calls.[154] Schrimsher hid for six days in the crawl space under Jane Roberts's house in order to make the recordings, camping out there until Roberts discovered him and called for help. At his trial, Schrimsher testified that he had investigated Roberts to determine his standing with her. His other testimony, however, suggested that he should have already known how she felt. Months before Schrimsher's stakeout, "Roberts told him to leave her alone and threatened to turn him over to her grandfather, who she said had underworld connections." Schrimsher said he also wanted to record Roberts's calls to ascertain whether she had lied about her grandfather.[155]

In addition, people have been successfully prosecuted or sued under state laws for secretly recording an intimate's phone calls.[156] A Texas court found Jack Duffy guilty of unlawful interception of electronic communication for spying on his wife, Darlene Duffy. Jack and Darlene were living in the same house, but were embroiled in a contentious divorce. Jack decided to record Darlene's phone calls so he could "see what [she] was up to." Darlene became suspicious that Jack, an executive at a telecommunications company, had bugged her phone since he "seemed to . . . know every move [she was] going to make before [she] made it." She searched the house for a recording device, found one that Jack had hidden behind books in a cabinet, and turned the matter over to the sheriff's office. Jack was prosecuted, convicted, fined $1000, and sentenced to two years in prison and two years of probation.[157]

Mary Lee Standiford successfully sued her ex-husband, James Standiford, for violating her rights under Maryland's Wiretapping and Electronic Surveillance Act. The trial revealed that James, a police officer, had covertly recorded Mary's phone calls as their marriage was deteriorating and used the information he gathered against her. This case illustrates how snooping on intimates can lead to blackmail when secrets are unearthed. James learned from his spying that Mary's aunt had committed adultery. He told Mary that he would inform the aunt's husband about the infidelity unless Mary signed some separation papers she did not want to sign. Mary sued James for recording her phone calls, and James had to pay her $12,500 in actual damages, $25,000 in punitive damages, and $9500 in attorney's fees.[158]

Just as many methods of unauthorized surveillance are legally prohibited, many types of information are legally shielded from an inquiring intimate's view without the subject's consent. It is a federal crime punishable with up to five years in prison to take, open, or destroy someone else's postal mail.[159] That was one of the strategies Annette Miller used to spy on her husband after they separated. She lied and told postal authorities that she lived in the same house as her husband and wanted the post office to hold the household's mail rather than deliver it. Miller would collect her husband's mail from the post office, sort through it, discard some items, and leave the rest in his mailbox so he would think a letter carrier had delivered his mail as usual.[160] This might have been an effective way to investigate her husband, but pursuing it made Miller vulnerable to federal prosecution.

Similarly, federal law protects the confidentiality of credit reports.[161] If a person obtains someone else's credit report under false pretenses or knowing that he does not have a statutorily permissible purpose, the consumer whose rights were violated can sue the wrongdoer for actual damages or $1000—whichever is greater—plus punitive damages, costs, and reasonable attorney's fees.[162] Someone who knowingly and willfully obtains a credit report under false pretenses is also subject to up to two years in prison, a criminal fine, or both.[163]

While scrutinizing a credit report can sometimes reveal an intimate's deceit, people have gotten themselves into legal trouble by obtaining an intimate's credit report without permission.[164] Patricia Ryan, an attorney with a credit union for a client, either used the credit union's computer to obtain her ex-husband's credit report or had a credit union employee acquire the report for her. Ryan later testified that she had wanted to verify that her ex-husband, Stephen Yohay, was no longer charging purchases to the joint credit card accounts they used during their marriage. Yohay discovered the unauthorized access to his credit information when he reviewed his credit records. He sued the credit union, which quickly brought Ryan into the litigation.[165] A federal trial court and a unanimous federal appellate court agreed that Ryan had violated federal law protecting the privacy of credit reports. Ryan had to pay Yohay $10,000 in punitive damages— plus $32,411 in attorney's fees and $957.90 in costs for the trial, with an additional award for appellate attorney's fees to be determined on remand.[166]

Phone records might also be very helpful in determining whether an intimate has been deceptive. However, the federal Telephone Records and Privacy Protection Act establishes criminal penalties for knowingly obtaining confidential phone records by making false statements to a phone company employee. The statute also makes it a federal crime to use the internet to access someone else's confidential phone records without the person's prior consent. Violators are subject to up to ten years in prison, a fine, or both.[167] This law criminalizes the practice popularly known as "pretexting," in which the pretexter deceives a phone company employee by impersonating a customer in order to access that customer's phone records.[168] Before Congress enacted this law, federal legislators repeatedly emphasized their determination to stop people from pretexting to acquire the phone records of a spouse or lover.[169]

Driver's license records similarly contain information that could be useful in ferreting out deceit, including a person's name, address, phone number, Social Security number, driver identification number, medical or disability information, and photograph.[170] However, the federal Driver's Privacy Protection Act enforces the confidentiality of driver's license records.[171] Knowingly obtaining or disclosing personal information from a driver's license record without a statutorily permitted purpose is unlawful.[172] Violators are subject to criminal fines.[173] Victims can also bring civil suits to recover liquidated damages of $2500 or actual damages if they are more than that—plus punitive damages and reasonable attorney's fees and costs.[174]

Shawn Schierts brought a successful suit under this statute. Schierts was embroiled in a custody dispute with his ex-girlfriend, Sarah Pretzel, who had primary physical custody of their son. Schierts lived in Arizona, but visited Wisconsin and went to see his son at daycare. Pretzel was at the daycare center at the time, and the parents began disputing custody. Someone called the police, and Officer Bart Engelking arrived at the scene. Pretzel and Officer Engelking corresponded about Schierts after this incident, and Pretzel told Engelking that she wanted to know Schierts's current address. Engelking located two addresses for Schierts by accessing his driver's license information without authorization. The officer emailed the addresses to Pretzel, writing: "You didn't get this info from me." Schierts discovered what had happened by accessing Pretzel's email account. Schierts sued Engelking and the city that employed him, and a federal district court agreed that the police officer had violated the Driver's Privacy Protection Act.[175] The court also noted that Pretzel could bring a subsequent suit against Schierts for violating the Stored Communications Act by snooping in her email.[176] Meanwhile, Officer Engelking had resigned by the time of the court's decision.[177]

Someone seeking to uncover deception might also acquire useful information about an intimate's veracity by examining the intimate's medical records, but federal and state laws make accessing medical records without the patient's consent difficult or impossible. Rules implementing the federal Health Insurance Portability and Accountability Act (HIPAA)[178] make clear that people are entitled to keep their medical records private, including from family members.[179] Some health care providers are so intent on protecting the confidentiality of medical records that they have apparently blocked family members from accessing those records even when the patient was incapacitated.[180] This regulatory regime means that most people will be unable to view an intimate's medical records if their intimate does not want them to have access. Some people have special opportunities to see medical records because they work in health care, but they can get into serious trouble for disregarding HIPAA rules. Mary Somogye, a registered nurse working in a cardiology department, was fired because she used the computer system at work to access her mother's and sister's medical records in violation of HIPAA's requirements.[181]

State laws add to the barriers to viewing an intimate's medical records without the intimate's authorization. Daniel Koch sought to access his wife's psychotherapy records as they were divorcing and disputing custody. A unanimous Florida appellate court held that a psychotherapist/patient confidentiality privilege protected the records, and Koch had no right to see them over his wife's objection.[182] Joshua Pierce, who was challenging his ex-wife for custody of their child, sought to access the medical records of his ex-wife's new husband. The Arkansas Supreme Court held that a physician/patient privilege protected the records, and Pierce could not access them without the new husband's consent.[183]

Examining an intimate's tax returns might likewise be an enormously effective way to determine whether an intimate is being deceitful. Tax returns could
reveal deception about finances, such as an intimate lying about his salary, savings, investments, or spending. Scouring tax returns might also help uncover
other forms of deceit that are often paired with financial deception. An article
in the *Houston Chronicle* encouraged married people to scrutinize the joint tax
returns they had filed with their spouses for possible evidence of deception
to hide adultery. Among other tips, the article—entitled *Return Has Wealth of
Infidelity Clues*—advised each reader to examine her joint return for indications
that her spouse had deceived her about the overtime he had worked, the wages
he had earned, the savings he had spent, and/or the investments he had sold.
The article's premise was that spouses might engage in such deceit to free up
time or money for extramarital escapades.[184] The *Chronicle's* proposed investigative strategy is perfectly legal. Anyone who has filed a joint federal income tax
return has the right to see that return, even if the other taxpayer would like to
block access. A person who files a joint return has automatically agreed to share
the enclosed information with his spouse.[185]

Joint returns aside, though, the federal government makes accessing someone
else's tax information without that person's permission very difficult. Federal law
provides that federal income tax returns and the information within them are
confidential.[186] Federal or state employees who willfully inspect a federal income tax return or return information without authorization are subject to up
to a year in prison, a fine of up to $1000, or both. Federal employees are also
subject to termination.[187] Federal or state employees who without authorization
willfully disclose a federal income tax return or return information are subject
to up to five years in prison, a fine of up to $5000, or both—and again federal
employees are also subject to termination. In addition, it is a federal crime to receive unauthorized access to a federal income tax return or return information in
exchange for willfully offering money or another item of material value for such
access. Violators are subject to up to five years in prison, a fine of up to $5000,
or both.[188] A taxpayer whose rights to confidentiality were violated can sue the
United States for damages if the wrongdoer was a federal employee or can sue
the wrongdoer directly if he did not work for the federal government.[189]

Congress strengthened legal protections for the confidentiality of tax returns
in response to evidence that Internal Revenue Service (IRS) employees were
not being adequately penalized for their unauthorized browsing through the
taxpayer data of family members, dates, friends, neighbors, and celebrities.[190] In
February 1997, for example, the unanimous United States Court of Appeals for
the First Circuit held that IRS employee Richard Czubinski had not committed
a felony under federal law. Czubinski had used his access to an IRS computer
system to take an unauthorized look at the tax return of a woman he had dated

and to peruse the tax files of various "friends, acquaintances, and political rivals," but had not done anything or intended to do anything with the information he learned.[191] Federal legislators were not pleased with the court's decision,[192] and that helped push Congress in August 1997 to criminalize the unauthorized inspection of tax returns.[193]

Employees at the National Security Agency (NSA) might have more access to information than anyone else. Perhaps unsurprisingly, at least a dozen people working for or with the NSA were discovered between 2003 and 2013 misusing their privileged access to NSA resources to investigate their intimates. One NSA employee used agency resources without authorization so he could monitor his foreign girlfriend's telephone number "to determine whether she was involved with any local government officials or other activities that might get him in trouble." Another NSA employee used agency resources without authorization so she could investigate a foreign phone number she had found in her husband's cellphone "because she suspected that her husband had been unfaithful." It should also not be surprising to learn that the wrongdoers suffered a variety of penalties, including reprimand, suspension without pay, withdrawn promotion, reduction in grade, denial of security clearance, resignation or retirement under pressure, and investigation by federal prosecutors.[194] The scandal was popularly dubbed "LOVEINT."[195]

This chapter has reviewed some of the many obstacles to uncovering intimate deception and learning the truth. Courts and commentators are often inclined to fault deceived intimates for having been duped. But even people of ordinary or above-average shrewdness and sophistication are not adept at detecting deception, and spotting an intimate's deceit may be especially hard. Strong social norms, moreover, discourage us from investigating our intimates. Even if we would like to override those norms and dig deeper, it is frequently challenging or impossible to investigate an intimate without the investigation itself threatening or ending the relationship because the intimate finds out about the detective work. Covert reconnaissance is often impracticable or illegal. Many people who have tried it have found themselves liable for damages, out of a job, and/or subject to criminal prosecution. The same legal system that blames plaintiffs for not uncovering deceit sooner prohibits and penalizes many forms of investigation. In sum, one answer to the question of why intimate deceivers often succeed in duping their targets is that unmasking an intimate's deceit can be much more difficult than courts commonly assume.

What Injuries
Can Intimate Deceivers Inflict?

Once someone succeeds in duping his intimate, the consequences of intimate deception begin to mount. This chapter examines the harms that intimate deceivers can inflict on their targets, as well as on third parties and society more generally. Courts denying remedies for intimate deception, and deceivers rationalizing their behavior,[1] often devote too little attention to those harms. But the injuries can be substantial—sometimes life-changing. Examining these injuries helps us understand the phenomenon of intimate deception and prepares us to consider its legal regulation.

We might reason about the damage that intimate deception can cause by drawing on abstract first principles. Almost by definition, deceit can infringe upon the deceived person's autonomy, diminish her control over her own decisionmaking, and warp and constrict her choices. Similarly, an intimate's deceit almost inevitably undermines trust, upends expectations, and destroys plans.

Examining first-person accounts, lawsuits, and the available social science research allows us to explore the injuries that intimate deception can inflict in more concrete and particular terms. These sources reveal recurring themes, even though there can be considerable variation in the type, extent, and severity of harm. The fallout from intimate deception can include financial losses, illnesses and infections, physical endangerment and abuse, violations of sexual autonomy and bodily integrity, unexpected vulnerability to criminal prosecution and other legal harms, wasted time, lost opportunities, and a range of psychological and emotional injuries.

Our culture and our legal system discourage deceived intimates from thinking of themselves as injured. The prevalence of deceit within intimacy, the tendency to blame deceived intimates for being fooled, and the law's commitment to shielding intimate deception can promote the sense that this deceit must be accepted and accommodated, rather than decried and condemned.

But it is nonetheless unsurprising that deceived intimates often conclude that they have been severely harmed. The injuries described in this chapter are burdens that few people would bear lightly. They cannot be plausibly dismissed as the complaints of the oversensitive.

We can start by examining financial and bodily injuries—the sorts of injuries that the law is usually most willing to redress—and then consider legal injuries, lost time and lost opportunities, psychological and emotional injuries, and harms that extend beyond the deceiver's primary target.

Financial Injuries

Courts and legislatures ordinarily find financial injuries relatively easy to understand and remediate. Intimate deception is not typically understood as a financial wrong. Yet it can inflict enormous economic damage. The consequences can be devastating, especially when the amount lost was a substantial portion of the deceived person's overall resources.

Financial injuries from intimate deception appear in myriad variations. Sometimes deceit causes a financial injury that is the flip side of the motivation for the deception. Someone deceives his intimate in order to acquire certain financial resources, and the duped intimate suffers the loss of those same financial resources.

Financial losses to con artists frequently take this form. William Allen Jordan, a career con artist who bilked women in the United States and the United Kingdom,[2] convinced one girlfriend, Mischele Lewis of New Jersey, that he worked for the United Kingdom's Ministry of Defence and she needed to pay $5000 for a security clearance so she could visit him. Lewis lost the $5000 that Jordan gained.[3]

Similarly, Johna Loreen Vandemore's victim lost the $95,850 that she extracted from him. Vandemore convinced a man she had briefly dated that she had become pregnant with his child, given birth, and was raising the girl on her own. She sent him a copy of the child's birth certificate and pictures of the girl as she grew. In return, the man sent Vandemore almost $100,000 in child support payments between 2007 and 2013 before learning that she had not been pregnant. The birth certificate was fake and the photographs showed the daughter of Vandemore's cousin.[4]

Janet Cook, a widowed church secretary, was wooed by a man she connected with via Match.com who said he was a German businessman named Kelvin Wells. He courted her with a steady stream of phone calls, emails, and promises of future travel together. Soon enough, Wells began telling Cook about numerous emergencies he supposedly faced and asking for her financial assistance. He swindled her out of almost $300,000.[5]

Cook's experience is not unusual. The FBI's Internet Crime Complaint Center tracks "suspected Internet-facilitated criminal activity."[6] In 2017 alone, the center received 15,372 complaints about "Confidence Fraud/Romance,"[7] defined as covering situations where "[a] perpetrator deceives a victim into believing the perpetrator and the victim have a trust relationship, whether family, friendly or romantic. As a result of that belief, the victim is persuaded to send money, personal and financial information, or items of value to the perpetrator or to launder money on behalf of the perpetrator."[8] The combined reported losses from these complaints totaled $211,382,989.[9]

Greedy deception by intimates who are not professional con artists often follows a similar pattern, with the deceived person losing the financial resources that his intimate duped him to obtain. For example, many married people have deceived their spouses in order to hide cash, property, or other assets.[10] Wallace Ridgway convinced his wife to agree to a less favorable property settlement at divorce by telling her that he had only $357 in cash, when he actually had $18,000 in a savings account, $10,000 in stock, "and a substantial amount of money in his partnership's checking account."[11] Joy Conrad allegedly lied about owning valuable timber harvesting rights in order to keep her husband from claiming a share of those rights at divorce.[12] James Sargent allegedly deceived his wife into accepting a much smaller divorce settlement by leading her to think that they had two million dollars in marital assets when he knew they had seventeen million.[13] Jesse Palacios hid from his wife that he had won a $5.38 million lottery jackpot so he would not have to share the prize money with her and could pay less child support for their two daughters—one with cerebral palsy. Palacios filed for divorce two days after learning he had won, quit his job, and presented himself to the divorce court as an unemployed truck driver.[14] In all these cases, the deception was designed to achieve a financial gain for the deceiver at the expense of a parallel financial loss for the deceived intimate.

Along the same lines, some married people intent on securing a financial advantage at their spouse's expense have deceptively concealed that they took their spouse's separate assets or expropriated their spouse's credit. Farrell Kahn reportedly deceived his wife to hide that he had used her separate property as collateral to obtain loans without her permission, had misappropriated the profits from the sale of her separate property, and had taken other funds from her.[15] Claire Wallace reportedly deceived her husband to hide that she had used his Social Security number and other personal information to acquire credit cards in his name without his knowledge or permission and to establish herself as an "authorized signer" on the cards, which allowed her to run up approximately $40,000 in bills that her husband would be responsible for paying.[16]

Sometimes a person practicing greedy deception dupes his intimate because he wants her to spend money on something that she would not or might not fund if she knew the truth. The deceit enables the deceiver to direct the money to his preferred use and costs the deceived intimate the chance to spend that money elsewhere.[17]

David Church allegedly deceived his wife, Jane Church, so she would continue to devote her financial and other resources to furthering his education. Jane reported that she paid for all or most of David's living and educational expenses while he attended medical school because the two had agreed that they would both benefit from the enhanced earning capacity that David would have as a doctor.[18] While Jane was working to support David, he was busy with a secret extramarital relationship that began in his second year of medical school and continued through his fourth year.[19] Once his four years of medical school were behind him, David told Jane that he wanted a divorce.[20]

Jane charged that David had deceived her to hide his affair and his plan to divorce her once he finished medical school because he wanted her continued help while he was still a student. Indeed, it seems likely that learning about David's infidelity would have prompted Jane to stop supporting him—whether because she would no longer have been interested in continuing their relationship or because she would have doubted whether David really intended to remain married to her and to share his income as a doctor.[21]

Intimate deception also frequently inflicts financial injuries that are not simply the flip sides of the economic benefits the deceiver obtains. People preparing to marry or live closer to intimates who were duping them to conceal something vitally important—such as an engagement to another woman—have quit their jobs,[22] sold their property,[23] and/or relocated.[24] The deceitful intimates in these cases did not acquire the money that the deceived people lost, and the deceivers might have preferred to avoid causing financial harm. Yet people nonetheless suffered economic losses because they relied on an intimate's deliberate misrepresentations.

Similarly, an intimate's deceit can lead people to forgo or postpone economic opportunities they would have otherwise pursued.[25] Aleksei Lodisev married Sandra Gubin after convincing her that he loved her and wanted to share his life with her.[26] Lodisev lived in the Soviet Union and Gubin, an American citizen, met him while participating in a cultural exchange program.[27] After their marriage, she devoted three-and-a-half years to helping her husband immigrate to the United States in the face of the Soviet government's persistent refusal to grant an exit visa.[28] In addition to the $15,000 she paid in expenses, Gubin worked on Lodisev's immigration problem for approximately twenty hours a week and delayed completing her doctorate, which would have increased her earning capacity.[29] She drew attention to her husband's situation by serving as spokesperson for the Divided Spouses Coalition, a group of Americans who had been separated from their Soviet spouses because the Soviet Union would not give their spouses permission to leave.[30] Gubin finally managed to secure her husband's release from the Soviet Union only to learn after he arrived in the United States that he had been misleading her about his true feelings and intentions and had just used her as a gateway to legal immigration.[31]

Deceived intimates also sometimes suffer economic penalties that their employers impose on them because of their association with a deceiver. Ann Sweeney married Robert Hunt, who had convinced her—and many other people—that he was a former astronaut and Marine aviator now working as a police detective. Hunt actually was a con artist who had fabricated his supposed accomplishments and careers. Sweeney and her family reportedly lost approximately $43,000 that Hunt swindled from them. Moreover, Sweeney lost her job because Hunt had taken her company credit card without her knowledge and used the card to finance his extravagant lifestyle.[32]

LeslieAnn Haacke lost her job as a lawyer for Utah's Department of Corrections because she married Mark Glenn. Haacke's employment gave her unrestricted access to criminal files, and the state considered it a serious conflict of interest for someone with such access to be married to a convicted felon. Unbeknownst to Haacke, Glenn had been convicted of theft in Alabama before they married. Glenn duped Haacke to conceal his felony record and to hide that he was using marital funds to pay fines and restitution he still owed. He explained the money he was spending and the frequent trips he was required to make to Alabama by falsely telling Haacke that he was taking care of child support obligations. The Department of Corrections discovered Glenn's criminal record and terminated Haacke because of her marriage. The department indicated that it would not consider rehiring Haacke unless she ended her marriage and convinced the department that she had not known about Glenn's felony conviction when she married him.[33]

Bodily Injuries

Deceptive intimates can also harm, jeopardize, or infringe upon the bodies of the people they are deceiving. Three broad, sometimes overlapping categories of injuries relating to the body predominate in first-person accounts and lawsuits. Sometimes intimate deception contributes to a deceived person contracting a sexually transmitted disease or bearing an increased risk of infection. Sometimes deceit otherwise threatens the health or physical safety of a deceived intimate by concealing danger or abuse. And sometimes deceit leads to a violation of the deceived intimate's sexual autonomy and bodily integrity.

Deception can facilitate the transmission of venereal disease in several ways. Most directly, someone who knows he has a sexually transmitted disease can deceive his sexual partner by falsely denying the infection or by deliberately remaining silent with the intent to mislead his partner into believing that he is uninfected. Numerous plaintiffs have reported that they contracted genital herpes,[34] human papillomavirus (HPV),[35] or human immunodeficiency virus (HIV)[36] from someone who subjected them to this sort of deceit. The consequences of such infections vary, but can be severe. They include pain and suffering, elevated cancer risks, reduced life expectancy, increased medical expenses, pregnancy complications, and the risk of transmitting the infection to one's children.[37] Plaintiffs have explained that they would have refrained from sex with their deceiver or taken more precautions against disease transmission if they had known the truth.[38]

Intimate deception can contribute to the transmission of venereal disease even when the deceiver does not know that she is infected. Plaintiffs have reported that their sexual partner infected them with a sexually transmitted disease after deceiving them to conceal infidelity.[39]

In addition, many people who were deceived about a sexual partner's infections or his fidelity have been subject to a greater risk of contracting a sexually transmitted disease, but have not become infected. People who have had this experience often report that they felt enormous anxiety, fear, and distress in the period between discovering the deceit and receiving their test results. This anxiety was especially acute in the era when HIV/AIDS was considered inevitably fatal.[40] One woman wrote that she "was furious" because her husband, who had deceived her to hide his extramarital relationships with men, "had played Russian roulette with our lives."[41]

Deception can also threaten the health and physical safety of deceived intimates by concealing other physical dangers or bodily abuse. For example, deception about a sexual partner's infertility can subject a deceived woman to unwanted pregnancy and its associated physical risks. Barbara Allen reported that she relied on John Gatfield's intentional misrepresentation that he was infertile when agreeing to sex with him. So deceived, she had intercourse with Gatfield and conceived. Allen suffered a life-threatening ectopic pregnancy, needed surgery to remove a fallopian tube, and became sterile.[42]

Daniel Hixon's deceit endangered his seven-year-old son, Nalin, and Nalin's grandparents, by allowing Hixon to contaminate their physical environment without their knowledge so they had no chance to stop him or escape. Deborah and Raymond Hansen cared for Nalin after his mother, the Hansens' daughter, committed suicide. The Hansens permitted Hixon to live on the bottom floor of their house so he could be with his son. Hixon deceived the Hansens—and Nalin—to conceal that he was producing methamphetamine in the Hansens' home.[43] This manufacturing process can start fires, spark explosions, and/or contaminate the surrounding area.[44] By the time law enforcement authorities inspected the Hansens' home, many of the rooms—along with the heating and air conditioning system—contained unsafe levels of methamphetamine. Tennessee quarantined the house and barred people from living there until a massive and expensive remediation project was completed.[45]

Michael Bradway's deceit enabled him to avoid suspicion for years as he physically and emotionally abused his young son.[46] Bradway was separated from his wife, Erika Hollander, and had custody of their child, Sam.[47] When Sam was around four or five, Bradway announced that the boy had cystic fibrosis, a potentially fatal disease. Sam himself was convinced, along with his mother, her parents, and many other people. Sam looked sick, and Bradway allegedly produced fraudulent medical bills to document the boy's treatment. Indeed, Bradway reportedly extracted $38,000 or more from Hollander's parents on the pretense that he needed the money for Sam's health care. But Bradway was lying when he insisted that Sam had cystic fibrosis. Law enforcement authorities believe that the child appeared ill because Bradway was severely restricting his son's access to food.[48] By the time Bradway's deceit came to light, Sam had spent four or five years believing that he had cystic fibrosis and was deteriorating. The boy's reaction to learning the truth was not made public. His mother was reportedly "beyond devastated."[49]

David Feltmeyer's alleged deceit endangered his ex-girlfriend's physical safety by attracting unwanted, potentially violent attention to her that she did not know was coming and had no chance to avoid. Law enforcement authorities believe that Feltmeyer deceived his then-girlfriend to hide that he was secretly recording their sexual interactions. After the relationship ended, Feltmeyer allegedly copied what he had recorded onto DVDs and distributed the discs on the windshields of parked cars he randomly selected. The DVDs listed his now-former girlfriend's name, address, and phone number. Men who saw the DVDs appeared at the woman's house thinking she wanted sex.[50]

Feltmeyer's ex-girlfriend apparently managed to send her unwanted visitors away. But many other cases of intimate deception have led to violations of the deceived person's sexual autonomy and bodily integrity. People often turn to deceit because they want to obtain or maintain sexual access to the person they are deceiving.[51] The frequent consequence of such deception is that the deceived person has sex with her deceiver when she would have refused sex if she had not been duped. Lawsuits and first-person accounts reflect the prevalence of this experience, with the exact deceptions ranging from the more commonplace to the more unusual.

Mary Neal's husband, Thomas Neal, deceived her to conceal that he was committing adultery.[52] We can probably be safe in assuming that he considered this a linchpin deception, meaning that Thomas knew or feared that his wife would end their relationship if she learned the truth. Indeed, Mary reported that she would have avoided sex with Thomas if she had known about his adultery because she considered sex with an unfaithful husband "offensive."[53] The couple began divorce proceedings after Mary discovered Thomas's deceit.[54]

Similarly, Nella Manko reported that Alex Volynsky told her that he was "unmarried and available" in order to induce her into a sexual relationship.[55] In reality, Volynsky was already married and did not plan to divorce or separate from his wife of more than two decades.[56] Manko explained that when she agreed to sex with Volynsky she relied on his "representation that this was the beginning of a lasting and loving relationship which [would] lead to marriage."[57]

Joyce Short's boyfriend lied about being unmarried and also deceived her about his age, religion, educational accomplishments, and military service.[58] She described her experience this way: "The man who had usurped both my sexual intimacy and my highest emotion, love, was totally an imposter, someone other than the man he portrayed. He had violated me with his perversion repeatedly for over three years to defraud me of sex, affection and caring. . . . I'd consented to sex with a fictitious man who wasn't the man he pretended to be, and who existed only through misrepresentation."[59]

Perhaps most starkly, Karrie Dulin contended that Floyd Hardesty had sex with her while deceiving her to conceal that he knew or had reasonable cause to believe that she was his daughter. In other words, Dulin reported that she unwittingly committed incest because of Hardesty's deceit.[60]

Legal Injuries

Deceptive intimates can also place the people they are deceiving into legal jeopardy or into greater legal jeopardy. In some cases, a person's interactions with her deceiver are the source of her criminal liability or vulnerability to criminal prosecution. For example, deceivers sometimes dupe their intimates into serving as unwitting accomplices to criminal activity or otherwise deceive their intimates so they do not realize they may be subject to criminal penalties because of their interactions with their deceiver.

Kevin Dolan allegedly deceived his girlfriend to conceal that he was robbing a bank and using her as his getaway driver.[61] Similarly, Juan Adame allegedly convinced an ex-girlfriend to drive him to and from Blanca Ortiz's apartment by telling the ex-girlfriend that he had to collect some items there. In fact, Adame planned to set Ortiz's apartment on fire because Ortiz had recently ended their relationship. His arson killed Ortiz's neighbor.[62]

Zachery Anderson's sexual interaction with a girl who lied about her age led to his prosecution for statutory rape, a jail term, probation, and registration as a sex offender. Anderson connected with the girl on a portion of the "Hot or Not" website that was designated for people eighteen or older. The girl was fourteen, but she lied and told Anderson she was seventeen. Anderson was nineteen and the girl presumably feared that he would lose interest if he knew her true age. The two decided to meet in person, Anderson picked the girl up at her home in Michigan, and they had sex at a nearby playground.[63] The girl's mother called the police while they were out because she did not know where her daughter had gone. The police learned about Anderson's sexual encounter with the girl and eventually arrested him for statutory rape.[64]

Statutory rape laws criminalize sex with an underage person, even if the sex would have been considered consensual and legal if both sexual partners had been above the age of consent. While some states provide that a person prosecuted for statutory rape can avoid conviction by establishing that his sexual partner lied about her age, that is not a valid defense in Michigan. The girl and her mother both opposed punishing Anderson, but he was prosecuted vigorously and sentenced severely nonetheless.[65] When the chief prosecutor for the county was interviewed later, he faulted Anderson for having been duped—contending that Anderson should have been "suspicious" of any information "in an online profile."[66]

Anderson ultimately pled guilty to fourth-degree criminal sexual conduct. The judge sentenced him to ninety days in jail, five years of probation, and a quarter century on Michigan's sex offender registry.[67] The terms of his probation prohibited him from using the internet, which meant he could no longer study computer science in college. Anderson's registration as a sex offender required him to remain in contact with law enforcement authorities even after his probation ended, to permit regular searches of his home, and to reside far from parks and schools. Anderson had been living with his parents and brothers before he went to jail, but he could not return to their home afterward because the house was too close to a public park to comply with the registry's requirements.[68]

Anderson's case attracted considerable public attention, and a Michigan court eventually vacated his sentence after he had served his time in jail and begun his probation.[69] Almost six months after he received his first sentence, Anderson was resentenced to the jail term he had already completed and two years of probation. The new terms of his probation imposed a nine p.m. curfew and limited his computer access, but permitted him to access the internet for schoolwork. The resentencing judge did not place Anderson on Michigan's sex offender registry.[70] Anderson's probation officer told him that he could not leave the county without authorization and needed to restrict his movements in order to avoid people younger than eighteen, with the exception of his younger brother.[71] Anderson's probation was later extended by six months.[72]

Anderson's interaction with his deceiver was the source of his criminal liability. In other cases, an intimate's deceit has kept the deceived person from knowing about a preexisting legal problem and from interacting with the legal system with that in mind—either by fixing the problem if possible or by hiding from legal authorities if not. For example, some parents and grandparents have deceived children to conceal that the children are undocumented residents of the United States. So deceived, the children did not take steps to avoid attracting unwanted attention from government officials.[73]

Heilit Martinez grew up in the United States and first thought she was a United States citizen. But her parents told her when she was twelve that she was actually a lawful permanent resident. That was a lie. As her parents knew, Martinez did not have a legal right to live in the United States. She had been in the country illegally since the age of two when her parents took her to the United States from Venezuela.

Martinez never suspected the truth. Her parents gave her a Social Security card, which helped her work at a McDonald's restaurant, obtain a driver's license, enroll at Utah State University, and win a scholarship.

Unaware of her legal vulnerability, Martinez joined other college students on a trip to Mexico for souvenirs. She first heard about her true immigration status when she tried to return home and border agents could find no record of her supposed lawful permanent residence. Immigration authorities detained Martinez and told her they were preparing to deport her.[74] She was eventually released from detention and permitted to return to the United States on a temporary, year-to-year basis. However, she had no right to stay in the country permanently and no legal right to work.[75] Senator Orrin Hatch introduced a private bill that would have made Martinez eligible for an immigrant visa or lawful permanent residence,[76] but Congress did not enact it.

Martinez's parents may have thought that lying to Martinez about her immigration status was a paternalistic deception that protected her. Her parents presumably knew from their own experiences as undocumented immigrants that living with that knowledge can be harrowing. They also presumably knew that they had no way to fix Martinez's legal problem. Even if her parents had been honest with her, Martinez would still have been an undocumented resident of the United States. In addition to the paternalism, her parents' deceit appears to be an example of deception from subordination, where disempowered people deceive their intimates because they see no better alternative. Until the truth came out, deceiving Martinez shielded her from feeling the weight of the family's vulnerability.

All that said, her parents' deceit ultimately added to Martinez's vulnerability because it kept her from knowing that she needed to avoid immigration authorities. One might argue, as a formal matter, that Martinez should not be considered injured because what her parents' deceit took from her she had no right to have. No one is entitled to evade detection for illegal conduct. In practical terms, however, her parents' deceit clearly harmed Martinez. In all likelihood, she would not have gone to Mexico on a trip for souvenirs if she had known that she had no legal right to return to the United States and might be detained at the border. Martinez had lived in the United States for years without attracting attention from immigration authorities. She entered their sights because she did not know she had to be careful.

Lost Time and Lost Opportunities

Deception can also cost deceived intimates lost time and lost opportunities. People use lies or other intentional misrepresentations to control how their intimates spend their days and select among potential choices. A deceived intimate may invest enormous amounts of time and energy in ways that she would have rejected if she had known the truth. Deceit routinely prevents or delays the deceived person from making the decisions she would have otherwise reached.

Deceived intimates describing their experiences in first-person accounts and lawsuits tend to make similar points in emphasizing how deception took their time and cost them opportunities. For example, people often turn to linchpin deceptions in order to maintain intimate relationships or draw someone into intimacy. After the truth emerges, deceived intimates frequently stress that deceit deprived them of opportunities to pursue other relationships by keeping them with their deceiver.[77]

Dina Matos McGreevey's husband—James McGreevey, New Jersey's governor from 2002 to 2004—deceived her to hide that he was gay. She described her lost time and opportunities this way: "What woman in her right mind—and believe me, I *am* in my right mind—would while away the best years of her life with a man who cannot really desire her? Or who cannot respond wholeheartedly to her desire? Not only would I not knowingly have married a gay man, but I would never have allowed a gay man to father my child. A marriage between a straight person and a gay person is by definition unstable, and the last thing I wanted was for my daughter to suffer the consequences of a broken home, as in fact she has."[78] Dina did not elaborate on what she meant by "the best years of her life." But the phrase suggests that Dina believed that the opportunity to pursue romantic relationships is particularly valuable when one is young, so losing that opportunity in one's youth is especially harmful.

In addition, many deceived intimates have stressed that deceit cost them the opportunity to have a child. In some cases, a person has intentionally misled his intimate about his willingness and/or ability to procreate. Brenda McCann reported that her husband, Franklin, falsely told her before they married that he wanted to have a child with her and deliberately concealed that a fertility test had revealed his sperm count to be "in the critically low range."[79] She explained that she never would have married Franklin if he had not duped her and that her reliance on his deceit caused her "to pass the age of child bearing without having a child."[80]

Similarly, Margie Conley reported that her boyfriend, Michael Romeri, deliberately misled her into thinking that he was willing and able to have children, when actually he had been sterilized and did not want more children.[81] She explained that Romeri knew she wanted to have a child, "knew she had little time in which to become a biological mother,"[82] and knew she would not be interested in a sexual relationship with him if she knew about his vasectomy.[83] Romeri's alleged deceit meant that Conley "wasted time" with him when "she was approaching the biological end of her childbearing capability."[84]

Other sorts of intimate deception can also lead to lost opportunities to have a child. Several women have reported that their sexual partners convinced them to have abortions by lying to them or making deceptive promises they never intended to fulfill. Lee Perry reported that Richard Atkinson, her married boyfriend, convinced her to have an abortion by promising to conceive a baby with her the following year, when he knew at the time he made the promise that he did not intend to honor it.[85] Along the same lines, M.N. reported that her married lover, D.S., convinced her to have an abortion by falsely telling her that he planned to obtain a divorce, marry her, and have children with her.[86] Joyce Short reported that her boyfriend, Brian Schecter, told her that he was the divorced father of two boys.[87] She became pregnant and he urged her to have an abortion. He explained that his ex-wife was dying of cancer and his children would be hurt if they learned that their father had a sexual relationship with another woman while their mother was terminally ill. Short agreed, only to learn after the abortion that Schecter was still married.[88]

Men have likewise reported that they lost the opportunity to have a biological child because of an intimate's deceit. Tina Hodge told Chadwick Craig that he was the only possible father of her son, Kyle. The couple married, raised Kyle together, and also parented Hodge's daughter, whom Craig adopted. Craig and Hodge decided they did not want more children, and Craig had a vasectomy. About eight years later, he discovered that Kyle was not his biological son. Craig reported that he would not have been sterilized if he had known there was a chance he was not Kyle's biological father.[89]

Other men have reported that intimate deception cost them the opportunity to have a relationship with their biological child.[90] Consider N.T.'s deception of M.P. after the two had sex and N.T. became pregnant. Early in her pregnancy, N.T. told M.P. that he was the father. But N.T. apparently decided later that she wanted to place the child for adoption without M.P. or her family knowing and having a chance to object.

N.T. moved from New York, where she had known M.P., to Kansas, where her parents lived. She remained in telephone contact with M.P., but refused to disclose her new address. Approximately two months after the move, N.T. falsely told M.P. that she had terminated her pregnancy. M.P. had doubts about whether N.T. had actually had an abortion, but N.T. insisted she had and temporarily cut off telephone communication with M.P. when he expressed skepticism.

In fact, N.T. carried her pregnancy to term, delivered a baby (A.A.T.), and surrendered the newborn for adoption. N.T. falsely told her mother, other relatives, and her friends that the child had died at delivery. As part of the adoption proceeding, N.T. signed an affidavit in which she provided a fake last name for the child's father, falsely stated that she did not know background information about the father, and claimed the father was unwilling to assist her during her pregnancy. She also falsely told a guardian ad litem that the father knew she intended to place their child for adoption and that she had not contacted the father since the second month of her pregnancy.[91]

N.T. did not tell M.P. the truth until six months after A.A.T.'s birth.[92] She testified later that she had lied to M.P. about having an abortion because she knew M.P. would refuse to place the child for adoption.[93] As N.T. had anticipated, M.P. did object to the adoption once he learned about it.[94] By that time, however, the child had been permanently adopted away from him. M.P.'s attempt to have the adoption set aside was unsuccessful.[95]

Psychological and Emotional Injuries

We turn to psychological and emotional injuries last, but not because those injuries are less important consequences of deceit. To the contrary, deceived intimates often report that their psychological and emotional injuries were the most harmful aspect of their experience. These injuries sometimes stand alone and sometimes accompany the other sorts of injuries that we have already considered.

It is hardly surprising that deceived intimates emphasize the psychological and emotional damage their deceivers inflicted. Deceit always has the capacity to wound in this way, and an intimate's deceitfulness may be especially likely to cause significant psychological and emotional harm because the deceived person will frequently have felt close to her deceiver and invested herself in their relationship.

Many people have stressed how devastating losing trust in a deceitful intimate can be. One man recalled that learning about his wife's deceit made him feel that he had never known her well: "My world crumbled in a moment and it seemed as though everything I thought to be true about my marriage and my life was nothing more than an illusion. In that same instant, I lost my identity as well as the identity of my wife. Who was this woman? Certainly not the woman I thought she was."[96] A woman who learned that her husband had deceived her likewise recalled that: "My lowest point was realizing that my husband was an adroit liar, and I had to question everything he had said to me over all the years of our marriage. I had always trusted him to tell me the truth, and loss of that trust was devastating."[97] Another deceived intimate described her feelings this way after learning the truth: "I am devastated. I feel betrayed, knowing I've spent the last 37 years living with a liar and a cheat. How can I ever trust him again? The bottom has fallen out of my world!"[98]

Indeed, deceived intimates frequently report that the betrayal of their trust is what hurt the most. One woman explained after discovering her husband's deceit that "[t]he hardest part to deal with was not the infidelity itself but the fact that he had lied to me for 2 years. I still cannot forget this."[99] Another woman similarly recounted that she realized "the trust-shattering impact of financial infidelity" after her "then-husband secretly withdrew all of [their] money from [their] shared bank account," even though she also recognized "how ultimately unimportant" money was to her.[100]

The relatively scant social science research that has been conducted in this area is consistent with these first-person accounts. Small-scale studies have found that people identify trustworthiness and honesty as the most important characteristics for a relationship partner to have,[101] and emphasize that deception erodes trust.[102]

People can feel that their deceptive intimates betrayed them and violated their trust even when they know that their intimates thought—or told themselves—they were helping.[103] Sherri Groveman's parents deceived her to conceal that she had Androgen Insensitivity Syndrome (AIS), which meant she was born with XY chromosomes and testes. Groveman discovered the truth at age twenty when she went to a medical school library to investigate aspects of her body that she wondered about.[104]

While Groveman's parents may have been trying to protect her, she concluded that their paternalistic deceit left her worse off. As she wrote, "learning the truth about AIS is traumatic. But learning the truth alone and scared in the stacks of a library is shockingly inhumane. When physicians and parents abdicate their responsibility to speak the truth they not only allow this to happen, they virtually ensure that it will."[105]

Groveman emphasized that the deception undermined her relationship with her parents because of how "disorienting" it was to learn that her parents had "lied and left [her] to [her] own devices to discover this truth."[106] In her words: "When I discovered I had AIS the pieces finally fit together. But what fell apart was my relationship with both my family and physicians. It was not learning about chromosomes or testes that caused enduring trauma, it was discovering that I had been told lies."[107]

Other deceived intimates have reported that losing faith in their ability to judge people was the most devastating aspect of being duped. As one deceived woman wrote, what she found "most disturbing" was that the "deepest feelings" of her fiancé and then husband had been "absolutely invisible to" her.[108] She explained that she was "shaken by the recognition that [she] hadn't been able to tell the difference between appearance and reality"[109] and reported that her "confidence in [her] own judgment" was what her husband had "most seriously damaged."[110]

People may often be overly confident about their ability to spot an intimate's deceit,[111] so discovering that you have been duped may actually leave you with a more realistic sense of how difficult detecting deception can be. Nonetheless, losing the comfort and security of overconfidence can be painful and inhibiting. Some people who were duped have reported feeling unable to begin new relationships and "trust anyone else."[112] This is how one man described the cruel dilemma confronting deceived intimates after the truth emerges: "On the one hand, we've learned some very difficult but valuable lessons about trusting others. But, the negative side is that too much distrust can prevent us from ever developing a loving relationship again."[113]

On a related note, many deceived intimates have reported that discovering they had been duped made them feel "humiliated" and "stupid."[114] One woman asked herself: "How come I was so blind and so vulnerable?"[115] Another woman recounted that she "felt deceived, foolish and extremely hurt. It was devastating to discover that a relationship that I had publicized to the world as life-affirming and built on mutual love was actually based on deceit, lies, and obtained by fraud."[116] A third woman explained that she "was mortified and [she] felt shame" after learning that her boyfriend had duped her. She thought, "I'm a college-educated person and I fell for it."[117]

Popular culture and legal authorities can encourage such feelings with their shared tendency to blame deceived intimates for their plight.[118] Indeed, some duped intimates have reported experiencing such criticism after their deceivers were unmasked. Observers armed with the clarity of hindsight insisted that they should never have been fooled or should have uncovered the truth much sooner.

One woman's husband deceived her to conceal his bigamy, financial swindling, and other wrongdoing.[119] Reflecting back, she wrote: "I trusted him, I believed in him, and yet I am branded 'stupid' for doing so. On top of losing everything I own and facing a future raising three children on my own, it is hard to know that society as a whole views me as some kind of fool."[120]

Some people have become so distraught after discovering an intimate's deceit that they have suffered physical harm or physically harmed themselves. Muriel Vance's husband, Arnold Vance, learned soon after their wedding that his divorce from his first wife had not been finalized when he married Muriel.[121] If Arnold had told Muriel the truth, the couple could have had another wedding after Arnold's divorce was complete and he was legally free to remarry. He chose instead to deceive Muriel for twenty years by concealing the legal invalidity of their marriage. Muriel did not learn about the two decades of deception until Arnold left her for another woman and sought an annulment on the ground that he had married Muriel while still married to someone else.[122] After that bombshell revelation, Muriel "went into a state of shock, engaged in spontaneous crying and for a period seemed detached and unaware of her own presence. She was unable to function normally, unable to sleep and too embarrassed to socialize." Along with her "emotional collapse and depression," Muriel experienced "symptoms of an ulcer."[123] Several other people have reported trying to kill themselves after learning about an intimate's deceit.[124]

Harms that Extend Beyond the Deceiver's Primary Target

Intimate deception can also harm people who were not the deceiver's primary target. For example, sometimes multiple people suffer the consequences of being deceived because a person intent on duping one intimate feels the need to deceive many other intimates as well in order to prevent discovery. This is one version of the deception to maintain a preexisting facade that Chapter 1 discussed.

A woman who wants to fool her husband into believing that he is the biological father of her child will probably also have to deceive the child in order to keep the truth from her husband. Such deceit may deprive the child of an opportunity to develop a relationship with her biological father during her formative years. Of course, the relationship the child develops with the man she thinks is her biological father may be just as rich and nurturing as the bond with the biological father would have been. But that connection is vulnerable to disruption if the man learns he was duped about biological paternity.

Some men have become less committed to parenting and more ambivalent about the child after discovering that they were deceived about biological paternity. Damon Adams openly told a national newspaper that his feelings toward his ten-year-old daughter shifted after he learned that he was not her biological father, reporting: "Something changes in your heart . . . . When she walks through the door, you're seeing the product of an affair."[125]

Some men have sought to sever all ties to a child after learning that the mother deceived them about biological paternity. William Doran and Billy Doran spent more than a decade thinking they were biological father and son. But William's wife had deceived him to conceal her adultery around the time of Billy's conception. When DNA testing revealed—just before Billy's eleventh birthday—that William and Billy were biologically unrelated, William sought to stop paying child support for Billy and demanded a refund of the child support he had already paid. William also "as gently as possible removed himself from the child's life in a way which he felt would cause the child the least amount of anguish and hurt."[126] William may have told himself that he orchestrated his exit well, but it seems improbable that Billy thought William had treated him "gently" in terminating their relationship.

That said, even if a man wants to stay close to a child after discovering that he has been deceived about biological paternity, children sometimes find sustaining relationships under those circumstances difficult. Deborah and James Cain were married when Deborah gave birth to Brian, but divorced shortly after Brian's birth. James and Brian believed they were biological father and son until Deborah told Brian, when he was about ten, that his actual biological father was another man. After this announcement, "the relationship between Mr. Cain and Brian suffered to the point that it eventually came to an end. Brian ultimately refused visits with Mr. Cain, refused to associate with him, and refused to communicate with him."[127]

Chadwick Craig arranged a DNA test and discovered that he was not the biological father of his fourteen-year-old son, Kyle.[128] After Kyle heard the news, Craig told Kyle that he wanted to maintain their relationship as it had been, but Kyle said "it's not the same now" and wanted to live with his mother.[129] Kyle later testified that he did not want to see Craig "at this moment."[130]

Other varieties of deceit can similarly cause ripples of injury that reach beyond the deceiver's primary target. Consider a man who is duping his wife to conceal that he has fathered a child with another woman. This deception is aimed at the man's wife, but is also likely to harm the hidden child as well as any other children the man has. A father who is trying to keep his child's existence secret from his wife is likely to spend little time with that child because the more time he spends, the harder his deceit will be to maintain. If the man has other children, their father's deceit will probably deny them an opportunity to develop a relationship with their hidden half-sibling. Former presidential candidate John Edwards reportedly deceived his wife, Elizabeth, to conceal that he had fathered a child, Quinn, with Rielle Hunter. Edwards did not publicly admit that he was Quinn's father until the media was deeply suspicious of his denials and the girl was almost two years old. Before that, Edwards apparently strove to keep Quinn and her mother far from his wife, which also kept Quinn from her father and her three half-siblings.[131]

Along the same lines, a person who is deceiving an intimate about his racial or religious background may decide to stay away from relatives who could reveal the deceit. This distance can damage or destroy the deceiver's relationships with the relatives he has left behind and also prevent the deceiver's new and old intimates from connecting with each other.

Tony Williams's deceit to hide his racial background affected both an intimate who knew what Williams was doing—his mother, Sallie—and intimates who did not—his sons, Billy and Mike. Williams deceived Billy and Mike to conceal that he had grown up as a black child in Muncie, Indiana. Williams and his children lived as white in Virginia until Billy was ten. Williams had little contact with his African-American relatives in Muncie during this period, and he made sure his children knew nothing about them. When Sallie traveled to Virginia, Williams presented her as an employee he had hired to work in his tavern and did not disclose that she was also his mother and his children's grandmother.[132]

As these examples suggest, society as a whole can suffer when one intimate dupes another. We all benefit when close relationships between intimates promote caregiving, cooperation, companionship, love, support, flourishing, fulfillment, respect, and joy. Trust can be both a strong bond between people and a firm foundation for social life and civil society. When deceit destroys the trust that intimacy needs to thrive, it can weaken or break those personal bonds and simultaneously erode that societal firmament. Similarly, when deceivers keep grandparents and grandchildren, or sisters and brothers, or parents and children apart in order to maintain their deceptive schemes, that separation can be a loss for society as well as for the people most immediately involved.

In sum, intimate deceivers can injure their targets, the people surrounding a deceived intimate, and society more generally. While the extent and nature of harm varies, the injuries associated with an intimate's deceit can be severe— even life-altering. Intimate deceivers can leave people with little money and no financial security. They can impair or endanger a deceived intimate's health and personal safety, violate her sexual autonomy and bodily integrity, make her vulnerable to legal penalties, cost her time and opportunities she will never be able to recapture, and inflict psychological and emotional pain, distress, and devastation. Intimate deceivers can also damage the relationships of people connected to a deceived intimate and deprive those people of their own opportunities to form or strengthen personal bonds. Yet as Part II will explore, the law routinely treats intimate deception differently than deceit outside of intimacy and insists that deceived intimates should not have access to the remedies available for deception in other contexts. With this in mind, let's turn from the social phenomenon of intimate deception to the law governing the field.

PART II

THE LAW OF INTIMATE DECEPTION

An enormous body of law regulates intimate deception. The size of this legal regime might seem surprising from one perspective, given courts' routine refusal to grant redress and the public exposure and expense involved in bringing suit. Plaintiffs have come forward with a steady stream of cases without much encouragement from legal authorities. But the size of this body of law is not at all surprising from another standpoint, in light of the frequency with which people deceive their intimates and the injuries such deceit can inflict. While the slim chances of legal victory have surely dissuaded many deceived intimates from pursuing legal remedies, many others have not been discouraged. Judges are regularly asked to decide how the legal system will respond to deceit within intimate relationships.

The law that governs intimate deception is not wholly coherent. In fact, it contains some notable internal tensions and inconsistencies that we will explore. But recurring themes run through this legal arena, providing guiding principles that courts reiterate, endorse, and enforce as they regulate myriad different instances of deceit within intimacy.

This part examines how the law treats intimate deception and explores how that treatment has changed over time. Chapter 4 places the law governing intimate deception in historical context by analyzing the contraction in legal remedies that has occurred since the early twentieth century. Chapters 5 through 7 uncover dominant patterns in the modern regulation of intimate deception. Chapter 5 explores an overriding premise that courts have embraced in creating this body of law—the assumption that people deceived within intimate relationships do not and should not have access to remedies that are available to people deceived in other contexts. This persistent differentiation of intimate deception has especially far-reaching consequences because judges tend to adopt expansive definitions of intimacy within romantic and/or sexual relationships, including people who did not know each other well. Chapter 6 focuses on the judicial determination to preserve existing norms and practices in courtship, sexual relationships, and marriage. It examines the distinction courts often draw between supposedly ordinary acts of deception within such relationships—which judges are intent on protecting for reasons they do not fully explain—and extraordinary deceit, which judges are sometimes willing to remediate—but only if providing redress will not jeopardize more commonplace deceivers. Chapter 7 considers the regulation of deception between intimates who are not each other's spouses, sexual partners, or romantic interests. Courts frequently strive to protect parents who have deceived their children, including their adult children. But courts are much more willing to provide remedies when adult children have deceived their parents, and courts empower parents to impose their own penalties on deceptive minor children. This chapter also explores how judges have excluded many family relationships beyond marriage and parenthood from their recognition of intimacy, routinely treating deceptive siblings, aunts, uncles, nieces, and nephews as if they were unrelated to the people they deceived and permitting plaintiffs to access remedies available for nonintimate deception.

A Legal History
of Intimate Deception

Both intimate deception and the law governing it have a long history. Indeed, I could devote an entire book to examining how the law's treatment of intimate deception has evolved over time. That legal history remains remarkably underexplored. This book, however, is primarily focused on how the law and practice of intimate deception operate now. Accordingly, this chapter uncovers an aspect of the legal history of intimate deception that is especially useful for placing modern regulation in context and understanding it better.

The current reluctance to provide legal remedies to deceived intimates is not a timeless, unchanging, and unchangeable feature of the law. Looking even a century back in time reveals that judges and lawmakers in the early twentieth century were often more willing than their modern-day counterparts to grant legal redress for intimate deception. Since then, some important legal remedies have disappeared or become much less valuable. There now appears to be proportionately less litigation about deceit within intimacy than there once was, even though many plaintiffs still file suit. That decline, in turn, helps explain the relative paucity of modern scholarly attention.

At least three sets of events contributed to the significant contraction in available legal redress for intimate deception that took place over the course of the twentieth century. First, a wave of state legislatures starting with Indiana in 1935 enacted so-called anti-heart balm statutes that abolished causes of action for seduction and breach of promise to marry that some women had been using to bring claims revolving around intimate deception. Since then, courts have relied on expansive interpretations of anti-heart balm laws in blocking an array of suits seeking damages from deceptive intimates. Second, changing social and legal norms about race and gender made courts unwilling to provide redress for some types of intimate deception that judges had once been willing to remediate. Third—and most significant in reducing the volume of litigation—the advent and rapid spread of no-fault divorce starting in 1970 meant that annulments or fault-based divorces because of intimate deception, even when still available, became much less important forms of legal relief than they had been when courts granted divorces only for cause. Let's examine each factor in turn.

The Rise and Fall of Heart Balm Suits

Judges and legislators in the nineteenth and early twentieth centuries were certain that sex outside of marriage endangered the parties involved—white, middle-class women especially—and threatened the broader public as well. Committing sin was a moral violation that could spread like contagion. Nonmarital sex also constituted a practical menace to social order. A woman's loss of virginity before marriage could diminish her marriageability in an era when remaining unmarried often meant that a woman would face economic hardship and social marginalization. More worrisome still, nonmarital sex could lead to childbirth outside of marriage at a time when widespread discrimination and scant welfare protections left many nonmarital children and their mothers impoverished and ostracized.

One way common law courts and state legislatures responded to these dangers was by developing special causes of action that allowed people to seek redress for harms stemming from nonmarital sex. Over time, legal authorities developed four basic causes of action, known collectively as heart balm or amatory torts: breach of promise to marry, seduction, criminal conversation, and alienation of affections. These actions sometimes relied on principles operating elsewhere in the law. For example, the doctrinal rules governing breach of promise to marry suits drew on some general tort and contract principles while diverging from others.[1] But the heart balm torts were unique and distinct causes of action directed exclusively at injuries within intimacy. They were not integrated and interwoven with the rest of the law.

Criminal conversation and alienation of affections were concerned about adultery and the destruction of marital relationships. Criminal conversation suits were, as an old joke observed, inaptly named because the litigation was neither criminal nor about conversation. Instead, a husband—redress for criminal conversation was an exclusively male prerogative—could sue his wife's lover for damages, even if the woman had pursued her affair with gusto.[2] Alienation of affections suits allowed a plaintiff—usually a husband, but sometimes a wife—to sue someone who had meddled in his marital relationship and caused him to lose the affection and exclusive sexual companionship of his spouse, even if the spouse had not committed adultery.[3] These claims did not require plaintiffs to prove deception, and I have not found suits where the plaintiff stressed whether the defendant had been deceitful.

I will focus here on two other heart balm torts, breach of promise to marry and seduction, because before legislatures began abolishing these torts in the mid-1930s, they provided vehicles that some plaintiffs used to sue intimates who had deceived them.

Breach of Promise to Marry and Seduction

Breach of promise to marry was a common law cause of action that allowed a person—in virtually every case a woman—to recover damages from someone who had promised to marry her and then not done it, in circumstances where the woman had committed no fault and the man had no legally recognized justification for breaking the engagement. Courts generally did not distinguish between promises to marry that were deceptive—meaning the promisor never intended to fulfill his promise even at the time he made it—and promises that were genuine when made but not fulfilled because the promisor subsequently changed his mind. In either case, the jilted fiancée could recover for breach of promise to marry.[4]

Breach of promise suits were nominally open to female and male plaintiffs alike. But the logic behind the cause of action reflected a gendered recognition of women's dependence on marriage in a world where viable alternatives were scarce. Courts adjudicating these suits in the nineteenth and early twentieth centuries understood that matrimony had particular economic and social benefits for women, as unmarried women usually found it difficult to support themselves in the market and establish themselves in society. After a broken engagement, a woman might be unable to marry at all or unable to marry someone with as much to recommend him as her first fiancé. Her prospects of marrying another suitor would be especially bleak if she had a child.[5]

While courts typically did not focus on whether the defendant in a breach of promise suit had been deceptive so much as the fact that a legally blameless woman had been jilted, some women used breach of promise suits as a way to win legal remedies and legal recognition for injuries inflicted through deceit. These plaintiffs reported that they had been subject to false promises to marry— promises men had never intended to carry out. The women usually suggested that their former fiancés had lied about their intent to marry because the men knew that the women would otherwise refuse to have sex with them.

Jessie Carter reported that James Rinker presented himself to her as "a widower" and "a man of wealth." By February 1907, the couple had decided to marry. They announced their engagement to Carter's family and friends. Once engaged, Carter consented to sex with Rinker "as his fiancée, and at his earnest solicitation, and in expectancy of said marriage." Their sexual relationship continued until March or April when Carter discovered that Rinker was already married. He had been living with his wife throughout the time he was seeing Carter and supposedly preparing to marry her. Not surprisingly, Carter reported that Rinker's conduct had left her "greatly humiliated" and "prostrated."[6] She sued him for breach of promise to marry and the federal Circuit Court for the District of Kansas agreed in 1909 that she had stated "a cause of action" and could pursue her suit.[7]

The seduction tort was initially very different from breach of promise to marry. But over time, seduction suits joined breach of promise actions as vehicles that some deceived intimates used to secure legal redress for their injuries. Courts originally structured the seduction tort as a cause of action that a father could bring against a man who had been sexually intimate with the plaintiff's unmarried daughter. The theory was that this nonmarital sex had interfered with the father's legal right to his daughter's services, in most cases because the woman had become less able to work and/or less employable due to pregnancy.[8] Nonmarital sex—especially if it led to pregnancy—also diminished the woman's chances of marrying, which meant that her father might have to support her for a longer period or indefinitely.

Between the 1850s and the 1910s, however, at least seventeen states or territories transformed their tort of seduction, establishing by statute or judicial decision that unmarried women could bring seduction actions in their own names. None of the laws that I have found defined what they meant by seduction when they granted women the right to sue their seducers.[9] But here too, some women used this cause of action to seek legal recognition that a deceptive intimate had wronged them and legal redress for their resulting injuries. These women reported that men had duped them in pursuit of nonmarital sex (often with insincere promises of marriage) and explained that without the deceit they would have refused sex outside of marriage—and avoided unwed pregnancy. Their asserted injuries turned on the biological reality that only women can bear children and the gendered social reality that nonmarital sex and especially childbearing outside of marriage stigmatized and burdened women while leaving men comparatively unscathed.

Nellie Swett reported that she was a "chaste and virtuous" seventeen-year-old when John Gray declared his love and promised "that he would soon marry her." Swett contended that Gray knew his statements were false at the time he made them. He wanted "to deceive [Swett] and take advantage of her love and affection for him and induce her to have sexual intercourse with him." As Gray had hoped, Swett agreed to sex "trusting and relying solely upon his said promise to marry her, and in the love and affection he professed for her, and influenced by his urgent importunity." She became pregnant, realized Gray had deceived her about his feelings and intentions, and sued Gray for seduction.[10] The California

Supreme Court agreed in 1903 that Swett's allegations, if proved, were sufficient to establish that Gray had seduced her.[11]

Ila Savage won a $2000 damages judgment in her seduction suit against Harvey Embrey, even though Embrey had never promised to marry her. Instead, Savage proved her claim by establishing that Embrey had deceived her into sex with "false protestations of love"—declarations he made knowing they did not reflect his true feelings. Savage was twenty-one at the time, while Embrey was a forty-year-old "traveling man."[12] She reported that she "believed and relied upon" Embrey's misrepresentations and consented to sex after two months of "his oft-repeated protestations of love."[13] Once he accomplished his goal, Embrey apparently was no longer interested in Savage. He left her pregnant with his child.[14] The Michigan Supreme Court, which reviewed Savage's suit in 1921, felt confident that Embrey would not have managed to dupe most women of Savage's age. But the court nonetheless upheld the jury's verdict that Savage had been seduced and had been injured as a consequence.[15]

Anna Busby reported that John Simons had deceived her into sex and she won $500 in damages in a seduction suit against him, even though she had not become pregnant.[16] Busby explained that Simons "falsely, fraudulently, and corruptly represented to her that he desired to marry her, and did promise to marry her." She was a virgin "of good social standing and respectability," but she agreed to premarital sex "believing that the defendant intended to marry her, and having full confidence in him and great love for him." Afterward, Simons "deserted her, refused to marry her, and publicly published the fact that he had had sexual intercourse with her." Busby emphasized her emotional distress ("agony of mind") and reputational injury ("her fair name has been destroyed, and her associates have forsaken her").[17] The Indiana Supreme Court upheld the damages award in 1889.[18]

Women also used seduction suits to secure legal remedies against men who had been both deceitful and violent in pursuing sex. Kate Verwers reported that she was lying in bed in the home of her future father-in-law when her supposed fiancé, Harley Carpenter, entered her room.[19] She apparently thought that Carpenter was just passing through on the way to his own room until he got into her bed.[20] Verwers "was unwilling to" have sex, but Carpenter "used physical force" and held her down.[21] Many modern readers would conclude that Carpenter raped Verwers. But when Carpenter climbed into Verwers's bed in 1909 and when the Iowa Supreme Court decided Verwers's seduction suit in 1914,[22] a rape conviction required proving that the woman had resisted the man's physical force to the utmost of her ability.[23] Verwers explained that Carpenter had deceived her by falsely promising to marry her.[24] She believed him and accordingly "did not resist as she would have done except for the promise of marriage and the love and affection she bore the defendant, resulting from his acts and artifices."[25] Verwers became pregnant and had a child who died soon after birth. Carpenter refused to marry her.[26] She sued him for seduction and the jury found in her favor, concluding "that physical force was used by defendant, but that plaintiff was induced to yield by reason of false promises."[27] The Iowa Supreme Court affirmed the verdict.[28]

By the mid-1930s, in short, suits for seduction and breach of promise to marry were part of a distinct set of torts that focused exclusively on injuries within intimacy. Some women were successfully using these torts to win legal remedies against intimates who had deceived them.

Anti-Heart Balm Laws

Heart balm torts may have been particularly vulnerable to political and popular attacks because they were special causes of action for intimates and were not integrated into the rest of the law. They were prone to attract attention, and legislatures could abolish them without much impact on the law governing life outside of intimate relationships.

Heart balm torts had their detractors even in the nineteenth century.[29] But criticism of heart balm began to resonate with state legislatures during the Great Depression, when tales of unscrupulous women and the threat they posed to men and their families may have seemed particularly frightening. Starting in 1935, a wave of states targeted these torts, enacting what were known as anti-heart balm statutes. This legislation blocked or narrowed an important pathway that some deceived intimates had been using to obtain legal redress.

Indiana was first. Roberta West Nicholson, the state's only female legislator, spearheaded the effort to pass an anti-heart balm law.[30] Nicholson was elected to the Indiana General Assembly in 1934, and she served in 1935 and 1936. Before that, she had been the elected secretary for the Indiana convention that ratified the federal constitutional amendment repealing prohibition.[31] Nicholson's election to the General Assembly was news in Indiana. She was not just a female lawmaker when that was rare, she was also a wife and mother of two school-age children. When the *Indianapolis Star* interviewed Nicholson soon after she took office, she stressed that her husband supported her political career and her father-in-law (a well-known writer and diplomat from Indiana) had inspired her political involvement. Nicholson also used this interview to name a range of legislative priorities, including regulating the newly legalized liquor industry and opposing child labor.[32] However, Nicholson ultimately became most known for her association with another cause. In her short legislative tenure, she achieved both political victory and national recognition in her campaign against heart balm torts.

Although Indiana's statute would reach more broadly, Nicholson—like many legislators after her—was most concerned about suits for seduction and especially breach of promise to marry, heart balm actions that women brought almost exclusively. Her arguments in 1935 against these causes of action previewed the assertions that would sweep statehouses in the years to come and added fire to contentions that had been appearing in the popular and legal press.

In advocating for her anti-heart balm bill, Nicholson said little about women who had actually been harmed within intimacy. Instead, she insisted that the women suing for breach of promise or seduction were fraudsters with fabricated claims designed to extract money from wealthy men. Nicholson was "firmly convinced" "that most actions for breach of promise and seduction have extortion as their chief motive. Surely a suit to recover money as damages for the broken romance cannot soothe a woman if love was genuine."[33] Heart balm plaintiffs were concealing their "itching palms in the guise of aching hearts."[34]

Nicholson did not present evidence that women were bringing droves of fabricated, fraudulent, and "extortion[ate]" heart balm suits. To my knowledge, no such evidence exists. Instead, Nicholson's logic was circular. Her proof that women suing for heart balm were conniving graspers advancing "blackmail suits" was the very fact the women had sued. As Nicholson explained to her fellow legislators, "self-respecting women" did not bring heart balm actions.[35]

Nicholson believed she was advancing women's interests, or at least the interests of the kind of women she cared about. She met with members of the Marion County Democratic Women's Club in February 1935 to encourage women to run for the Indiana Legislature and to assert that her anti-heart balm bill "protected wives and feminine members of the family of men who suffered from the often unfounded blackmailing machinations of unscrupulous women."[36] Nicholson's comments may have been especially resonant given contemporary concerns about the strains the Great Depression was placing on men and their connections to their families.

She also showed no hesitation about claiming to speak for all women, even as she moved to abolish causes of action that some women had been using to secure legal remedies. When Nicholson urged the other members of the Indiana House to pass her bill, she simultaneously distanced herself from organized movements for women's equality and spoke as if every woman supported the abolition of heart balm torts. She contended: "Women do not demand rights, gentleman, they earn them, and they ask no such privileges as these which are abolished in this bill."[37]

Many of Nicholson's colleagues in the Indiana Legislature embraced her arguments. State Senator Leo Smith declared "that 999 out of 1,000 breach of promise and alienation of affection suits were nothing but shakedowns."[38] He advised his fellow lawmakers that the anti-heart balm bill would end "dastardly rackets"[39] and urged them to "eliminate this evil from the good old state of Indiana."[40] State Senator Jesse Wade added criticism of plaintiffs' attorneys, who might have been particularly ripe targets in an economic climate that left many lawyers hungry for work and perhaps less discriminating about the cases they took. He asserted that "[t]housands on thousands of dollars are being taken by unscrupulous jackleg lawyers in such cases."[41]

Some Indiana lawmakers wanted to keep the heart balm torts in place. State Senator William Dennigan declared that Nicholson's bill was "wrong" and asked: "Do you mean to tell me you will help women by taking away their civil rights against philanderers and men who prey upon them?"[42]

But the proponents of Indiana's anti-heart balm bill did not have to wait long for legislative victory. On March 11, 1935, Indiana abolished breach of promise to marry, alienation of affections, and criminal conversation as causes of action in the state and limited seduction suits to cases where the woman was injured before turning twenty-one.[43] The measure passed by large margins, eighty-seven to seven in the House and thirty-one to fifteen in the Senate.[44]

Even before Indiana enacted its anti-heart balm statute, lawmakers in other states were asking Nicholson for copies of her bill and beginning to consider similar or identical legislation.[45] Nicholson commented wryly on all the attention. She seemed to acknowledge implicitly that having female leadership in a movement to take away legal options from women provided protective cover for the men rallying to her cause. Nicholson quipped: "It looks like I've become the standard bearer of a crusade to make the world safe for men."[46]

New York was the next state to pass an anti-heart balm law. On March 29, 1935, New York prohibited suits seeking money damages for alienation of affections, criminal conversation, seduction, or breach of contract to marry.[47] The lawmakers responsible for New York's statute echoed Nicholson's critique of heart balm and contended—without presenting the evidence needed to support such an assertion—that many or most heart balm plaintiffs were bringing fraudulent claims. The text of the New York law declared—in phrases that would be repeated or paraphrased in the anti-heart balm statutes of New Jersey (1935),[48] Colorado (1937),[49] Wyoming (1941),[50] Nevada (1943),[51] Maryland (1945),[52] and Florida (1945)[53]—that heart balm remedies had "been subjected to grave abuses, causing extreme annoyance, embarrassment, humiliation and pecuniary damage to many persons wholly innocent and free of any wrongdoing, who were merely the victims of circumstances," had "been exercised by unscrupulous persons for their unjust enrichment," and had "furnished vehicles for the commission or attempted commission of crime and in many cases ha[d] resulted in the perpetration of frauds."[54] Governor Herbert Lehman similarly asserted in signing New York's anti-heart balm bill into law that "[f]or many years these actions have been used to extract large sums of money without proper justification. They have been a fruitful source of coercion, extortion and blackmail."[55]

While the New York statute abolished all four heart balm torts, legislators appear to have been most concerned about the types of suits women brought, especially breach of promise to marry actions. State Senator John McNaboe, who sponsored and championed the anti-heart balm bill that became law in New York,[56] declared that the law was targeting "a tribute of $10,000,000 paid annually by New York men to gold-diggers and blackmailers" and charged that "[n]ine out of ten recent breach of promise suits have been of the racketeer type."[57] The term "gold-digger" was a gendered pejorative used in this era to describe the supposedly rapacious and conniving women who sued for breach of promise to marry. McNaboe condemned both the women who sued and the purportedly low-class, unseemly, and unscrupulous attorneys who represented them, describing both groups in terms usually reserved for gangsters or other criminals. He announced in a radio broadcast that New York "refuses to be a party to blackmail any longer; the great Empire State will not be a coconspirator of a certain type of lawyer, who, working in cahoots with the modern female racketeer, seeks to become rich at the expense of reputation, embarrassment, and wide-spread publicity."[58]

By the end of 1935, at least seven states had enacted anti-heart balm laws, all of which prohibited suits for breach of promise to marry and five of which either prohibited seduction actions or limited them to plaintiffs who were younger than a specified age when injured.[59] By the end of 1945, at least nine more states had enacted anti-heart balm laws that prohibited or limited breach of promise suits. Four of those states also prohibited or limited seduction suits.[60] By the end of the twentieth century, at least twenty-nine states and the District of Columbia had enacted statutes prohibiting or limiting suits for breach of promise to marry and/or seduction.[61]

The flurry of legislative activity in the 1930s and 1940s responded to and helped encourage the condemnations of heart balm suits that appeared in newspapers, magazines, books, legal treatises, and law journals. Like state legislators, popular and scholarly critics of heart balm actions in the first decades of the twentieth century had remarkably little to say about why women who had actually been harmed within intimacy did not deserve legal remedies. Instead, critics devoted almost all their time to asserting—rather than proving—that seduction and especially breach of promise to marry suits were usually fraudulent and extortionate.

Heart balm's opponents in the media and the legal profession relied on the same circular logic evident in state legislatures. On their reasoning, the simple fact that a woman had sued for breach of promise to marry revealed that she was probably a "gold-digger"[62] because only an "indelicate, scheming, enterprising" woman would be willing to sue.[63] Heart balm critics were certain that "a woman of modesty and good breeding" who had "been actually wronged" would "never" bring a breach of promise claim.[64] She would not "air in a court of law the fact that she had been jilted by some man" and she would not "lay herself open to the slurring attacks in public of the man's lawyer."[65] A "respectable" woman would know "that suffering can never be paid for in cold dollars and cents,"[66] that "no amount of money" could "cure or even salve" the injury a breach of promise to marry inflicted.[67] Indeed, some critics compared breach of promise plaintiffs to prostitutes.[68] As one wrote, "[a]ny sophisticated person knows that decent women do not sue for breach of promise. We are all familiar with the type of female who sets a monetary value on her body. The price makes no difference. Neither does the means of collection."[69]

Critics had less to say about seduction actions, but when their attention turned there they similarly charged that "[f]raud, oppression, and blackmail are manifest dangers, as is abuse at the hands of gullible and sympathetic juries. As in the case of breach-of-promise suits, the [seduction] action will often fail to protect those who need it most. Women with refined sensibilities will not bring action."[70] One critic asserted that a seduction action was "even less likely to be commenced by a self-respecting and innocent woman than an action for damages for breach of contract" because of the "incidents of unpleasant notoriety" associated with seduction litigation. In his view, seduction suits were "more likely to be abused by women of questionable character and motives."[71]

Such arguments reflected a long history of reasoning about gender in ways that divided women into the virtuous and the wanton, placed rigid expectations on each type of female, and presumed that a woman seeking legal redress from a man was lying about the man's misconduct. These ideas were culturally engrained and their pull was perhaps especially strong in a time of so much uncertainty, upheaval, and worry. Even someone as committed to advancing women's welfare as Eleanor Roosevelt seemed to endorse these canards. When she spoke in support of New York's anti-heart balm bill a few days before the governor signed it into law, the First Lady told reporters: "I don't think anyone who was really hurt would ever sue."[72]

Yet some critics of breach of promise to marry and seduction suits nonetheless contended in the 1920s and 1930s that eliminating those causes of action was a thoroughly modern idea, consistent with "[t]he modern tendency toward equalization of men's and women's social, economic, political, and legal rights."[73] These critics asserted that women's status had been transformed so that a breach of promise to marry suit had become "an anomaly in this twentieth century"[74] because "times have changed."[75]

In retrospect, it seems vastly—even absurdly—overstated to contend that women in the 1920s and 1930s were no longer "dependent upon matrimony for [their] welfare and subsistence."[76] Indeed, such a declaration appears to be in tension with the law's longstanding efforts to hold men responsible for the economic support of women and children, so government authorities need not be. The success of the anti-heart balm movement is anomalous from that perspective, as these statutes barred women who had been left without the financial and social protection of marriage from making economic claims on the men who had made them so vulnerable.

To be sure, assertions that women deprived of heart balm remedies would be able to support themselves in the market without men's help were more plausible than they would have been a century earlier. Some women in the 1920s and 1930s were managing to earn a living—including presumably some of the female journalists who urged the abolition of heart balm torts. Heart balm critics in this era could emphasize that "[w]omen now have the legal right to collect their own wages, enter into business contracts," and "own property in their own name."[77] Moreover, women had finally won a suffrage amendment in 1920.[78]

That said, describing 1920s and 1930s America as "an era in which women work alongside men as competitors"[79] ignored the persistent reality that men's and women's work was starkly divided and unequal. Legal policies and social practices operated together to ensure that gender pervasively constrained the jobs open to women, the compensation women received, and the working conditions women experienced. Women were segregated into work that paid little and demanded much and were excluded from most of the occupations open to men, especially if they were lucrative, rewarding, and/or prestigious.[80] If a woman became pregnant and did not want to carry her pregnancy to term— perhaps because she would be unable to support herself and her child—she confronted statutes that criminalized abortion in every state.[81] Federal law did not prohibit employment discrimination against women until the 1960s.[82] The Supreme Court would not strike down any law on the ground that it denied women equal protection until 1971.[83] The Court would not recognize constitutional limits on the power of legislatures to restrict women's access to abortion until 1973.[84] Moreover, the rigidly gendered norms that pervaded the popular and legislative attack on heart balm actions hardly suggested the triumph of "modern ideas" about "the equality of the sexes."[85]

While critics cited the "new era dawn[ing] for women" as grounds for eliminating heart balm torts,[86] the concerns about unmarried women's vulnerability that lay behind these torts were as pressing in the 1930s as they had been in the late nineteenth century—perhaps even more pressing given the economic desperation and unemployment that pervaded the Great Depression years. Prohibiting suits for breach of promise to marry or seduction did not make it any easier for unmarried women to support themselves in the market, much less lighten the burdens weighing on nonmarital children and their mothers.

Banning these causes of action simply blocked legal pathways that some women had been using to seek remedies for injuries within intimacy, including injuries stemming from deception.

Judicial Enforcement of Heart Balm's Abolition

After legislatures enacted anti-heart balm statutes, courts helped intensify the impact of those statutes. Judges enforcing anti-heart balm laws might have contented themselves with ensuring that plaintiffs no longer won suits designated as claims for breach of promise to marry or seduction and no longer relied on precedents created when courts recognized heart balm torts. Instead, however, courts have been much more active in policing, even expanding upon, the abolition of heart balm. Judges have scrutinized lawsuits between intimates to assess whether plaintiffs bringing claims under still-viable causes of action are "really" pursuing heart balm actions by another name, and judges have dismissed suits alleging significant injuries when they think they have found a heart balm case in disguise. Courts have not always been consistent with each other in what they take anti-heart balm statutes to prohibit.[87] But from the 1930s to the present day, courts have repeatedly relied on anti-heart balm laws—and far-reaching judicial interpretations of those laws—in barring a variety of suits revolving around intimate deception. If a plaintiff sues someone she once planned to marry but did not, courts are inclined to insist that any claim alleging any type of deceit falls within statutory bans on breach of promise suits. Courts have even read statutory prohibitions on breach of promise litigation as grounds for blocking suits about deception between people who married, where no promise to marry was breached at all. These expansive interpretations of anti-heart balm laws, frequently unmoored from the statutory text, have been significant obstacles for deceived intimates seeking redress. Part III argues that judicial interpretations of anti-heart balm legislation should track the actual language in the statutes. Before we get there, this section reveals how aggressively courts have used anti-heart balm laws.

Deceived intimates felt the impact of anti-heart balm statutes right away. In 1938, a unanimous New York appellate court held that the state's ban on breach of contract to marry suits meant that Frances Sulkowski could not sue her ex-fiancé, John Szewczyk, to recover for the injuries his misrepresentations reportedly inflicted on her.[88] Sulkowski contended that Szewczyk had proposed while falsely presenting himself as unmarried and concealing that he already had a wife. She sued him "to recover damages for false representations."[89] Nonetheless, the court insisted that her suit was actually "based upon breach of contract to marry." The judges also suggested that Sulkowski had fabricated her allegations,

although they could cite no evidence to support that charge and Szewczyk's preexisting marriage was presumably a matter of public record. The court stated that
"Plaintiff's suit is one of those in which the service of the summons or merely the
threat to do so is sufficient to cause a settlement even when there is not any merit
in the alleged cause of action."[90]

A federal district court in Pennsylvania, subsequently affirmed unanimously
on appeal, similarly concluded in 1940 that the abolition of breach of promise
to marry suits in New York and Pennsylvania meant that A.B. could not sue her
former fiancé, C.D., for "fraud and deceit."[91] A.B. reported that C.D. had promised to marry her knowing at the time he made the promise that he did not intend
to carry it out.[92] She recounted that she spent over $10,000 "in contemplation of
the supposedly impending marriage"—including gifts she gave to C.D.—only to
learn from him after almost three years that he had been deceiving her. A.B. sued
seeking compensation for her financial outlays.[93] The judge dismissed her suit,
explaining that he was reading the legislative prohibitions on breach of promise
to marry actions "broad[ly]" and would "guard against resort to the action of
deceit as a subterfuge and attempt to circumvent the statutory prohibition."[94]

The California District Court of Appeal held in 1964 that California's prohibition on "breach of promise of marriage" suits barred Hazel Boyd from suing her
allegedly deceptive husband, John Boyd—even though John had married Hazel
and so no promise to marry had been breached.[95] Hazel reported that John had
promised to live with and support her. Instead, however, John departed two days
after the wedding and refused to cohabit or provide support. She contended
that John had never intended to fulfill his promises and had knowingly inflicted
an extraordinary economic hardship on her through his deceit. As John knew,
Hazel had been widowed by her first husband and had been collecting monthly
Social Security and veterans' benefits based on that relationship. The federal government stopped making those payments once Hazel married John. Hazel sued
John seeking damages for the injuries his deceit had caused.[96]

The California court recognized that some of the California Legislature's
concerns about breach of promise suits did not apply to Hazel's case. Hazel was
certainly not making "a trumped-up" allegation when she reported that John had
agreed to marry her as "the existence of marriage vows [was] a conceded fact."[97]
Yet the court was nonetheless intent on protecting the legislature's ban on breach
of promise suits from all possible incursions—even to the point of holding that
"the occurrence of a marriage ceremony does not affect operation of the statute."
The court held that just as Hazel could not have sued John for damages if he
failed "to undergo a marriage ritual," she also could not sue John for damages
when he failed "to fulfill matrimonial obligations and expectations."[98] The court
did not bother to mask the gendered hostility and suspicion it directed at wives
who accused their husbands of deceiving them. The opinion explained that

Hazel might seek an annulment, divorce, or legal separation from John, but "a wronged woman" would not be permitted to sue her husband for damages stemming from his deceit because that would allow her "to secure additional money, vengeance or both."[99]

Judges have continued to treat anti-heart balm statutes as barriers to legal claims involving intimate deception.[100] Consider five more recent decisions in which courts relied on anti-heart balm laws—and expansive judicial interpretations of those laws—in blocking plaintiffs from pursuing remedies against intimates who had reportedly deceived them.

The first case, Brown v. Strum,[101] illustrates how judges examine suits between former intimates on the assumption that they may really be heart balm actions in disguise. If courts decide that they detect the presence of heart balm, they refuse to allow the litigation to proceed—even when the plaintiff invokes modern tort law and alleges substantial injury. Cleveland Brown reported that Adam Strum induced her into a sexual relationship by falsely presenting himself as unmarried.[102] She explained that Strum emailed her when they were both using the Match.com dating service. She viewed his profile, saw he listed himself as divorced, and responded to his message. When they spoke on the phone later, Strum told Brown that he was divorced and wanted to remarry and have additional children. The two began dating and had sex. Brown reported that throughout the relationship "Strum kept reinforcing her belief that he was divorced and interested in marrying her." However, Brown eventually learned that Strum was still married and did not intend to divorce. She sued him for fraud and intentional infliction of emotional distress.[103]

The federal district court in Connecticut announced that it had ferreted out a heart balm action by another name and would not permit Brown to pursue redress. The opinion explained "that a plaintiff may not circumvent the statutory prohibition on heart balm actions by recharacterizing them as emotional distress or fraud claims. To determine whether a plaintiff has a bona fide claim or is simply using an emotional distress claim to evade the anti-heart balm statute, courts look to the underlying factual allegations of the complaint."[104] After scrutinizing Brown's suit, the court held in 2004 that the ban on seduction and breach of promise to marry actions in Connecticut (where Brown lived) and New York (where Strum lived) barred the litigation.[105]

The next two cases illustrate how expansively courts interpret anti-heart balm laws when considering litigation between people who once planned to marry but did not. Courts tend to insist in these suits that statutes barring breach of promise claims should also be read to block any claims that these plaintiffs bring about any sort of deception.

In M.N. v. D.S.,[106] M.N. reported that D.S.—her married lover—deceived her so she would have an abortion rather than bear his child. As she recounted,

D.S. told her that if she terminated her pregnancy, he would divorce his wife, marry her, and have a child with her later. These promises convinced her to abort when she otherwise would have carried her pregnancy to term.[107] After the abortion, she discovered that D.S. had never intended to have a child with her or to leave his wife.[108] M.N. sued him "for intentional and negligent infliction of emotional distress, battery, and fraud and misrepresentation."[109]

The Minnesota Court of Appeals held in 2000 that M.N. could not pursue any of her claims because her suit violated Minnesota's statutory prohibition on breach of promise to marry actions.[110] As the unanimous court acknowledged, M.N. charged that D.S. had deceived her about more than a promise to marry. Moreover, the harm that M.N. emphasized most was not that D.S. refused to marry her, but that she aborted a pregnancy based on his misrepresentations.[111] Nonetheless, the court read Minnesota's ban on breach of promise actions as also precluding other claims, contending that this was a simple matter of logic without explaining why. As the court concluded, "if no cause of action can exist in tort for a fraudulent promise to marry, then logically no cause of action can exist for a fraudulent promise by a married man to leave his wife and impregnate a woman who is not his wife."[112]

Smith v. National Railroad Passenger Corporation[113] similarly exemplifies the judicial inclination to read anti-heart balm statutes broadly enough to cover all allegations of deceit that plaintiffs bring against former fiancés, whether or not the claims are directly about breaching a promise to marry. Susan Smith reported that Fred Weiderhold had deceived her about two crucial issues. First, he told her that he planned to marry her when he knew that was not true. Second, he misrepresented the personnel policy at Amtrak—where he was the Inspector General and she worked in human relations—by falsely telling Smith "that they could not work together at Amtrak once they were planning to marry." Smith resigned from her job only to discover a few months later that Weiderhold had been deceiving her. She tried to get rehired at Amtrak, but was unsuccessful. Smith sued Weiderhold for "Misrepresentation," explaining that after she resigned from Amtrak based on Weiderhold's false statements she "suffered and continues to suffer loss of employment, loss of income, loss of retirement benefits, severe emotional distress, pain and suffering, mental anguish, inconvenience, loss of enjoyment of life, and other non-economic losses."[114]

A federal district court in Pennsylvania dismissed her suit in 1998 on the ground that it contravened Pennsylvania's anti-heart balm statute and "the strong legislative policy of Pennsylvania" expressed in that law. Smith had focused her claim for damages on the allegation that Weiderhold had tricked her into quitting. This claim was distinct from her contention that Weiderhold had agreed to marry her knowing he would not do it. Terminating her employment with Amtrak would probably have hurt her financially even if she had married Weiderhold. The court mentioned no evidence that Weiderhold was so extraordinarily wealthy that Smith would not have needed to support herself if they wed. But the court nonetheless insisted that Smith's suit was really "for breach of promise to marry," asserting that her "loss is inextricably bound to defendant's broken promise to wed her."[115] Smith could not pursue her suit and Weiderhold appears to have paid little, if any, price for his alleged deceit. He remained Amtrak's Inspector General until 2009.[116]

Judicial hostility to litigation between people who were once engaged can extend to lawsuits that parents bring against their child's former fiancé. In *Yang v. Lee*,[117] Helen and Edward Yang sued Holden Lee, who had been engaged to the Yangs' daughter, Janet.[118] The plaintiffs reported that Holden had intentionally misled all three Yangs by concealing that he was gay and having sex with men.[119] Janet and Holden had been in a long-distance relationship, with Janet in Hong Kong and Holden in California. He proposed after about three years of dating, taking care to request and receive approval from Janet's parents first. Janet accepted Holden's proposal and moved to San Francisco to live with him, leaving her job as Director of Salomon Smith Barney for Asia.[120] None of the courts that eventually reviewed the history of the relationship discussed how the couple decided that Janet would relocate. But the result was that Janet—like Susan Smith—sacrificed career opportunities and financial prospects, while Holden—like Fred Weiderhold—was able to pursue his career "in the fields of development and private investment" without interruption. Janet had been earning half a million dollars annually in Hong Kong, but the job she obtained in California paid a comparatively paltry $70,000 a year.[121]

A few weeks before the wedding date, Janet found love letters that men had written to Holden. She reported that this discovery "utterly shocked" her and left her feeling betrayed. She would attempt suicide several times, although the precise timing of those attempts is unclear.[122]

Janet seems to have told both Holden and her parents about finding the letters. In the immediate aftermath of Janet's discovery, Holden apparently still wanted to marry her. He met with Janet and her parents and admitted that he was gay and had been having sex with men.[123] Helen and Edward (understandably) felt at this point that marrying Holden would be a "high risk" proposition for their daughter.[124] But Holden signed a written agreement stating that he would give Janet's parents $500,000 so they could hold this money in trust "as security in the event that he violated his marital obligations to Ms. Yang." However, Holden told Helen and Edward the next day that the wedding would not take place after all. Holden eventually sued Janet in California because he wanted the engagement ring and some other assets back from her. Janet's parents then filed a federal suit against Holden in Maryland, where Helen and Edward lived.[125] Among other counts, Helen and Edward contended that Holden had injured them through his intentional misrepresentation and intentional infliction of emotional distress.[126]

Helen and Edward did not argue that Holden should have married their daughter.[127] Indeed, it is not clear whether Janet still wanted to marry Holden after discovering his deceit.[128] Instead, Helen and Edward charged that Holden had asked for their approval before proposing to Janet while intentionally misleading them about his sexual orientation and sexual history.[129] They also emphasized the emotional distress they experienced because of Holden's behavior toward them and their daughter.[130]

One might think that Helen and Edward were not the best plaintiffs to sue Holden and should have left any litigation to Janet. Nonetheless, the federal district court in Maryland that decided this case in 2001 made clear that Janet would not have fared better if she had brought the suit herself.[131]

The district court—later affirmed unanimously by the Fourth Circuit—held that Helen's and Edward's claims for intentional misrepresentation and intentional infliction of emotional distress were barred under Maryland's anti-heart balm law, "which is remedial in nature and must be construed liberally."[132] The court did not fully explain its reasoning, but its argument seems to have been that this litigation constituted a breach of promise to marry suit because one of the many things that Holden did in his long series of interactions with Janet and her parents was "breach[] his promise to marry Janet"—meaning, presumably, that Holden was the first one to declare the wedding off.[133] If a couple planned to marry but never did, courts are inclined to insist that any litigation about deceit between the formerly betrothed—or even about deceit between one former fiancé and the parents of the other—is really a breach of promise suit, regardless of whether the plaintiffs complain about the broken engagement.

Indeed, courts have interpreted statutory prohibitions on breach of promise litigation so expansively that they have read these statutes to bar suits between people who actually married—where the promise to marry was kept rather than breached.[134] In *Summers v. Renz*,[135] Debra Summers reported that Frederick Renz, Jr., had duped her into marriage by lying about his criminal record, employment history, military service, and treatment of his first wife, among other matters. Before they married, Renz allegedly told Summers that he was a certified public accountant, a former partner at Arthur Young, a decorated war hero, and a retired Air Force pilot. He also allegedly told her that he was law-abiding and that his first marriage had generally been happy and had ended in an amicable divorce.[136] Summers explained that she eventually discovered after marrying Renz that he had fabricated all of this supposed personal history and deceived her about many other issues besides.[137] Most disturbingly, Renz had reportedly concealed from Summers that he had been convicted of felony atrocious assault for attempting to kill his first wife by shooting her while she slept with their three-year-old child.[138]

Summers contended that she never would have married Renz, remained his wife, or transferred any assets to him if she had not been deceived.[139] She sued him, "seeking to undo or be compensated for" various financial transactions in which she had given assets to Renz "under a fraudulently induced belief that she had married a highly accomplished and rectitudinous individual." Summers also sought damages for the emotional distress she reportedly experienced upon learning about Renz's attempt to kill his first wife and comprehending "the magnitude of [his] deceit."[140]

The California Court of Appeal unanimously held in 2004 that California's anti-heart balm laws blocked Summers's effort to secure "financial vindication of her erroneous marital expectations that her husband was a man of a certain caliber and character." Summers's suit involved no actual breach of a promise to marry, as Renz had married Summers. Rather than complain about a broken engagement, Summers wanted damages to help restore her to the financial position she would have occupied if Renz had not duped her into marriage. Nevertheless, the court insisted that "[i]nsofar as [Summers's] lawsuit attempts . . . to seek remedies for her failed marital expectations as a result of [Renz's] alleged fraud regarding his own personal history, we conclude it is nothing more than a latter-day incarnation of a breach of promise suit."[141]

The arguments that led to a wave of anti-heart balm laws prohibiting breach of promise to marry and seduction suits do not fare well in the light of modern scrutiny. Yet those statutes are not dusty relics. Courts continue to rely on them in blocking litigation from deceived intimates. Indeed, courts have interpreted anti-heart balm statutes expansively, extending their reach well beyond breach of promise to marry claims. Anti-heart balm laws—and aggressive judicial interpretations of those laws—help explain the contraction in available legal remedies for intimate deception that occurred over the twentieth century.

Changing Norms About Race and Gender Undercut Some Intimate Deception Claims

A second factor that helps explain the diminution in legal remedies for intimate deception centers on evolving norms about race and gender. Some types of lawsuits have not been legislatively prohibited, but have nonetheless died out because courts have concluded that recognizing the injuries at stake as legally compensable harms would contravene modern commitments to equality—whether by endorsing racial caste systems or condoning the treatment of women as "the personal chattels of men."[142] By the last decades of the twentieth century, changing attitudes about racialized and gendered subordination had made plaintiffs less likely to bring certain intimate deception claims and judges unwilling to grant redress they had once provided.

A Legal History of Intimate Deception About Race

Deception about race provides a striking example of how changing norms have undercut some intimate deception claims that judges were once willing to remediate. Courts through the middle of the twentieth century repeatedly insisted that white people deserved legal redress when they were deceived into intimacy with people who were not white. Judges reaching that conclusion were reflecting and reinforcing foundational aspects of American law and culture that have since shifted significantly—albeit not entirely.

Before the establishment of the modern civil rights regime, explicit racial segregation and legalized race discrimination in public and private life meant that classification as a white person versus a person of color had tremendous legal as well as economic and social consequences. White Americans often justified the Jim Crow system to themselves by insisting that racial differences were real. But white legal authorities simultaneously constructed and defined those differences. One way many states expressed and enforced white supremacy was by adopting so-called one-drop rules, which provided that even a small proportion of nonwhite ancestry was sufficient to deny someone legal status as a white person.[143] This exclusionary definition of whiteness meant that a person could look white, yet not "really" be white according to the metrics of a one-drop rule.[144] The prospect that a person of color could pass as white and dupe a white person into marriage was a source of considerable cultural anxiety and fascination. It sparked memoir,[145] and it propelled the plots of numerous novels and films through the middle of the twentieth century.[146]

Concerns about intimate deception over race also generated many lawsuits in which people whose whiteness was unquestioned charged that they had been duped into marrying or becoming engaged to someone who was not white.[147] From the nineteenth century through the middle of the twentieth, courts routinely presumed and reaffirmed that a white person suffered a legally cognizable injury if he married someone who was concealing nonwhite ancestry. The issue arose most often in annulment cases, where plaintiffs asked courts to nullify their marriages.

Some white people actually secured annulments by arguing that they had unknowingly wed someone who was hiding her "true" racial status as a person of color.[148] Protecting and promoting white supremacy mattered so much to judges that they nullified marriages to defend that regime, even though annulments were otherwise difficult to obtain. Cyril Sunseri initiated an annulment suit in 1936 New Orleans against his wife, Verna Cassagne.[149] He charged that his wife—who insisted she was white and apparently looked white—was in fact "a person of color, having a traceable amount of negro blood." Sunseri admitted that Cassagne's paternal ancestors from her great-great grandfather to her father were all white men. His claim that Cassagne was a person of color under Louisiana law rested on the contention that her great-great grandmother, Fanny Ducre, "was a full-blooded negress," rather than "an Indian" as Cassagne claimed.[150]

The Louisiana Supreme Court scrutinized the available evidence to determine Cassagne's racial status in the eyes of the law. As the court noted, Cassagne was born in "a white maternity ward" and "was educated in the white public schools of New Orleans." Local Catholic churches treated her and her mother as white.[151] Both women used "the seats reserved for white persons" on public transportation. "Their friends and associates [were] apparently exclusively of the white race."[152]

But the unanimous court ultimately gave more weight to evidence indicating that Cassagne was not legally white.[153] Several witnesses had testified that Ducre's descendants were known to be black.[154] Even more crucially, Cassagne's birth certificate identified her as "colored," and the marriage certificates of two aunts identified the aunts as "colored."[155]

Once the court determined in 1940 that Cassagne was not white, its decision to annul Cassagne's marriage to Sunseri was automatic.[156] Louisiana prohibited marriages between "white persons and persons of color" and declared such marriages "null and void."[157] The state's ban on interracial marriages would remain in place until the United States Supreme Court found all such prohibitions unconstitutional in 1967.[158]

Florence Godines also won an annulment after claiming racial deception.[159] Godines sued in 1935, reporting "that she had been induced to marry" her husband, who was Filipino, based on "the fraudulent representation that he was of Spanish Castilian descent." Godines had married in New Mexico, where marriages between whites and Filipinos were permitted, but she brought her annulment suit in California, which prohibited such marriages. California law allowed a married person to obtain an annulment based on premarital "fraud" if she stopped living with her deceptive spouse once she discovered his fraud and the fraud was "vital to the marriage relation." The unanimous California District Court of Appeal declared in 1936 "that a misrepresentation by a Filipino that he is a Spaniard is a fraud that touches a vital spot in the marriage relation and constitutes, therefore, a cause for annulment."[160] Godines received an annulment,[161] although the matter did not end there. She was subsequently convicted of perjury for falsely stating in her annulment complaint that she had permanently separated from her husband upon learning about his deceit.[162] Her once-husband was the prosecution's star witness.[163] The District Court of Appeal had occasion to discuss Godines's annulment because the court considered her appeal of the perjury conviction (and ordered a new trial).[164]

The logic of white supremacy similarly structured many unsuccessful annulment suits through the middle of the twentieth century. The plaintiffs in these suits had the law on their side. Courts agreed with them that a white person was entitled to an annulment if he had been duped into marrying someone who was not white. These plaintiffs lost because they could not establish the necessary facts.

In some cases, judges or juries concluded that the spouse whose racial status had gone on trial was legally white.[165] Judicial decisionmakers were well aware that whiteness was a precious commodity in a nation that tied opportunity to race. They often did not want to "consign" an apparently white person "to the association of the colored race" if such a result could be avoided.[166] Frank Ferrall sought to terminate his relationship with his wife, Susie Ferrall, relying on a North Carolina statute that declared void any marriage "between a white person and a person of negro or Indian descent to the third generation inclusive."[167] Frank contended that he had married Susie believing she was white like him, only to discover later that she was not. The North Carolina Supreme Court ruled in 1910 for Susie, upholding a jury's verdict that she was not "of negro descent within the third generation."[168] Chief Justice Walter Clark agreed "in all respects with the opinion of the court" and wrote a separate concurring opinion that emphasized how white Susie and her children looked and how devastated they would have been by a legal determination that Susie was "negro." If Frank had won his suit, he would have been freed from any obligation to support his once-wife. Moreover, the "innocent children" of Susie and Frank would have been "brand[ed] . . . for all time by the judgment of a court as negroes—a fate which their white skin [would] make doubly humiliating to them."[169]

White judges and jurors may also have been reluctant to suggest that a person of color could have spent years successfully posing as white, living undetected in white society with a white spouse. Such an acknowledgment would have been in tension with the white supremacist tenet that racial classifications reflect real differences, rather than social and legal constructions. "[S]ome of the best people in Frankfort," Kentucky—meaning, presumably, the best white people—testified on behalf of Lillian Theophanis,[170] who maintained that she was white when her white husband of almost a decade sought an annulment on the ground that she was "a mulatto" and had concealed that from him before they married.[171] Theophanis's witnesses reported that she was "kind, affectionate, patient, well-mannered, and altogether charming."[172] The Kentucky trial and appellate courts that unanimously concluded in 1931 and 1932 that Theophanis was white may have been unwilling to believe that Frankfort's white elite could have failed to sense a woman of color amongst them.[173]

Other annulment suits were unsuccessful because judges or juries found that the plaintiff had known about his fiancée's racial background before marriage and accordingly had not been misled.[174] A plaintiff seeking an annulment in a state that prohibited interracial marriages could escape an interracial union without proving deceit. If one spouse was white and the other was not, their marriage was void. But a plaintiff seeking an annulment in a state that permitted interracial marriages needed to show that he had been deceived about his fiancée's race. For example, Leonard Kip Rhinelander's New York annulment suit against his wife, Alice Jones Rhinelander, was unsuccessful because the jury concluded that Alice had not deceived Leonard before their wedding by denying or concealing "that she was of colored blood."[175]

Rhinelander v. Rhinelander was by far the most well-known annulment case involving charges of racial deception. It attracted relentless media attention as it unfolded in the 1920s and has since been the subject of books and articles— as well as an inspiration for a highly fictionalized film.[176] Leonard came from a wealthy, socially prominent, and long-established New York family.[177] Alice "was working as a housemaid" when she met him.[178] After years of courtship, the couple married on October 14, 1924, without telling Leonard's father, Philip Rhinelander.[179]

Leonard's family—and the nation—learned of the wedding soon enough. Word of the nuptials hit the newspapers one month after Alice and Leonard married. The *New York Times*, the *Washington Post*, the *Chicago Daily Tribune*, and other papers thought the news was so remarkable that they trumpeted it on their front pages, with headlines like "Society Youth Weds Cabman's Daughter."[180] The articles stressed that Alice was not just working class, but racially questionable as well. Her father, George Jones, was "said to be of West Indian descent"[181] and he had signed a document that identified him as a "colored man" when he applied for United States citizenship. Alice's sister, Emily, was similarly classified as "colored" on her marriage license application, which Emily had signed.[182]

Leonard left Alice on November 20, 1924,[183] a few days after the press began reporting on the wedding and Alice's possible "Negro Taint."[184] Alice believed that Leonard's father was keeping Leonard away from her.[185] She would later sue Philip for alienation of affections.[186]

Alice hoped Leonard would return to her,[187] but instead he filed an annulment suit on November 26. Leonard contended that Alice had duped him into marriage by falsely telling him "that she was white and not colored and had no colored blood" when she knew this was untrue. Leonard maintained that he had married Alice believing she was white.[188] Even though New York permitted interracial marriages, New Yorkers still took the law's foundational commitment to white supremacy for granted. Both Alice's lawyers and Leonard's assumed that Leonard was entitled to an annulment if Alice had deceived him about her race.[189] When Leonard's annulment suit went to trial a year later in November 1925, the central question at issue was whether Leonard had been so deceived.[190]

Alice's attorney declared at the start of the trial that Alice had "some negro blood in her veins," but insisted that Leonard knew Alice's racial background before he married her.[191] Alice's family members testified during the trial about the time Leonard had spent with them before marrying Alice. A former Rhinelander chauffeur also reported that he had questioned Leonard's courtship of Alice by asking: "Don't you know her father is a colored man?" According to the chauffeur, Leonard replied: "I don't give a damn if he is."[192] Leonard lost his annulment suit because the jury concluded in December 1925 that Alice had not misled him.[193]

Even after Alice won the annulment trial, however, Leonard kept trying to end their marriage. He attempted to get the New York appellate courts to set aside the verdict and order a new annulment trial.[194] When that did not work, Leonard obtained a Nevada divorce in 1929 without Alice's participation.[195] Alice and Leonard (and Philip Rhinelander) eventually negotiated an agreement in 1930. Alice then had her attorney appear in a Nevada court and recognize the divorce decree, modified to provide that Alice would receive some financial support from the Rhinelanders. Alice dropped her pending lawsuits seeking support from Leonard and damages for alienation of affections from Philip. She also agreed to stop calling herself Alice Rhinelander.[196] Alice had prevailed in the annulment suit, but Philip Rhinelander had won the war for Leonard's loyalty.

Modern Judicial Treatment of
Intimate Deception About Race

While there once was a robust jurisprudence adjudicating legal claims about intimate deception over race, such claims have now virtually disappeared. Deception about race may have become less common after the dismantling of Jim Crow racial segregation and the enactment of civil rights statutes prohibiting many forms of race discrimination. People deceived about an intimate's racial background may also be less inclined to seek a legal remedy on that basis, as articulating a claimed injury is difficult without drawing on commitments to white supremacy and racial purity that have become socially unacceptable in many circles. Modern courts have not had many opportunities to address intimate deception about race or related topics, like caste. On the occasions that have presented themselves, however, courts have made clear that they are unwilling to grant the redress they once provided.

Patel v. Navitlal, a New Jersey annulment decision from 1992, is the modern case that perhaps comes closest to presenting the sort of intimate deception claim about race that plaintiffs once advanced with some regularity. Hitesh Patel was committed to the values of "the Indian caste system." He explained that within this system "individuals occupy a certain status within a particular caste making them more or less desirable as a spouse." Patel went to India in the spring of 1990 "and contacted a marriage broker for purposes of obtaining a wife of the same caste to live with him in the United States."[197]

While the Indian caste system differs in many respects from the system of legalized white supremacy and racialized subordination that developed in the United States, the two regimes share important characteristics. The caste system is hierarchical and members of the lowest castes experience systematic discrimination and disadvantage.[198] Castes are hereditary and people usually cannot move from the caste to which they were born, although they can be expelled from it.[199] The caste system also imposes strong social prohibitions on marrying someone from another caste.[200]

Patel found his bride, Varsha Navitlal, through the marriage broker he used in India. After Patel and Navitlal met in person twice, they agreed to marry and they wed in June 1990.[201] In the fall of 1991, however, Patel learned that Navitlal's mother, although still married to Navitlal's father, was living with another man who came from a different caste.[202] Patel sued for an annulment, contending that Navitlal had duped him into marriage because she wanted to immigrate to the United States. Patel testified that the "intercaste relationship" of Navitlal's mother "constitutes a violation of the caste system that has embarrassed both him and his family and had he known of it, he would not have married" Navitlal.[203]

The Chancery Division of the New Jersey Superior Court refused to grant an annulment.[204] The court acknowledged that caste was very important to Patel. As the opinion noted, "[t]he unrebutted proofs show that the plaintiff went to India and employed a marriage broker for the sole purpose of securing a spouse of the same caste."[205] The court also observed that "[p]ublic policy encourages full disclosure of pertinent facts especially in contemplation of entering a bond as significant as marriage."[206]

But the court was nonetheless unwilling to hold that concealment of a mother's intercaste relationship would constitute "fraud as to the essentials of the marriage" that would entitle Patel to an annulment.[207] Rather than empathize with Patel, the court was most concerned about his alleged deceiver, Navitlal, and insisted that treating caste as essential would be unfair to her. The court stressed that there was no evidence suggesting that Navitlal "was unable or unwilling to act as a wife to [Patel] nor that she did not want to create for herself the status of wife." In the court's view, granting Patel "an annulment for reasons which remain outside the control of one of the parties to the marriage would result in a miscarriage of justice." The phrase is striking because Navitlal's alleged deceit was within her control. She could have revealed her mother's intercaste relationship to Patel before marrying him. What was beyond Navitlal's control was her mother's behavior and her family's caste status. The court specifically noted that its decision was not "recogniz[ing] the Asian-Indian caste system" or accepting the premise that transgressing this caste system could constitute "a deficiency in a character trait."[208]

The judge sent Patel off with a version of the admonishment that courts frequently deploy when rejecting an intimate deception claim,[209] advising Patel that he should have conducted a more thorough premarital "investigation" to determine whether marrying Navitlal would be consistent with the caste system's tenets.[210]

Patel's New Jersey court, perhaps unused to considering federal constitutional matters, did not cite any precedent from the United States Supreme Court. Supreme Court precedent might also have seemed less relevant because *Patel* did not feature the black/white binary that has dominated the Supreme Court's thinking about race. Nonetheless, one of the Supreme Court's decisions supports the *Patel* holding by strongly suggesting that lower courts should not provide redress for harms stemming from intimate deception about race.

Palmore v. Sidoti (1984)[211] involved a dispute between two white parents, Linda Palmore and Anthony Sidoti, who each wanted custody of their daughter, Melanie.[212] Palmore had obtained custody when she and Sidoti divorced, but a little more than a year later Sidoti attempted to win custody. His petition stressed that Palmore was living with an African-American man, whom she soon married.[213]

The Florida court that considered Sidoti's custody petition noted Sidoti's "evident resentment of the mother's choice of a black partner." Nonetheless, the Florida court held that it was in Melanie's best interests to leave her mother's home and live with her father, reasoning "that despite the strides that have been made in bettering relations between the races in this country, it is inevitable that Melanie will, if allowed to remain in her present situation and attain[] school age and thus [become] more vulnerable to peer pressures, suffer from the social stigmatization that is sure to come."[214]

As the United States Supreme Court remarked in reversing the state court's judgment, it was "clear" that the Florida court would have kept Melanie with her mother if the mother's new husband had been a white man "of similar respectability."[215] Palmore lost custody "because of her remarriage to a person of a different race."[216]

One of the guiding principles that runs through family law—constantly reiterated even if not always honored in practice—is that courts should decide custody disputes between parents according to the best interests of the child.[217] Yet the Supreme Court in Palmore departed from placing utmost priority on the Florida court's assessment of Melanie's best interests because the Court was convinced that "the Constitution's commitment to eradicating discrimination based on race" was at stake.[218] The Supreme Court unanimously held that the Fourteenth Amendment's Equal Protection Clause prohibited a state court adjudicating a parental custody dispute from taking into account "the reality of private biases and the possible injury they might inflict"— even if disregarding the fact of persistent social prejudice against interracial marriage meant that Melanie might "be subject to a variety of pressures and stresses not present if the child were living with parents of the same racial or ethnic origin." As the Supreme Court explained, "[t]he Constitution cannot control such prejudices but neither can it tolerate them. Private biases may be outside the reach of the law, but the law cannot, directly or indirectly, give them effect."[219]

If the Supreme Court insists that the judiciary cannot tolerate the racial biases of private individuals, it is hard to see how any lower court could grant a remedy for intimate deception about race. How could a court hold that such deceit inflicts a legally cognizable injury without recognizing—and functionally accommodating—social prejudices against interracial intimacy? The legal redress once available for intimate deception about race has become normatively, even constitutionally, unacceptable.

Evolving Gender Norms
Undercut Some Intimate Deception Claims

Social norms about gender have also shifted considerably, if incompletely, since the early twentieth century. Where women's subordination was once legal, pervasive, and widely endorsed, such subordination is now routinely recognized—at least in principle—as a legal, constitutional, and moral wrong. Evolving norms of sex equality have sometimes made courts unwilling to provide redress for harms inflicted through intimate deception that they might have once remediated. Anti-heart balm statutes do not block these claims, but courts believe that awarding damages would be inconsistent with contemporary legal commitments to upholding women's equal humanity.

A Legal History of Reasoning About Women as Commodities in a Marriage Market

Courts in the late nineteenth and early twentieth centuries were comfortable comparing women to property, whether farm animals or objects. This inclination to reason about women as if they were commodities in a marriage market sometimes structured how judges thought about intimate deception.

Consider *Gring v. Lerch*,[220] which the Pennsylvania Supreme Court decided in 1886. Clara Lerch and Charles Gring became engaged in November 1882, but Gring broke the engagement four months later. When Lerch sued him for breach of promise to marry, Gring insisted that he was legally blameless for canceling the wedding.[221] Gring explained that Lerch was unable to fulfill the sexual "duties of a wife" because of "a physical incapacity." He contended that Lerch did not reveal this incapacity until the month after they were engaged. Gring further reported that Lerch promised to have corrective surgery, but then let three months pass without having the operation as the wedding date approached.[222] Two doctors testified at trial to confirm that Lerch had known about her "physical defect"—an unusually "thickened hymen"—and the need for surgery if it was to be remedied.[223]

The Pennsylvania Supreme Court agreed that Lerch's "failure to perform her promise to have the operation performed absolved [Gring] from his contract."[224] The unanimous court's explanation stressed male sexual prerogatives and envisioned marriage as a straightforward exchange in which husbands provided support in return for sex. In the court's blunt language, "[a] man does not court and marry a woman for the mere pleasure of paying for her board and washing. He expects and is entitled to something in return, and if the woman with whom he contracts be incapable by reason of a natural impediment of giving him the comfort and satisfaction to which as a married man he would be entitled, there is a failure of the moving consideration of such contract, and no court ought to enforce it by giving damages for its breach."[225]

The court also took care to note that Gring would have been similarly entitled to break the engagement if he had discovered Lerch's secret before the wedding without her telling him about it. The court's reasoning compared Lerch, "an imperfect woman," to a defective cow and compared Gring to a man about to buy that cow. The opinion declared: "To conceal such a thing from him until after marriage would be a fraud. It would be a fraud to sell a cow with such a defect without making it known to the purchaser."[226]

The *Gring* court analogized Lerch to livestock in the course of ruling against her. Yet judges in this era could reason about women in property terms even when ruling in their favor. *Moore v. Moore* (1916),[227] which granted Mary

Moore an annulment, is illustrative. The New York trial court found that Mary had a sexual relationship with John Moore that left her pregnant at eighteen. John agreed to marry Mary, at the urging of her friend. But John took Mary to her mother's house after the wedding ceremony, left her there, and never returned. He then promptly moved from where he had been living. By the time Mary sought an annulment, she had neither seen nor heard from her husband in over six years.[228] The court held that Mary was entitled to an annulment "on the ground of fraud" because John had deceived her by concealing his intent "to at once abandon her and never perform those obligations and duties the law imposed on him."[229]

Mary won her suit, but the court had more pity for her than respect. Its reasoning compared Mary to goods stolen through deceit: "A man purchases merchandise with the purpose and intent of never paying for it. It constitutes such a fraud on the seller that he may rescind the sale and recover the goods sold. One who buys goods on credit impliedly represents he intends to pay for them, and if he in fact intends not to pay for them he is guilty of fraud. So one who goes through the marriage ceremony represents in so many words his intention and purpose to fulfill all the obligations of a husband to the woman he marries."[230]

An Illinois appellate court in *Beckley v. Beckley* (1904)[231] similarly reasoned about Ella Beckley in property terms while deciding in her favor. Ella's husband, John Beckley, had sought an annulment,[232] contending that Ella had "represented to him that she was a great church worker and sabbath-school worker, and that she was a good, religious woman" when she actually "was a woman of bad repute and a prostitute."[233] The unanimous court held that John had "utterly" failed to prove that Ella "was a prostitute" and denied the annulment. But the court saw no irony in describing Ella as a commodity nonetheless. *Beckley* reported that John found Ella by writing "to a broker in the matrimonial market in Ohio and [receiving] a list of fifty articles in that market that were for sale." The court proceeded to explain that John "got possession of the same flesh and bones he bargained for," even if he later became dissatisfied with his choice—and she was dissatisfied with him.[234]

Denying Intimate Deception Claims to Recognize Women's Equal Humanity

Reasoning about women in property terms became less acceptable after the rise of the modern women's rights movement and the establishment of constitutional and statutory prohibitions on sex discrimination. By the end of the twentieth century, concerns about respecting women's equal humanity sometimes led courts to reject suits seeking redress for injuries stemming from intimate deception, even when an anti-heart balm statute did not bar the litigation.

Perhaps the clearest example is *Singh v. Singh*,[235] which the Ohio Court of Appeals decided unanimously in 1992. Notably, *Singh*—like *Patel*—involved litigation between Indian Americans. Both cases illustrate how ideas about gender, race, and national origin can overlap and influence each other. The courts in *Singh* and *Patel* described the disputes as revolving around "the social values of another culture"[236] or "other cultures."[237] This perception may have made judges particularly inclined to use their opinions as opportunities to declare and enforce modern America's commitment to equality. The chance to present legalized subordination as a foreign idea, rather than one with the deepest American roots, may have been especially appealing.

Kuldeeph Singh, the defendant in *Singh*, had helped his sister-in-law, Satinder Kaur, find a husband by advertising on her behalf in *India Abroad*. Harbhajan Singh (who was not related to Kuldeeph) responded to the ad and wed Satinder "shortly thereafter." The marriage ended less than three years later. The displeased ex-husband then sued the man who had helped arrange the match, alleging "fraud and intentional infliction of emotional distress." Harbhajan charged that Kuldeeph had "fraudulently induced" him to marry Satinder by deliberately concealing that she had "an incurable disease, which adversely impairs her ability to have normal sexual relations."[238] The phrase "incurable disease" makes the mind race with possibilities. The plaintiff's amended complaint revealed that he was complaining about his ex-wife's "lower back problems."[239]

The court agreed with Harbhajan that Ohio's anti-heart balm statute did not bar his suit.[240] But the court nonetheless dismissed the case because the court refused to "enforce or condone" "the marketing of brides."

Where *Gring, Moore,* and *Beckley* had taken male supremacy for granted, the *Singh* court emphasized the state's commitment to women's equality. Indeed, *Singh* glossed over a much more complex history containing decades of legalized subordination to contend that Ohio had accomplished the legal emancipation of women more than a century earlier. The court explained that the Ohio "Married Woman's Act of 1887 effected a radical change in the rights of married women while removing most of their common-law disabilities. Married women were given equal rights with their husbands to contract, take, hold and dispose of property without their husband's consent, and to sue or be sued alone. The intent of the Act was patently to emancipate women and to place them on equal footing with men in respect to their rights and liabilities."

Gring, Moore, and *Beckley* had not hesitated to reason about women in property terms and to envision women as items for sale in a marriage market. But *Singh* condemned "Harbhajan Singh's attempt to craft a 'defective-bride' cause of action" for going "against public policy" by treating "female persons as goods and

subject[ing] others to suits if the women themselves are found unacceptable."
The court rejected Harbhajan's suit because "women may not be considered the
personal chattels of men, whether they are merchandised by relatives in magazine advertisements or otherwise. Persons who adhere to such customs are free
to pursue them, but should they ultimately be dissatisfied with a wife so selected,
we hold it is against the public policy of this state to treat these agreements as
enforceable."[241]

In short, even when anti-heart balm laws do not block suits revolving around
intimate deception, courts sometimes conclude that granting redress would
contravene modern legal and social norms of equality.

Divorce Law's Impact on Intimate Deception Claims

The success of the anti-heart balm movement and the ascension of equality
norms that made some intimate deception claims unacceptable helped contribute to the contraction in legal remedies for intimate deception over the
course of the twentieth century. But a third factor—the advent and swift spread
of no-fault divorce laws—has been most responsible for diminishing the volume
of litigation. Many people who might have litigated intimate deception claims
under a fault-based divorce regime did not sue once no-fault divorce was available. When plaintiffs do sue, moreover, some courts have cited the advent of
no-fault divorce as a reason to rule against people seeking damages for injuries
inflicted through a spouse's deceit.

Fault-Based Divorce

In the nineteenth century and for most of the twentieth, obtaining a divorce was
difficult or even sometimes impossible. South Carolina did not make divorce
available at all until 1949 (except for a brief period during Reconstruction).[242]
New York limited divorce to cases of proven adultery until 1967.[243] Most states
were somewhat more generous. But even so, fault-based divorce meant that a
person could not obtain a divorce unless she could establish that her spouse had
committed at least one of the transgressions her state recognized as grounds for
divorce, such as adultery, cruelty, desertion, drunkenness, or felony conviction.[244]

Many people in this era attempted to secure divorces by contending that they
had been duped into marriage. Sometimes divorce petitioners could cite statutory provisions specifically concerned about deceit. Kansas's 1931 law "setting forth the grounds upon which divorce may be granted" listed "fraudulent

contract" as a ground for divorce. That statute also permitted divorce "when the wife at the time of marriage was pregnant by another than her husband," a scenario likely to have involved some deceit on the woman's part.[245] An 1872 Maryland law permitted divorce "when the woman before marriage has been guilty of illicit carnal intercourse with another man, the same being unknown to the husband at the time of the marriage, and when such carnal connection shall be proved to the satisfaction of the court."[246] An 1853 California statute allowed divorce "[w]hen the consent of either of the parties to the marriage was obtained by force or fraud, upon the application of the injured party."[247]

In other cases, petitioners claiming that they had been duped into marriage obtained divorces with the help of statutory provisions that did not directly address the possibility of deceit. The District of Columbia Supreme Court in 1888 granted James Caton a divorce from his wife, Annie Caton, under a D.C. law permitting divorce "[w]here either party is matrimonially incapacitated at the time of the marriage."[248] James established that Annie had married him without revealing that she was pregnant by another man.[249] The court held that Annie had been "absolutely incapacitated" when she married because she was "already pregnant and [could not] conceive again by her husband while she [was] in that condition."[250]

The restrictions on divorce also made annulment a prized option for people seeking to end their marriages. Annulments could be especially appealing to men because they usually meant that a man would owe no support obligations to the woman who had once been his wife, unless a state statute specifically provided otherwise.[251] For the same reason, pursuing an annulment was a costly choice for a woman. Annulment judgments did not provide damage awards for injuries inflicted through deceit and usually meant that a woman would not have a support claim against her once-husband. But even for women, the fact that annulments could end marriages made them a valuable form of redress in an era when obtaining a divorce was difficult.

Scores of litigants sought annulments on the ground that they had been duped into marriage (deceit after the wedding was irrelevant for purposes of winning an annulment).[252] Courts agreed that some, but not all, kinds of premarital deception justified annulling a marriage.[253] Over the course of decades and hundreds of cases, they developed an annulment jurisprudence—now all but forgotten—that regulated deceit by premarital intimates, deciding which forms of deception the law expected people to endure and which provided grounds for escaping a marriage.

Judges repeatedly explained that "[f]raud sufficient to vitiate a marriage must go to the essence of the marriage relation. The degree of fraud sufficient to vitiate an ordinary contract will not afford sufficient ground for the annulment of a marriage. It is not sufficient that the complainant relied upon false

representations and was deceived."[254] While there was never complete consistency between and within jurisdictions, courts often envisioned the necessary
components of marriage in similar ways and reached similar conclusions about
which forms of premarital "fraud or trickery"[255] went "to the very essence of the
marriage relation."[256] Deception about the ability or willingness to have marital
sex,[257] or the ability or willingness to have children,[258] was almost always sufficient to secure an annulment. In contrast, courts were almost never willing
to grant annulments for premarital deception about finances.[259] A man could
typically secure an annulment by establishing that his wife had deceived him
to conceal that she was pregnant when they married, even though she had not
engaged in premarital sex with her husband.[260] It was more difficult for a man to
win an annulment after marrying a woman while she was faking a pregnancy,[261]
in part because these plaintiffs necessarily acknowledged their premarital intercourse with their wives—which did not endear them to the judiciary.[262] Courts
disagreed about whether a woman was entitled to an annulment when her fiancé
had deceived her to hide his criminal record and/or ongoing criminal activity.[263]

New York counterbalanced its particularly restrictive divorce law by granting
an atypical number of annulments and developing an especially liberal annulment jurisprudence. The federal government collected statistics on annulments,
with all or almost all states reporting. In 1932, New York granted 1025 (26.26%)
of the 3903 reported annulments nationwide. In 1958, New York granted 3417
(27.25%) of the 12,541 reported annulments nationwide.[264] New York judges
often drew the boundaries of cognizable fraud more capaciously than their
counterparts in other states, permitting annulments when other jurisdictions
would probably have denied relief. For example, New York courts granted
annulments where a fiancée had lied about her marital history,[265] or had concealed past childbearing,[266] or had lied about having enough money to establish
a business her husband could run.[267]

Whether in New York or outside it, though, the fault-based divorce regime
helped generate a seemingly endless supply of cases revolving around intimate
deception. In this era, a substantial portion of the people who went to court
declaring that an intimate had deceived them were there because they wanted to
end their marriages.

The Advent of No-Fault Divorce

In 1970, California became the first state to institute no-fault divorce.[268] The in-
novation spread rapidly through the nation.[269] Under this new divorce regime,
someone who wished to end her marriage no longer needed to prove that her
spouse had committed a legally recognized transgression. A person who wanted

a divorce could secure one, even if her spouse was legally blameless and preferred to stay married. While annulment remained a possibility in every state and some states retained fault-based divorce as an option, both forms of redress became much less valuable and important.

Changes in annulment law further diminished the incentives to pursue one. Traditionally, two of the most common reasons a person sought an annulment rather than a divorce were the difficulty of obtaining a divorce and/or the desire to avoid some of the economic consequences of divorce, such as support obligations and property distribution. But state law on annulments has shifted over time so that the consequences of annulment more closely resemble those of divorce, including with respect to support and property. A divorce is now easier to secure than an annulment and both routes to ending a marriage often have the same practical results.[270]

Some people still seek annulments on the ground that they were duped into marriage.[271] Annulments can appeal to people who have religious reasons for wanting to avoid divorce. People also may pursue annulment rather than divorce because they believe that annulments better signify a fresh start.

Judges in recent years have occasionally been willing to grant annulments that earlier courts would have refused. These decisions are not numerous, but they constitute some recognition that the dynamics of any particular marriage and the desires of the people within that union can vary more than the common law presumed. One woman received an annulment not because her husband had deceived her to conceal how sick he was, but because he had deceived her to conceal how healthy he was. He had falsely claimed to be terminally ill in order to convince his ex-wife to remarry him.[272] Another woman won an annulment not because she was duped into marrying someone who was determined to avoid parenthood—a traditional concern of annulment law—but because she was duped into marrying someone who was intent on having children.[273]

However, the flow of litigation seeking annulments or fault-based divorces has diminished exponentially. Many people who would have once brought intimate deception claims to court now obtain no-fault divorces instead.

When plaintiffs do seek legal remedies for harms stemming from intimate deception, moreover, the existence of no-fault divorce has sometimes proven to be an obstacle. A no-fault divorce ends a marriage, but does not provide any redress linked to the fact that one spouse deceived the other. Indeed, one premise of no-fault divorce is that courts presume or insist that marital or community assets will be divided evenly at dissolution. Some courts have cited the adoption of no-fault divorce as grounds for rejecting suits pursuing damages for injuries reportedly sustained because of a spouse's deceit.[274] Part III argues that this line of reasoning is misguided and that providing remedies for deception within marriage is consistent with the availability of no-fault divorce. For our purposes

now, however, we can focus on how courts have used the advent of no-fault divorce as a reason to deny redress.

Mary Mims sued her then-husband, Robert Mims, "for compensatory and
punitive damages." She charged that Robert had duped her into marriage "with
false and fraudulent protestations of love," only to separate from her after ten
days of marriage, insist that she leave the home he had bought, and threaten
violence. Mary contended that Robert had acted "with wilfulness and malice"
and maintained "that he intended to cause her severe emotional distress and
that he succeeded in this aim."[275] I suspect that Mary would have found it difficult to prove at trial that Robert had deceived her, rather than just changed his
mind. But Mary never got that far. The unanimous Florida appellate court that
dismissed Mary's suit in 1974 insisted that "to permit this complaint to stand
would simultaneously be to destroy the beneficent effects of the 'no-fault' dissolution statute and to turn every, or almost every, dissolution case into two
cases—one to secure a dissolution from the chancellor, and another, to secure
damages from a jury or trial judge, for the 'wrongs' done by a tortious spouse."[276]

The California Court of Appeal relied on similar reasoning in dismissing
Ronald Askew's fraud suit in 1994.[277] Ronald reported that his wife, Bonnette
Askew, had told him before marriage that she loved and desired him, but years
later admitted—in and out of court—that she had not felt sexual desire for him
before or during their marriage. Ronald contended that he relied on Bonnette's
misrepresentation when he gave her joint ownership of some of his separate
property, on the purported understanding that she would hold this property for
the benefit of Ronald and his children from a prior marriage.[278] The unanimous
court emphasized in rejecting Ronald's suit that the litigation was incompatible
with California's no-fault divorce regime. As the court explained, "[t]he limited
recovery available in dissolution actions is easily circumvented if spouses are
allowed to sue each other because of love-related promises. As in the present
case, a couple undergoing the unpleasantness of a dissolution could wind up in
civil court litigating the very emotional underpinnings of the marriage itself in a
'fraud' action. This is just another name for 'fault' divorce."[279]

The availability of no-fault divorce has helped dissuade some deceived
intimates from bringing their stories to court and has simultaneously helped make
some courts unreceptive to the intimate deception claims that are presented to
them. One way some courts have marked the move from fault-based to no-fault
divorce is by rejecting suits complaining about deception within marriage.

In sum, the twentieth century saw a significant contraction in the legal
remedies that were available for intimate deception and in the practical importance of the remedies that remained. This shift was fueled by the legislative abolition of heart balm torts and expansive judicial interpretations of anti-heart balm
statutes, the rise of equality norms that made some intimate deception claims

unacceptable to the judiciary, and—above all else—the advent of no-fault divorce. The contraction helps explain why the law's treatment of intimate deception has received relatively little attention in recent years. That said, a steady stream of litigation persists, even though the proportion of cases revolving around intimate deception appears to have declined over time. This remains a highly active site of legal regulation, one whose outcome is usually to deny deceived intimates redress and protect their deceivers. Let's turn to the modern law of intimate deception.

Modern Law's Sharp Divide
Between
Deception Within and Outside Intimacy

Modern courts repeatedly assume and insist that the law should treat intimate deception differently than deception outside of intimacy. Judges invoke this refrain across myriad contexts, relying on it to shape their regulation of marital and nonmarital relationships and financial and sexual deception. The premise that deceived intimates should not have access to remedies that are available to redress, deter, and condemn deception in other contexts has especially far-reaching consequences because judges often define intimacy broadly in romantic and/or sexual relationships to include people who did not know each other well.

Courts routinely deny deceived intimates remedies and shield their deceivers. Indeed, courts frequently stress their overarching commitment to protecting intimate deception from legal redress even when ruling for the occasional plaintiff. For example, judges emphasize that they are allowing a deceived intimate to pursue damages only because permitting that particular lawsuit advances other public policy goals, such as promoting public health by curbing the spread of sexually transmitted disease.

This chapter explores how courts persistently differentiate intimate deception from deception outside of intimacy. It begins with decisions rejecting plaintiffs' attempts to secure remedies and then turns to cases where judges permitted plaintiffs to seek redress.

Treating Intimate Deception Differently

The judiciary's recurring refusal to subject intimate deceivers to the legal rules governing deception elsewhere is an overriding, if understudied, feature of the law. That core theme is visible in doctrinal arenas ranging from the regulation of disputes between nonmarital sexual partners, to the law governing financial deception within ongoing marital relationships, to the rules on granting annulments. Courts tend to assume rather than explain the wisdom of treating intimate deception differently, but judges have briefly offered a rotating set of (unsatisfying) rationales.

Nonmarital Sexual Relationships

We can start by examining cases where people sued their former sexual partners for reportedly harming them through deception. Courts commonly refuse to provide these plaintiffs with remedies ordinarily available to victims of fraud and deceit. Judges sometimes contend that this divide keeps the law from intruding on intimate relationships and sometimes treat the divide as a matter of indisputable common sense too obvious to require justification.

Consider the Massachusetts Appeals Court's unanimous 2004 decision holding that Margie Conley could not pursue tort damages for the injuries that Michael Romeri allegedly inflicted on her through deception.[1] Conley had a sexual relationship with Romeri when they were both in their early forties and divorced. She was childless and had recently started a business. He had four children and was a director at a management consulting firm.[2]

Conley reported that Romeri knew she wanted to have a baby, "knew she had little time in which to become a biological mother," and knew she would end their relationship if she learned about his vasectomy.[3] Romeri also reportedly knew that deceiving Conley about his sterility was likely to cause her emotional distress.[4]

Conley contended that Romeri nevertheless concealed his vasectomy and intentionally misled her into thinking that he was able and willing to have more children.[5] For example, he asked Conley approximately a month after they first had sex "whether he had gotten her in trouble," even though he was well aware that he could not have impregnated her.

Conley explained that she relied on Romeri's misrepresentations and would not have had sex with him if she had known about the vasectomy.[6] She also reported that the revelation of Romeri's deceit approximately eight months into their relationship "emotionally devastated her, that she suffered a major depressive disorder and incurred medical expenses, and that she was unable to reverse the economic position of her company."[7] She sued him for fraud, negligent and intentional infliction of emotional distress, and assault and battery.[8]

The Massachusetts Appeals Court stressed the importance of avoiding judicial intrusion into romantic relationships in holding that Conley could not sue her former lover for fraud because the deception she reported was intimate.

Conley refused "to assess the emotions, expectations, and commitments inherent in a developing romantic relationship."[9] The Massachusetts Appeals Court also declared in *Conley* that another state appellate court had been "instructive and persuasive" when it contended in an intimate deception decision from 1980 that "[c]laims such as those presented in this case arise from conduct so intensely private that the courts should not be asked to nor attempt to resolve such claims."[10]

When the *Conley* court emphasized its desire to avoid intervening in an intimate relationship, that was not a neutral stance designed to help both parties protect and preserve their ties. The court advanced this argument while discussing a relationship so extinguished that one former intimate was suing the other. Conley had come to court because she wanted legal recognition that Romeri had harmed her through wrongful conduct and she wanted to collect damages for the injuries that Romeri had reportedly inflicted on her. Conley's lawyer also told the *Boston Globe* that Conley—who was still childless when the Massachusetts Appeals Court issued its opinion—had pursued her appeal in the hope of establishing a precedent that would help other people subject to similar deceit.[11] Arguments about nonintervention systematically served to impede Conley's pursuit of redress and to advance Romeri's interest in avoiding liability.

The *Conley* court also cited its desire to stay out of intimate relationships without explaining why shielding deceptive sexual partners represented sound public policy. Romeri allegedly duped Conley into a sexual relationship and then used the fact that he had established intimacy to avoid legal consequences for his deceit. Invoking nonintervention concerns to uphold Romeri's freedom to deceive had a price, which Conley paid. The court's ruling meant that Conley had no right to be protected from Romeri's deceit as she decided whether to pursue a relationship with him.

Moreover, the *Conley* decision did not actually keep the law out of intimate relationships. Indeed, such a goal was impossible from the start. The Massachusetts Appeals Court could not stay out of the dispute between the former lovers—whether the court ruled for Conley or Romeri. Either way, the court would be establishing the parties' legal rights and obligations, setting legal ground rules for future intimate relationships, and structuring incentives. When the court blocked Conley from pursuing her fraud claim, it shaped those legal rights, responsibilities, baselines, and incentives in ways that protected deceivers and denied deceived intimates relief. *Conley*'s holding meant that Romeri could use deception about his procreative abilities and desires to lure Conley into maintaining a relationship with him, without rendering himself liable for fraud damages. Similarly, *Conley* established that any other person in Massachusetts can similarly deceive a sexual partner about his ability and desire to have children without fear that the duped intimate could win redress for her resulting injuries by successfully suing her deceiver in tort for fraud. Siding with Romeri made the law's role in shaping intimate life less visible than if the court had ruled for Conley, and denying a claim always involves less work for the judiciary than allowing one to proceed. But the law was structuring the terms of intimacy nonetheless.

The Massachusetts Appeals Court disposed of Conley's other claims quickly, apparently relying on little more than its own starting assumption that deception within romantic and sexual relationships is naturally beyond the law's concern. The court held that Conley could not pursue a negligent infliction of emotional distress claim against Romeri because proving negligence requires establishing that the defendant has breached a legal duty. The court argued that Romeri did not breach a legal duty by deceiving Conley because people "in a dating relationship" do not have a legal obligation to tell each other the truth. The court did not see the need to explain why no such duty exists, beyond briefly suggesting that this conclusion reflected "existing social values and customs and appropriate social policy." Instead, the court took for granted that the legal rules governing intimate relationships should not expect and require the truthfulness that the law sometimes demands elsewhere.[12]

The court similarly drew on its own common sense in holding that Conley could not pursue her intentional infliction of emotional distress claim. The court announced that "[e]ven if the impact of the defendant's revelation was intended, and even if the defendant had created false expectations about his future relationship with the plaintiff, nothing in his conduct throughout the relationship can be said to rise to the high order of reckless ruthlessness or deliberate malevolence required for a showing of conduct that is intolerable."[13]

This declaration was a conclusion rather than an explanation. But note what the court expected Conley to tolerate. On Conley's account, Romeri knowingly caused her severe emotional distress with financial consequences by luring her into a sexual relationship through deception about a matter that he knew was a linchpin for her. She had sex with someone she would have otherwise avoided and lost precious time she could have spent trying to conceive. But here again the court returned to its baseline presumption that harms inflicted through deceit within intimacy are not legally redressable. The court quoted a classic torts treatise to proclaim that "[i]t does not lie within the power of any judicial system to remedy all human wrongs. Many wrongs which in themselves are flagrant— ingratitude, avarice, broken faith, brutal words, and heartless disregard of the feelings of others—are beyond any effective legal remedy."[14]

Conley also brought a battery claim, contending that Romeri's deceit about his ability to have children "was a fraud that vitiated her consent to sexual relations." The court appeared loathe to dwell on this claim and dismissed it quickly, concluding, "as a matter of law, that the plaintiff's consent was not vitiated." The court's reasoning was underdeveloped. But the court seemed to

argue that Conley had presented no evidence that Romeri had been deceptive "with the intent to induce [Conley] to have sexual intercourse." The court
maintained that Conley's allegations indicated that Romeri had deceived her
"only as an inducement to continue dating." The court attempted to support
this assertion by noting that Romeri's alleged deceit began after just a few
dates, when sex with Conley was only a future possibility.[15] Yet the supposed
distinction between deceiving to date and deceiving for sex could not easily
be read into Conley's allegations, as Conley reported that Romeri had turned
to deception early and then continued duping her as they became sexually
intimate—knowing that Conley would end the relationship if she learned
about the vasectomy.[16] On the most straightforward reading of Conley's
allegations, at least one of the reasons why Romeri deceived her about his vasectomy was because he wanted sex and realized she would refuse him if she
knew about his sterility. This contention apparently made the court deeply
uncomfortable, however, and the Conley opinion labored to avoid confronting
the charge. The court knew it wanted to deny Conley a remedy, but that determination was more visceral than reasoned.

Let's turn to the unanimous 1987 decision from the California Court of
Appeal that disposed of Lee Perry's suit against Richard Atkinson. This opinion
similarly revolved around assumptions that the law should treat intimate deception differently and assertions about nonintervention.

Perry reported that she had a sexual relationship with Atkinson, became
pregnant after about a year, and wanted to carry the pregnancy to term. But
Atkinson, who was married to another woman, allegedly convinced Perry to
have an abortion by promising to conceive another child with her the following
year—either the old-fashioned way or via assisted insemination if their relationship had ended. Perry contended that Atkinson never intended to fulfill
this promise and wanted Perry to rely on his misrepresentation to her detriment. His purported scheme worked, and Perry underwent an abortion that
caused "her physical and mental pain." After discovering that Atkinson had
duped her, Perry reportedly "became depressed, requiring psychiatric treatment, incurring extensive medical bills and losing six months of earnings."
She sued him "for fraud and deceit and intentional infliction of emotional distress."[17] They reached an out-of-court settlement on Perry's emotional distress
claim, but litigated her fraud and deceit claim.[18]

Perry lost in the California trial and appellate courts. Both courts held that
she could not use tort law to seek damages for injuries inflicted though fraud and
deceit because the deception she alleged was intimate in nature. The lower court
maintained that "public policy prohibits a cause of action for fraud and deceit
concerning intimate matters involving procreation." It "concluded that to control the promises of the parties by legal action would constitute an unwarranted

governmental intrusion into matters affecting the individual's right to privacy."[19] The California Court of Appeal affirmed this line of reasoning, declaring that "[p]ublic policy compels our holding no cause of action exists for Atkinson's fraud and deceit."[20] The unanimous appellate court explained that "[a]lthough Atkinson may have deliberately misrepresented his intentions to Perry in order to persuade her to have the abortion, their procreative decisions were so intensely private that we decline to intervene."[21]

Here again, it is worth dwelling on the assertion that courts should exclude deceived intimates from the ordinary protections of tort law in order to prevent the legal system from intruding on intimate relationships. Like the Massachusetts court in *Conley*, the California court in *Perry* declared its determination to stay out of intimate relationships while discussing a relationship that had ended and left one of the former participants asking for legal redress for her alleged injuries. Perry did not want to keep quiet about her experiences or to hide them from public view. To the contrary, Perry hoped to persuade other people—both inside the judiciary and out—that the law should recognize and condemn the wrongfulness of the deceptive behavior she reported. In addition to advancing her lawsuit, Perry spoke with the media to stress the harm that deceitful intimates can inflict. She told the press that "[t]he kind of representations we make in our personal relationships should be as honest as those we make in other relationships, particularly if it's the kind of lie that could affect somebody's physical well-being." Perry also drew an analogy between using deception to control someone's decisionmaking and using violence for the same purpose, arguing that "[t]o be able to do with a lie what you are not permitted to do with a fist is wrong."[22]

Atkinson, of course, would surely have been delighted if Perry had never sued or told anyone about her experiences. Her silence would have kept him out of court and protected his reputation. Perry was an assistant professor of psychology at Harvard when she filed suit and Atkinson was the chancellor of the University of California at San Diego. The prestige of those positions helped draw attention to the litigation. Atkinson held a press conference after Perry sued him, taking his wife along for the occasion. He insisted to the media that Perry's allegations were "false and . . . far-fetched."[23] However, Atkinson's desire to avoid litigation, legal liability, and negative publicity did not distinguish him from almost any other defendant in any case.

The Court of Appeal also did little to explain why supposedly keeping the law out of intimate relationships by denying remedies to Perry would constitute sound public policy. The court summarily announced that "[t]ort liability cannot apply to the choice, however motivated, of whether to conceive or bear a child."[24] But it would be difficult to describe *Perry* as a victory for reproductive autonomy—at least women's reproductive autonomy. To the contrary, the court's ruling undercut a woman's freedom to reach her own decisions about childbearing without interference from a man's deceit. Perry insisted that she would have chosen to carry her pregnancy to term if Atkinson had not manipulated her decisionmaking by lying in order to "fraudulently induc[e] her to have an abortion."[25] The court's holding protected that manipulative interference with Perry's procreative choices from legal redress.

Moreover, the court's decision in *Perry v. Atkinson* did not actually keep the law from intervening in intimate relationships and such a goal was unattainable in any event. The Court of Appeal could not stay out of the conflict between the former lovers, whether it sided with Perry or Atkinson. Either way, the court had to decide their dispute and it did, simultaneously establishing the legal rules that governed Atkinson's reported behavior toward Perry and the rules that govern other California couples in similar situations. The *Perry* decision means that men in California can use deception to convince their girlfriends to have abortions without concern that the women will be able to recover damages by suing their deceivers in tort for fraud and deceit. *Perry* is designed to discourage rather than spark future litigation, but the decision nonetheless regulates intimacy— structuring entitlements and incentives in ways that shield deceivers and leave deceived intimates unprotected.

In short, both *Conley* and *Perry* began from the premise that people deceived within a romantic and sexual relationship do not and should not have access to legal remedies that are available to redress deceit in other contexts. Both courts reasoned from that assumed baseline, whether they justified the distinct treatment of intimacy using arguments about (supposedly) avoiding judicial intervention or took it for granted as a matter of common sense.

Financial Deception in Marriage

The judiciary's response to deceit within marriage also pivots on the recurring presumption that the law should sharply differentiate between intimate deception and deception outside of intimacy. Courts routinely emphasize that a spouse deceived during an ongoing marriage does not have access to remedies for deceit that are available elsewhere, or even access to remedies that are available when a spouse is duped after her marriage has already deteriorated irrevocably. This persistent differentiation of marital deception extends to cases where the defendant reportedly used deceit to redistribute marital assets to his own purposes and to inflict financial harm on his spouse. The law often finds financial injuries relatively easy to understand and redress. Marriage is an economic relationship in addition to a social one. Indeed, it is frequently the most important economic relationship in a married person's life, and a deceptive spouse can inflict far-reaching economic injury. But courts are reluctant to award remedies when financial deception occurs within marriage.

Ollen Smith's unsuccessful suit against his former wife, Bonita Smith, provides a useful illustration. Ollen charged that Bonita had "used marital funds for her adulterous affairs," apparently without his knowledge or consent. The couple divorced, but Ollen reported that the divorce court divided their marital assets without considering Bonita's financial deceit. Ollen then sued Bonita for breach of fiduciary duty among other claims,[26] asserting that his financial injury exceeded $10,000. His argument before the North Carolina Court of Appeals stressed that the legal treatment of financial deception in marriage should track the law's response to financial deception in business partnerships. Ollen contended that "since a business partner could be required to account to the partnership for misappropriated partnership funds, [Bonita] should likewise be held accountable for misappropriated marital funds."

The North Carolina appellate court unanimously dismissed Ollen's claim in 1994, summarily rejecting his "attempt to analogize the marital relationship to a business partnership." The court declared: "Although we believe that the relationship between married persons demands the highest level of integrity, we refuse to impose on it the strict duties of a business partnership."[27] The internal tension in that statement would seem to call out for explication. If the court was convinced that marriage "demands the highest level of integrity," why wouldn't the court enforce that demand by holding a spouse liable for deceptively misappropriating funds? But the court took for granted that duped spouses should not have access to remedies that would be available for deception in other contexts. That premise apparently seemed too obvious and well-established to require elaboration or defense.

The Florida District Court of Appeal likewise denied Martha Beers tort remedies in 1998 because the deceit that allegedly caused her enormous financial injury was committed by her then-husband, David Beers, during their marriage. Martha reported that David had deceived her to conceal that he had used more than $600,000 in marital assets to further "an adulterous relationship."[28] Her suit starkly illustrates how deceit to hide infidelity can be entangled with financial deception. Martha sued for constructive fraud and breach of fiduciary duty, among other claims. She explained that suing David "in tort for fraud" allowed her to seek punitive damages, which are available in tort litigation but not divorce proceedings.[29] Like Ollen Smith, Martha Beers contended "that married couples should be held to the same standard as business partners, who have a fiduciary duty to account to the partnership for misappropriated partnership funds."[30]

The Florida appellate court unanimously rejected Martha's argument and dismissed her claim, announcing that "there simply is no cognizable tort claim for constructive fraud for a concealed dissipation of marital assets."[31] *Beers v. Beers* declared that "it is beyond dispute that the utmost integrity and honesty should inhere in a marital relationship."[32] Yet the court would not protect and promote those supposed norms with tort law. *Beers* refused to apply legal remedies for deception outside of intimacy to cases of deception within marriage and held that Martha could not access tort remedies because her husband's alleged deceit had involved "depletion of marital assets during the marriage."[33] Here again, the court apparently believed that an extended defense of the differential treatment of marital deception was unnecessary.

The deception that Carole O'Neill experienced was somewhat more unusual than the adultery leading to financial deceit that Ollen Smith and Martha Beers reported. But the Illinois Supreme Court similarly denied Carole redress because her husband's deceit occurred within an ongoing marital relationship.

When Carole's husband, Stephen O'Neill, was prosecuted for attempted rape, he lied and told his wife he was innocent. Stephen presumably had many reasons for lying. But one likely motivation was that he wanted to use marital funds to pay his legal fees and feared that Carole would attempt to keep her half of the marital assets for herself if she knew Stephen was guilty. After Stephen lied to Carole about his innocence, the couple spent $15,000 on Stephen's unsuccessful defense, using joint savings, insurance money they had received after a car accident, and a $7000 loan from Carole's father that almost certainly would not have been available to Stephen without Carole's cooperation. The year after his conviction, Stephen finally told Carole that he was guilty of the attempted rape. The O'Neills lived together in disharmony for about another year and a half, until Stephen left the family home and ultimately filed for divorce.

Carole apparently did not bring a tort suit against her husband for the harm his deceit had inflicted. Instead, she sought redress within their divorce proceeding. The divorce court had awarded Carole and Stephen equal shares of the couple's marital property and marital debts.[34] Carole relied on the Illinois Marriage and Dissolution of Marriage Act to contend on appeal that the judicial allocation of the couple's assets at divorce should have compensated her for the $15,000 spent on Stephen's legal defense.[35] This statute instructed courts distributing marital property to take into account "the contribution or dissipation of each party in the acquisition, preservation, or depreciation or appreciation in value, of the marital and non-marital property."[36] Carole argued that Stephen had dissipated marital assets because he falsely told her that he was innocent in order to convince her that they should spend $15,000 on his legal defense.[37]

The Illinois Supreme Court refused to award Carole compensation for the financial injury Stephen's deceit had caused. The court held that the $15,000 did not count as dissipation of the couple's assets because the Illinois General Assembly purportedly "intended for the term 'dissipation' to refer only to a spouse's improper use of marital property during the time in which the marriage is undergoing an irreconcilable breakdown."[38] Phrased plainly, Carole could not use Illinois divorce law to secure remedies because Stephen had duped her while their marital relationship still was ongoing. More generally, the court's reading of the Marriage and Dissolution of Marriage Act meant that anyone in Illinois could deceive his spouse in order to control spending during an ongoing marriage and that deceit—even if about something vitally important—would not count as dissipation of marital assets entitling the deceived spouse to compensation at divorce.

The Supreme Court's interpretation of the Illinois statute had a remarkably shaky foundation. Indeed, two Illinois Justices dissented on the ground that the majority had misinterpreted the statute.[39] The text of the Marriage and Dissolution of Marriage Act drew no distinction based on when the dissipation of marital assets took place and did not indicate that the timing of the dissipation mattered. Moreover, the statute discussed marital contributions and dissipations together, directing courts to take into account "the contribution or dissipation of each party." It would be implausible to suppose that a court distributing marital property should only consider the contributions each spouse made after the marriage was irrevocably broken. All marital contributions at any point during the marriage were clearly relevant. So the Illinois Supreme Court's reading of the statute left contributions interpreted broadly and dissipations interpreted narrowly, even though the act's structure suggested that both should be treated the same way. The intermediate appellate court in this case had also found that "nothing in the legislative history of the Act supports the irreconcilable breakdown rule."[40]

The Illinois Supreme Court did not explain why narrowing the definition of marital dissipation was a good idea, other than to note that several lower Illinois courts over the years had also imposed this limit on the statute.[41] But the Supreme Court appeared certain that the state legislature would not have wanted to remediate Stephen's conduct because it occurred during an ongoing marital relationship, and the court read that restriction into the law. Protecting deception within marriage from legal redress apparently seemed like common sense.

The Virginia Circuit Court similarly denied Annette Whelan a remedy for her husband's alleged financial deceit because that deceit purportedly occurred before their marital relationship had irrevocably broken down.[42] Annette's husband, Edward Whelan, owned and operated a construction company, where Annette also worked on occasion. The couple separated between late May and early September 1998, but then lived together again until separating permanently in June 2000. During the 1998 separation—when the possibility of divorce was presumably looming in Edward's mind—Edward sold the construction company to his father for $100,000. Edward's father apparently did not transfer a cent to Edward to pay for this purchase, but instead gave Edward a promissory note that was payable in 2005. After the sale, Edward continued to work at the construction company and earned the same salary as before. Annette reported that Edward deceived her to conceal what he had done and that she did not learn about the sale until her divorce litigation with Edward was underway.[43]

If the Virginia Circuit Court had permitted Annette to conduct discovery on this issue and present evidence,[44] she probably would have established that Edward transferred the construction company to his father for less than fair market value in order to deny Annette her share of that marital asset if they divorced. Virginia law provided that a spouse who has "wasted or dissipated" a marital asset "in anticipation of" divorce or separation should be "held account-able for" that waste when a court makes "an equitable distribution" of marital property at divorce.[45] Dividing property equitably means dividing it fairly. But the judge held that Annette was not entitled to redress for Edward's alleged financial deceit, even if she could prove all her factual allegations.[46]

The court's conclusion rested on two claims. First, the court insisted that marital waste could occur only "when the marriage is undergoing an irreconcilable breakdown." Second, the court asserted that the Whelan marriage could not have been irreconcilably broken during the 1998 separation because the couple subsequently lived together for almost two years.[47] Both claims are worth exploring.

Whelan v. Whelan more assumed than defended the wisdom of denying remedies for marital waste that happened before the relationship was irreconcilably broken. The court warned that the judiciary needed to avoid the "slippery slope" of providing redress for waste that reportedly "occurred during a period of marital strife" while the marriage was still ongoing.[48]

In fact, Annette's marital waste claim would have been easy to distinguish from most litigation seeking remedies for waste during an ongoing marriage. The Whelans were not simply unhappy and feuding when Edward sold the construction company. They had separated. Moreover, the sale had no discernable purpose other than to advantage Edward at divorce. But shielding financial deception within marriage from legal redress was the court's presumed baseline. With that in mind, the court was ready to see slippery slopes everywhere.

The court also used the fact that the Whelans lived together after Edward sold the construction company as grounds for concluding that their marriage could not have been irreconcilably broken at the time of the sale, without exploring *why* the couple cohabited after their 1998 separation. In all likelihood, Annette would not have reconciled with her husband in September 1998 if she had known that he had secretly transferred the construction company to his father. That covert transaction betrayed Annette's trust and learning about the betrayal would surely have undermined Annette's confidence in Edward. Moreover, an attorney would probably have advised Annette that she could improve her chances of securing compensation for Edward's deceit by promptly filing for divorce because that would help establish that her marriage was irredeemably over when Edward sold the company away from her. Edward managed to keep Annette in their marriage by duping her. And in keeping her there, he prevented Annette from obtaining redress for his deceit.

Annulment

The differential treatment of intimate deception also looms large when people ask courts to end their marriages through annulment rather than divorce. From the nineteenth century to the present day, courts have repeatedly insisted that many examples of deceit that would be sufficient to "vitiate the ordinary contract" are insufficient to win an annulment nullifying a marital contract.[49]

Judges and treatise writers in the nineteenth and early twentieth centuries repeatedly offered two interlocking explanations for this different response to deception. The first explanation assumed that marriage was the foundation of the social order, worried that any dissolution of a marital bond threatened that foundation, and sought to sharply differentiate marriage from nonmarital relationships. An influential 1862 opinion from the Massachusetts Supreme Judicial Court defended the difficulty of obtaining an annulment based on premarital deceit by declaring that "[t]he law, in the exercise of a wise and sound policy, seeks to render the contract of marriage, when once executed, as far as possible indissoluble. The great object of marriage in a civilized and Christian community is to secure the existence and permanence of the family relation, and to insure the legitimacy of offspring."[50] Joel Bishop, who wrote some of the nineteenth century's most prominent treatises on family law, reasoned similarly in 1891. He observed: "If one has cheated another through a fraudulent contract of the ordinary sort, whether executed or not, only individual property interests are injured. No new status, the abrogation whereof would be disturbing to the community, has been established."[51] A 1931 law review article likewise stressed that annulment jurisprudence promoted "morality" and set "an example, not only to the interested litigants, but to the community at large as well," by making clear "that a system would not be tolerated where the fruits of marriage might be enjoyed promiscuously and the formal relationship which permitted such enjoyment, could be readily dissolved for frauds of minor import."[52]

The second early explanation for why annulment law needed to disregard deception that would provide grounds for undoing an ordinary contract emphasized the common law rule providing that an annulment rendered the former couple's children illegitimate. This rule meant that an annulment could have devastating consequences in an era when nonmarital children and their mothers experienced pervasive legal, economic, and social marginalization.[53] Bishop made the point vividly, declaring that when a court considered whether to nullify an "ordinary" contract "[u]nborn children do not cry out from the mother's womb, demanding that they may not be bastardized, lose a father, and know only a disgraced mother."[54]

Neither explanation for the differential treatment of deception in annulment cases is as compelling today as it was in the nineteenth or early twentieth centuries. First, a legal system that permits no-fault divorce has manifestly abandoned the view that any marital dissolution jeopardizes social order. The law no longer attempts to make marriages "as far as possible indissoluble,"[55] but instead gives people wide-ranging freedom to sever their marital ties through divorce. If marital dissolutions do threaten social order, moreover, that danger has already materialized and the ease or difficulty of securing annulments will do little to alter the danger's magnitude. Second, state statutes on annulment now routinely override common law doctrine to provide that an annulment does not make the couple's children illegitimate.[56]

The original logic behind distinguishing between annulment suits and other efforts to nullify agreements has become strained or has evaporated entirely. Yet judges still presume that their annulment decisions should deny redress for most linchpin deceptions that convinced a person to marry when she would have rejected the defendant if she had known the truth. For example, winning an annulment based on premarital deception about finances remains extremely difficult. When someone lies about the financial resources and assets he is bringing to a business partnership, courts routinely allow the deceived partner to rescind the partnership agreement.[57] But when a fiancé lies about the wealth and financial resources he is bringing to his marital partnership, courts almost never allow the deceived spouse to secure an annulment nullifying the marriage.[58]

Consider Ann Meagher's unsuccessful attempt to win an annulment from Malekpour Maleki, who before their marriage "misrepresented his financial status and fraudulently induced her to invest in a business venture with him, with the intent to gain control of her assets."[59] When Meagher married Maleki, she had $1 to $1.5 million in assets along with "substantial equity in her expensive home."[60] Meagher thought that Maleki was "a well-educated millionaire with expertise in real estate and finance."[61] He convinced her before they married to invest in a real estate venture that would give them equal ownership of several properties.[62] The trial court found that Maleki falsely told Meagher "that he was contributing equally to the parties' business venture," when actually "other than Maleki's initial contribution of approximately $100,000 to $125,000, everything of material value that went into the venture was hers."[63]

Meagher discovered after the wedding that Maleki had deceived her about his wealth and his plans for her assets. Less than three years into the marriage, he told her that they did not have enough money to pay their living and business expenses.[64] He announced about two months later that he would seek a divorce unless she placed all her assets into joint tenancy and gave him complete power over them. "Meagher began to doubt what Maleki had been telling her about his financial situation and about how he was running their business venture" and ultimately "began to suspect that Maleki had married her just for her money." Meagher had "religious reasons" for wanting to avoid divorce. She sued for an annulment.[65]

The trial court found that Maleki "fraudulently misrepresented his financial circumstances to Meagher prior to the marriage" and lied about his financial contributions to their business venture.[66] The trial court also "determined that not only the business venture but also the parties' marriage was based on Meagher's reliance upon Maleki's representation that he had great wealth and that he would take care of her, and not that he expected through a series of transactions to divest her of at least half an interest in several million dollars' worth of property."[67] Maleki did not contest the trial court's factual findings, but contended that his deceit provided Meagher with insufficient legal grounds for an annulment.[68]

The California Court of Appeal agreed with him. The appellate court's unanimous 2005 opinion began by noting that "[t]he law in California has long been that an annulment of marriage may be granted on the basis of fraud only in an extreme case where the particular fraud goes to the very essence of the marriage relation."[69] Indeed, the appellate court's language throughout the opinion echoed nineteenth-century jurisprudence, with its assumption and insistence that annulment law would provide far fewer remedies for deception than are available in other suits seeking escape from agreements with deceitful partners. The court returned to the common law refrain that "the fraud relied upon to secure a termination of the existing [marital] status must be such fraud as directly affects the marriage relationship and not merely such fraud as would be sufficient to rescind an ordinary civil contract."[70]

The court did not defend that proposition on its own merits or explain why it was sound public policy to shield someone who had schemed before and during marriage to betray his wife's trust and take her assets. Instead, the court simply emphasized that denying Meagher an annulment was consistent with a long line of judicial decisions treating deception differently in the annulment context. The opinion's discussion of why Meagher could not obtain an annulment concluded this way: "[Meagher] cites no authority . . . either in California or elsewhere, for the proposition that annulment can be granted based on fraud or misrepresentation of a purely financial nature. As already noted, the cases are entirely to the contrary. Accordingly, we agree with Maleki that the fraud established in this case, as a matter of law, was not of the type that constitutes an adequate basis for granting an annulment."[71]

The United States Territorial Court of the Virgin Islands relied on similar reasoning in refusing to grant Kyle Francis an annulment in 1985. Kyle reported that her husband, Kade Francis, intentionally misled her during premarital counseling sessions by concealing his debts and falsely telling her that he did not owe any past due rent or child support.[72] In fact, Kade owed $11,753 to creditors and had fallen behind on his rent and child support payments. Kyle reported that she was duped and relied on Kade's premarital misrepresentations about his financial condition when she married him.[73] She explained that she would have refused to marry Kade if she had known the truth and that she stopped living with him soon after their wedding once she discovered that he had deceived her.[74] She also reported that her reliance on Kade's deceit had caused her "embarrassment, grief, and financial damage." Kade conceded the accuracy of Kyle's allegations.

Kyle's annulment suit was based on a Virgin Islands statute providing that "fraud in the inducement of a marriage is grounds for an annulment."[75] The *Francis* court acknowledged that "a reading of Virgin Islands law and [this statute] might suggest that marriages can be terminated almost at will."[76] Yet the court denied Kyle an annulment nonetheless, insisting that the annulment statute's concern about "fraud" had to be interpreted narrowly in a way that excluded Kade's misrepresentations.[77]

In explaining this holding, the judge briefly noted the societal significance of marriage, which the judge described (quoting a New York decision from 1952) as "more than a personal relation between a man and woman" and "an institution involving the highest interests of society."[78] Beyond that generalized pronouncement about marriage, the *Francis* opinion offered little defense of its narrow reading of the annulment statute. The court did not explain how the specific marriage at issue, which was founded on Kade's deceit, furthered any important societal interests.

Instead, the court just assumed the continued wisdom of the common law consensus that annulment jurisprudence should provide less redress for deception than would be available for deceit in other contexts. The court found it to be "well settled in a majority of the states that the term 'fraud' as used in annulment proceedings is not to be construed as broadly as it is to void an ordinary contract. Courts in most states have ruled that before fraud will be sufficient to allow an annulment it must be shown that the fraud concerns the essentials of the marital relationship, such as cohabitation or consortium."[79] *Francis* fell in line with many earlier common law decisions in holding that "[m]isrepresentations of financial matters . . . do not concern the essentials of a marriage relationship and as such have been specifically rejected as grounds for annulment."[80]

Francis also contended that "even assuming financial misrepresentation could provide a basis for annulment, the misrepresentations alleged here are not flagrant enough to form the basis for an annulment."[81] This last comment presumably reflected the court's assessment that the scale of Kade's deceit was relatively small. Deception to hide less than twelve thousand dollars in debt might seem like small potatoes to a judge with a law degree and a prestigious professional perch. Yet Kade's deceit concealed from his fiancée that he was unable to support himself and to meet his financial obligations, even if those obligations appeared modest from the perspective of a wealthier person. When Kyle learned of the deception, moreover, she had good reason to conclude that Kade was untrustworthy as well as debt-ridden. The *Francis* court echoed its common law predecessors in discounting and minimizing the deception Kyle experienced, but that deception could easily constitute a linchpin from Kyle's perspective.

Intimacy, Broadly Defined

The judiciary's commitment to treating intimate deception differently has especially far-reaching consequences because of how broadly courts can define intimacy, applying that classification to relationships in which the deceiver took advantage of the fact that the parties did not know each other well.

The Illinois Supreme Court's unanimous 2012 decision in *Bonhomme v. St. James*[82] is a stark illustration of the judicial inclination to define relationships as intimate and refuse remedies on that basis—even when the relationship at issue lacks important indicia of intimacy, such as extended time spent together. Paula Bonhomme unsuccessfully sued Janna St. James over conduct that occurred largely before the two ever met. For much of the time they interacted, St. James deliberately avoided face-to-face contact with Bonhomme and communicated instead via the internet, mail, and phone.[83]

Not surprisingly, this approach can sometimes facilitate deceit that would be harder to pursue in person.[84] St. James's strategic avoidance of personal meetings allegedly enabled her to subject Bonhomme to a relentless campaign of deception and abuse for almost two years.[85]

The two women reportedly first communicated in April 2005 in an internet chatroom for fans of the Deadwood television series.[86] St. James initially registered in this chatroom using the name "Ms. Magnolia," but she registered again in June 2005—identifying herself this time as a man named "Jesse James."

St. James apparently began deceiving Bonhomme in July 2005. That month, St. James used her "Jesse" alias to communicate with Bonhomme in the chat room and via email. At the same time, St. James used her own name to email Bonhomme and claim that she knew the fictional "Jesse" as well as many of his associates.

St. James maintained and expanded this scheme over the next year. Between July 2005 and July 2006, "Jesse" exchanged emails, photographs, letters, gifts, and phone calls with Bonhomme. St. James used a device that disguised her voice so she sounded like a man on the phone. St. James also continued to communicate with Bonhomme under her own name, still presenting herself as someone who knew "Jesse." Moreover, St. James invented about twenty additional aliases in order to pose as other people who supposedly knew "Jesse," including his ex-wife, son, and friends. She used those supplemental aliases to send even more emails, letters, photographs, and packages to Bonhomme. Bonhomme, meanwhile, sent more than ten thousand dollars in gifts to St. James and her various aliases.

Bonhomme's financial losses and emotional suffering from St. James's deceit had only begun, however. "Jesse" made plans to meet Bonhomme in person, although St. James knew such a meeting could never take place. After "Jesse" canceled those plans around September 2005, St. James told Bonhomme that "Jesse" had tried to kill himself. Bonhomme reported that learning about this suicide attempt caused her severe emotional distress, leading her to incur more than five thousand dollars in therapy bills.

St. James was still not done with Bonhomme. By April 2006, "Jesse" had convinced Bonhomme to move in with him. Bonhomme spent about seven hundred dollars getting ready for that move. Of course, any real-life meeting between Bonhomme and "Jesse" remained as impossible as ever. In July 2006—the month scheduled for the relocation—St. James posed as "Jesse's" sister, "Alice," to tell Bonhomme that "Jesse" had died from liver cancer. St. James used some of her other aliases to send Bonhomme condolence letters.

Bonhomme reported that news of "Jesse's" death left her depressed, "experiencing headaches, exhaustion, inability to sleep, and inability to focus on job-related tasks. She also contracted a recurring infection known as MRSA (multidrug resistant staphylococcus aureus) because her immune system was so weakened."

St. James kept contacting Bonhomme even after killing off "Jesse." With "Jesse" safely dead, St. James apparently wanted to meet Bonhomme in person and dupe her at close range. She convinced Bonhomme to take a trip with her in September 2006 so they could visit places supposedly connected to "Jesse." St. James used this trip to present Bonhomme with a letter purportedly from "Jesse." The letter declared that "Jesse" loved Bonhomme and explained his last wishes.

St. James visited Bonhomme's home in February 2007—after Bonhomme had spent a thousand dollars readying her home for St. James's arrival, which required installing "a handrail, sliding chair, and medical bath assist devices." During that visit, some of Bonhomme's real friends uncovered St. James's deceit and confronted her.[87] St. James acknowledged on video that she had subjected Bonhomme to "an emotional ringer for maybe a year and a half."[88] Bonhomme reported that she stayed in therapy after the revelation of St. James's deceit, accumulating therapy bills and losing earnings because of her "affected mental state."[89]

Bonhomme sued St. James for fraudulent misrepresentation and her case reached the Illinois Supreme Court.[90] Bonhomme's allegations appeared to satisfy each element of the fraudulent misrepresentation tort, which requires a plaintiff to establish "(1) a false statement of material fact; (2) known or believed to be false by the person making it; (3) an intent to induce the plaintiff to act; (4) action by the plaintiff in justifiable reliance on the truth of the statement; and (5) damage to the plaintiff resulting from such reliance."[91] Nonetheless, the Illinois Supreme Court dismissed Bonhomme's suit.[92] The court's argument was underdeveloped, but had two basic components.

First, the court started from the familiar premise that legal remedies for deception outside of intimacy are not and should not be available for deception within intimacy. The court insisted that the tort of fraudulent misrepresentation was designed to provide remedies in "cases involving business or financial transactions between parties" and could not help a plaintiff who had been deceived "in a setting that is purely personal in nature."[93]

The wisdom of this stark divide was assumed rather than defended. *Bonhomme* took for granted that the law is rightly concerned about deception within commercial relationships, but has no interest in redressing deception within personal relationships—even when that deceit causes considerable injury. The court declared that "the veracity of representations made in the context of purely private personal relationships is simply not something the state regulates or in which the state possesses any kind of valid public policy interest." This statement suggested that the law can and does leave personal relationships untouched. But the court's decision in *Bonhomme* was unavoidably going to establish ground rules regulating deceit in personal relationships, whether the court ruled for Bonhomme or St. James. In siding with St. James, the court set a legal baseline in Illinois that shielded deceivers rather than their targets. *Bonhomme* means that a person can inflict significant harm through deception in a personal relationship without worry that she could be held liable for fraudulent misrepresentation.

The second part of the court's argument insisted that it was not "difficult" to conclude that Bonhomme and St. James had "a purely personal relationship," with "absolutely nothing of the commercial, transactional, or regulatory at work." On the court's account, Bonhomme and St. James had shared "intimacy, trust, mutual beneficence, emotional support, affection, disappointment, and even grief."[94] The court evinced no hesitation about defining intimacy capaciously enough to cover a situation in which Bonhomme's most intense interactions were with "Jesse," a fictional character whom Bonhomme (of course) never met. St. James sometimes operated under her own name when communicating with Bonhomme, but those interactions were more limited and they focused on "Jesse" and St. James's supposed connection to him.

It is also striking that the court concluded that there was "absolutely" no commercial aspect to the interactions between Bonhomme and St. James. Identifying all of St. James's motivations for her cruel barrage of deception would be difficult, if not impossible. But one likely reason (among many) for the torrent of deceit was that St. James wanted to extract financial resources from Bonhomme. Moreover, she did extract such resources. Before her scheme was uncovered, St. James reportedly received more than ten thousand dollars in gifts from Bonhomme. St. James and Bonhomme were involved in multiple financial transactions—albeit transactions that allegedly benefited St. James much more than Bonhomme.

Nonetheless, the court found that Bonhomme and St. James had a relationship that was entirely personal and not at all commercial. With that finding in place, the Illinois Supreme Court joined many other courts in quickly concluding that Bonhomme could not access legal remedies that are available to people deceived in other contexts.[95]

Protecting Public Health
Rather than Deceived Intimates

Courts are so committed to the premise that the law should shield intimate deceivers from legal liability that they frequently stress that presumption even when ruling for particular plaintiffs. Consider the case law on deception about sexually transmitted diseases. Multiple courts have allowed plaintiffs who contracted such diseases to sue the defendants who reportedly duped and infected them. However, these opinions routinely emphasize the judiciary's tremendous reluctance to provide redress to deceived intimates. Judges make clear that the plaintiffs winning favorable rulings have presented exceptional cases in which courts need to depart from their usual response to intimate deception in order to safeguard public health by deterring the spread of sexually transmitted infection.

We can begin by examining two decisions in which the California Court of Appeal unanimously ruled in favor of plaintiffs who were allegedly infected by deceptive sexual partners. In *Kathleen K. v. Robert B.*,[96] Kathleen reported that she contracted genital herpes from Robert, who knew he had herpes and falsely told her that he had no sexually transmitted diseases. She contended that she would have refused sex with Robert if she had known about his infection. The court held in 1984 that Kathleen could pursue her suit against Robert for fraud, negligence, battery, and intentional infliction of emotional distress.[97] Even in ruling for Kathleen, though, the court stressed its general commitment to (supposedly) staying out of intimate relationships by denying remedies to deceived intimates. The *Kathleen K.* opinion made clear that the court was making an exception in this case because Robert's alleged deceit had led Kathleen to contract a "serious and (thus far) incurable" disease.[98] The California court may have been particularly concerned about how sexually transmitted disease can threaten public health because the AIDS crisis was coming into view in 1984. The court compared genital herpes to AIDS, writing that "[l]ike AIDS it is now known by the public to be a contagious and dreadful disease."[99] In short, "the interest of this state in the prevention and control of contagious and dangerous diseases" was at stake in Kathleen's suit.[100]

When the California Court of Appeal in 1987 blocked Lee Perry from pursuing her suit against a former lover who had allegedly duped her into having an abortion, the *Perry* opinion quoted this last phrase from *Kathleen K.* to explain why it was disposing of Perry's suit after having permitted Kathleen's litigation to proceed. *Perry* agreed with *Kathleen K.* that suits involving the reported spread of sexually transmitted infection required special treatment. As the *Perry* decision stressed, "[t]he tortious transmission of a contagious disease implicates policy considerations beyond the sexual conduct and procreative decisions of two consenting adults."[101]

The California Court of Appeal confirmed again in *Doe v. Roe* (1990)[102] that it understood cases revolving around sexually transmitted infection to be exceptions that did not undercut the judiciary's general hostility to litigation alleging intimate deception. Jane Doe reported that she contracted genital herpes from Richard Roe, who had deceived her to conceal his infection.[103] She testified that she would not have agreed to sex with Richard if she had known about his herpes.[104] Jane sued Richard for fraud and negligence,[105] and the Court of Appeal affirmed the trial court's judgment ordering Richard to pay $150,000 in damages to Jane for "negligent transmittal of the virus herpes simplex II."[106] The appellate court cited its earlier decision in *Kathleen K.* in emphasizing that the judiciary's usual concerns about (purportedly) avoiding intrusion into intimate relationships would not block Jane's suit because of "the strong interest of the state in preventing the spread of communicable sexual diseases." In this context, the court declared that "the right of privacy is not absolute and must yield where outweighed by the state's right to enact laws which promote public health and safety."[107]

The Minnesota Court of Appeals reasoned similarly in allowing R.A.P. to sue his ex-wife, B.J.P., "for negligent and fraudulent transmission of genital herpes." R.A.P. reported that B.J.P. came into their relationship knowing she had herpes and infected him before they married, but did not disclose her infection until after they had wed.[108]

The court's decision helped R.A.P. But the court's unanimous opinion nonetheless accepted the premise that providing remedies to deceived intimates could threaten the judiciary's supposed commitment to nonintervention in intimate relationships, highlighting the worry that granting such redress could constitute "an undue invasion of the law into the most private aspects of personal life."[109] Rather than challenge the judiciary's typical way of thinking about intimate deception, *R.A.P. v. B.J.P.* emphasized why that case was special. The 1988 opinion detailed the menace that genital herpes posed to public health, a danger absent from ordinary intimate deception cases. As the opinion elaborated: "Genital herpes is a contagious and debilitating disease. It is extremely painful, and often leads to serious physical and psychological complications. It is presently incurable, and is spreading at an alarming and dangerous rate. Genital herpes thus poses a severe threat to the public health."[110] The court concluded that "[o]n balance, we believe that society's interest in preventing the spread of a dangerous, incurable disease justifies some intrusion into personal privacy."[111]

The United States District Court for the Western District of Michigan also adopted this mode of argument in allowing another suit to proceed against a defendant who had allegedly deceived his sexual partner to conceal his sexually transmitted infection. The anonymous "Jane Doe" plaintiff in this suit reported that she had contracted human immunodeficiency virus (HIV) from Earvin Johnson, Jr.,[112] the celebrated former professional basketball player popularly known as Magic Johnson.[113] Doe brought multiple claims against Johnson, including fraud, battery, negligence, and intentional infliction of emotional distress.[114] Her fraud claim alleged that Johnson knew or should have known that he had HIV and did not disclose his infection because he wanted Doe to believe he was uninfected.[115] She also reported that Johnson refused to use a condom.[116] The district judge held that Doe could pursue her suit to the extent she alleged that the sex without disclosure took place at a time when Johnson knew he had HIV, knew he had already experienced symptoms associated with HIV, or knew that at least one of his previous sexual partners had been diagnosed with HIV.[117]

In reaching this decision, however, the federal court made plain its deep reluctance to grant legal remedies for intimate deception. The opinion worried that "court supervision of the promises made by, and other activities engaged in [by], two consenting adults concerning the circumstances of their private sexual conduct is very close to an unwarranted intrusion into their right to privacy."[118]

More generally, the opinion emphasized and endorsed a sharp division in the legal regulation of intimate versus nonintimate relationships. The court stressed that the law typically does not require sexual partners to be trustworthy or to protect each other—even though people do have such legal obligations in some commercial relationships. The opinion explained that Johnson owed "[n]o special duties" to Doe based on their "single consensual sexual encounter." The court elaborated with a remarkable turn of phrase suggesting that the law expects and allows sexual relationships to be less safe than public spaces like hotels and trains: "this case does not illustrate a special relationship where one entrusts himself or herself to the protection of another and relies upon that person to provide a place of safety, e.g., landlord-tenant, innkeeper-guest, common carrier-passenger."[119]

Doe v. Johnson left little doubt that the court was allowing Doe's litigation to proceed because her suit presented the unusual case where intimate deception could have lethal consequences for this plaintiff and for "future plaintiffs" who might be subject to the same sort of deceit.[120] The district court decided this case in 1993, as the death toll from AIDS was rising in the United States and anxiety about the epidemic was escalating.[121] The judge stressed that "at this point in history there is no cure for the HIV virus. Moreover, as far as I am aware, the HIV virus often (if not always) leads to AIDS—and ultimately death. Thus, society certainly has a strong interest in preventing the spread of this disease."[122] After the district court issued its opinion, the parties settled their dispute out of court.[123]

In sum, the law routinely assumes and enforces the premise that deceived intimates should not have access to legal remedies that are available to people duped in other contexts. This common refrain has shaped the regulation of marital and nonmarital relationships across multiple arenas. The judiciary's visceral commitment to the differential treatment of intimate deception has an especially far-reaching impact because of how broadly courts can define intimacy, including relationships in which the deceit was made possible by the reality that the parties did not know each other well. The determination to treat intimate deception differently even shapes decisions in which a particular plaintiff manages to win a ruling in her favor. Even in those cases, courts often emphasize their general opposition to providing remedies for intimate deception and make clear that the lawsuit at issue is exceptional.

6

The Legal Protection of Ordinary Deception in Courtship, Sex, and Marriage

Denying remedies for intimate deception creates no incentives for deceivers to change their ways. One might wonder whether judges refusing redress are concerned about leaving intimate deception unchecked. But courts evince remarkably little interest in reducing deceit within courtship, sexual relationships, or marriage. Instead, they routinely assume, accept, and uphold existing practices. Judges start by presuming that deceit pervades romance, sex, and marriage, and they contend with little—if any—explanation that courts should accordingly protect commonplace intimate deception from legal redress.

This commitment to the supposed status quo means that judicial assumptions about which kinds of deceit are typical in intimate relationships have important practical consequences. Plaintiffs are much less likely to win redress when courts think the deception is ordinary and more likely to win redress when courts believe the deception is unusual and deviant. In short, judges presuppose that many forms of deceit are widespread in romance, sex, and marriage, and they help make that so—normalizing the deception by shielding it from legal condemnation and legal remedies.

Moreover, the judicial determination to protect assertedly ordinary deception can shield even extraordinary deceivers. Courts sometimes refuse to provide redress for manifestly extraordinary examples of intimate deception on the ground that the judiciary needs to guard against creating a slippery slope that could ultimately expose more commonplace deceivers to liability.

Indeed, the judiciary's commitment to protecting supposedly ordinary intimate deceivers is so powerful that courts have stressed this commitment in deciding cases with defendants who deceived government officials or business rivals. Judges have reasoned from the premise that the legal system should not jeopardize commonplace intimate deception when they have rejected or limited statutes whose impact extends well beyond intimacy, such as a law penalizing false claims about military awards and a law against computer fraud and abuse.

I began this project suspecting that courts might deny remedies to deceived intimates out of a belief that intimate deception is insufficiently important to merit judicial concern. But judges deciding intimate deception cases often appear convinced that this regulatory arena is vitally important. More specifically, judges seem to think that it is crucial to govern intimate deception in ways that maintain and reinforce current norms and practices in courtship, sexual relationships, and marriage. Courts are intent on upholding the status quo in intimacy, although they never quite explain why the status quo is worth protecting so fiercely if deceit is as common in intimate relationships as judges assume.

Protecting (Supposedly) Ordinary Intimate Deceivers

We are living in an era that often valorizes marriage and romantic life. Odes to the glories of wedlock and recitations of the legal advantages tied to marriage abounded in the most successful civil rights effort in recent years, shaping advocacy supporting marriage equality and judicial decisions holding that prohibitions on same-sex marriage are unconstitutional. The Massachusetts Supreme Judicial Court struck down the state's ban on same-sex marriage in 2003 while emphasizing that "marriage provides an abundance of legal, financial, and social benefits," "nurtures love and mutual support,"[1] "fulfils yearnings for security, safe haven, and connection that express our common humanity,"[2] and constitutes "a highly public celebration of the ideals of mutuality, companionship, intimacy, fidelity, and family."[3] The 2015 United States Supreme Court decision establishing "[t]he right of same-sex couples to marry"[4] throughout the nation likewise stressed "the constellation of benefits that the States have linked to marriage"[5] while declaring that "marriage is essential to our most profound hopes and aspirations," "offers unique fulfillment," and "always has promised nobility and dignity to all persons, without regard to their station in life."[6]

Courts and commentators reasoning about intimate deception frequently accept and protect a much bleaker vision of marriage, courtship, and sexual relationships. This account presumes that deceit is ubiquitous within intimacy—even natural, timeless, and inevitable. A columnist for the *San Francisco Chronicle* wrote that deceiving people—women, more specifically—to induce them to have sex "has been going on since the first caveman invited the first cavewoman up to see his wall etchings." He asked: "Where would common, ordinary, everyday seduction be without fraud and misrepresentation?" He contended that deception was so central to heterosexuality that trying to stop such deceit could threaten to "wipe out the human race."[7] Another commentator stated flatly in the *Chicago Tribune* "that everything in romance is lying."[8] An editorial in the New Jersey *Star-Ledger* summarized human history by declaring that "[f]or thousands of years, men have been lying to woo women to bed."[9]

Many courts denying legal relief for deception within courtship, sexual relationships, or marriage similarly rely on the twin assertions that courts should protect ordinary intimate deceivers from legal redress and the defendant is an ordinary intimate deceiver. Rather than attaching legal benefits and advantages to marriage and other intimate relationships, courts adjudicating deceit take intimacy as grounds for denying access to remedies that are available in other contexts. The law governing deception is a prime arena where courts define what constitutes ordinary behavior within intimacy and enforce their understanding of normalcy by shielding what judges take to be commonplace intimate deception from legal remedies.

Consider Cory Starr's unsuccessful suit against Alisha Woolf seeking damages for the emotional and financial injuries her deceit allegedly inflicted on him. Starr reported that he had a sexual relationship with Woolf in February and March 2002. He ended that relationship and shortly thereafter met his future wife, Michelle Jackson. Starr and Jackson married on July 3, 2002. Woolf allegedly destroyed the newlyweds' happiness just five days after the wedding.[10]

On Starr's account, Woolf falsely told him that she was pregnant with their baby, which led him to tell his wife about the pregnancy.[11] Woolf also reportedly lied to Starr's wife directly by telling her that Starr had continued his sexual relationship with Woolf even after he married Jackson.[12]

Woolf's machinations apparently succeeded in enraging Jackson. Starr's wife reportedly assaulted her new husband and damaged his car. She committed suicide a few days later and left a will bequeathing just $1.50 to her husband.[13]

Starr reported that he would not have told his wife about Woolf's purported pregnancy if he had known she was not pregnant. He contended that as a result of Woolf's deceit and his reliance on her misrepresentations "he suffered extreme emotional distress, lost his wife to suicide, incurred $12,000 worth of damage to his BMW, lost money on real estate transactions, and lost money on the $25,000 engagement ring that he purchased."[14]

After Jackson's suicide, moreover, Woolf kept contacting Starr and contending that she planned to sue him for child support.[15] Woolf also taunted Starr about his wife's death, blaming him for the suicide and threatening to name the baby after Jackson.[16]

Woolf later admitted under oath that she had known as early as October 2002 that she was not pregnant.[17] Nonetheless, Woolf allegedly told Starr in mid-November that their baby was due on January 3, 2003.[18] She reportedly maintained this deceit until January 2003, the month when the child was supposed to appear and did not.[19]

Starr charged that Woolf had falsely told him that she was pregnant with their baby in an effort to extract money from him.[20] He sued her for intentional and negligent misrepresentation and intentional and negligent infliction of emotional distress.[21]

The California Court of Appeal unanimously dismissed Starr's suit in 2005.[22] The court repeatedly insisted that the type of deceit Woolf reportedly committed was common and assumed that commonplace intimate deception should not trigger legal liability.

The court summarized the case by emphasizing that Starr "presents facts depicting the messy aftermath that *all too often* follows casual sexual encounters and failed romances. A couple has unprotected sex; they go their separate ways; the woman learns she is pregnant and informs the man, or perhaps claims to be pregnant in an attempt to reconnect or to compensate for the man's rejection; the man lashes out at the woman as if she alone caused his dilemma; the woman retaliates and threatens to tell the man's current lover or wife; the man tries to limit the damage by telling his lover or wife first; the lover or wife reacts unfavorably. Unfortunately, the scenario is *not unusual*. For the court to intervene in such personal matters, there must be some conduct by the defendant that is particularly egregious, which causes serious injury to the plaintiff. As we shall explain, this case does not present such egregious circumstances."[23]

Similarly, the court stressed in rejecting Starr's intentional infliction of emotional distress claim that Starr's "complaint and exhibits thereto reflect the *all too typical* immature behavior that often follows a failed relationship. Although the behavior may be unseemly, it is not outrageous, even if the claim of pregnancy was false. Regrettably, false accusations of pregnancy by women are *not uncommon*, and neither are false denials of paternity by men. The fact such conduct is *not unusual* undermines any claim that it is outrageous. In other words, it is not conduct which would arouse the resentment of an average member of the community and lead him to exclaim, 'Outrageous!' Hence, it is not the type of misconduct for which the court system offers redress."[24]

As this book makes clear, intimacy and deception are frequently intertwined. But the court's insistence that Woolf's alleged deceit was unexceptional and insufficient to spark outrage is striking nonetheless. On Starr's account, Woolf spent about half a year falsely claiming to be pregnant with their child—continuing this deceit even after Starr's wife killed herself.[25] Woolf also falsely told Jackson that Starr had been unfaithful and then taunted Starr about Jackson's suicide.[26] Nonetheless, the court contended that Woolf's alleged deceit was not "particularly egregious" and did not cause Starr "serious injury."[27] The court showed no hesitation about asserting that false claims of pregnancy like the ones Woolf allegedly made "are not uncommon" and "not unusual."[28]

Once the court classified false claims of pregnancy as ordinary rather than extraordinary, the court took it as common sense that the judiciary should not disturb this existing practice by providing remedies. The *Starr v. Woolf* opinion characterized Woolf's reported deceit as regrettable and "unseemly" without exploring how dismissing Starr's suit might accommodate and facilitate false claims of pregnancy by shielding such deception from legal penalties and normalizing it.[29] The court was content to protect this deceit from redress and uninterested in fostering change.

Let's turn to the New Jersey Superior Court's 1986 rejection of Melida Tobon's annulment suit against Guillermo Sanchez. Tobon contended that Sanchez had deceived her before they married to conceal that he already had two children and wanted no more.[30] The New Jersey court that dismissed Tobon's suit required her to present "clear and convincing evidence" proving her allegations.[31] Even under this exacting standard, the court found that Sanchez had deceived Tobon to hide that he had children. (The court held that Tobon had insufficient proof that Sanchez had a "fixed" premarital determination to have no children with her.)[32]

The court insisted that Sanchez's deceit to conceal his children was insufficient for an annulment, asserting that such deception was too commonplace to entitle Tobon to legal redress. As the opinion explained: "The Court is unwilling to hold that the failure to disclose the existence of out-of-wedlock children born prior to the marriage would, on its own and without more, be grounds for annulment. Such a rule would likely make a substantial number of marriages voidable. For example, a mother who secretly gave up a child for adoption or a father who concealed a child left behind in wartime in a foreign country would each find a subsequent marriage voidable through annulment if this were the rule."[33]

The court's statement took the supposed frequency of deception to hide children's existence as an obvious reason to refuse redress for that deception. One might think that the law would not want to accommodate a father who left his child "behind in wartime" and then concealed that he had a child. But the court presumed that the judiciary should shield such men from legal penalties for their deceit because their brand of deception was (purportedly) relatively common.[34]

The court also accepted the prevalence of deceit to conceal parenthood as an external fact that the judiciary should recognize, without exploring how the law might be influencing the frequency of such deceit. Yet the court's own examples suggest how the law often facilitates deception to hide that one has had a child. Whatever the other benefits or disadvantages of closed adoption, that legal arrangement can help a birth parent intentionally mislead others—including intimates—into thinking that she has not had a child. Likewise, United States citizenship law facilitates deception to conceal "a child left behind in wartime."[35]

Consider the citizenship status of children born outside the United States to unmarried parents, with fathers who are United States citizens and mothers who are not. The United States makes it very difficult for these children to become citizens unless they have their fathers' cooperation, as expressed in a timely acknowledgment or establishment of paternity and an agreement to provide support until the age of majority. If an American man wants to hide that he has a nonmarital child who was born abroad, federal law helps the father successfully deceive his intimates by granting the father a significant measure of control over whether his foreign-born child will ever have legal authorization to live and work in the United States. That legal privilege applies whether the citizen father traveled internationally as a soldier or a civilian.[36] But as the Supreme Court emphasized in upholding this aspect of federal law, the available evidence suggests that American servicemen fathered many of the nonmarital children who were born abroad to one citizen parent and cannot obtain United States citizenship because they do not have the requisite paternal cooperation.[37]

Of course, the *Tobon v. Sanchez* decision also facilitates deception about progeny. *Tobon* refused to grant an annulment for Sanchez's deceit. More broadly, the *Tobon* court accepted such deception as a relatively common practice that the law should accordingly protect.[38]

Similar reasoning shaped the Connecticut Superior Court's 2006 decision denying Kirsten LaBranche an annulment.[39] Kirsten reported that her husband, Norman LaBranche, fraudulently assured her before they married that he would be able to get a full-time job and did not reveal the magnitude of a back injury that impaired his ability to work. The court assumed that fiancés often "deliberately concealed frailties" and that legal redress was inappropriate for commonplace intimate deception. The *LaBranche v. LaBranche* opinion quoted *Nerini v. Nerini*, a 1943 Connecticut Superior Court decision, to suggest that granting Kirsten an annulment would be as wrong as voiding a marriage for such purportedly ordinary deceits as a fiancé falsely denying that he has a "glass eye or a set of pearly false teeth."[40]

Nerini also proclaimed—in a passage that the *LaBranche* court cut around to avoid quoting[41]—that "[n]o Draconian law could or should be formulated to stop a man or a maid from pursuing during courtship the harmless deceptive arts to which both almost universally resort by wrapping themselves in an aura which is not strictly theirs to use."[42] This statement contained the triple assertions that deception is almost universal and perhaps inevitable in courtship, that premarital deception is harmless, and that the law should deny redress for such deceit. The passage illustrates how the judge thought courtship proceeded and simultaneously helped entrench those expectations into law. One reason the

LaBranche court may have avoided quoting this passage from *Nerini* is that the *LaBranche* case demonstrates how even commonplace intimate deception can inflict significant injury. Norman's alleged misrepresentation of his ability to support himself and others had concrete financial repercussions for his wife and her three children from a prior marriage.[43]

As *Nerini* suggests, the judicial determination to uphold existing norms and practices in courtship by refusing to attach legal penalties to supposedly ordinary deception has at least decades of history behind it. Some of the courts that labored to preserve this status quo reasoned in explicitly gendered and heterosexual terms, insisting that deception was particularly natural and normal when a man courted a woman. These accounts presented deceit as a core expression of masculinity and assumed that denying legal remedies for such deceit was essential to preserving appropriate gender relations.

The New Jersey Court of Chancery refused in 1925 to grant Rhoda Woodward an annulment from Emile Heichelbech, who had duped her before they married by falsely claiming "that he had an important position in a large company," earned seventy-five dollars a week, had more than two thousand dollars in a bank account, and had two cars.[44] Heichelbech had misrepresented his ability to support a family, in an era when rampant discrimination and job segregation severely restricted women's wage-earning opportunities. But the court characterized his blatant lies about employment and assets as nothing more than a man "paint[ing] the lily in his courtship." The opinion emphasized in denying redress that Heichelbech had behaved like many other men intent on "the winning of a bride": "It is fair to say that under such circumstances a man always puts his best foot forward to impress the woman of his choice with his desirability as a mate."[45] Rather than express concern for women who were duped into marrying men they would have otherwise rejected, the court was intent on protecting and preserving men's courtship strategies—even if those strategies manipulated women and distorted their decisionmaking.

A New York trial court reasoned similarly in refusing to grant Helen Jones an annulment in 1947. Helen reported that her husband, Donald Jones, had deliberately concealed that he was "a heavy drinker" because he realized Helen would not marry him knowing the truth.[46] She explained that Donald's premarital deceit had been a linchpin in her decision to marry him because she feared "a home life marred by drunkenness."[47] On Helen's account, in other words, Donald's deceit had changed the course of her life by skewing one of the most important decisions she ever made. Nonetheless, the court insisted that Helen's injury did not exist in the eyes of the law. The judge explained Helen's defeat this way: "It is to be expected that every suitor will put his best foot forward. It would be contrary to human nature if he did not paint himself in glowing colors, and did not fully utilize all the 'seller's puff,' to borrow a phrase from the law of contracts, which was at his command. Boastfulness and self approbation are as natural and as much to be expected under such circumstances as the strut of the rooster in the barnyard."[48] The court characterized Donald's alleged deceit as nothing more than puffery, a harmless bit of male exaggeration, display, and self-promotion that every woman should know to discount. The judge maintained—echoing and anticipating the arguments of many other courts—that the judiciary should protect such premarital deception from legal redress because the deception was supposedly ordinary, normal, expected, even inevitable when men courted women. Donald was behaving as naturally as any male farm animal luring a mate. The court would not fault men for deceit in courtship, expect them to behave differently, or help the women they duped.

Remedies for (Some) Extraordinary Intimate Deception

One way courts express their commitment to preserving existing norms and practices in courtship, sex, and marriage is by denying relief for what judges take to be commonplace deception. Another way courts express this commitment is by emphasizing when they do grant redress in a particular case that the deception at issue is atypical, abnormal, and distinct from ordinary intimacy. Judicial responses to bigamy and con artistry provide revealing illustrations. Let's begin with bigamy.

Even if falsely presenting oneself as unmarried is a relatively common practice in sexual and romantic relationships,[49] actually marrying again without first securing a divorce is clearly more unusual. Every state criminalizes bigamy and provides that bigamous marriages are void. A steady stream of judicial decisions has enforced those criminal and civil provisions—usually against men, who constitute almost all bigamy defendants.[50]

This case law reveals the enormous injuries that bigamy can inflict on a duped spouse. Frederick Erb deceived Emma Welsh to conceal that he married her while still married to—and apparently still living with—another woman. Erb explained his absences from home by falsely claiming to work for "Naval Intelligence." Welsh discovered Erb's deceit after more than a year and a half when she visited him in the hospital and encountered his other wife.[51] When Pennsylvania successfully prosecuted Erb for bigamy, Welsh told the court about the funds she had expended to support her supposed husband and the unpaid domestic services—cooking, cleaning, washing, and ironing—she had provided to care for him.[52] She also testified about her emotional suffering and distress, explaining that "this crime to me is worse than a murder or a mugging or even a robbery because you can replace material things. But you cannot replace your affections. And I have been, you know, really in a state since this thing has happened."[53]

The recognition that bigamists often deceive their spouses may be one reason why lawmakers have criminalized bigamy. As a federal district court in Utah noted in 2013, "the policy behind this ancient prohibition of polygamy seems to have centered on the often fraudulent nature of a polygamous marriage: Such an act defrauds the state and perhaps an innocent spouse or purported partner."[54]

In turn, the criminalization of bigamy has probably helped bolster the judiciary's willingness to provide tort remedies to people duped into marrying a bigamist. With criminal law's condemnation of bigamy as a backdrop, courts have been receptive to plaintiffs seeking redress from defendants who duped them (or almost duped them) into bigamous unions. These decisions routinely stress that bigamy is unusual and deviant, rather than commonplace and expected.

Consider the unanimous 2012 decision from the Maryland Court of Special Appeals that upheld a jury verdict awarding Dara Bradley $469,000 in compensatory and punitive damages from Ronald Bradley. Ronald had told Dara before they began dating in 2004 that he and his wife had been separated for years and were in the process of divorcing. Ronald proposed to Dara at the end of 2004, with the apparent understanding that they would marry after he was divorced.[55] Dara subsequently resigned from her job at Ronald's request to help care for his children.[56] Ronald announced in September 2006 that his divorce had become final. He showed Dara a plaque displaying an official-looking document entitled "Judgment of Absolute Divorce." The document included a court seal and a (forged) signature from the court clerk. Dara and Ronald married in April 2007.[57]

Ronald proved to be a violent husband. After he had assaulted her twice, Dara searched the Maryland judiciary's online database in 2008 to investigate Ronald's involvement in other domestic violence cases and discovered that Ronald's divorce was not in the database. Dara then hired a lawyer, who verified that Ronald had never divorced his first wife.[58] She sued Ronald for an annulment and also sought tort damages for intentional and negligent misrepresentation, intentional infliction of emotional distress, and battery.[59]

One might think that Dara's suit bore a closer resemblance to a breach of promise to marry case than some of the litigation (described in Chapter 4) that courts have blocked as falling within statutory bans on breach of promise actions. Ronald agreed to marry Dara and purported to marry her, knowing that he was not legally free to marry and that their marriage would be legally invalid. But the trial court not only granted Dara an annulment—a foregone conclusion as a bigamous marriage is void—it also upheld the jury's hefty damages award,[60] concluding that Maryland's statutory prohibition on breach of promise to marry litigation did not bar Dara from suing Ronald for misrepresentation.

The trial judge's explanation emphasized the importance of denying remedies for commonplace intimate behavior, while stressing that Ronald's deceit was not commonplace. The judge assumed that damages were inappropriate where a plaintiff had simply experienced "broken expectations [because] of not getting married" or complained about the sort of "breakdown of expectations" that is present in "every divorce case."[61] However, the trial judge was convinced that Ronald's deceptive bigamy could not be contained within these everyday categories. Instead, Ronald's false statement "that his divorce is final" paired with his decision to marry Dara knowing that he was still married to his first wife constituted an unusual deceit that subjected Dara to the extraordinary shock of discovering "that she's not legitimately married and that this is a sham or a fraud."[62] The Maryland appellate court held that "the trial judge properly interpreted Maryland case law," agreeing that Dara had presented valid claims for misrepresentation that did not fall within Maryland's prohibition on breach of promise to marry litigation.[63]

The Utah Supreme Court's 1995 decision permitting Ranay Jackson to sue Scott Brown for intentional infliction of emotional distress similarly stressed that Brown's behavior was unusual rather than ordinary.[64] Brown deceived Jackson to hide that he was already married to another woman. But he was not just another run-of-the-mill philanderer who falsely presented himself as unmarried so he could attract a girlfriend. Brown asked Jackson to marry him and did not break their engagement until the morning when their wedding was supposed to take place. Even when he canceled the wedding, he did not disclose that he already had a wife.[65]

In short, Brown's deceit had left Jackson on the verge of marrying a bigamist. The court's decision allowing Jackson's intentional infliction of emotional distress suit to proceed emphasized how extraordinary and abnormal Brown's web of deception had been: "Brown has conceded that during the period in question, he was already married; at no time during his relationship with Jackson was he able, legally, to marry her. Yet he proposed, scheduled a ceremony, acquired a license, and apparently offered every appearance of going through with the wedding. He withdrew his promise only hours before the time scheduled for the ceremony. These actions may very well be considered outrageous and intolerable in that they offend against the generally accepted standards of decency and morality."[66]

Let's turn to con artistry. As we have seen, courts are often reluctant to provide remedies in cases of greedy deception, where a person deceived his intimate for financial gain. That result is perhaps not too surprising, given the judiciary's interest in protecting types of deception that judges assume are common within intimacy. However, courts are more willing to grant redress when they are convinced that the defendant is not an ordinary intimate deceiver, but instead is a

professional con artist whose overriding purpose in forming a relationship was
to drain his target's bank account and expropriate her assets. Con artistry—
telling lies for a living—and commonplace serial intimate deception—living by
telling lies—can have more overlaps than many of us would like to acknowledge.
But when judges penalize con artists for their deceit, they routinely stress how
the defendants' actions were distinct and deviant from everyday intimacy—
criminal and pathological rather than normal and expected.[67]

Consider the successful prosecution of Kevin Jennings for mail fraud. The
unanimous United States Court of Appeals for the Seventh Circuit repeatedly
emphasized in upholding his sentence how the defendant was not an ordinary
intimate deceiver and how his actions fell outside the realm of normal courtship.[68] As the court explained, Jennings was a violent convicted felon who
was "locked in a prison" when he embarked upon his "villainous" plan "to defraud unsuspecting women outside of prison of thousands of dollars." "[T]he
criminally-minded" Jennings subscribed to magazines with personal ads "from
single women seeking serious relationships with men." He scammed women
he found there by writing them letters brimming with lies about why he was
in prison, his need for money, his love for them, and his desire to marry them.
Women sent Jennings a total of $13,378 before the federal government uncov-
ered his "devious" scheme.[69]

The Seventh Circuit was confident that Jennings had pursued his letter writing
campaign in the interest of generating money rather than genuine relationships.[70]
The court also had "no trouble concluding that if Jennings' victims knew the truth
behind his lies, they would not have sent him one red cent."[71] After highlighting
the distance between the defendant's deceit and ordinary intimacy, the Seventh
Circuit affirmed the district court's judgment sentencing Jennings to an additional twenty-seven months in prison and requiring him to pay $13,378 in
restitution.[72]

The Wisconsin Supreme Court similarly stressed that James Lambert's career
of deceit was extraordinary and abnormal in unanimously upholding Lambert's
conviction and sentencing for six counts of theft by fraud.[73] Lambert proposed
to at least seven women in the span of less than three years. Once the women had
accepted or were considering his proposals, he set about extracting money from
them. He deployed a variety of stories, usually explaining that he had a pressing
debt, wanted to pursue a business opportunity, and/or needed to pay various
expenses in anticipation of marriage.[74] Several different women simultaneously
thought Lambert was preparing to marry them.[75] Lambert concealed that he was
already married, and his wife cooperated in this deceit.[76]

The Wisconsin Supreme Court condemned Lambert as a "con artist,"[77] "cal-
lous,"[78] and "palpably fraudulent."[79] Indeed, the Supreme Court approvingly

quoted the trial judge's conclusion that Lambert was an "outrageous liar" and an incurable social pathogen who needed to be quarantined so he could inflict no more harm: "I don't believe there is any hope for rehabilitation for this man. I believe he has to be separated from this society, like you would separate a person contaminated with a dangerous disease."[80] Having highlighted Lambert's deviance, the Supreme Court had no problem affirming Lambert's sentence to twenty-four years in prison and a decade of probation.[81]

In short, courts are sometimes willing to impose penalties on extraordinary intimate deceivers. But they routinely emphasize the abnormality and unusualness of the defendants' deceit, making clear that commonplace deception is not at issue.

Slippery Slope Arguments Protecting Extraordinary Intimate Deceivers

Moreover, even extraordinary intimate deceivers can benefit from the judicial commitment to shielding ordinary deceit. Courts sometimes refuse to grant redress for extraordinary intimate deception on the ground that providing remedies might create a slippery slope that would ultimately jeopardize more commonplace deceivers. These arguments typically assume without explanation that protecting ordinary deception is vitally important and worth the cost of allowing unusually reprehensible intimate deceivers to escape legal penalties.[82]

Susan Kerr's unsuccessful suit against Dan Boyles, Jr., for negligent infliction of emotional distress is illustrative. Kerr and Boyles had a sexual relationship when she was nineteen and he was seventeen. Boyles and his friend, Karl Broesche, agreed that Broesche would surreptitiously record Kerr and Boyles having sex. Boyles deceived Kerr so she would not discover this plan and the hidden video camera that Broesche and two accomplices used to record Kerr and Boyles. Afterward, Boyles took custody of the video and screened the recording three times, permitting ten additional people to watch it. Boyles continued to deceive Kerr to conceal the video's existence and his display of the recording.[83]

Gossip about Kerr's video appearance spread like wildfire, including at the schools Kerr and Boyles attended. The talk was apparently pervasive enough to reach Kerr herself about four months after the secret recording. Kerr's friends and acquaintances wrongly assumed that she had consented to the video and asked her why she had participated. Some of Kerr's "friends" (frenemies?) derided her as a "porno queen." Kerr confronted Boyles, who eventually told her the truth and surrendered the recording.[84]

Kerr reported "that she suffered humiliation and severe emotional distress from the videotape and the gossip surrounding it," which "affected her academic performance" and "made it difficult for her to relate to men." She began psychological counseling,[85] and a psychologist concluded that she had post-traumatic stress disorder.[86]

Kerr sued Boyles, Broesche, and Broesche's two accomplices for negligent infliction of emotional distress. The jury agreed that all four men had been grossly negligent. It awarded Kerr $500,000 in actual damages and $500,000 in punitive damages, with $350,000 of the punitive damages levied against Boyles.[87] Boyles was the only defendant to appeal.[88]

The Texas Supreme Court denied Kerr recovery in 1993, holding that the court would not recognize "negligent infliction of emotional distress as an independent cause of action."[89] The court conceded that Boyles's behavior had been "truly egregious" and "that Kerr's injuries were not a trifle." Yet the court nonetheless ruled against Kerr on the theory that permitting the jury's award to stand would create a slippery slope that would ultimately place more ordinary miscreants in legal jeopardy for "conduct far less outrageous than that involved here." The court proclaimed "that tort law cannot and should not attempt to provide redress for every instance of rude, insensitive or distasteful behavior, even though it may result in hurt feelings, embarrassment, or even humiliation."[90]

The court never explained how ruling for Kerr would lead to successful lawsuits for mere rudeness, or why protecting rudeness, insensitivity, and distastefulness was so important. But the court took it to be common sense that the law needed to prioritize shielding ordinary wrongdoers from tort liability. On the court's account, it was better to deny Kerr access to a cause of action that would provide her with redress for Boyles's admittedly egregious deceit than to risk creating a precedent that might interfere with everyday humiliation.

Protecting Ordinary Intimate Deception When Regulating Beyond Intimacy

Courts are so determined to protect everyday intimate deception that they have reasoned from that baseline when deciding cases with defendants who deceived government officials or business rivals. Judges have used the premise that ordinary intimate deceivers should not be vulnerable to legal penalties as a reason to reject or narrow statutes reaching far beyond courtship, sex, and marriage, such as a law criminalizing false claims about military awards and a law protecting against computer fraud and abuse.

Let's start with the 2012 Supreme Court opinions in *United States v. Alvarez* holding that the Stolen Valor Act was inconsistent with the First Amendment's protection for free speech.[91] This statute established federal criminal penalties for falsely claiming "to have been awarded any decoration or medal authorized by Congress for the Armed Forces of the United States."[92] Federal prosecutors indicted Xavier Alvarez under the Stolen Valor Act because he lied about having won the Medal of Honor,[93] "the highest military award for valor against an enemy force."[94] Alvarez pled guilty, while reserving his right to challenge the statute's constitutionality.[95]

Alvarez told the lie that triggered his prosecution at a public meeting of a California water district board. He was a member of that board and the audience for his falsehood presumably included the other board members along with any members of the public attending the government meeting. Alvarez's prosecution did not rest on evidence about whether he had ever lied to an intimate by falsely claiming military decorations.[96] Nonetheless, the judicial opinions reviewing Alvarez's case as it wound through the federal courts repeatedly condemned the Stolen Valor Act on the theory that upholding the law would permit criminal prosecutions for deception within intimate relationships.[97] That pattern held in the Supreme Court. Both the four-Justice plurality opinion and the two-Justice concurring opinion that found the Stolen Valor Act unconstitutional dwelled on intimate deception.

The plurality's argument that the Stolen Valor Act violated the First Amendment importantly turned on the claim that the statute placed ordinary intimate deceivers in legal jeopardy. The plurality read the statute as reaching beyond lies "made in a public meeting" to "apply with equal force to personal, whispered conversations within a home." The plurality seemed to take for granted that Congress could not hold people criminally liable for lying to their intimates about their military honors, declaring that "the sweeping, quite unprecedented reach of the statute puts it in conflict with the First Amendment." In the plurality's view, the hypothetical possibility that the federal government could successfully prosecute commonplace intimate deception under the Stolen Valor Act demonstrated that Congress had overreached its constitutional authority.[98]

Justice Stephen Breyer's concurrence echoed the plurality. He agreed that the Stolen Valor Act applied to intimate deception and took that as telling evidence that the statute was unconstitutionally overbroad. Where the plurality had simply assumed that the law should protect intimate deception about military honors, Breyer offered a reason for shielding such deceit. He wrote that "[a]s written, [the Stolen Valor Act] applies in family, social, or other private contexts, *where lies will often cause little harm.*" Breyer cited no evidentiary basis for that empirical assertion, presenting it as a matter of common sense.[99]

Investigating intimate deception readily reveals how lies about military honors can inflict injury. Recall (from Chapter 4) Frederick Renz, Jr., who allegedly lied to his fiancée and then wife, Debra Summers, about his military awards (among other matters), falsely claiming to be a decorated war hero and a recipient of the Medal of Honor. Summers reported that Renz's lies about military decorations and other signs of good character induced her to marry him, stay married to him, and use her assets, earnings, and inheritance on his behalf when she would have acted otherwise if she had known the truth.[100] Similarly, remember (from Chapter 1) William Barber—the "Don Juan of con" in the *New York Post*'s immortal prose[101]—who had been imprisoned for deserting the Army, but falsely claimed to be a war hero as he lured women into purported marriages, betrayed their trust, and stripped them of their assets.[102]

However, no member of the Court was interested in exploring how intimate deception about military honors can inflict harm. Instead, all six Justices voting to strike down the Stolen Valor Act reasoned from the unquestioned assumption that the law should protect ordinary intimate deceivers.

The United States Court of Appeals for the Ninth Circuit began from the same premise in narrowly interpreting the Computer Fraud and Abuse Act (CFAA). *United States v. Nosal*[103] reviewed the federal government's indictment of David Nosal under a provision of the CFAA that authorizes federal criminal penalties against "[w]hoever" "knowingly and with intent to defraud, accesses a protected computer without authorization, or exceeds authorized access, and by means of such conduct furthers the intended fraud and obtains anything of value, unless the object of the fraud and the thing obtained consists only of the use of the computer and the value of such use is not more than $5,000 in any 1-year period."[104]

Nosal had decided to start an executive search firm that would compete with his former employer, Korn/Ferry. He enlisted some former colleagues who were still at Korn/Ferry. These colleagues downloaded confidential information from a database on the Korn/Ferry computer system and gave it to Nosal.[105] Korn/Ferry had authorized Nosal's accomplices to access this database in the course of doing their work for the company, but prohibited them from divulging confidential data.[106]

The federal government argued that Nosal had violated the CFAA because his accomplices "exceed[ed]" their "authorized access" to the Korn/Ferry computers when they used those computers to extract confidential information for a competitor. On the government's reading of the statute, the CFAA's statutory language about exceeding authorized access applied "to someone who has unrestricted physical access to a computer, but is limited in the use to which he can put the information. For example, an employee may be authorized to access customer lists in order to do his job but not to send them to a competitor."[107]

The en banc Ninth Circuit rejected the government's argument in 2012,[108] holding that Nosal could not be prosecuted under the CFAA for his accomplices' misuse of the Korn/Ferry computer system.[109] The court interpreted the statute "narrowly," insisting that the term "exceeds authorized access" refers only to "hacking"—accessing information that the person is not authorized to access for any reason.[110]

The Ninth Circuit's decision to limit the CFAA's reach was inextricably linked to the court's assumption that the law should and would safeguard ordinary intimate deception. The phrase "exceeds authorized access" appears multiple times in the CFAA, and the court contended that the phrase must have the same meaning each time.[111] The court argued that accepting the government's interpretation of this phrase in Nosal's case would allow federal prosecutors in future cases to use another part of the CFAA to pursue ordinary intimate deceivers on the ground that they exceeded their authorized access to a website when they violated the site's terms of use by knowingly posting false information about themselves on the site.[112]

Nosal emphasized the pervasiveness of intimate deception online, while highlighting examples meant to make the practice seem innocuous. The court explained that although "numerous dating websites" have "terms of use" prohibiting "inaccurate or misleading information,"[113] "[l]ying on social media websites is common: People shave years off their age, add inches to their height and drop pounds from their weight."[114]

With the ordinariness of intimate deception made vivid, the Ninth Circuit took it as given that the government's statutory interpretation was implausible if it would threaten such commonplace deceit. There is little reason to think that federal prosecutors enforcing the CFAA would be eager to indict ordinary daters for lying about their appearance. But the court wrote as if the federal government was intent on such prosecutions, warning: "Under the government's proposed interpretation of the CFAA, . . . describing yourself as 'tall, dark and handsome,' when you're actually short and homely, will earn you a handsome orange jumpsuit."[115]

Even the dissenting judges agreed that the law should protect commonplace intimate deception. Rather than dispute that premise, the dissenting opinion insisted that Nosal's prosecution did not threaten the security of ordinary intimate deceivers. The dissent stressed the commercial nature of Nosal's wrongdoing and the significant economic injury he sought to inflict on his former employer. Here's how the dissent began: "This case has nothing to do with playing sudoku, checking email, *fibbing on dating sites*, or any of the other activities that the majority *rightly values*. It has everything to do with stealing an employer's valuable information to set up a competing business with the purloined data, siphoned away from the victim, knowing such access and use were prohibited in the defendants' employment contracts."[116]

Neither the majority nor the dissent in *Nosal* explained the value of safeguarding commonplace intimate deception. They assumed that value as a given and used this baseline to guide their interpretation of a statute that reached far beyond intimacy. Nosal, like Alvarez, was prosecuted for conduct that did not involve deceit within an intimate relationship. But both men avoided penalties they were facing because courts were concerned about even the hypothetical possibility of jeopardizing ordinary intimate deceivers.

In sum, courts routinely demonstrate a deep, if often unexplained, determination to protect commonplace deception in intimate relationships. Courts accept many forms of deceit as ordinary and expected in courtship, sexual relationships, and marriage and help make that so—normalizing the deception by shielding it from legal redress and condemnation. Courts are sometimes willing to provide remedies for intimate deception that judges consider deviant and abnormal, but they make clear that more typical deceit is not at issue. Moreover, even an extraordinary intimate deceiver can benefit from the judicial commitment to preserving the status quo. Courts worry about slippery slopes and protect unusually egregious deceit to avoid creating precedents that might ultimately threaten more ordinary deceivers. Indeed, judges are so committed to the premise that the law should safeguard commonplace intimate deception that they reason from that baseline when deciding cases whose impact extends well beyond intimate life.

7

Intimate Deception Outside of Romantic, Sexual, or Marital Relationships

The preceding chapters in this part have focused on deceit within romantic, sexual, and marital relationships. This chapter turns to types of intimate deception that have been even less explored, focusing on cases involving family members who are not each other's spouses, sexual partners, or romantic interests.

The assumption that courts need to protect intimate deceivers from legal consequences is still visible in this context, but it appears almost exclusively in judicial decisions considering parents who have deceived their children—including their adult children. Courts are frequently unwilling to penalize parents for their deceit and inclined to blame children for having been duped. In fact, judges sometimes write as if parents have a legal prerogative to deceive their children and keep that right even after their children become legal adults. In contrast, courts are often eager to order redress when adult children have duped their parents, and courts grant parents wide-ranging authority to impose their own punishments on deceptive children who are still minors.

Exploring intimate deception outside of romance, sex, and marriage also reveals significant boundaries on judicial understandings of intimacy. As we have seen, judges thinking about deception within romantic and/or sexual relationships frequently define intimacy expansively, classifying people as intimates when they did not know each other well. But judges tend to define intimacy narrowly when considering deceit within familial relationships, excluding family members other than spouses, parents, and children. Courts routinely treat deceitful relatives not connected by marriage or parenthood—such as siblings, aunts, uncles, nieces, and nephews—as if these family members were unrelated to the people they duped.

Parents Deceiving Children

The law gives parents tremendous control over their children, including when parents exercise that power in ways that may undercut their children's best interests. The legal authority that parents wield over their minor children's custody, education, employment, safety, and punishment is fairly well-known.[1] Much less attention has focused on how the law protects parents when they lie to their children or otherwise intentionally mislead them. Without attracting much notice, judges sometimes decide cases as if parental prerogatives include the right to deceive. While a parent's prerogatives generally end when a competent child reaches the age of majority, courts have shielded parental deception even when that deception extends into or begins during the child's adulthood.

Let's begin with a historical example and then turn to some more recent cases. The Minnesota Supreme Court in 1924 dismissed Susanna Miller's suit against John and Susanna Pelzer, which charged that the defendants had "procured [Miller's] labor and services" through "fraud and deception."[2] Miller explained that the Pelzers had raised her from infancy and that she had remained on their farm for almost seven years after becoming a legal adult, not leaving to marry until she was nearly twenty-five.[3] Miller reported that the Pelzers had duped her into believing that she was their biological child when she was actually their foster child and the Pelzers had received money from the county to care for her until she reached eighteen.[4] She contended that the Pelzers had never told her the truth, but had confided in Miller's husband before he married her, while asking him to keep Miller in the dark. Miller's husband reportedly shared the secret with his wife when she was almost thirty-four years old.[5]

The Pelzers may have thought they were protecting Miller by deceiving her about their biological and legal relationship—although their failure to adopt Miller is puzzling if they really were committed to protecting her. In any event, the Minnesota Supreme Court was convinced that Miller was "better served" when she was not "told the truth." The court dwelled on the stigma associated with Miller's "illegitimacy" and "unknown parentage."[6] That stigma was undeniably powerful in this era. But Miller—like many people subject to paternalistic deception—did not agree that the deception served her interests.

Her suit maintained that the Pelzers' deceit had denied her the opportunity to make informed choices about where to live and work once she became a legal adult. Miller argued "that it was the legal duty of [the Pelzers] on her eighteenth birthday to disclose to her the fact that she was not their natural daughter."[7] She asserted that she had worked for the Pelzers for free after reaching adulthood and had delayed marriage because the Pelzers had duped her into thinking that they were her biological parents. Miller estimated that her nearly seven years of uncompensated adult labor on the Pelzers' farm—"a woman's work in the house and a man's work in the field"—were worth a total of $2500, and she sought that amount in damages.[8] Her claim illuminated how parental deception can circumvent limits on other parental prerogatives. The Pelzers could no longer directly control Miller's labor once she became an adult, but Miller maintained that the Pelzers' deceit enabled them to expropriate her labor nonetheless.

The unanimous Minnesota Supreme Court emphasized in reviewing Miller's suit that it would never permit children to sue their parents "for personal injuries suffered" while a child was still under the age of majority.[9] In fact, *Miller v. Pelzer* was one of the earliest judicial opinions announcing a common law doctrine of parental tort immunity, which shielded parents from tort liability for harming their minor children through intentional conduct or negligence.[10] Of course, such a pronouncement hardly decided Miller's case. Miller did not fault the Pelzers for duping her while she was young. Her complaint focused exclusively on what happened after she became a legal adult.

The court rejected Miller's fraud claim in two steps. The opinion began by making clear that the Pelzers would receive the same judicial deference granted to "natural parents." To be sure, the Pelzers were not Miller's biological or legal parents. Indeed, Miller's lawsuit rested on that fact. But the court declared that "[t]his family relation for all practical purposes was just as sacred as if plaintiff had been the natural daughter."[11]

With that asserted, the court quickly concluded that the Pelzers were free to deceive Miller into adulthood and had no obligation to compensate Miller for the injuries their deceit reportedly inflicted. As the court announced, it was "largely within the discretion of the foster parents" to decide whether they would reveal their legal status or intentionally misrepresent themselves. While the court used the caveat "largely," the opinion did not identify any actual limits on parental prerogatives to deceive. Even if Miller had provided the Pelzers with unpaid labor only because the Pelzers deliberately misrepresented their blood connection, the Pelzers did not need to pay Miller for her work.[12]

Modern courts have continued to protect a parent's prerogative to deceive his child—including his adult child—about matters of vital significance. Consider Dawn Harkness's unsuccessful 1997 suit against her parents, Lawrence and Kathleen Fitzgerald.[13] Harkness contended that her father physically, emotionally, and sexually abused her from the ages of two to sixteen, and that both parents deceived her so she would not report the abuse. She explained that she had repressed all memories of the sexual abuse and that her parents had intentionally misled her into believing that the physical and emotional abuse was legitimate "punishment" that her father had a right to inflict.[14] She also reported that her mother "often blamed" her for the abuse.[15] According to Harkness, her parents never told her the truth, even when she was an adult.[16] However, she eventually realized what her parents had "fraudulently concealed from her" and sued her father for assault and battery and both parents for intentional and negligent infliction of emotional distress.[17]

Like Miller's claim, Harkness's complaint illustrates how deception can enable parents to circumvent limits on their authority. The Fitzgeralds had no right to abuse their daughter, but Harkness contended that her parents' deceit allowed them to continue their abuse for much of her childhood—without apparently ever being arrested or prosecuted—and to avoid legal liability after she reached adulthood.[18] Harkness argued that her parents had a legal obligation "to disclose their wrongdoing" to her and that their deceit had delayed her litigation.[19] The Maine Supreme Judicial Court flatly rejected Harkness's argument, however, holding unanimously that the Fitzgeralds had no "duty to disclose" the truth to their adult daughter and were free to deceive her.[20]

A New Jersey Superior Court was likewise eager to protect parents' freedom to deceive. A group of adult adoptees sued the state to challenge the constitutionality of New Jersey laws that placed the original birth certificates of adopted children under seal and barred adoptees from seeing their own birth records unless a court agreed that the adoptee had "good cause" to view the information.[21] These laws denied adoptees the automatic access to their birth records that other adults and children had "as a matter of course."[22] The plaintiffs argued that the statutory provisions violated their "constitutionally protected right to privacy and to receive important information" and denied them "equal protection of the law."[23] The court in *Mills v. Atlantic City Department of Vital Statistics* (1977) rejected this constitutional challenge.[24]

Mills repeatedly asserted the importance of safeguarding the prerogatives of parents to deceive their children, including their adult children. The court presumed that many parents who had surrendered a child for adoption and later raised other children had deliberately misled the children they kept so those children would not know they had a biological full or half-sibling who was adopted away. Indeed, the court assumed that a birth parent's desire to maintain that false impression would be the key reason why she would not want her adopted away child to find her. The reappearance of a surrendered child would threaten to reveal the truth to the birth parent's family members, including her adult children.

The court took for granted that the law should place enormous value on shielding such deceit from discovery. The court rejected the adoptees' privacy argument, but described a birth parent's prerogative to deceive to hide an adoption as falling within a zone of privacy that was statutorily and constitutionally protected.[25] As *Mills* explained, "[i]t is highly likely that [a birth parent] has chosen not to reveal to his or her spouse, children or other relations, friends or associates the facts of an emotionally upsetting and potentially socially unacceptable occurrence 18 or more years ago. This natural parent has a right to privacy, a right to be let alone, that is not only expressly assured by the provisions of [the challenged New Jersey laws] but has also been recognized as a vital interest by the United States Supreme Court."[26]

The court recounted Florence Fisher's testimony to illustrate the importance of protecting parental deception about adoption. Fisher was an adult adoptee and the founder of the Adoptees' Liberty Movement Association (ALMA),[27] which sought to establish the right of adult adoptees to have "free access to [their] original birth certificates and the records of [their] adoption."[28] She had spent much of her life trying to learn the truth about her adoption. Fisher's adoptive parents had repeatedly lied to her to deny that she was adopted, and she was already an adult before another relative confirmed what she had long suspected.[29] Fisher then set out to locate her birth mother, but her adoption file was sealed.[30] Finding her birth mother took twenty years of searching in which the law was an enormous obstacle.[31] After their reunion, Fisher discovered that her birth mother wanted to maintain the illusion that she had never placed a child for adoption by continuing to deceive her husband and two other children— Fisher's biological half-siblings—to conceal Fisher's existence.[32] Here's how the *Mills* court described what happened next: "after waiting a period of 4½ years for her mother to 'do the honorable thing' and inform the family, Ms. Fisher decided that she had an absolute right to approach her half brother and reveal her identity to him. She did in fact do so. Although her encounter had a positive result, such an action in direct disregard of the wishes of the natural parent is an invasion of that parent's privacy." One might take this example as evidence that siblings separated by adoption can forge constructive connections if they meet in adulthood. But the court presented the testimony as a cautionary tale that demonstrated how granting adoptees "unlimited access" to their birth records "may result in unwarranted intrusions," where "the interference of the adoptee" hampers the birth parent's ability to continue to mislead her other children.[33]

None of this is to deny that a birth parent can have powerful reasons for wanting to make her intimates think that she has never placed a child for adoption. Keeping an adoption secret can spare a birth parent the emotional pain that might come from discussing the adoption. Deceit to conceal an adoption could also be an example of paternalistic deception, where a birth parent deceives because she believes—rightly or wrongly—that her family will be happier and more content not knowing that they have a biological relative who was adopted away. In addition or alternatively, deceit to hide an adoption could be a form of deception from subordination. A birth parent may intentionally mislead her intimates because she fears being stigmatized, shamed, and shunned—whether for having a child outside of marriage, for surrendering a child, or both.

That said, protecting such deception can inflict significant harm. The plaintiffs were adult adoptees, meaning they had already waited at least eighteen years to learn about their biological origins. They testified about the deep psychological and emotional injuries they experienced when blocked from knowing the identities of their biological parents and prevented from pursuing potential connections with their biological family members.[34] Indeed, they argued "that as adults the information regarding their natural parents is part of their identity as human beings."[35] The children who never knew about their adopted away siblings also lost any chance to connect with those siblings, although they would remain unaware of that loss if their parents' deceit was successful. In short, upholding parents' prerogatives to deceive their children can have a steep price.

The New Jersey Superior Court in *Mills* focused on protecting parents who had deceived their intimates to hide that they had surrendered a child for adoption. The New Jersey Supreme Court was equally interested in shielding parental prerogatives to deceive, but focused on parents adopting a child. The Supreme Court in 1981 interpreted a New Jersey law regulating the new birth certificates that children received when adopted. This law provided that the new birth certificates would list the adoptive parent(s), the child's adoptive name, and the child's date and place of birth.[36]

In re Adoption of a Child by L.C. considered the portion of a new birth certificate that identified the adopted child's birthplace. New Jersey law permitted the listing of a false birthplace—where the adoptive parent(s) lived at the time of the adoption, rather than where the child really was born—so long as the child was actually born somewhere in the United States, the adoptive parents lived in New Jersey at the time of the adoption, and a court agreed with the adoptive parents that there was "good cause" for listing a false birthplace.[37]

A statute authorizing knowingly inaccurate information on official documents is unusual, to say the least. But New Jersey lawmakers were willing to allow false records in order to help adoptive parents deceive their children. As the court noted, the provision on false birthplaces was "intended as a means of concealing the fact of adoption from the adopted child and anyone else who sees the birth certificate."[38]

The New Jersey Supreme Court wholeheartedly endorsed the legislature's commitment to protecting and enabling deception by adoptive parents. The court's interpretation of the statute's "good cause" requirement was meant to facilitate such deceit, with the court declaring "that a finding of good cause will be the rule, not the exception, when a child is adopted at such an early age that he is unaware of his adoption." On the court's reading, the "desire of parents to exercise control over the circumstances in which an adopted child learns that she was adopted is 'good cause' for ordering a change of birthplace." This statement implied that adoptive parents would eventually tell their children they were adopted. But neither the statute nor the court placed any obligation on adoptive parents to share the truth with their children. Choosing whether to communicate "the fact of adoption" was a "parental decision."[39] Adoptive parents were free to deceive their children, even after their children became legal adults.

The court identified only one situation where other legislative priorities would constrain adoptive parents' prerogatives to deceive. It explained that New Jersey's birth certificates for children adopted internationally needed to list the children's actual birthplaces—not to protect these children from deceptive parents, but to prevent interference "with the federal government's methods for proving citizenship" because federal law expects people born outside the United States "to have birth certificates indicating their real place of birth."[40]

As we have seen, courts making parental prerogative arguments to shield deception focus on parental discretion and authority. Judges uphold parents' decisionmaking, even when parents choose to deceive their children—including their adult children—about matters that are crucially important to the children, the parents, or both. Another set of arguments that courts invoke to protect deceptive parents from legal consequences focuses on blaming deceived children for having trusted their parents. The law generally assumes and endorses children's tendency to have faith in their parents, which helps create strong bonds of love, care, and mutual support. But when a child seeks redress for the harm a deceptive parent has inflicted, judges often discount children's propensity to trust and write as if the law should discourage such reliance.[41]

Let's start with John Collins, Sr., and his three adult sons, Jack, Robert, and Thomas, who shared a family brunch on the first Easter after John lost his wife and the sons lost their mother.[42] John used the occasion to summon each son one-by-one into the kitchen for a private conversation/confrontation.[43] He insisted that his sons sign a document "for the bank," but would not let them read it.[44] The sons questioned their father, but he refused to elaborate and "harshly persisted" in his demand.[45] Each son signed the document that day. The oldest and youngest sons signed because that was what their father wanted.[46] The middle son signed "because his father was so upset and hostile, and because Robert, at least on this morning, did not want to argue the point."[47] The sons learned about their father's deceit after his death around a decade later, when they discovered that they had unknowingly signed a deed giving away their partial ownership of the family home. The sons sued to challenge the deed's validity and lost.[48]

The trial judge found that John "did intentionally misrepresent the nature of the document which he asked (or more accurately, demanded) his sons to sign."[49] The judge further found that all the sons "no doubt trusted their father,"[50] and that the youngest son—"known affectionately in the family as Meathead"—thought of "his father as the ruler."[51] John had also shrewdly chosen to trick his sons on a day when they would be especially infused with feelings of love, respect, obedience, and conciliation. As the plaintiffs noted, they were "cheated by their father on the first Easter after their mother's death, in the presence of their wives and children."[52]

Nonetheless, the trial judge held that it "was not reasonable" for the sons to rely on their father's misrepresentation "that the document was for the bank."[53] The Massachusetts Appeals Court unanimously affirmed in 2003.[54] The courts faulted the sons for complying with their father's demand that they sign—without reading—the document he presented.[55] The legal burden was on the sons to verify what their father told them, rather than on their father to refrain from intentional misrepresentation. In the eyes of the law, the sons were wrong to trust their father. When they did trust him, they had no remedy for the injuries their father's deceit inflicted.

The Tennessee Court of Appeals relied on similar arguments in 2008 while rejecting Annette Hanna's suit against her father, Scott Sheflin. Hanna was in a car accident when she was approximately eighteen and "sustained serious and debilitating injuries." She spent two years recuperating in her parents' home before leaving to marry. While she was still recovering with her parents, Hanna received a sixty-three thousand dollar settlement from the driver of the car in which she had been riding. She entrusted those funds to her father. Hanna knew that her father spent some of the settlement money to cover her medical bills and to buy her a car,[56] but also "knew her father was still in possession of a substantial amount of her settlement proceeds when she moved out of her parents' home."[57]

Hanna was trusting and initially did not ask about the remaining settlement money.[58] She reported that her parents lied to her when she did inquire. Hanna testified that she asked about the money approximately nine years after leaving home only to have her mother tell her that "the funds were being held in an investment account for her benefit."[59] Hanna wrote her parents about three years later "after hearing a rumor that her parents had spent all of the money." She contacted a lawyer when her parents did not reply. The attorney wrote Hanna's father, and her father responded by contending that he had spent all the settlement money in paying Hanna's medical bills and buying her car. When Hanna (or her lawyer) investigated, however, Hanna learned that her father's assertions were false.[60] As Hanna's parents later admitted to the court, thirty thousand dollars of settlement funds had remained after the medical bills and car purchase, and Hanna's parents had kept this money for themselves.[61] Hanna sued her parents for conversion and charged that they had deceived her "to fraudulently conceal their wrongful actions."[62] The trial court dismissed her case, and Hanna appealed the dismissal of her suit against her father.[63]

She lost.[64] The unanimous appellate court held that the three-year statute of limitations on her conversion claim began running the moment Hanna left her parents' home to marry.[65] Even if Hanna's father did everything Hanna reported, his deceit was insufficient to trigger the doctrine providing that the court will toll the limitations period when the defendant fraudulently concealed the cause of action against him.[66] As a practical matter, it seems exceedingly unrealistic to suppose that a young adult who had just spent two years recuperating with her parents would be sufficiently independent of her parents—not to mention savvy and wary enough—to demand that her father "make an accounting and deliver the remaining funds to her" right after she left her parents' home.[67] To the contrary, one would expect a young adult in such a situation to have enormous faith and confidence in her parents. Indeed, the legal system typically seeks to encourage such trust, which can promote children's flourishing and strengthen their bonds with their parents. Would Hanna have recuperated as well if she had suspected that her parents might defraud her?

Nevertheless, the Tennessee Court of Appeals blamed Hanna for not promptly investigating her father, faulting this trusting daughter for not devoting more "care and diligence" to "discovering her father's alleged conversion of the funds."[68] The court's decision functioned to reward deceit. Hanna's father may have used strategic silence to deceive his daughter into thinking that he had not taken her money—and he admittedly lied when confronted—but he bore no legal responsibility for pocketing Hanna's funds because he managed to keep her in the dark for long enough.

Of course, judges do not always refuse to hold parents responsible for injuries they inflict on their children by deceiving them. Deceptive parents sometimes lose in court. But the judiciary's reluctance to provide redress is often palpable and courts tend to rule for deceived children in limited circumstances. For instance, courts are notably more inclined to hold deceptive parents liable when the parents perpetuated their deceit with the help of deep-pocketed third parties and those third parties are likely to be the source of any money damages the child actually collects.[69]

Michelle Tucek's suit against her father, Garlan Mueller, and the people and companies who reportedly helped him deceive and defraud her is illustrative.[70] When Tucek was nineteen, she was a passenger in a one-car accident that left her comatose for eight days and hospitalized for six weeks.[71] The driver's insurance policy authorized paying up to one hundred thousand dollars in claims. The insurer retained an adjusting company to investigate and negotiate a settlement with Tucek.[72]

The insurance adjuster arrived while Tucek was still "in a neurology ward, physically and mentally incapacitated."[73] Mueller's finances were in a shambles at the time, and he seized the chance to profit at his daughter's expense.[74] Mueller told the adjuster that he would negotiate Tucek's claim on her behalf and the two men swiftly settled the claim for seventy thousand dollars, thirty thousand below the maximum payout Tucek could have received from the driver's insurer.[75]

Mueller did not have the legal authority to make decisions for his adult daughter.[76] Nonetheless, Mueller never informed Tucek about what he was doing and never received her permission to proceed. She did not know settlement negotiations were underway, much less concluded.[77] The insurance adjuster knew that Mueller was in "economic dire straits" and anxious to settle Tucek's claim quickly, and the adjuster appears to have taken advantage of that knowledge to settle Tucek's claim for less.[78] The adjuster bargained only with Mueller and never consulted Tucek.[79]

After Mueller and the insurance adjuster reached an agreement, Mueller needed Tucek's signature on a release form to finalize the deal.[80] Mueller reportedly forged his daughter's signature on the release.[81] Mueller told a notary at his bank that Tucek was waiting outside and the notary was willing to act illegally by notarizing Tucek's supposed signature without seeing her.[82] The notary knew that Tucek had recently been comatose and that Mueller had "cash flow problems" and owed the bank money.[83]

Mueller's deceit continued. He managed to take his daughter and the notarized release to the insurance adjuster's office so they could collect the settlement money. It is not clear what Mueller said or did to get Tucek there. Tucek went to the bank afterward and thought she was depositing the settlement checks into personal savings and checking accounts from which only she could make withdrawals. Neither Mueller nor the bank told her that they had arranged matters so that the accounts Tucek believed were hers alone were actually joint accounts that authorized Mueller to write checks as well. Mueller spent Tucek's money for his own purposes, writing checks for thousands of dollars.[84]

Mueller used some of the money he purloined from his daughter to pay off a past due loan he had at the same bank (for his bowling alley). He also bought himself a van and treated himself to "a grand vacation to Florida." It is unclear how much, if any, money was left for Tucek after she paid more than thirty thousand dollars in medical bills.[85]

Tucek eventually learned about her father's scheme. She sued her father for fraud, deceit, and conversion, and also brought fraud and deceit claims against the bank, the notary, the insurer, the adjusting company, and the insurance adjuster who negotiated with Mueller rather than Tucek.[86]

The trial court found Mueller liable for $230,400 in damages and he did not appeal.[87] The South Dakota Supreme Court in 1994 expressed unmitigated support for Tucek's litigation against her father. The Supreme Court repeatedly described Tucek as "an innocent victim" and Mueller as a scoundrel who had behaved "unscrupulously" and "defrauded his own daughter."[88] The court also held that Tucek could pursue her suit against the various other defendants and go before a jury to seek damages for their fraud and deceit.[89]

One factor that surely fueled the Supreme Court's enthusiasm for Tucek's suit is the sheer outrageousness of her father's scheme. Mueller took advantage of his daughter's grievous misfortune to negotiate an inadequate settlement without her knowledge and then stole the money from her.

In addition, Tucek's litigation may have appeared less threatening to parental prerogatives because she had her mother's support and assistance. Tucek's mother had told the insurance adjuster that it would be "several years" before Tucek could settle her claim.[90] After the adjuster and Mueller came to an agreement anyway, Tucek's mother found out that Mueller had settled Tucek's claim for below the insurance policy's limit, with the help of Tucek's forged signature on the release.[91] Tucek's suit did not feature a child challenging the unified judgment and decisionmaking of her parents. It pitted the good sense of one parent against the nefariousness of the other.

Perhaps most importantly, Tucek's suit was ultimately directed more at the people and companies that helped her father perpetrate his deceit than at Mueller himself. Mueller did not contest his daughter's suit. She won a default judgment against him, rather than a litigated judgment that required prevailing over his arguments and defenses.[92] One likely reason for Mueller's passivity is that he was probably judgment proof by the time Tucek sued, meaning that he was not too worried about being subject to a damages award because he knew he had no money left to lose. Tucek's chances of actually collecting much, if any, money from her father were probably equivalent to the likelihood of wringing blood from a stone. As a practical matter, Tucek's suit appears to have been aimed at winning damages from the third parties whose actions facilitated her father's scheme because those third parties had the resources to pay an award. The sole dissenting Justice emphasized this aspect of the litigation. The dissenter agreed that Mueller was a "villain," but argued that "this court should not open up the vaults of the bank or the insurance company to pay for his despicable conduct in converting his daughter's settlement for his personal use."[93]

In short, courts are willing in some contexts to hold parents legally responsible for injuries they inflict by deceiving their children. But it helps if third parties are on the hook at least as much as, or more than, the deceitful parent himself. Courts are inclined to protect parents who deceive their children—including their adult children—and prone to blame children for having been deceived. Indeed, judges sometimes write as if parents have a legal prerogative to dupe their children, one that persists into the children's adulthood.

Children Deceiving Parents

At least in theory, the law embraces symmetrical norms in governing deception within romantic, sexual, and marital relationships. Courts are not supposed to treat deceptive girlfriends more harshly than deceptive boyfriends, or deceptive wives more harshly than deceptive husbands. The judiciary will not always achieve such equity, but it is supposed to be a goal. In contrast, courts manifestly treat children who have deceived their parents more severely than parents who have deceived their children. This imbalance is commonly presumed and often explicit. The asymmetry begins when deceptive children are below the age of majority, when the law routinely assumes and enforces a hierarchical relationship between parent and child. However, the harsher treatment of deceptive children persists after children reach maturity, when children and parents are both independent legal adults. Let's first consider deceptive minor children and then turn to adult children's deceit.

Not surprisingly, parents rarely, if ever, sue their minor children for injuries inflicted through deception. Few minor children have any financial resources of their own, and there are obvious obstacles to holding minor children civilly liable for their behavior toward their parents when the law generally recognizes that minors cannot be held fully responsible for their actions because of their immaturity.

Instead, the legal system protects parents whose minor children deceive them by empowering parents to impose their own penalties. The parent of a minor child has wide-ranging authority to restrict his child's movements,[94] switch his child's school,[95] and inflict other punishments that deceived people are usually unable to impose. Moreover, parents can cast their children out once the children reach legal adulthood.[96] A young adult without her parents' financial and emotional support often faces grim prospects, and children who are deceiving their parents have reported that they expect and fear that their parents would throw them out if they discovered the deceit.[97] These powerful tools can help parents guide their children in better directions—in part by giving children concrete incentives to avoid displeasing their parents. But parents enjoy these prerogatives even when they exercise them in ways that may be contrary to their children's best interests.

Parents also have a right to resort to violence in response to a minor child's deceit, a legal prerogative that other private individuals—including deceived children—do not have when they discover that they have been deliberately misled. Courts routinely hold that parents are entitled to inflict reasonable corporal punishment on a deceptive minor child, while defining reasonableness expansively.

Consider the Hawaii Supreme Court decision concluding that Ijeva Matavale was within her rights to strike her fourteen-year-old daughter multiple times because the child had deceived her.[98] Matavale's daughter was performing poorly in high school and began receiving tutoring to help.[99] But the girl (whom the court kept anonymous) soon began lying to her mother to hide that she was regularly skipping tutoring to spend time at a mall with her friends. After a few months, the child received another abysmal report card.[100] She deliberately left the report card at school and lied to her mother about it that afternoon, pretending that she had forgotten to take the report card home.[101]

Matavale was suspicious and questioned her daughter, who eventually confessed to lying about the tutoring and the report card.[102] Matavale used violence during and after this interrogation. She hit her daughter repeatedly on the arm and hand with objects that were nearby: "a plastic backpack," "a plastic hanger," "a small car brush," and "an unspecified tool." Matavale believed her daughter "was dishonest, and felt deceived."[103]

The child stayed out of school afterward, first at her mother's direction and then with her mother's permission. Matavale appears to have been worried about school authorities seeing her daughter's injured arm. The child did not return to school until six days after the violence. Even then, her arm was still visibly injured. The school called the police.[104] After a three-day trial, a jury found that Matavale had abused her daughter.[105]

The Hawaii Supreme Court reversed Matavale's conviction in 2007,[106] holding that Matavale's violent response to her daughter's deceit fell within parental prerogatives.[107] The opinion emphasized that the deceitful child had flouted her mother's rightful authority, and the court accepted violence as a permissible means of steering children toward obedience and respect. Matavale had "disciplined" her daughter "for her continuously defiant behavior in refusing to answer [Matavale's] questions and in lying to her."[108] As the opinion elaborated, "the uncontroverted evidence demonstrates that Daughter had been lying to [Matavale] for about two and a half months, telling [Matavale] she was attending her tutoring classes when, in fact, she was hanging out at the mall with her friends without supervision. Daughter lied to [Matavale] about forgetting her report card at school when, in fact, she 'purposely' left her report card at school because of her low grades. Daughter repeatedly refused to answer [Matavale's] questions concerning her report card, the reasons for the grades not improving, and whether she was attending her tutoring classes. Given these circumstances, it would not be unreasonable for a parent in [Matavale's] position to conclude that Daughter needed disciplining for lying to, misleading, and disrespecting her mother."[109] In short, Matavale was well within her rights to respond to her daughter's deceitfulness with violence.

Two Justices dissented, arguing for more deference to the jury's fact-finding.[110] But even the Justice who wrote the dissent stressed her empathy for parents who react violently to their minor children's deceit, making plain that she felt "discomfort with condemning [Matavale] for her actions in the present case. Most assuredly, even the most pious of parents are susceptible to the unique aggravation caused by the disrespect, disobedience, or deception of their offspring, capable of triggering an uncharacteristic parental reaction."[111] The child had defied her mother by deceiving her and even the dissent was reluctant to condemn a violent rejoinder.

The Pennsylvania Commonwealth Court similarly held in 2005 that William Smith had acted within his legal authority when he responded to the deceit of his fourteen-year-old daughter, J.S., by striking the child hard enough to cause short-term hearing loss.[112] J.S. deceived her father to conceal that she had recently been suspended from school and had received a bad report card two weeks earlier.[113] J.S. also lied so her parents would think she was going to an afterschool swim practice.[114] She wanted to avoid a confrontation with her parents and seems to have thought that postponing her return home would be a good strategy.[115]

It didn't work. J.S.'s school called her father and told him about the suspension and report card.[116] Then J.S.'s mother apparently discovered when she called her daughter that J.S. had gone to a friend's house after school rather than to swim practice.[117]

William reacted to the revelation of J.S.'s deceit by hitting his daughter three times.[118] The first blow landed on J.S.'s ear and knocked her to the ground.[119] William then struck his child two more times on the ear while she was sitting on the floor.[120] J.S. reported "difficulty hearing" afterward and still had "muffled" hearing more than a week after the attack.[121] She later testified that her father's violence made her "scared."[122]

J.S.'s forehead and ear were bruised and swollen.[123] Her friend saw that J.S. was injured and told a social worker.[124] J.S. had at least three medical appointments to monitor her recovery.[125] The local county in Pennsylvania filed a child abuse report with the state's "Childline Registry."[126]

William successfully sued to have his name expunged from the registry.[127] The unanimous Commonwealth Court agreed that William's violent response to his daughter's deceit fell within his authority to inflict corporal punishment.[128] The court's opinion emphasized William's prerogatives as a parent and J.S.'s failure to act as a daughter should. The court declared that "[p]arents must be permitted, in fact encouraged, to discipline their children" and stressed that it was "well established in [Pennsylvania] that parents are permitted to use corporal punishment as a means of discipline."[129] The court sympathetically described William as "a concerned parent who has tried everything in his means to control his child" and observed that he "was frustrated because of his daughter's continuous misconduct."[130] Indeed, the opinion dwelled on J.S.'s "misconduct and defiance." The court highlighted J.S.'s admission "that her grades are poor, she lies to her parents, and has skipped swimming practice to be with her friends without her parents' knowledge."[131] The court also took the time to note that William had been "summoned to the child's school because Administrators discovered that the child had condoms in her purse." Moreover, months before the violence in question, William had "discovered that J.S. had a boy in her bedroom and saw a male figure fleeing from the home."[132] While the opinion did not explicitly mention gender norms, these indications of sexual activity may have been particularly disturbing—for both William and the court—because J.S. was a daughter rather than a son.

In short, the court devoted much of its energy to detailing J.S.'s bad behavior (her deceitfulness, disobedience, defiance, and deviance), while rationalizing and permitting her father's (his violence). The court made plain that when minor children deceive their parents, the parents have far-reaching discretion to respond as they see fit—including with blows.

Let's turn to adult children's deceit, which does trigger parental lawsuits. Although courts are predisposed to protect parents who have duped their children, that inclination to shield deception dissipates when the parties are reversed. To the contrary, courts commonly show no hesitation about providing remedies when an adult child's deceit has harmed his parent. Indeed, courts sometimes insist that such deception especially deserves legal condemnation and legal redress.

Some of the deceived parents who have won legal relief were ailing or otherwise especially vulnerable when their adult children duped them. For example, courts unanimously awarded remedies to "an elderly widow who never attended school and understood little English" when her son duped her into selling her house to him for below market value and then evicted her from it,[133] to a mother and father who were past ninety and "in poor health" when their son duped them into giving him real estate by falsely promising that he would care for them in his home for as long as they lived,[134] and to a mother with "little formal education" who was seventy-four and possibly "in failing health" when her son duped her into signing away her life estate in a farm she had sold him.[135]

However, many of the parents who have successfully sued their deceptive adult children appear to have been no more vulnerable to an intimate's deceit than anyone else.[136] Courts are eager to provide even mothers and fathers who fit this description with redress. Rather than express concerns about subjecting intimate deceivers to legal liability, judges trumpet their righteous indignation on behalf of deceived parents and condemn duplicitous adult children. Adults who duped their parents have found themselves subject to large financial penalties and sometimes left with hardly a dollar to their names.

Consider Mary Lopez's successful fraud suit against her adult son, Adam Taylor.[137] Lopez had agreed when she divorced to pay half of her son's college expenses, including half of his tuition, dues, books, and room and board.[138] She dutifully gave Taylor the funds.[139] But Taylor deceived his mother about the price of his tuition, overstating the cost so Lopez would give him more money.[140] Taylor duped his mother into overpaying him for three semesters, for a combined overpayment of $3590.[141]

She was suspicious by the time her son overstated his college expenses for a fourth semester.[142] In fact, Taylor was so exaggerating his expenses by this point that if Lopez had paid half of the figure Taylor cited, she would have given Taylor more than his entire college expenses for the semester.[143] Lopez questioned her son and he would not respond.[144] Rather than pay, she sued Taylor for fraud— and also successfully sued her ex-husband for breach of contract and fraud for working with their son to deceive her.[145]

The Tennessee Court of Appeals in 2005 expressed only empathy for Lopez and only contempt for her deceitful son. The unanimous court detailed the weight of Lopez's financial burden. Her annual earnings during the relevant period were between $22,000 and $26,000, less than a third of her ex-husband's $90,000 in annual earnings.[146] Nonetheless, Lopez paid $12,674 in college expenses over two academic years, $9084 of which was actually due and $3590 of which was an overpayment.[147] Lopez reported that she had to withdraw money from her Individual Retirement Account (IRA) to cover these expenses, which triggered tax liability.[148] Meanwhile, her son was "unrepentant" and offered no "sound explanation for" his deceit. Indeed, Taylor reported that one reason he duped his mother was that he did not want her in his life.[149] Taylor apparently did not recognize that his deceit increased his mother's involvement in his life—by tricking her into financing more of it.

The court had no qualms about penalizing Taylor for his deceit, swiftly holding that he "forfeited his right to have" his mother pay for college when he defrauded her. Taylor's deceit freed Lopez from "any further obligation to pay her son's college expenses."[150]

The United States Bankruptcy Court for the District of Colorado was equally eager to award Martin Wagner remedies in 2013 and to condemn his deceptive son, William Wagner.[151] Martin owned a cabin that he agreed to let his son use as collateral on a $194,000 loan.[152] William told his father that he planned to sell his home and promised Martin that he would pay off $100,000 of the loan with proceeds from that sale.[153] William concealed from his father that he had already negotiated the sale of his home and was scheduled to close on the deal approximately four days after he obtained the $194,000 loan.[154] William pocketed more than $93,000 in cash from selling his home, but he did not devote any of that money to reducing the balance on the loan secured with Martin's cabin.[155]

William defaulted on the loan after about a year, which meant that the bank would foreclose on Martin's cabin unless Martin paid off the loan himself.[156]

Martin successfully sued his son in state court only to see William file for bankruptcy before paying what he owed.[157] Debts are generally discharged in bankruptcy. Indeed, freeing people from the legal obligation to pay their accumulated debts is a core purpose of personal bankruptcy. However, bankruptcy law protects creditors in situations where the debtor made a misrepresentation intending to deceive the creditor and the creditor justifiably relied on the misrepresentation and suffered a loss because of the misrepresentation.[158] Martin sued William in bankruptcy court, arguing (among other claims) that his son's debt to him was not dischargeable because of William's fraud.[159]

The bankruptcy court's disdain for William and respect for his father were both manifest. The judge described William as "an individual who will say virtually anything the situation seems to require,"[160] someone with a "propensity to tell whatever 'truth' suits his particular purpose at any given moment."[161] The court found that William meant to deceive his father and never intended to use proceeds from selling his home to pay off $100,000 of the loan.[162] The court also found that Martin's agreement to have his cabin be collateral on a $194,000 loan for William depended on William's false promise about paying off the $100,000. Without that misrepresentation, Martin would have agreed to have his cabin be collateral on a $94,000 loan for William.[163]

Having stressed William's deceitfulness, the court emphasized Martin's honorable motivations and reasonable judgment. Martin testified that he fell for his son's deceit at a time when he thought they had "a good" relationship and "he felt closer to [William] than he did to his other children." After recounting this testimony, the court concluded that Martin "had good reason to rely on the good faith and truthfulness of [William's] stated intention to pay down the Cabin Loan with equity received from the sale of [William's home]."[164]

The court held that William had a legal obligation to compensate his deceived father that was not dischargeable in bankruptcy.[165] The court required William to pay Martin $100,000 in "fraud damages," "plus interest from the date of default." With interest, William's debt to his father had already reached more than $148,000 by the time of the court's order. If William did not pay immediately, additional interest obligations would accumulate at a rate of 4.95% a year.[166]

That was a significant—probably overwhelming—financial burden for a son who had already reached the point of seeking bankruptcy protection. But the court was determined to hold William responsible for duping his father and did not hesitate to subject William to the full force of the law.

The successful suit that Early Mae and Henry Sykes brought against their son, Bezell Sykes, similarly illustrates the judiciary's willingness, even eagerness, to protect deceived parents and punish their deceitful adult children. Early Mae and Henry had wanted to purchase a house for themselves, but were unable to obtain a mortgage in their own names—presumably because they had lost their previous house. They struck a deal with their son that Bezell would buy the property in his name and then transfer the title to his parents.[167] The down payment for the house and almost all the mortgage payments came from Early Mae and Henry, who lived in the house.[168] But Bezell never transferred the house's title to his parents, notwithstanding repeated entreaties from his father.[169] Indeed, Bezell ultimately sought to evict his parents after they had been in the house for more than three decades. Early Mae and Henry responded by suing Bezell for "fraud and deceit," among other claims.[170] The jury concluded that Bezell had made a misrepresentation and that his parents had justifiably relied on that misrepresentation. It awarded Early Mae and Henry $100,000 in compensatory damages for fraud and $42,000 in punitive damages for fraud.[171] The trial court held that Bezell had to transfer the house's title to his parents, in addition to paying those damages.[172]

The California Court of Appeal unanimously affirmed in 2004, showing no qualms about upholding a damage award that would leave Bezell on the verge of indigency, bankruptcy, or both. The appellate court agreed that Early Mae and Henry were entitled to the house because their bargain with their son provided that they would receive it.[173] The court also agreed that Early Mae and Henry were entitled to money damages because of Bezell's "fraud and deceit." The court was confident that Bezell had never intended to transfer the house's title to his parents and emphasized that Bezell had obtained additional loans on the house during the three-plus decades when he kept legal ownership for himself. The court had no doubt about "his parents' resulting emotional distress."[174]

Bezell argued that the punitive damages award was excessive, but the court was unsympathetic. Bezell reported a net worth of $146,200 (excluding the house his parents claimed). Paying $42,000 in punitive damages would cost Bezell about 28.7% of his net worth. Indeed, Bezell would be left with essentially no assets once he paid compensatory and punitive damages to his parents— not to mention fees to his attorneys. But the court expressed no concerns about Bezell, noting that it was "satisfied that this award of punitive damages was not excessive in light of Bezell's conduct and was in proper proportion to the award of $100,000 in compensatory damages."[175] Bezell had deceived his parents and the law would make him pay the price, even if it devastated him financially.

In short, courts are prone to protect parents who deceive their children. But that inclination to shield deceit dissolves when the parties are reversed. Children who dupe their parents should not expect much, if any, sympathy from the judiciary. To the contrary, judges enthusiastically come to the aid of deceived parents and penalize deceptive adult children for their betrayal.

Deceit from Other Family Members

Let's turn to deceitful family members not connected by marriage or parenthood. Courts and legislatures constructing and enforcing family law tend to dwell endlessly on spouses, parents, children, and (sometimes) their functional equivalents, while sparing remarkably little attention for other relatives. That narrow perspective perpetuates a common law tradition that took marriage and parenthood to be the key familial relationships and had almost nothing to say about other family ties.[176] The legal regulation of intimate deception presumes and reflects family law's overriding tendency to focus on marriage and parenthood to the virtual exclusion of other relationships. Judges adjudicating deceit routinely assume that family ties beyond marriage and parenthood fall outside the borders of legally recognized intimacy. Indeed, courts often take these family ties to be so patently irrelevant that judges do not even bother to explain that they will extend no special treatment to deception in such relationships. Courts simply proceed to treat deceitful siblings, aunts, uncles, nieces, and nephews as if they were unrelated to the people they deceived and allow plaintiffs to access remedies available for nonintimate deception.[177]

Leang Ly's successful suit against her four brothers is illustrative.[178] Ly testified that she agreed to spend $150,000 on purchasing a car wash only because her brothers, David, Khim, Quang, and Moses Lee, promised that she would receive an equal ownership share of the business in return.[179] Indeed, Ly reported that she contributed more than $150,000 because she also loaned Quang $80,000 and Moses $50,000 to help them pay their $150,000 contributions. Ly charged that her brothers duped her. As the Lees later admitted in court, they took larger shares of the car wash for themselves when incorporating the company. Once they had their sister's money, moreover, the brothers denied that Ly's loans to Quang and Moses had to be repaid. The California Court of Appeal did not explicitly consider the possibility that gender played a role in the Lee brothers' decision to dupe their sister out of an equal share of the business. But it is striking that Ly provided a total of $280,000, yet was left with "a lesser share in the car wash than any of the men in the family."[180]

After the car wash business failed, David, Khim, and Quang sued Ly, her husband, and Moses. David, Khim, and Quang ultimately dropped their suit. But by that point, Ly and her husband were suing all four Lee brothers.[181] After over ten days of trial, the trial judge awarded Ly and her husband $150,000 in damages for intentional misrepresentation, $130,000 in damages to compensate for the outstanding loans, and another $25,000 in damages for various other claims.[182] The trial court also absolved Ly and her husband of any obligation to pay the debts the failed car wash had left behind.[183]

When the California Court of Appeal unanimously affirmed in 2002, it noted (of course) that Ly was the sister of the men she was suing.[184] The appellate court observed that the litigation revealed "the sad details of family strife" and recounted that Ly "broke down emotionally" at one point during the trial.[185]

But the Court of Appeal never suggested that Ly should have fewer or different remedies for intentional misrepresentation because the defendants were her brothers. To the contrary, the court assumed that the sibling ties between Ly and her brothers were legally irrelevant. The appellate court emphasized that the trial judge had found Ly's testimony credible and readily agreed that Ly had presented "substantial evidence" of misrepresentation.[186] In short, the court treated the Lee brothers as if they were unrelated to the sister they had deceived and assumed that the wisdom of this approach was too obvious to require explanation.

The South Dakota Supreme Court similarly presumed that sibling ties were legally irrelevant in granting Margaret Conway redress in 1992 for the injuries her brother, Gerald Conway, had inflicted through deception.[187] Margaret, Gerald, and a third sibling, Glen, had each inherited a two-ninths share of one hundred and sixty acres of farmland and their mother, Loretta, had inherited a three-ninths share.[188] The Conways understood that Loretta would keep all the rental income from the farmland for the rest of her life so she could use that money to support herself.[189] Loretta accordingly collected rent for decades. After about twenty-seven years of collections, however, she transferred her share of the farmland to Gerald so she would be eligible to receive larger Social Security payments.[190] Margaret (who lived out of state) learned about this transfer more than two years after it happened, but thought her mother was still collecting all the rental income because that had been the family's understanding.[191]

In fact, Gerald started collecting all the rental income and depositing it in his own bank account once he acquired his mother's share of the farmland. Gerald eventually bought Glen's share of the land.[192] However, Margaret still owned a two-ninths share and was receiving none of the rent. The court observed that it was "clear from the record that Gerald made a conscious decision to remain silent about [his] receipt of rental income in order to conceal this fact from Margaret."[193]

Margaret did not discover Gerald's deceit until after their mother died.[194] At that point, Gerald had been pocketing Margaret's share of the rent for more than eight years.[195] Margaret asked for her share and when Gerald would not surrender it, she sued him and won.[196]

The South Dakota Supreme Court made clear that it would decide Margaret's suit against her brother using the same rules that govern litigation between any two "tenants in common"—i.e., two people who each own partial shares of the same property. The unanimous court explained that "one co-tenant will not be permitted to obtain a secret profit to the disadvantage of the other co-tenants where all must act in unison." Gerald's "fraudulent concealment" that he was collecting all the rent stopped the statute of limitations from running on Margaret's claim. The court would not permit Gerald to "profit from his own wrong."[197] He would have to give his sister her share of the rent he had collected and her share of the rent going forward.[198] In other words, the court treated Margaret and Gerald like any other co-tenants. The opinion did not even consider the possibility that the law should respond to Gerald's deceit differently because he was Margaret's brother.

Courts similarly presume that family ties are no obstacle to providing redress when considering deception between relatives who are further apart on the family tree than siblings. Consider the Massachusetts Appeals Court's 2008 decision permitting Adam Rimscha to pursue his suit against his allegedly deceptive brother-in-law, Napoleon Suprenant.[199] Adam reported that he had a close relationship with his brother, Edward Rimscha, and was living in Edward's house when Edward was hospitalized.[200] Napoleon and Edward married while Edward was in the hospital, and Edward died the following day.[201]

It is unsurprising that one of the earliest intimate deception cases to involve a same-sex marriage arose in Massachusetts, the pathbreaking state that in 2004 became the first to permit same-sex couples to marry.[202] However, Adam's claim did not revolve around how Napoleon had treated his husband. It centered on how Napoleon had allegedly treated Adam, his brother-in-law.

On Adam's account, Napoleon knew that Adam and Edward were close, but nonetheless deceived Adam by "actively" concealing that Edward had died.[203] Rather than telling Adam about Edward's death and funeral, Napoleon allegedly lied to Adam twice, each time offering false assurances that Edward "was still alive and getting better." Adam also reported that Napoleon "abruptly removed him from" Edward's house the day after Edward's death and sent Adam to his son in Florida, which presumably helped Napoleon keep Adam from learning the truth.[204]

Adam sued Napoleon for intentional infliction of emotional distress after he discovered Napoleon's deceit. The unanimous Massachusetts Appeals Court held that Adam could pursue his suit.[205]

Recall (from Chapter 5) that the Massachusetts Appeals Court had previously rejected Margie Conley's lawsuit seeking redress for the injuries that Michael Romeri had allegedly inflicted by deceiving her to conceal his vasectomy.[206] Conley reported that Romeri had used deceit about his sterility to induce her into a sexual relationship that she would have avoided if she had known the truth, causing her enormous emotional distress that ultimately hurt her financially.[207] In rejecting all of Conley's claims, the Massachusetts appellate court emphasized its common sense intuitions and its desire to avoid intruding

on intimate relationships—as if that was possible.[208] The court insisted when
dismissing Conley's claim for intentional infliction of emotional distress that
Romeri's alleged behavior did not "rise to the high order of reckless ruthlessness or deliberate malevolence required for a showing of conduct that is
intolerable."[209]

Four years after *Conley*, the Massachusetts Appeals Court was much more
sympathetic to Adam's intentional infliction of emotional distress claim. The
court held that if Adam proved his allegations, a jury could reasonably find
that Napoleon's "conduct was extreme and outrageous, having a severe and
traumatic effect upon plaintiff's emotional tranquility." Accordingly, Adam—
unlike Conley—was "entitled to an opportunity to prove the allegations he has
made."[210]

To my mind, Romeri's alleged deceit seems at least as outrageous as Napoleon's.
But one reason the Massachusetts Appeals Court may have been more willing to
condemn Napoleon's alleged deceit was that the court clearly had no worries in
Rimscha v. Suprenant about intruding on intimate relationships. *Conley* had been
intent on (supposedly) keeping the judiciary out of intimacy by denying Conley
remedies for deception. Yet the same court expressed no doubt that the family
tie between Adam and Napoleon was beyond the boundaries of intimacy. The
court saw this as a deception suit between legal strangers, so the law's ordinary
approach to an intentional infliction of emotional distress claim applied.

The Texas Court of Appeals likewise took the family connection between a deceitful uncle and deceived nephew to be legally irrelevant to the nephew's fraud
claim.[211] When James Gayle was fifteen, he inherited his grandfather's house and
his uncle, Joe Maeberry, became his legal guardian until he turned eighteen.[212]
Gayle contended that about six months after he became a legal adult, Maeberry
tricked him into giving away his house.[213] Maeberry reportedly instructed Gayle
to sign a legal document that Maeberry described as "guardianship papers."[214]
Gayle believed him and signed, but the document actually stated that Gayle was
selling his house to Maeberry for just ten dollars.[215] Gayle testified that he did
not receive even those ten dollars from his uncle. In any event, the house was
worth nineteen thousand.[216]

The Texas Court of Appeals held in 1997 that Maeberry had no special
obligations to Gayle once Gayle turned eighteen, even though Maeberry was
both Gayle's former guardian and his uncle.[217] To be sure, the court noted the
kinship between the defendant and plaintiff, observing that "Maeberry was essentially the only remaining family that Gayle had." Yet the court's analysis did
not turn on that family tie. To the contrary, the court applied standard legal
principles to Gayle's claim that Maeberry had taken the house through fraud,
explaining that "[t]he elements of fraud are a material representation, which
was false and was either known to be false when made or was asserted without

knowledge of its truth, which was intended to be acted upon, which was relied upon, and which caused injury."[218] The trial judge had believed Gayle's testimony, and the appellate court agreed "that there was legally and factually sufficient evidence that Maeberry obtained the deed by making a false, material statement to Gayle, which was intended for Gayle to rely on and which Gayle did rely on to his detriment."[219]

Maeberry was liable to Gayle under the same legal standards that govern fraud suits between people with no family connections. He had to return the house, compensate Gayle for the rental income that Gayle could have earned in the period when Maeberry had wrongful possession, and pay punitive damages and Gayle's attorney's fees.[220] In the law's eyes, the family tie between Maeberry and Gayle did not register as an intimate connection triggering differential treatment.

In sum, examining the legal regulation of intimate deception outside of romantic, sexual, or marital relationships reveals aspects of the field that otherwise would not be visible. The presumption that courts should protect intimate deceivers still appears in this context, but it is almost exclusively confined to cases about parents who deceived their children—including their adult children. Courts are often reluctant to penalize deceitful parents and prone to fault children for having been fooled. Indeed, courts sometimes write as if parents have a legal prerogative to deceive their children, one that parents retain even after their children reach legal adulthood. In contrast, judges are frequently eager to grant remedies when an adult child has duped her parents and courts empower parents to inflict their own penalties on deceptive minor children. Examining deception beyond romance, sex, and marriage also illuminates boundaries on how judges understand intimacy. Courts routinely assume that family members not connected by marriage or parenthood fall beyond the borders of legally recognized intimacy. Judges treat deceitful siblings, aunts, uncles, nieces, nephews, and the like as if they were unrelated to the people they deceived and give plaintiffs access to remedies available for nonintimate deception.

PART III

REFORMING THE LAW
OF INTIMATE DECEPTION

Parts I and II focused on the present and the past, examining deceit within intimacy as a persistent part of life and a consistent issue for the law. Intimate deception and its legal regulation have attracted remarkably little critical attention, but exploring these subjects reveals the prevalence and impact of deceit in intimate relationships. People can inflict significant—even life-altering—injuries on their sexual partners, spouses, and family members by deceiving them, including financial losses, illnesses and infections, physical endangerment and abuse, violations of sexual autonomy and bodily integrity, unexpected vulnerability to criminal prosecution, lost time, missed opportunities, and psychological and emotional pain, distress, and devastation. The law's response to such deceit pivots to a remarkable extent on whether judges classify the deceiver and deceived as intimately connected. Courts routinely assume that a deceived intimate will not and should not have access to remedies that are available to redress, deter, and repudiate deceit in other contexts. Judges are fiercely determined to protect what they identify as ordinary acts of deception within intimacy and inclined to define commonplace intimate deception expansively.

The law has placed too much emphasis on shielding intimate deceivers and too little importance on helping intimates who have been deceived. People should not lose the law's protection from deceit when they enter intimate relationships or are duped into them. Legal vulnerability should not be the price of intimacy. This part turns to the future, exploring how courts and legislatures can improve their treatment of intimate deception.

8

Work to Be Done

One way legal authorities shape deception within intimate relationships is by deciding whether, when, and why to provide remedies in court. Judicial decisions set legal rules, distribute rights and responsibilities, establish baselines, and enforce normative judgments—whether courts side with people seeking redress from duplicitous intimates or protect their deceivers. The law's role in governing intimate deception is especially visible when courts issue judgments. But as we have seen, the legal regulation of intimate deception also operates before litigation begins, structuring the incentives to deceive and the ease with which someone acting deceitfully can succeed in duping his intimate and taking advantage of her.

Legal reform will be most transformative and effective if it extends to the multiple ways that the law governs intimate deception. Courts should be more receptive to suits seeking redress from deceptive intimates who have caused harm. At the same time, the law should pursue reforms that reach beyond improving the prospects of plaintiffs who report injuries from intimate deception. Preventing harm is better than providing remedies after the fact. Instead of creating, exacerbating, or accommodating incentives to deceive an intimate, legislatures and courts should work to counter such incentives. Instead of promulgating and enforcing legal rules that help intimate deceivers execute their schemes, lawmakers and judges should seize opportunities to adjust the law in ways that will thwart deceivers while not unduly burdening everyday transactions and still respecting privacy, liberty, and security.

In short, the law should do much more to recognize, remediate, and prevent harms inflicted through intimate deception. This chapter begins by considering how to augment the relief available to deceived intimates in court and then turns to other potential improvements in the legal treatment of intimate deception.

More Remedies for Deceived Intimates

Judges are more likely to make wise decisions if they start with a rebuttable presumption that the law will provide remedies for deception within an intimate relationship when redress would be available for an equivalent example of deception outside of intimacy. If a plaintiff could sue a deceptive stranger for fraud, misrepresentation, battery, intentional infliction of emotional distress, or the like, courts should begin by assuming that the plaintiff can sue an intimate who is equivalently deceptive for the same causes of action. The exact amount of damages would vary case-by-case. In some instances, the fact that the defendant duped his intimate rather than an acquaintance might be reason for a judge or jury to conclude that the plaintiff suffered more harm. But the judiciary's starting presumption would be that the same doctrinal standards, tests, rules, and evidentiary requirements apply to cases involving intimate deception as govern equivalent cases involving deceit outside of intimacy.

To be sure, establishing such a rebuttable presumption would be the beginning of a conversation rather than the end. There would be disputes about what counts as equivalent kinds of deception within and outside of intimacy. There would also be debates about whether, when, and why to override the rebuttable presumption and subject specific types of intimate deception to special legal treatment. This chapter elaborates on my answers to those questions, but I do not anticipate perfect alignment between my answers and every conclusion courts would reach after applying the rebuttable presumption. In fact, I am confident that judges with different normative commitments, or simply with different perspectives on the facts of a case, would endorse some conclusions that I would have rejected. Nonetheless, I am convinced that the rebuttable presumption provides a better initial baseline than the law's current, largely unexamined assumption that intimate deception is categorically unlike deception outside of intimacy and should be subject to different legal rules. A presumption in favor of treating intimate deception like deception outside of intimacy would prod judges and litigants to ask better questions, even if they would not necessarily agree on the answers.

This section considers the strengths and limitations of the rebuttable presumption I propose. It then provides examples of how the presumption could work in practice before exploring why the most likely counterarguments in defense of preserving the status quo are unconvincing.

Creating a rebuttable presumption in favor of treating intimate deception like deception between nonintimates would help promote compensation, deterrence, and recognition. These three goals are important and mutually reinforcing.

Giving deceived intimates access to the remedies available for deception in other contexts would help plaintiffs secure compensation for injuries their intimates have inflicted through deceit. Money damages are the usual means of redress in civil litigation, although sometimes equitable remedies (like injunctions) are available as an alternative or additional means of redress. Here as elsewhere in the law, money damages would rarely be able to restore a plaintiff to the same position she occupied before the defendant harmed her. But judges and juries have considerable experience with assigning dollar values to personal injuries that are hard to quantify in monetary terms, and money damages do offer some measure of relief for plaintiffs who have suffered financially, physically, emotionally, and/or otherwise. The desire to secure at least partial compensation through money damages is one reason why many people have already sued intimates who duped them, notwithstanding the judiciary's present hostility to such claims.

Increasing the chances that deceptive intimates will have to face legal consequences for their conduct should also help promote deterrence to some extent. I do not believe that the law could ever completely deter intimate deception and would never promise that the incidence of intimate deception would decline by a certain amount if courts adopt my proposed approach. Myriad factors constrain the law's ability to deter, including that many potential defendants do not understand the law or believe—rightly or wrongly—that the people they are harming will never sue or will never prove their cases in court if they do sue. Many people will continue to inflict significant injuries on their intimates through deceit, under any conceivable legal regime. That said, even a few well-publicized damage awards could jolt some people into worrying about whether deceiving their intimates could trigger legal liability, or simply cause some deceivers to reassess the wisdom and justness of their actions. Judicial victories for deceived intimates are especially likely to attract widespread media coverage and popular notice given the cultural fascination with intimate deception. At least some people thinking about duping their intimates in ways likely to inflict harm might reconsider, especially if their deceit involves sustained planning over time rather than a spur-of-the-moment decision. Some other people might continue to be deceptive, but adjust their behavior to inflict less injury. For example, someone falsely presenting himself as unmarried could reduce the harm this deceit causes by dissuading his new "fiancée" from quitting her job and selling her home to move closer to him.[1]

In addition, greater judicial openness to claims revolving around intimate deception would be an important and public way for the law to recognize that people can inflict wrongful and severe injuries on their intimates by deceiving them. Deceived intimates have been making that point for years, in and out of courtrooms. Legal acknowledgment and legitimation of such arguments—after a long history in which the law discounted and dismissed the claims of deceived intimates and blamed them for being duped—can be important to plaintiffs whose injuries are taken seriously and whose deceivers are held accountable. Such recognition can also be uplifting to deceived intimates who never sue.

Moreover, the rebuttable presumption would not simply improve plaintiffs' chances. It would bolster those prospects by giving deceived intimates access to the same remedies available for deception outside of intimacy. Mainstreaming intimate deception has at least three advantages over attempting to help plaintiffs by creating special causes of action that exclusively apply to injuries inflicted through deception within intimate relationships.

First, deceived intimates' claims should be more secure if they are brought into the heart of the legal system, rather than consigned to its peripheries. Special remedies for injuries within intimacy can be extraordinarily vulnerable to attack and elimination, as the history of heart balm torts and anti-heart balm legislation suggests. One likely explanation for the wildfire success of anti-heart balm activism is that the heart balm torts were separate causes of action for intimate injuries that legislatures could abolish without having to restructure tort law more generally. Allowing deceived intimates to access the causes of action that redress deception outside of intimacy would integrate deceived intimates into the rest of the law instead of isolating them outside of ordinary legal doctrine. Deceived intimates do not need special protections or privileges, which can be criticized and condemned as such. They need the ordinary protections that the law provides against injuries inflicted through deceit.

Second, starting with a rebuttable presumption that deceived intimates will have the same remedies that are available for nonintimate deception would allow courts adjudicating intimate deception claims, and parties litigating those claims, to draw on well-established and developed bodies of law detailing the elements a plaintiff has to prove, the harm a plaintiff has to show, the standard of proof, the statute of limitations, and more. The presence of intimacy could be relevant in applying some of these rules and standards. For example, suppose a state's judges have defined the elements of a claim so a plaintiff must prove that her reliance on the defendant's misrepresentations was reasonable. Or suppose courts have a doctrine instructing judges to toll the statute of limitations governing a claim when the plaintiff's reasonable reliance on the defendant's misrepresentations justifies the plaintiff's delay in discovering the defendant's misconduct. A plaintiff might be able to draw on the intimateness of her connection with the defendant in arguing for the reasonableness of her reliance. Chapter 2 detailed the obstacles to detecting intimate deception, and I think that reliance is often more reasonable when the deceiver is intimately connected to the person she is deceiving. I would advise courts to be receptive to such arguments, in recognition of the reality that ordinary, reasonable people frequently believe what their intimates tell them only to discover later that they have been deceived. That said, courts would be asking the same ultimate questions—about the reasonableness of the plaintiff's reliance, for instance—whether or not the case involves intimates. This consistency in doctrinal rules and standards should facilitate judicial decisionmaking and help make the case law on intimate deception more stable and predictable. Courts would be using the same tools they use outside of intimacy.

Third, aligning the legal regulation of intimate and nonintimate deception would mean that judicial preconceptions about the boundaries of intimacy would become much less important. Such preconceptions matter enormously when the law's response to deception pivots on whether judges believe the plaintiff and defendant were intimately connected. As we have seen, judges are inclined to think about intimacy expansively when considering deceit in romantic and/or sexual relationships, classifying people as intimates when they actually did not know each other well.[2] In contrast, judges are inclined to think about intimacy narrowly when considering deceit in familial relationships beyond marriage and parenthood, excluding family members like siblings, aunts, uncles, nieces, and nephews.[3] Neither of these tendencies is wholly satisfactory or defensible. Starting with a presumption that deceived intimates can access the same law that governs deception outside of intimacy would mean that most cases would not turn on how judges draw the dividing lines between intimates and others—lines that will always be debatable and debated.

I think the advantages of a rebuttable presumption treating intimate deception like equivalent deception outside of intimacy outweigh the limitations inherent in this approach. Nonetheless, those limitations should be understood at the outset.

First, the law's regulation of deception outside of intimacy is (of course) imperfect. Under my proposed approach, deceived intimates will be subject to the same imperfections in legal doctrine that people now confront when strangers deceive them. For example, tort law systematically privileges financial and physical injuries and makes recovering for emotional damage more difficult.[4] Allowing deceived intimates to access the causes of action available for equivalent deception outside of intimacy would improve the law's treatment of intimate deception. But this reform would not solve every overarching problem in tort law, including the pervasive undervaluing of emotional injuries. Plaintiffs bringing suits for injuries stemming from intimate deception—like plaintiffs bringing any claim—would still be more likely to win damage awards to the extent they could show that the defendants' conduct harmed them financially and/or physically, in addition to emotionally. This disparity is itself a worthy subject of reform, but one that extends far beyond the regulation of deception within intimacy.

Second, the rebuttable presumption will be easiest to employ when the intimate deception at issue has a clear equivalent outside of intimacy and harder to apply when possible nonintimate equivalents are less manifest. Indeed, courts may conclude in some cases that an intimate was subject to deceit that has no equivalent outside of intimacy at all, so judges have to weigh the benefits and costs of providing redress without being able to rely on the rebuttable presumption in favor of treating intimate and nonintimate deception alike. Even if the rebuttable presumption does not help in every case, however, it will provide immediate guidance much of the time. As my examples will illustrate, many instances of intimate deception can be quickly paired with nonintimate equivalents.

With these strengths and limitations in mind, let's turn to examples of how the rebuttable presumption could work in practice. These examples address some common situations and provide guidance for how to think about other circumstances.

One straightforward scenario involves plaintiffs who can establish all the elements of a claim for fraud, misrepresentation, battery, intentional infliction of emotional distress, or the like—but were deceived by an intimate rather than a stranger. Courts now routinely assume that the presence of intimacy is an obstacle to recovery. Under my proposed approach, in contrast, courts would start by presuming that these plaintiffs can successfully pursue their claims without regard to whether they were intimates of the defendants when deceived.

Bonhomme v. St. James[5] provides a helpful illustration. Recall (from Chapter 5) that Janna St. James allegedly deceived Paula Bonhomme by falsely presenting herself through electronic and other communications "as a man named Jesse James" and then using this fake persona and additional aliases to dupe Bonhomme for almost two years, emotionally abuse her, and extract more than ten thousand dollars in gifts from Bonhomme.[6] The Illinois Supreme Court unanimously held that Bonhomme could not sue St. James for fraudulent misrepresentation—even if Bonhomme could prove all the elements of that tort—because the relationship St. James lured Bonhomme into was supposedly "purely personal," with "absolutely nothing of the commercial, transactional, or regulatory at work." Like many judges before them, the Illinois Justices assumed and insisted that the law should deny deceived intimates access to remedies that the law provides for deception outside of intimacy.[7] Courts would begin with the opposite presumption under my approach. Bonhomme would win her claim for fraudulent misrepresentation if she could prove the same elements of the tort that someone would be required to establish when suing a nonintimate.

The rebuttable presumption could also help restrain judicial interpretations of anti-heart balm laws. Consider a plaintiff who has brought a claim involving deception and can prove all the elements ordinarily required to establish the claim. Her demand for damages does not rest on the allegation that the defendant fraudulently promised to marry her. However, the plaintiff and defendant were once engaged and ultimately did not marry. Judges are now inclined to interpret statutory prohibitions on breach of promise to marry litigation expansively, citing these laws as reasons to block plaintiffs with broken engagements from suing their former fiancés for any claim that implicates any sort of deceit.[8] Courts applying my approach would start by presuming that a plaintiff who can prove all the ordinary elements of a cause of action should be able to present the same evidence and win the same claim, whether she is suing a stranger or someone to whom she was once engaged. Statutory prohibitions on breach of promise to marry litigation would not immunize everything that happens between two people simply because the parties once planned to wed. Instead, judges should interpret these prohibitions in ways that reflect the actual language of the statutes—limiting the reach of the bans to claims that are actually about breaches of promises to marry, such as claims contending that the defendant fraudulently promised to marry the plaintiff or broke their engagement without cause.

Smith v. National Railroad Passenger Corporation[9] offers a useful illustration. Recall (from Chapter 4) that Susan Smith sued Fred Weiderhold for misrepresentation, contending that he "fraudulently induced" her to quit her job at Amtrak. Weiderhold, who was Amtrak's Inspector General, allegedly misrepresented Amtrak's personnel policy by falsely telling Smith "that they could not work together at Amtrak once they were planning to marry." Smith explained that she relied on that misrepresentation in resigning from her job and suffered financially and otherwise as a result.[10]

A federal district court held that Smith could not sue Weiderhold for misrepresentation because her suit assertedly fell within Pennsylvania's statutory prohibition on breach of promise to marry litigation.[11] Smith did report that Weiderhold had promised to marry her while never intending to fulfill that promise.[12] But her claim that Weiderhold had duped her into resigning did not depend on whether Weiderhold married Smith or not, or agreed to marry her knowing that he would not honor that commitment. Even if Weiderhold had become Smith's husband, his alleged misrepresentation about Amtrak's personnel policy would still have injured Smith by inducing her to leave her job. The court offered no reason to believe that Weiderhold was so wealthy that Smith would not have needed to support herself if she married him.

Under my proposed approach, the fact of a broken engagement between plaintiff and defendant would not bar a legal claim involving deception—so long as the claim does not directly contravene an anti-heart balm statute by requiring a court to decide whether a promise to marry was genuine or whether the reasons behind a broken engagement were legitimate. Suppose Weiderhold had duped another Amtrak employee, whom he had never dated, into quitting by misrepresenting Amtrak's personnel policy. If that now-former Amtrak employee could sue Weiderhold for misrepresentation, Smith should be able to bring the same cause of action.

A rebuttable presumption in favor of treating intimate deception like equivalent deception outside of intimacy could similarly transform the law of annulment. Courts now take for granted that many examples of deception that are sufficient to undo an ordinary contract are insufficient to undo a marital contract. The baseline assumption that annulment law will usually not remediate premarital deceit is more insisted upon than explained, with modern courts relying on old precedents whose reasoning retains little persuasive force. Judges and treatise writers in the nineteenth and early twentieth centuries wanted to preserve restrictions on annulment because they believed that any marital dissolution threatened the social order. This was a coherent position in a legal regime that severely limited the availability of divorce, when judges knew that some unhappy spouses would pursue annulments in the hopes of evading divorce restrictions. But no-fault divorce is now available throughout the United States. If marital dissolutions jeopardize the social order, that danger is already with us and annulment doctrine can do little about it. Similarly, judges and treatise writers in the nineteenth and early twentieth centuries wanted to restrict access to annulment because of common law doctrine providing that an annulment made the former couple's children illegitimate, which was likely to leave the children and their mother destitute and ostracized. However, state laws have transformed the consequences of annulment. The former couple's children now remain legitimate if a marriage is annulled.[13] Moreover, the economic consequences of annulment now more closely resemble the consequences of divorce, including with respect to support obligations and property distribution.[14]

Courts applying my rebuttable presumption would begin by assuming that the law's treatment of deception in the formation of marital contracts should track the law's treatment of deception in the formation of ordinary contracts. In considering whether to grant an annulment for premarital deception, a court would first assess how the plaintiff's claim would fare if she had been equivalently deceived outside of intimacy and was seeking to break an ordinary contract. Not every annulment plaintiff would be able to establish that the defendant's deceit would have provided legally adequate grounds for rescinding an ordinary contract. The effort involved would probably lead many potential annulment plaintiffs to conclude that they should instead pursue the easier route of no-fault divorce. For example, an annulment plaintiff may find it difficult to prove that the defendant deceived her, that she relied on the defendant's deceit in deciding to marry, and that she would have rejected the defendant if she had known the

truth. However, if a plaintiff could prove that she would have been entitled to escape an ordinary contract with the defendant because of his deceit, courts would
start with the presumption that she should be able to dissolve her marital contract
on the same grounds. In some instances, judges might find convincing reasons to
deviate from this presumption in favor of treating intimate deception like deception outside of intimacy. But those would be exceptions that defendants would
have to argue for and courts would have to justify. Courts should have to explain
why ordinary contract rules should not govern a particular annulment case. The
turn-of-the-last-century rationales for treating annulments differently do not
make sense anymore, yet courts continue to rely on them reflexively.

We can use *In re Marriage of Meagher and Maleki*[15] to explore how this change
could operate in practice. Recall (from Chapter 5) that Ann Meagher unsuccessfully sued Malekpour Maleki for an annulment. Maleki "misrepresented his
financial status" before marriage, presenting himself as "a well-educated millionaire with expertise in real estate and finance." Before the wedding, he had already
"fraudulently induced" Meagher "to invest in a business venture with him, with
the intent to gain control of her assets."[16] The trial court found "that not only the
business venture but also the parties' marriage was based on Meagher's reliance
upon Maleki's representation that he had great wealth and that he would take
care of her, and not that he expected through a series of transactions to divest
her of at least half an interest in several million dollars' worth of property."[17] The
unanimous California Court of Appeal nonetheless refused to grant an annulment, citing common law precedents insisting that many deceitful schemes—
including deceit about finances—that would provide grounds for rescinding an
ordinary contract do not provide grounds for rescinding a marital contract.[18]

In all likelihood, Meagher would have been able to escape her contract with
Maleki if he had used the same strategies to dupe her into a commercial partnership.[19] Maleki lied to Meagher about his financial assets and his plans to strip
her of her assets, and he wanted Meagher to rely on his lies. She did rely and
would not have married him if she had known the truth. Under my approach, a
court would accordingly begin by presuming that Meagher is entitled to void her
marital partnership through annulment. To successfully oppose an annulment,
Maleki would have the burden of convincing a court to deviate from this initial
baseline.

The rebuttable presumption could also transform what counts as crucial in
suits about intimate deception. The fate of many cases involving deceit in courtship, sexual relationships, or marriage often turns now on whether judges think
the deception at issue is typical or atypical. Judges are much less likely to provide redress for supposedly commonplace deceit and more likely to grant relief
when they believe the deceit is deviant and unusual. This practice protects and
normalizes what courts characterize as ordinary deception in courtship, sex, and

marriage. Judges have enforced an expansive vision of ordinary deception that has shielded deceit as significant as faking a pregnancy, hiding that one has children, or intentionally misrepresenting one's capacity to work. Indeed, the fierce judicial commitment to the presumed status quo in intimacy can also protect deception that is patently extraordinary and extraordinarily harmful. Courts sometimes refuse to remediate even extreme examples of intimate deception on the ground that doing so might create a slippery slope that could ultimately imperil more ordinary deceivers.[20]

Denying redress for ordinary intimate deception simultaneously classifies harmful deceit as commonplace and helps make that so. Courts are so determined to safeguard ordinary intimate deception that they seemingly never consider the possibility that the prevalence of a type of deception—the fact that a category of behavior currently causes many people harm—could be a reason for the law to be more, rather than less, concerned about providing remedies and promoting deterrence.

The prevalence or rarity of a type of intimate deception would not be pivotal under my approach. Rather than asking how many other intimates do what this particular defendant did, courts would begin by presuming that the law should provide the same redress for intimate deception—whether unusual or commonplace—that the law would provide for equivalent deception outside of intimacy.

Neal v. Neal,[21] which the Idaho Supreme Court decided in 1994, offers an illuminating illustration. Mary Neal's husband, Thomas Neal, deceived her to conceal that he was having a sexual relationship with another woman.[22] Mary eventually learned of Thomas's deceit and sued him for battery, among other claims.[23] She argued that her consent to sex with Thomas while he was duping her to hide his affair should be considered legally "ineffective." Mary contended that she would not have agreed to sex if she had known about her husband's "sexual involvement with another woman" because "sexual relations under those circumstances would have been offensive to her."[24]

Most judicial decisions discussed in this book are examples of how I think courts should not proceed. *Neal's* response to Mary's battery claim constitutes a rare example of a court not succumbing to the usual judicial assumption that intimate deception is categorically unlike deception outside of intimacy and requires unique legal rules. This decision suggests how courts should respond to suits seeking redress for injuries inflicted through an intimate's deceit.

The Idaho Supreme Court did not ask whether Thomas's conduct was ordinary or unusual—an inquiry that surely would have led the court to conclude that deceit to conceal adultery is commonplace, as is reliance on linchpin deceptions to dupe someone into agreeing to sex that she would have refused if she had known the truth. Rather than concerning itself with how Thomas's conduct fit within the spectrum of intimate behavior, the court focused on how Mary's battery claim fit within the law on battery.

The *Neal* court took for granted that it would subject Mary's battery claim to the same doctrine that applies when a plaintiff sues a stranger for battery. With that foundation in place, the unanimous court explained that winning a battery claim requires the plaintiff to prove that the defendant inflicted "an intentional, unpermitted contact upon the person of" the plaintiff that was "either unlawful, harmful or offensive." A plaintiff who agreed to the contact at the time it occurred can still establish her "lack of consent" as a legal matter by proving that the defendant secured her agreement through "fraud or misrepresentation" that rendered her consent legally invalid.[25] After reviewing this basic doctrine governing the battery tort, the court held that Mary could pursue her battery claim and attempt to prove that the sex at issue should be considered "nonconsensual" because of Thomas's deceit.[26] Of course, there would be no guarantee that Mary would be able to establish at trial that her consent to sex was invalid. Realistically, I anticipate that plaintiffs bringing suits that involve common forms of intimate deception would face significant skepticism from factfinders, whether juries or judges. We live in a society that is used to shielding intimate deceivers and blaming deceived intimates for having been fooled. I am not contending that all plaintiffs subject to prevalent forms of intimate deception would, or even should, prevail. But the *Neal* court was right to allow Mary to access ordinary tort doctrine on battery. Mary's obligation to prove all the elements of her battery claim put her in the same position as any other plaintiff. Rather than bar Mary from bringing suit as a matter of law, the court left her to litigate her battery claim on the facts.

Consider one last example of how the rebuttable presumption could work in practice. Starting with an assumption that the law will treat intimate deception like deception outside of intimacy could reshape how the judiciary regulates parents who have deceived their adult children. Courts sometimes reason as if parents have a legal prerogative to dupe their offspring and retain that right throughout their children's adulthood. Judges are reluctant to provide remedies to children injured through their parents' deceit and eager to protect parents' ability to deceive. Opinions stress parents' authority over their children and blame children for having been fooled.[27]

I am well aware that courts reviewing the behavior of parents who deceived their minor children are very likely to override any rebuttable presumption in favor of treating intimate deception like equivalent deception outside of intimacy. One can question the wisdom of parental decisions to dupe minor children in ways that would lead the children to reflect back as adults and conclude the deceit injured them. My own view is that the soundness of such decisions varies widely between cases—turning, for instance, on the subject of the deception and the particular child's maturity and development at the time she was deceived. That said, the premise that parents should be able to deceive their children when the children are below the age of majority fits within a legal regime that—for better or worse—grants parents sweeping power over their minor children as a matter of both policy and constitutional doctrine. State and federal laws systematically imbue parents with wide-ranging authority to determine how they raise their minor children.[28] Moreover, the United States Supreme Court has long held that the Constitution protects parents' far-reaching control over their minor children.[29] While the Supreme Court has issued no opinions directly on point, a parent's choice to deceive his minor child arguably falls within the scope of parents' established constitutional rights.

However, any special prerogative that parents have to deceive their children should end when children reach the age of majority. This would track the law's usual practice of terminating parental prerogatives when a competent child reaches adulthood and be consistent with the existing constitutional precedents on parental rights, which focus on parental autonomy over minors. Under my approach, parents would have no special rights to dupe their adult offspring. Courts would begin by presuming that an adult suing her parent for injuries inflicted through deception in adulthood has access to the same causes of action that would be available when suing an equivalently deceptive stranger.

As this discussion makes clear, establishing a rebuttable presumption in favor of treating intimate deception like deception outside of intimacy would constitute a significant legal transformation. I will conclude this section by identifying potential arguments against creating such a presumption and explaining why I find them unconvincing. My reading of the existing case law on intimate deception leads me to think that this is how courts and critics would be most inclined to defend the status quo, although I cannot predict with certainty. To date, judges in this arena have tended to rely on visceral commitments and common sense intuitions as much as, or more than, reasoned arguments.

I am not worried that granting deceived intimates access to the same causes of action they would have if equivalently deceived outside of intimacy would allow the law to intervene in intimate relationships. First, civil litigation—by definition—begins at the plaintiffs' request. Judges hearing suits about intimate deception are not swooping in without invitation. They are deciding disputes that one party has brought to the courthouse. The plaintiffs have asked the judiciary for help.

Second, the premise of these suits is that the defendant has harmed the plaintiff. Denying deceived intimates remedies in the name of nonintervention would leave their injuries unredressed, even when the law would provide relief for an equivalent injury inflicted outside of intimacy. The appeal of leaving the status quo intact turns on what the law is preserving. Here, the law would be ignoring injuries simply because they took place between people who were once intimately connected.

Third—and most fundamentally—the law always and inescapably regulates our intimate lives, whether courts side with plaintiffs or defendants in litigation over injuries stemming from intimate deception. Rejecting plaintiffs' claims leads to fewer lawsuits than granting redress. But either way, the law is setting rules, establishing baselines, determining rights and responsibilities, and making normative judgments. As we have seen, courts are already deciding which relationships count as intimate and which do not, what legal consequences flow from forming an intimate relationship or being duped into one, and which types of intimate behavior are normal and which are deviant. The relevant questions are not about whether the law will intervene in intimacy. They are about how, when, why, and where the law will intervene and in whose interests. The law presently offers enormous protection to people who dupe their intimates. The rebuttable presumption I propose would do more to help people injured through intimate deceit and less to shield their deceivers.

I am also not worried that granting deceived intimates access to more remedies would discourage reconciliation. By the time a plaintiff files a lawsuit, any intimate ties that once connected the plaintiff and defendant have usually been severed—often because the plaintiff discovered that the defendant was duping her. I agree that reconciliation between the parties is unlikely after litigation. That is one reason why someone who wants to preserve her relationship with the person who deceived her is unlikely to sue. I have no quarrel with deceived intimates who decide not to pursue litigation in the interest of maintaining relationships. At the same time, I do not think that the law has a stake in encouraging the rekindling of all intimate connections, even when the plaintiff has chosen to seek redress for injuries her once-intimate inflicted. If a relationship is nasty and brutish, the law should not object if it is short.

I am not worried that creating a rebuttable presumption in favor of treating intimate deception like deceit in other contexts would encourage deceived intimates to feel aggrieved when they otherwise would accept their lot. The law currently gives deceived intimates little, if any, incentive to think of themselves as injured. Nonetheless, many people are already well aware that their intimate's deceit has harmed them financially, physically, emotionally, and/or otherwise. They are not waiting for legal authorities to alert them to that reality. Of course, some deceived intimates may take their injuries more seriously once the law does as well. That can happen whenever courts are willing to hear a claim and whenever lawyers are willing to consider taking a client's case rather than dismissing the possibility of litigation at the outset. I would be pleased, rather than concerned, if providing more remedies for intimate deception prompted some people to realize that they deserve better than to suffer at the hands of a duplicitous intimate.

I am not worried that giving deceived intimates access to the same causes of action they would have if equivalently deceived outside of intimacy would "open the floodgates" and overwhelm the judiciary with new cases. As an initial matter, it is worth noting that numerous factors would constrain the increase in litigation about intimate deception. While the advent of a more favorable legal regime for deceived intimates would attract widespread attention, that news would not reach every potential plaintiff. Even when deceived intimates were aware of their improved prospects for success in court, many would remain unwilling to subject themselves to the stress and public exposure involved in pursuing a lawsuit and the feelings of embarrassment that can arise from revealing that one has been duped in a culture that tends to blame deceived intimates for having been fooled.

Moreover, structural features of the American litigation system would continue to discourage lawsuits. Most potential plaintiffs lack the desire and ability to represent themselves. This means that filing suit entails either the considerable expense of paying an attorney—which may be an uncomfortable burden, perhaps an impossible one—or the challenge of finding a lawyer who will work for a contingency fee. A would-be plaintiff may be reluctant to pay a lawyer, and an attorney will be disinclined to work on contingency, if winning a large damage award is unlikely or if the potential defendant lacks the means to pay. In general, lawyers are most willing to work on contingency when the would-be plaintiff has suffered substantial injuries and can present strong evidence to support her allegations and when the would-be defendant has the resources to provide compensation for the harm he caused. Some of the barriers to entry in our litigation system—like the usual need to hire lawyers—help sort stronger from weaker claims before any suit is filed. At the same time, some of these same barriers— like the expense of litigation and the importance of lawyers—disproportionately exclude people with less money, less savvy, and fewer connections. People with fewer resources are less able to pursue litigation. People with fewer resources are also more likely to be in intimate relationships with other poor people, who do not have the money to pay a damage award—so suing them is not worth a lawyer's time. There are myriad good reasons to criticize unequal access to justice. But the persistence of structural barriers to pursuing civil litigation is an issue that extends well beyond the regulation of intimate deception. These barriers are likely to remain in place for the foreseeable future—whether or not courts bring deceived intimates into the law governing deception in other contexts.

Recall too that the rebuttable presumption I propose would not alter tort law's systematic undervaluing of emotional injuries, meaning that plaintiffs who have not been injured physically and/or financially would still face significant obstacles to winning damage awards and might have little economic incentive to sue. In short, numerous constraints would limit the increase in litigation from courts embracing a rebuttable presumption in favor of treating intimate deception like deception elsewhere.

More fundamentally, however, I reject the implicit normative premise underlying warnings that the floodgates would open if deceived intimates had more remedies. Such arguments not only predict a flurry of new cases if legal reform is implemented, they also assume that those cases would not really be important enough to merit the judiciary's attention—that the added cases would burden judges, rather than presenting courts with a valuable opportunity to redress a pervasive source of injury. Yet many examples of intimate deception cause much more harm than the run-of-the-mill contract disputes and tort suits that consume much of the judiciary's civil docket. The mere fact that deception occurs within an intimate relationship does not make the resulting injuries less severe or less worthy of judicial time.

I am not worried that deceived intimates may file suit in part because they dislike, even hate, the people they are suing. First, such dislike is not independent from the deception at issue; the defendant's deceitfulness may be why the plaintiff loathes him. Second, I suspect that plaintiffs commonly feel animosity toward the individuals they are suing, no matter what the subject of the litigation. As just discussed, suing someone can be emotionally and financially taxing. That helps explain why the vast majority of people with potential tort claims never sue, despite all the myths about America as a litigious society.[30] Would-be plaintiffs may be more willing to bear the burdens of litigation when they dislike the person who injured them. For example, the available evidence suggests that less likeable physicians may be sued more often for medical malpractice.[31] The law does not ordinarily bar litigation because of the possibility that the plaintiff dislikes, or even detests, the defendant. If the legal system took such a position, there might not be many lawsuits left. Third, if a suit actually is frivolous and motivated by spite alone, the law already has means of dealing with that problem. Plaintiffs bear the burden of proof in civil litigation. If they cannot prove their allegations and establish their injuries, they lose. Courts can impose sanctions on attorneys who litigate frivolous claims and/or can order a plaintiff to pay the defendant's legal fees. The judiciary has already focused tort law on physical and financial injuries rather than emotional damage, in part because courts recognize the possibility of frivolous or fraudulent suits and think that physical and financial injuries are easier to prove or disprove. Finally, civil litigation should give plaintiffs a calmer and safer forum for expressing any animosity than many of the extralegal alternatives that a person might pursue in the absence of a legal remedy, such as the violence, mayhem, and destruction that we have seen some deceived intimates inflict after they discover the deceit.[32]

I am not worried that treating intimate deception like deception outside of intimacy would be inconsistent with no-fault divorce. Establishing the legal right to end an unhappy marriage was a crucial advance for liberty and autonomy. But the availability of no-fault divorce does not and should not mean that conduct within marriage falls outside the reach of civil law, so there is no remedy for injuries one spouse inflicts on another. If that was the case, then the availability of no-fault divorce would suggest that a person beaten during her marriage cannot obtain redress from her abusive spouse for the damage and suffering he caused. Such a position would be deeply unappealing. No-fault divorce protects the freedom to dissolve a marriage. It neither guarantees nor rests on the "freedom" to harm one's spouse and escape the legal consequences that would attach to such behavior if directed at a nonintimate. While marriage is a union, it no longer marks the disappearance of individual personhood—for women or men. Marrying should not mean losing your rights to pursue ordinary civil remedies when injured. That is one reason why the vast majority of states have abolished interspousal tort immunity, which had allowed married people to inflict a wide variety of injuries on their spouses—including intentional violence—without fear of tort liability.[33] Marriage no longer immunizes people from the reach of tort law.

Lastly, I am not worried that providing more legal redress for intimate deception would undermine people's intrinsic motivations to treat their intimates well, weakening their internalized sense that deceiving intimates is wrong and their internalized commitment to avoiding such deceit. A growing literature in recent years has explored circumstances where the use of external incentives arguably crowds out and undercuts intrinsic motivations to behave in socially positive ways, perhaps even to the point that the imposition of external incentives is counterproductive. The crowding out literature has most commonly focused on situations where providing monetary rewards for socially desirable behavior might weaken intrinsic motivations to engage in that behavior.[34] I think it is extremely unlikely that a similar dynamic would operate in the context of legal reform offering more remedies for intimate deception.

First, the risk that creating legal incentives for good behavior might inadvertently undermine people's intrinsic motivations is most concerning in contexts where those intrinsic motivations are currently robust and effectively inspire people to behave in socially positive ways, even without the aid of legal carrots or sticks. Some people do refrain from deception because harming their intimates through deceit would violate their own sense of morality and their personal commitment to their intimates. But overall, the available evidence suggests that deception is widespread within intimacy and frequently causes significant injury. Intimate deception has flourished under a regime that creates few legal incentives to avoid such deceit. Crowding out arguments worry about disrupting the status quo that prevails before the creation of external incentives, but the status quo here is unsatisfactory and ripe for disruption.

Second, even the most ardent proponents of crowding out theories do not contend that the *usual* response to legal reform taking a source of injury more seriously is for people to conclude that the harm is less important than they previously thought. Crowding out arguments have attracted attention by asserting that external incentives can have counterproductive consequences in some instances, when classic economic theory would predict that such counterproductivity never materializes. Much more commonly, however, the law's expression and enforcement of normative judgments helps move popular opinion in the same direction. Think about the legal campaigns designed to detect, penalize, and discourage domestic violence and drunk driving. Those campaigns build on—but also promote and bolster—social norms condemning domestic violence and drunk driving as wrongful. I see no reason why that ordinary dynamic would not apply to legal reform treating intimate deception as seriously as deception outside of intimacy.

Exceptional Contexts Where Judges Should Deny Redress for Harmful Intimate Deception

Creating a rebuttable presumption that deceived intimates will have access to the same causes of action as people equivalently deceived outside of intimacy should fundamentally improve the law's regulation of deceit in intimate relationships. In advocating for this starting presumption, however, I do not mean to suggest that courts should grant redress for every instance of intimate deception that causes harm, even severe harm. I have already discussed how courts are highly unlikely to provide redress where parents have deceived their minor children. This section is devoted to exploring two other exceptional contexts where judges should deny remedies to plaintiffs harmed by an intimate's deceit, and compelling arguments for additional exceptions may emerge over time. The first exception involves situations where providing redress would inflict significant injury on a blameless third party, such as a child. The second involves scenarios where telling the truth would have placed the deceiver or a third party in imminent physical danger.

We can explore how denying remedies to deceived intimates can protect innocent third parties from significant harm by considering suits seeking redress for deception about paternity or deception about contraception or sterility that led to the birth of a child. Many men have sued for fraud, intentional infliction of emotional distress, or similar causes of action seeking damages from a woman—frequently the plaintiff's former wife—who allegedly deceived the plaintiff into believing that he was the biological father of the defendant's child.[35] A man pursuing such litigation commonly argues that he would not have devoted "time, emotion, and money" to the child in question if he had known the child was not his biological offspring.[36] Plaintiffs also frequently emphasize the distress they experienced upon discovering that they had been duped.[37] Such assertions are often very plausible. Deception about biological paternity can be tremendously consequential—even life-changing—for a deceived man.

Similarly, multiple plaintiffs—mostly men, but also a few women—have brought suit for fraud, intentional infliction of emotional distress, or the like seeking damages from a former sexual partner who allegedly deceived the plaintiff into believing that the partner was sterile or using contraception. These plaintiffs report that they relied on the defendant's deceit, only to find that sex with the defendant resulted in pregnancy and the birth of a child.[38] People bringing such litigation explain that they did not want to have a child with the defendant.[39] Male plaintiffs tend to focus on the financial burden of paying child support.[40] Female plaintiffs tend to identify a wider range of injuries that reflects both the biological reality that only women experience the tribulations of pregnancy and childbirth as well as the social reality that these women will devote their energy along with their money to caregiving.[41] Both male and female plaintiffs emphasize their distress after learning that they had been deceived.[42] These suits draw power from the reality that becoming a parent can be life-changing, meaning that deceit leading to childbearing can have life-changing consequences.

In my view, however, courts should nonetheless refuse to provide remedies if there is reasonable cause to believe that granting redress would significantly harm the child at issue. Moreover, I anticipate that judges will have strong grounds for reaching such a conclusion in any suit where the plaintiff's claim for damages rests on injuries he allegedly suffered because the defendant's deceit pushed the plaintiff into a relationship with a child. The law cannot make a person want a meaningful relationship with a child, but the legal system can shape the incentives it creates and the roles it plays. The law should not give people incentives to describe their relationships with children as injuries to themselves that they would have avoided if they had known the truth. Courts should refuse to become vehicles for encouraging, amplifying, and formalizing such messages. Even if—or especially if—such contentions accurately describe the plaintiffs' feelings, they are bound to wound the children, who are not responsible for the deceit and who are inherently more vulnerable than adults. Litigation identifying the plaintiff's relationship with a child as a source of injury can only further harm and humiliate the child in question and further strain her relationship with the man she once thought was her biological father (in suits over deception about paternity) or the plaintiff who is her biological parent (in suits over deception about contraception or sterility).

Some courts already refuse to provide remedies for deception about pater-nity,[43] although not every court has taken that position.[44] Plaintiffs have not been successful in securing remedies for deception about contraception or sterility that led to the birth of the plaintiff's biological child with the defendant.[45] Yet even courts that reach the right conclusion often do so for the wrong reasons or do not clearly articulate the best argument for denying redress—protecting chil-dren from significant harm.

Courts should not deny redress to keep the law from intervening in inti-mate relationships. Judges have often invoked that line of argument in refusing to provide remedies to plaintiffs who contended that they were injured by a sexual partner's deceit about contraception or sterility, which led to the birth of a child.[46] Stephen K. sued Roni L. "for fraud, negligent misrepresentation and negligence," reporting that he had sex with her while relying on her false repre-sentation that she was using birth control. The intercourse left Roni pregnant and Stephen made clear that he considered the resulting baby "unwanted."[47] The unanimous California Court of Appeal emphasized nonintervention arguments in dismissing Stephen's claims in 1980.[48] The court stated that it did not want to "define any standard of conduct" with respect to deception about contracep-tion,[49] "attempt to resolve such claims,"[50] or "encourage unwarranted govern-mental intrusion."[51] Yet keeping "the practice of birth control" cleanly "free from any governmental interference"[52] was not a realistic possibility, whether or not the court ruled for Stephen. Either way, the court would be establishing the legal ground rules that govern deception about contraception, setting baselines, and structuring incentives. Either way, the court would be adjudicating the dispute between the former sexual partners—now antagonists rather than intimates. When the court dismissed Stephen's suit, it decided that people are free to de-ceive their sexual partners about contraception and will bear no tort liability for harm inflicted through such deceit.

Courts should not deny redress by blaming deceived intimates for failing to protect themselves. This argument has also frequently appeared in decisions refusing to provide remedies to plaintiffs who reported deception about contra-ception that led to the birth of a child. Judges declare that the plaintiffs should have insisted on condoms, no matter what a sexual partner allegedly said about her use of other contraception. Opinions proclaim that "no good reason appears why [the plaintiff] himself could not have taken any precautionary measures" to avoid "fathering a child he did not want,"[53] or that the plaintiff "was free and able to practice contraceptive techniques on his own" if he "did not desire children."[54] Such arguments tend to fault people for the ordinary behavior of trusting their intimates. Moreover, these arguments overlook the obstacles to using visible contraceptives like condoms after a sexual partner has declared them unnecessary. In such circumstances, attempting to protect oneself from the consequences of possible deceit by insisting on condoms could be seen—with good reason—as an expression of distrust that could itself destabilize a relationship. Recall (from Chapter 2) the public health studies reporting that some people think that agreeing to sex without condoms is a powerful way to demonstrate trust that a sexual partner is honest and monogamous.

Courts should not block deceived intimates from suing by asserting that recognizing a claim would "serve as a vehicle for much vexatious and fraudulent litigation."[55] Some courts have made such pronouncements in dismissing suits seeking redress for deception about contraception that led to the birth of a child—even though the courts can cite no evidence that the plaintiffs have fabricated their allegations.[56] Fraudulent complaints are possible whenever the law recognizes any cause of action. But one of the judicial system's central roles is to distinguish fraudulent from meritorious claims, in part by holding trials that place the burden of proof on plaintiffs. Here, as elsewhere, some plaintiffs will have difficulty meeting this burden—whether because they invented their allegations or because they simply cannot present sufficient evidence to support their claims.[57] That should not be a reason to deny every plaintiff reporting deception about contraception the chance to prove his case if he can.

Courts should not deny redress through overly broad interpretations of prohibitions on heart balm litigation.[58] "John Doe" sued "Jane Doe" for fraud and intentional infliction of emotional distress, reporting that she deceived him to conceal that he was not the biological father of two of the three children born during their marriage.[59] The unanimous Maryland Court of Appeals dismissed the case in 2000, relying on the state's ban on suits for criminal conversation.[60] Recall (from Chapter 4) that the common law tort of criminal conversation authorized a cuckolded husband to sue his wife's paramour for damages. The Maryland legislature never prohibited criminal conversation suits, but the Maryland Court of Appeals abolished the tort in 1980.[61]

At this point, we should hardly be surprised to learn that a court has prevented a deceived intimate from seeking legal remedies by contending that the litigation is incompatible with a prohibition on heart balm suits. The judiciary has an oft-demonstrated tendency to read such prohibitions expansively. Yet it distorts John's case to assert that he was using the facade of "different tort labels" in an attempt to resuscitate the criminal conversation tort.[62] John's complaint pivoted on Jane's alleged deceit.[63] In contrast, criminal conversation suits were about adultery rather than deception. Even the Maryland court dismissing John's suit acknowledged that success in a criminal conversation case did not turn on whether the plaintiff had been duped. The fact that a wife had committed adultery without her husband's consent was sufficient to establish criminal conversation, whether or not the wife and/or her lover bothered to hide her infidelity from her husband.[64]

The Maryland Court of Appeals could have awarded John redress while maintaining its commitment to denying "tort damages based upon adultery."[65] John argued—very plausibly—that Jane's deceit about the paternity of two of her children (twins) harmed him.[66] This deceit may have overlapped with Jane's adultery, but was distinct from it. If Jane had told John about her affair, he would have known that he might not be the twins' biological father. John would not have been duped and he could have made more informed decisions about whether and how to embark on relationships with the twins.

There was a good reason to dismiss John's case. Namely, allowing John's suit to proceed could have inflicted significant harm on the twins by conveying and publicizing the message that John considered himself injured by their existence. However, John's claim about misrepresented paternity was not the same thing as a complaint about adultery and the court should not have treated that claim as inconsistent with a prohibition on criminal conversation suits.

Finally, courts should not deny deceived intimates redress by invoking un-specified public policy considerations. Simply declaring that a suit seeking remedies for deception about paternity is contrary to public policy does not clearly state the real problem with such litigation, which is that it may cause the child in question significant harm. Consider Peter Nagy's suit against his ex-wife, Sabina Nagy, for fraud and intentional infliction of emotional distress.[67] Peter contended that Sabina duped him into believing that he was the biological fa-ther of Christopher, who was born during their marriage.[68] Sabina allegedly did not reveal her deceit until Christopher was more than three and a half years old and the Nagys were in the process of divorcing. Peter stressed that he relied on Sabina's misrepresentation about paternity in "developing a very close and inti-mate relationship with Christopher," in which he "performed all acts that a father would towards a son."[69] The California Court of Appeal asserted in dismissing the suit in 1989 that permitting Peter to pursue his fraud claim "would be con-trary to public policy."[70] The opinion declared that "allowing a non-biological parent to recover damages for developing a close relationship with a child misrepresented to be his and performing parental acts is not a 'damage' which should be compensable under the law."[71] But the court did not make explicit that dismissing Peter's claim—and discouraging future litigation from similarly deceived men—could help protect children from the harm of having a once-father describe their relationship as a source of injury.

A few courts have made the case for denying redress plainly.[72] The Nebraska Supreme Court's unanimous 2002 opinion rejecting Robert Day's suit against his ex-wife, Robin Heller, is exemplary.[73] Heller bore a son, Adam, while mar-ried to Day and allegedly deceived Day to conceal that another man was the biological father. Day reported that he obtained DNA testing about eight years after his divorce, when Adam was almost twelve. Day's interest in continuing his relationship with Adam apparently vanished once he saw the test results. Approximately a month after learning that Adam was not his biological child, Day agreed to have Heller's new husband adopt the boy. The adoption took place soon after Adam's twelfth birthday.[74] Day then turned to suing his ex-wife for fraud, assumpsit, and intentional infliction of emotional distress.[75] In refusing to allow Day's suit to proceed, the court stressed how the litigation could harm Adam. As the opinion aptly observed, "a tort or assumpsit claim that seeks to recover for the creation of a parent-child relationship has the effect of saying 'I wish you had never been born' to a child who, before the revelation of biological fatherhood, was under the impression that he or she had a father who loved him or her." The court rightly refused to permit Day "to use a tort or assumpsit claim as a means for sending or reinforcing this message."[76]

The unanimous Washington Court of Appeals was similarly insightful in dismissing Robert Moorman's suit against Tracy Walker.[77] Moorman had a child with Walker after the couple had unprotected sex. Moorman sued Walker for misrepresentation, contending that she deceived him into believing that she was infertile.[78] The Washington court emphasized in dismissing Moorman's suit in 1989 that it would "not collaborate in conduct that disparages an innocent child." As the court explained, allowing "parents to disparage their child by claiming in open court that the child's existence has damaged them" could cause "emotional harm to the child." The court insisted that "[p]arents must put their children's interests above their own."[79]

None of this is to deny that deception about paternity or deception about contraception or sterility can cause the deceived person enormous harm. Such deceit can inflict tremendous damage, and I would not hesitate to argue for redress if courts could provide a remedy without harming a child. The clearest opportunity to provide remedies without injuring a child appears when there is no child.[80] For example, courts should provide remedies for harm inflicted through deception about infertility when such deception results in the plaintiff's unwanted pregnancy, but not the birth of a live baby. Consider Barbara Allen's tort suit against John Gatfield.[81] Allen reported that Gatfield lied to her about being sterile to induce her to have sex with him.[82] She conceived and it was a life-threatening ectopic pregnancy.[83] Allen needed surgery that removed her fallopian tube and left her infertile.[84] The California Court of Appeal was right to hold in 1983 that Allen could sue Gatfield for battery and deceit because her allegations satisfied all the ordinary elements of those causes of action.[85] Allowing the lawsuit to proceed gave Allen an opportunity to prove that Gatfield had duped her and caused her "physical, emotional, and financial" harm.[86] At the same time, the litigation would not make a child feel that she was unwanted, unloved, or a burden on her parents because Allen's pregnancy did not lead to the birth of a child.[87]

Given the injuries that intimates can inflict through deception related to childbearing, and the likelihood that permitting tort suits for such deception would harm the children in question, the legal system should look for alternative ways of mitigating the damage from deceit. Instituting routine DNA testing at birth is one approach that lawmakers could take to counter deception about biological paternity, and it would operate before father-child relationships develop. I think lawmakers should seriously consider whether to implement such a policy.

The federal government sets standards for states in this area by mandating state compliance with federal rules as a condition of receiving federal funds. Federal law currently requires DNA testing in certain contested paternity cases. But if a man accepts a mother's representation that he is the biological father of her child, the man can become the child's legal father without first confirming the blood tie.[88] In fact, federal law actually prohibits states from insisting on DNA testing before a man can voluntarily acknowledge paternity and become a child's legal father.[89]

This legal regime makes duping a man about paternity easier to accomplish because it leaves DNA testing as an option that men have to pursue, rather than a default procedure. A man who cares deeply about whether he is a child's biological father might not ask for a DNA test because he trusts his partner and believes he has no reason to doubt his biological paternity. Even a man without complete confidence in his partner's monogamy may be unwilling to demand DNA testing out of concern that voicing doubt by asking for a test could destabilize his relationships with the mother and child—even if he proves to be the biological father.

The federal government could remove the prohibition that prevents states from making DNA testing a prerequisite to the establishment of legal paternity. States could then choose to make DNA testing a routine part of newborn procedures. For example, a state could provide that one of the requirements for being named as a legal parent on a child's birth certificate will be that the parent must have either undergone DNA testing that confirms his genetic connection or signed a notarized statement acknowledging that he is not the child's genetic parent. A state could potentially apply this requirement to mothers and fathers alike and have the requirement operate in the same way regardless of whether a woman was married when she gave birth.

The approach just outlined would not mean that only genetic parents could be listed on a child's birth certificate. The policy would not prevent both members of a same-sex couple from being identified as legal parents on a child's birth certificate, for instance, or mean that a woman could not be named as a legal mother because she used someone else's eggs to bear a child. It would not bar a man from becoming the legal father of a child who was not his biological offspring.

Making DNA testing routine at birth would neither force a man deceived about biological paternity to leave the child's life nor compel him to remain involved. Instead, a state would attempt to ensure that a person knows whether he is a child's genetic parent before his name appears on a birth certificate as a legal parent.

Once a person signed a notarized statement acknowledging the absence of a genetic connection, he could not later use the lack of genetic ties as grounds for severing his legal relationship with the child or reducing his legal responsibilities to the child. Similarly, once a genetic parent agreed that someone without genetic ties to the child should be named as a legal parent on the birth certificate, genetics could not subsequently be a reason to privilege the genetic parent over the nongenetic parent in legal proceedings.

States could further provide that adult children will have the right to access the information in their birth records about whether they are genetically related to one or both of their legal parents—information that would not appear on the birth certificate itself for all to see. If an adult child chose to request the information, she could learn whether her parents underwent DNA testing that confirmed their genetic relationship to her or signed affidavits stating that they were not her genetic parents. This would be the adult child's own choice to make, and government officials would not inform the child's parents about her request for the information in her birth records.

Routine DNA testing at birth would have the considerable advantage of generating information about biological paternity sooner rather than later. A man would know before embarking on the life-altering work of parenting a child whether he was that child's biological father. Testing biological paternity at the outset of a child's life would be a more powerful and effective means of countering the injuries that deception about paternity can inflict than offering deceived men redress after the fact.

Establishing biological paternity at the beginning of a child's life can also protect that child from later shocks and disruptions. Some men who discovered years after a child's birth that they were deceived about biological paternity have responded by reducing their commitment to and engagement with the child.[90] Indeed, some men have reacted by seeking to sever their ties with children they had been parenting.[91] After Gerald Miscovich learned that he was not the biological father of the child his ex-wife bore during their marriage, he shared the news with the four year-old and "ceased all contact with the child."[92] Franklin Simmons told the Texas courts that once he discovered that his ex-wife had deceived him about biological paternity "his attitude toward [the teenager] changed to such an extent that it is not in the child's best interest to continue the parent-child relationship."[93]

I will not minimize the harm these men experienced when they were deceived about biological paternity, but also will not defend how they behaved after learning the truth. I would have urged them to set their own emotions and injuries aside and do everything in their power to maintain their relationships with the children they had been parenting—for the children's sake, if not their own.

Nonetheless, a parent intent on abandonment, or even partial disengagement, can devastate a child left behind. If a man is going to discontinue or curtail contact with a child because the two lack a biological connection, that rejection will cause less emotional harm to the child if it occurs during infancy rather than after the child has developed a lived relationship with the man she considers her father. Chandria's once-loving father cut off contact when she was eleven after discovering that Chandria's mother had deceived him about biological paternity. Nine years later, Chandria reported that the experience "kind of wrecked my self-esteem." She explained that: "Even now, I worry about being a burden on people. I don't want to be in the way. I don't want to be anybody's problem. It's made me apprehensive about getting attached to people, because one day they're there and the next day maybe they won't be. You can't help but be careful."[94]

The routine DNA testing at birth that I have outlined here would also have the advantage of making it more difficult for legal parents to deceive their adult children by falsely presenting themselves as genetic parents when they are not. States should never compel adult children to order their complete birth records, but states could help adult children who conclude that they are better off knowing the truth. Many people want to know their genetic origins, for a multitude of reasons including that they want to understand how they came into the world, want to meet their biological parents and biological siblings, and/or want to be informed about genetic health risks they may face.[95] Some people have even pursued litigation as a means of confirming or uncovering the identity of a biological parent.[96] One adult child, Jeanne Tedford, sued a man who had an affair with her mother around the time of conception and convinced a court to order DNA testing that established his biological paternity.[97] Another child sued his mother while he was still a minor in an unsuccessful attempt to learn the identity of his biological father.[98] No plausible legal regime could ensure that every adult child knows the identities of her genetic parents. But the approach outlined here would permit many adult children to learn whether their legal parents are their genetic parents. Moreover, this policy would give parents strong incentives to share the truth about genetic parenthood with their children as they grow up because parents would know that children could discover the facts on their own once they reached adulthood.

I think the advantages of instituting routine DNA testing at birth are significant and make this policy possibility worth serious consideration. That said, potential objections and disadvantages need to be explored as well. I will begin with some objections that I find less troubling and then turn to some objections I find more concerning.

One potential objection to routine DNA testing at birth is that such a policy would place undue emphasis and attention on genetics. I agree that routine DNA testing at birth would not make much sense if people attached little importance to whether they have genetic connections to children. However, many people are intensely interested in whether they are a child's genetic parent. Discovering that the genetic relationship they thought existed is not actually there would impact their subsequent decisionmaking about involvement with the child precisely because of the significance they attribute to genetics. Of course, not everyone places the same weight on genetics, and the weight any particular person gives to genetics may vary by context. But the approach outlined above would neither fault people for caring about genetic connections nor compel people to emphasize genetics when they would prefer to prioritize other considerations in deciding whether to become a child's legal parent. The proposed approach would not require a genetic connection between legal parents and their children. Instead, it would help disclose whether a genetic connection exists.

Another potential objection to routine DNA testing at birth is that some marriages and nonmarital relationships would be shaken—or shattered—by the revelation that a woman has conceived a child with someone other than her husband or primary partner or the news that a man has fathered a child with someone other than his wife or primary partner. That bombshell would be enough to destroy even some long-term bonds and would swiftly end many relationships where the couple has little in common except for the child. Routine DNA testing would not force adults apart. But it would thwart deception that could be keeping them together. I do not derive any pleasure or satisfaction from the prospect of marriages or nonmarital relationships ending. I would not want to understate the associated heartache, and I am not advising people that they should break up if DNA testing reveals deceit. However, the likelihood that routine DNA testing at birth would lead to some divorces or nonmarital dissolutions does not present a compelling argument against such testing. Government policies designed to enhance the stability of intimate relationships between adults are often well-founded. Such stability can foster human flourishing, caregiving, community, and joy. But a government's legitimate interests in relationship stability do not extend to promoting the preservation of adult relationships that can be maintained only if one party successfully dupes the other about an issue that the deceived person would consider vitally important. The law should not help keep deceit under wraps in order to preserve adult relationships that would end if a linchpin deception was unmasked and the facts came out.

Another set of potential objections to routine DNA testing at birth centers on practicalities and logistics. In theory, lawmakers could overcome these obstacles through careful regulatory design. But what is theoretically possible does not always match what is realistically achievable. Routine DNA testing at birth would have to be implemented well to be an appealing policy option.

The first, and perhaps greatest, practical challenge is financial. A state, or the federal government, would have to pay for the DNA testing and the administrative costs associated with incorporating DNA testing into newborn procedures—either all the time or at least when the parties are unable to pay. Making DNA testing routine at birth will not work if lawmakers are unwilling to devote adequate financial resources to such a regime. States cannot create a system where people are unable to establish their legal parenthood because they cannot afford DNA testing.

A second logistical challenge concerns privacy. Lawmakers would need to make clear that the people who provide their DNA samples for testing own those samples. Lawmakers should require testing facilities to destroy the samples after using them to confirm or disprove genetic parenthood. No one should be permitted to view, retain, or use the DNA records for other purposes, such as law enforcement. I would not support routine DNA testing at birth if the policy served as a vehicle for government officials to acquire and retain genetic information about an increasingly large proportion of the population.

A third practical challenge concerns quality control. Lawmakers making DNA testing routine at birth would need to regulate testing facilities to safeguard against mistakes and to subsidize immediate retesting when a party believes that a DNA test result is inaccurate. Routine DNA testing would be counterproductive if the results from that testing were not reliable.

A fourth practical challenge centers on protecting particularly vulnerable people. A state implementing routine DNA testing at birth would have to make provisions for victims of domestic violence who need to be protected from their abusers if DNA testing of their newborns reveals infidelity. Offering meaningful police protection and social support to people subject to domestic violence is always a good idea. A firm commitment to such policies, and sufficient funds to make them a reality, should be part of the implementation of routine DNA testing at birth. I would be very reluctant to endorse routine DNA testing at birth if a state is unwilling or unable to provide real protection and support to victims of domestic violence.

These practical and logistical challenges are substantial, but states could overcome them with sufficient money, time, and commitment. Perhaps the most concerning aspect of instituting routine DNA testing at birth is the likelihood that such testing will leave some children worse off. Consider a situation where the absence of routine DNA testing helps a woman successfully deceive her husband or boyfriend about biological paternity for a lifetime. So deceived, a man could become a legal father and have a wonderful influence on his child's life—with the relationship never disrupted by learning the truth about biological paternity. Routine DNA testing at birth will expose such subterfuge and the discovery that a child is biologically unrelated will push some men away from children that they would have otherwise raised. In some cases, moreover, the child's biological father will be an inadequate parent and a poor substitute for the mother's husband or boyfriend who disengages from the child upon learning that there is no biological tie. While a single mother may be able to provide for all of her child's emotional and financial needs, the persistence of women's economic inequality and the scant government support for parenting in the United States will make that more difficult.

I do not want to discount or minimize this troubling scenario. Lawmakers could reasonably decide against instituting routine DNA testing at birth because they are concerned about children's welfare. That said, there are also strong arguments on the other side that I find persuasive. First, it is worth putting concerns about children's welfare in context. If instituting routine DNA testing at birth will leave some children worse off, so will the absence of such testing. Failing to test DNA at birth is most likely to operate to a child's benefit in cases where the mother's deceit will never be uncovered, so the child's relationship with her legal father will never be roiled by discovering the absence of a biological connection. While one can hypothesize such a scenario, there is no guarantee that any actual situation will unfold that way. In real life, the absence of routine DNA testing at birth means that there will always be the chance that the truth about biological paternity will emerge later in a child's life—with potentially more calamitous consequences for the child.

Second and more fundamentally, I believe that a man has a legitimate interest in not being deceived about whether he is a child's biological father—even if such deceit would produce a commitment to parenting that would vanish if the man knew the child was not his biological offspring. Parenting can be a life-changing responsibility and many people consider the fact of a biological connection pivotal to their willingness to undertake that responsibility. One might wish that people would place less weight on biological ties, but the law does not ordinarily expect adults to take individual responsibility for children who are not their biological progeny simply because the children would benefit from the help.

I think a policy designed to make DNA testing routine at birth deserves serious consideration, whether or not lawmakers ultimately decide to implement such an approach. Routine DNA testing at birth represents a potential strategy for countering deception about biological paternity that operates before father-child relationships develop.

Let's turn to situations where courts should refuse to provide redress for injuries inflicted through intimate deception because telling the truth would have placed the deceiver and/or a third party in imminent physical danger. Being honest can often expose someone to negative consequences that she would like to avoid. An exception permitting intimates to escape legal responsibility for harmful deception whenever they resorted to deceit because they feared what would happen if they told the truth would be so far-reaching that it could defeat any effort to provide more redress for intimate deception. Such a sweeping exception would also be inconsistent with the law's usual practice of holding competent adults responsible for their decisions, including many decisions reached under challenging circumstances. If truth-telling would place the deceiver or another person in imminent physical danger, however, the threat spurring the deception is sufficiently immediate and serious that providing redress would be inappropriate. This level of risk is also rare enough that the exception will not overwhelm the general presumption in favor of providing more remedies to deceived intimates.

Many of the cases falling into this exception will involve domestic violence. People experiencing domestic violence often resort to deceit to avoid triggering their abusers' wrath.[99] Expecting someone to place herself or another in that much jeopardy by telling the truth is unrealistic and unreasonable. Moreover, a person who uses brutality to get his way should not have cause to complain if the people he abuses respond with deceit. Instead, the legal system should seek to counter this type of deception by augmenting the law's efforts to protect and empower abused intimates so they are out of danger. The fact that domestic violence frequently leads to deceit provides one more reason among many others for the law to deter and penalize that violence and help the people who experience it.

In short, courts should begin with a rebuttable presumption that plaintiffs deceived within intimacy will have access to the same causes of action they would have if equivalently deceived by a stranger. However, courts should override that baseline presumption when granting redress would inflict significant injury on a blameless third party or when telling the truth would have placed the deceiver or a third party in imminent physical danger.

Reforms to Improve the Legal Regulation of Intimate Deception Before Litigation Begins

Establishing a rebuttable presumption that judges will treat intimate deception like deception outside of intimacy would be an important advance. But the law can do more. The legal system should improve how it regulates intimate deception before litigation begins. Avoiding harm is better than having a right to legal redress after the injury has been inflicted and many deceived intimates will not sue, even if their chances of prevailing in court improve. The law helps shape the incentives to deceive and should do more to counter those incentives. The law also helps determine the ease with which intimate deceivers can accomplish their plans and should do more to thwart deceivers. Let's turn to thinking about reform beyond the courtroom.

Countering Incentives to Deceive

People often have enormous incentives to be deceitful within intimacy. The law itself has created or exacerbated some of those incentives, and the law can help lessen their magnitude and impact.

One strategy should center on adjusting legal rules that currently push people toward deceiving their intimates—or toward deceiving people into intimacy. For example, recall (from Chapter 1's discussion of gateway deception) that federal immigration law gives noncitizens who would like legal authorization to live and work in the United States tremendous incentives to dupe a United States citizen into marriage. Most people in the world have little, if any, chance of legally immigrating to the United States unless they marry a United States citizen.

In theory, the federal government could reduce the incentives to deceive citizens into sham marriages for immigration purposes by increasing the opportunities for legal immigration that are open to people who are not closely related to United States citizens. In practice, though, Congress is unlikely to expand immigration opportunities by the orders of magnitude that would be needed to make a noticeable dent in the incentives to dupe a citizen into marriage.

Whether or not Congress is willing to overhaul its general approach to immigration, the federal government should restructure its regulation of sham marriages. Federal law penalizing people who enter into sham marriages currently focuses on defending the integrity of the immigration system, without attempting to remediate the harms inflicted on deceived intimates. Someone who entered a sham marriage in cahoots with a willing accomplice is subject to the same legal penalties as someone who duped an unwitting citizen into a marriage that the citizen believed was genuine. Yet the latter set of offenders cause much more injury because they ensnare individual victims in the course of evading immigration requirements. The federal government should recognize that additional harm and do more to counter the incentives that the law creates to inflict it. To the extent that immigration officials and federal prosecutors have limited resources to devote to the problem of sham marriages, they should prioritize pursuing cases where the citizen was duped.

Congress could also rewrite federal law to provide that citizens deceived into sham marriages for immigration purposes are authorized to sue their deceivers in federal court for money damages. To be sure, many of these potential defendants will be judgment proof—meaning without sufficient assets to make suing them worthwhile, always a practical constraint on tort law. But some potential defendants will have resources. To prevail in such a suit, a plaintiff would have to prove that her spouse duped her to conceal that he had no intent to share his life with her and was using their marriage as a scheme to evade immigration requirements. Federal courts already have extensive experience evaluating such claims, as federal prosecutors enforcing prohibitions on sham marriages have to prove that their defendants schemed to evade immigration requirements by marrying.[100] If a citizen plaintiff proved her case, the statute could specify that she would automatically win a minimum damage award (perhaps $5000 and reasonable attorney's fees) and could win a larger award by establishing that her actual damages exceed the statutory minimum. For example, a damage award could compensate the plaintiff for any money she spent to help her spouse immigrate, any funds she expended for their wedding, and any economic opportunities she sacrificed or postponed because of their marital relationship.[101] If noncitizens who dupe citizens into sham marriages were subject to civil suits in addition to the usual legal penalties for marriage-related immigration fraud, that might help dissuade some people from pursuing such fraud—or at least convince them to find a willing partner in crime rather than preying on an unwitting dupe.

Another way the law can mitigate the incentives to deceive is by taking steps to counter the legalized inequality that can spur deceit within intimate relationships. Recall (from Chapter 1's discussion of deception from subordination) that some intimates resort to deception because they are disempowered and see deceit as a way to seize greater control over their lives. Inequality's role in fostering intimate deception constitutes yet another reason for the law to fight against subordination and discrimination.

Consider stay-at-home wives (or husbands) whose spouses refuse to give them cash or severely limit the cash they provide. As Chapter 1 explored, such enormous power imbalances can prompt cashless spouses to resort to deception in order to obtain funds that they can spend on their own or save for their own purposes. The law should look for opportunities to promote more egalitarian marital relationships—a policy goal with much to recommend it, including that reducing marital domineering should also diminish deceit designed to resist such domineering.

The good news is that the law has many ways to encourage and facilitate more egalitarian marriages in which both spouses have direct access to cash and similar economic opportunities. Indeed, exploring all the possibilities would require another book. For example, the law could pursue policies—like paid family leave and subsidized child care—that make it easier for both parents to work in the market. The law could do more to counter employment and wage discrimination based on sex, pregnancy, race, sexual orientation, national origin, and other illegitimate criteria. At the same time, the law could improve the bargaining power of spouses who do not work in the market by reforming divorce law so that married people who prioritize domestic responsibilities over market work do not need to fear impoverishment if they divorce.

Tax law also offers opportunities to promote more egalitarian marital relationships, and I will explore one such possibility at more length because it may be less intuitive. When a married couple files a joint federal income tax return, the federal government currently taxes the couple as if each spouse earned half of the total marital income—whether or not that is really the case.[102] This income-splitting for tax purposes creates little or no tax advantage when the two spouses actually earn similar incomes; their incomes are already divided evenly or almost evenly in real life.[103] But income-splitting for tax purposes can be enormously advantageous for wage-earners married to people who do not work in the market, allowing wage-earning spouses to move to lower tax brackets than the ones they would occupy if single.[104] Married people receive the benefits of income-splitting for tax purposes without having to present any evidence that each spouse controls half of the marital income. A wage-earning husband who refuses to give his stay-at-home wife access to cash enjoys the same tax advantages as a wage-earning husband who deposits his salary into a joint account that both spouses access equally.[105]

Family law runs through the federal tax code, one area among many where Congress uses tax laws to advance its social policy goals and to incentivize taxpayers to act in socially desirable ways.[106] With this in mind, Congress could adjust the tax code to create incentives for married people to arrange their finances on more egalitarian terms. Congress could provide that spouses may split their income for tax purposes only to the extent that they actually split their income in real life. In order to reap the tax advantages associated with an even division of marital income, a married couple would have to present evidence showing that each spouse has equal access to, control over, and ownership of the marital income.[107] As with all of tax law, administering such a system perfectly and ferreting out all noncompliance would be impossible. But tax administrators could focus on key pieces of evidence, like who owns and controls bank accounts, investment accounts, and major assets. Linking income splitting on tax forms to income splitting in real life would make it more expensive and/or more difficult for a wage-earning spouse to deprive his stay-at-home spouse of access to cash. The reform would simultaneously promote egalitarian marital relationships and reduce the incentives to deceive that inequality can foster.

Thwarting Intimate Deceivers

Countering incentives to deceive is an important strategy for diminishing the prevalence of deceit in intimate relationships. But even with such efforts, many people will still deceive their intimates in ways likely to inflict significant harm. With that in mind, the law should also pursue reforms designed to lessen the injuries that intimates experience when they are deceived. Deception generally causes less harm if it is unmasked sooner rather than later. So the law should make it easier for intimates to learn whether they are being deceived when such facilitation can be accomplished without jeopardizing privacy, liberty, or security. Similarly, deception will be less harmful if the law limits what a deceitful person can do without his intimate's knowledge and consent. So the law should make it harder for one intimate to take, sell, encumber, or otherwise expropriate jointly owned assets without the other intimate's permission when such safeguards can be erected without unduly burdening everyday transactions.

Let's start with making it easier to uncover deceit sooner. No one should be faulted or legally penalized for acting as an ordinary person would and trusting his intimates. Both human psychology and social norms push us toward such trust, and faith in our intimates can help foster human flourishing, caregiving, cooperation, and social bonds. The law should neither expect nor desire the end of trust within intimacy. That said, it should be abundantly clear after reading this book that sometimes people would be well-advised to be skeptical about what their intimates tell them and would be well-served by attempting to confirm their intimate's veracity and trustworthiness for themselves. Chapter 2 reviewed some of the myriad practical and legal obstacles to investigating an intimate and discovering whether he is being deceptive. As that chapter observed, many of these obstacles to investigation help protect important values of privacy, liberty, and security. I do not advocate giving people unrestricted access to information about their intimates—even if such transparency would substantially reduce deceit within intimate relationships. Tax returns, credit reports, medical records, private communications, and the like should not be open to the prying eyes of the suspicious or curious.

However, the law should look for opportunities to help people learn whether an intimate is deceiving them when that can be accomplished without infringing on privacy, liberty, or security, or creating other public policy problems. For example, many supposedly public records are often hard to access in reality. As a practical matter, they are most available to people with expertise, money, time, stamina, and/or luck—all resources unevenly distributed amongst us.[108] The states working together, ideally with the help of the federal government, could consolidate at least some public records and make them more accessible without unduly threatening privacy, liberty, or security. For instance, creating a centralized registry recording all marriages and divorces in the United States—as well as all bigamy convictions—would make it easier to determine a person's marital status and marital history, frequent subjects of deception when someone is trying to attract or retain a romantic partner. Such a centralized database could help individuals check whether their date—or fiancé—is as unmarried as he claims to be. The database could also be a resource for dating services that would like to verify the marital status and marital history of their users. Moreover, such a database would be a boon for scholars and researchers. At the same time, it would be difficult to argue that consolidating marriage and divorce records would seriously infringe on privacy, liberty, or security because those records are already public documents recording state action. In short, creating an accessible centralized registry for marriages and divorces would be valuable from many perspectives. I suspect the main obstacles would be logistical and financial. Lawmakers could ease those practical burdens by not attempting to include existing marriages and divorces in the centralized registry and instead operating the registry prospectively, so the registry would become more comprehensive and useful over time.

Let's turn to thinking about how the law could make it harder to harm an intimate without the intimate's knowledge. The legal system will not always have a realistic chance to place roadblocks in front of deceitful schemers, but should seize the available opportunities. For example, someone intent on taking, selling, encumbering, or otherwise expropriating a jointly owned asset without the knowledge and consent of his co-owner will often need the assistance of third parties, such as banks, mortgage companies, or credit card companies. The law can use this dependence on third parties to help thwart such deceivers, while creating safeguards to avoid unreasonable burdens on quotidian transactions.

Consider financial deception in marriage. Numerous judicial decisions discuss married people who deceived their spouses to conceal that they had bought a house with joint assets,[109] sold or given away a jointly owned home,[110] mortgaged a jointly owned home,[111] or accumulated credit card debt.[112] An unwitting spouse can pay a steep price for what happened without her knowledge or consent. Some courts have refused to let duped spouses escape financial liability for credit card debts or loans they did not know about or authorize.[113] I think courts should hold deceptive spouses responsible for the consequences of their financial deceit. But even when a deceptive spouse is punished after the fact, that penalty often does not return the duped spouse to the position she occupied before she was deceived. By that point, the damage has been done and the money to compensate the deceived spouse is often long gone. Thomas Garrison forged his wife's signature so he could secretly mortgage the family home. He then defaulted on the mortgage, which led the mortgage holder to foreclose on the home and sell it. Garrison was ultimately disbarred, but that punishment did not protect his wife and children from being forced to move.[114]

Deceitful spouses would inflict less injury if the law did more to stop them before they expropriated jointly owned assets without the other spouse's knowledge and permission. To be sure, insisting upon mutual spousal consent for every decision affecting jointly owned property would be impractical. Such a requirement could mean that both spouses would have to agree to—or even witness—every transaction with an impact on joint assets. Mandating constant marital togetherness or consultation in order to conduct ordinary business would be inefficient, even annoying. However, the law should look for opportunities to thwart the deceptive expropriation of marital assets when such safeguards would not unduly undermine the convenience and efficiency of everyday transactions.

For example, legislatures could require mutual spousal consent before a married person could use marital assets as collateral for a bank loan. Lawmakers could require mutual spousal consent before any real estate transaction—purchases, sales, mortgages, gifts, and the like—involving jointly owned assets. Legislatures could require mutual spousal consent before a married person could open a credit card account for which both spouses will be liable.

Such restrictions should be relatively easy to understand, publicize, and enforce. Some deceptive spouses would seek to evade them, but legislatures would not have to fight those evasions on their own. Lawmakers could give third parties powerful incentives to block deceptive spouses from accomplishing their plans. Legislatures could require banks to ensure that both spouses have consented before their joint assets are used as collateral for a bank loan. Lawmakers could similarly impose a legal duty on mortgage companies to ensure that both spouses have agreed to mortgage transactions involving jointly owned assets. If a bank or mortgage company violated this legal obligation, the law could subject the offending business to fines or, better yet, require the bank or mortgage company to compensate the deceived spouse for her losses. Along the same lines, legislatures could require credit card companies to obtain consent from both spouses before opening a credit card account that both spouses will be liable to pay off. If a married person did not consent in advance to the credit card account, he would not be obliged to pay off the charges. Lawmakers could also require credit card companies to send separate monthly statements to each spouse on a joint credit card account—ideally to separate email addresses, rather than the same postal address—increasing the chances that each spouse will be able to track activity on the joint account.

One way to verify the consent of both spouses would be to require signed and notarized authorizations from each spouse if the spouses do not personally appear to declare their consent. However, some people have forged their spouse's signature and managed to get it notarized—or notarized the forgery themselves.[115] Requiring the actual presence of both spouses to verify consent would provide more protection and accordingly could be worth the added inconvenience for the most consequential transactions. Transactions involving the sale or mortgaging of jointly owned real estate, or the purchasing of any real estate with joint funds, would be likely candidates for an actual presence requirement.

Such a regime promoting transparency between spouses would strengthen the protections the law offers against one spouse covertly seizing joint assets for himself. Consider community property states, which provide that both spouses jointly own community property during their marriage. Every community property state currently gives each spouse far-ranging authority to manage, control, and dispose of community property without informing the other spouse— much less obtaining her consent. Existing laws tend to create only a few limited exceptions to this regime, most commonly designed to ensure that both spouses consent to transactions involving jointly owned real estate.[116] Some community property states have statutory provisions specifying that a married person making decisions about joint assets has a duty to act as a fiduciary for his spouse or a duty to act in good faith.[117] That is a good start and more states should codify such requirements. Yet giving duped spouses a cause of action after the fact is no substitute for stopping duplicitous spouses before they can inflict injury in the first place. The legal system can and should do more to thwart intimate deceivers who seek to use joint assets for their own purposes.

In sum, the law has spent too much time and energy shielding people who deceive their intimates and placed too little emphasis on protecting people who are deceived. When a plaintiff sues a deceptive intimate, judges should begin with a rebuttable presumption that the plaintiff will have access to the same causes of action that would be available if she was equivalently deceived outside of intimacy. Before litigation begins, legislatures and courts should strive to counter intimate deception by fighting against the incentives to deceive, helping duped intimates discover the deceit sooner, and limiting the harm that the duplicitous can cause without their intimates' knowledge. Inside and beyond courtrooms, the law can and should do more to recognize, prevent, and redress injuries inflicted through deception within intimate relationships.

Conclusion

Deception pervades intimacy. The potential topics are innumerable, ranging from fidelity to finances, contraception to education, marital status to military service, fertility to criminality, to anything else that someone in an intimate relationship cares about. The consequences can be enormous, up to and including reshaping the fundamentals of a deceived person's life. Of course, harmful deceit does not mar every sexual, marital, or familial relationship. But the unsettling truth is that deception is common in intimate relationships and its victims are not confined to the particularly gullible or vulnerable.

One reason intimate deception is so prevalent is that people can often secure tremendous concrete and material benefits by deceiving their intimates or by deceiving someone into intimacy. People deceive to lure intimates in and to keep them from leaving. They dupe someone into marriage so they can obtain legal rights and privileges that are otherwise out of reach, such as legal immigration, Social Security spousal benefits, or government benefits for the spouses of veterans. They deceive their intimates to take advantage of them financially or sexually. They deceive to exercise power and control over their intimates or to resist such domination. They deceive their intimates because they are already deceiving someone else, or everyone else, and want to maintain the facade they have constructed.

Courts routinely blame deceived intimates for having been duped, misunderstanding and underestimating the obstacles to uncovering deceit and learning the truth. Human psychology, social norms, practical realities, and legal rules can all make intimate deception difficult to detect—even for a person of ordinary or above-average shrewdness and sophistication. The same legal system that faults plaintiffs for not unmasking their deceitful intimates sooner often creates many legitimate barriers to investigation. People who turned to covert reconnaissance in the hopes of determining whether an intimate was deceiving them have found themselves paying damage awards, out of a job, or even criminally prosecuted for their efforts. The civil and criminal penalties that the law imposes on intimates who investigate without consent help protect privacy, liberty, and security, but also help the duplicitous avoid discovery.

When an intimate is duped, the deceit can diminish his control over his life—reducing his autonomy, distorting his decisionmaking, constricting his choices, and upending his plans. Intimate deception can undermine financial security, imperil health and personal safety, violate sexual autonomy and bodily integrity, create unexpected vulnerability to criminal prosecution, waste time, destroy opportunities, and cause psychological and emotional pain, distress, and devastation. Our legal system and our culture discourage deceived intimates from sharing their experiences by denying them legal redress and blaming them for their plight. But it is nonetheless unsurprising that many intimates have publicly described the harm their deceivers caused. Deception within intimate relationships can inflict injuries that few of us would take lightly.

Intimate deception is an unavoidable issue for the law because it is such a perennial aspect of life. Courts and legislatures constantly have to decide how to anticipate, control, and respond to deceit within intimacy. In the process, these authorities have created a wide-ranging legal field that reflects, shapes, and enforces social norms. This is a key site where the law draws boundaries between intimate and other relationships, establishes the consequences of forming intimate ties, determines what constitutes acceptable behavior in intimacy, and regulates the meaning of gender, race, class, national origin, and other divides.

Courts routinely deny redress to deceived intimates and protect their deceivers. Indeed, the available remedies for intimate deception have contracted significantly since the early twentieth century or become much less valuable, with the enactment of anti-heart balm statutes that courts have interpreted expansively, the evolution in norms about race and gender, and the advent of no-fault divorce laws that have made annulment and fault-based divorce far less important.

The presumption that courts should treat intimate deception differently than deceit outside of intimacy runs through modern law. Judges repeatedly assume and insist that remedies available against deceptive strangers are not available to redress damage that deceptive intimates have caused. The persistently differentiated response to intimate deception means that legal regulation pivots on whether a court concludes that the plaintiff was intimately connected to the defendant at the time of the deceit. Judges rely on their own intuitions more than reasoned analysis in defining legally recognized intimacy. They are inclined to define intimacy broadly when sex and/or courtship are at issue, including people who did not know each other well. In contrast, judges tend to define intimacy narrowly in the context of familial relationships beyond marriage and parenthood, treating deceptive siblings, aunts, uncles, nieces, and nephews as if they were unrelated to people they deceived.

I suspected when I started this project that judges might deny redress for intimate deception on the assumption that such matters are unworthy of their notice, time, and concern. But in fact, judges repeatedly emphasize the importance of this regulatory arena in the course of turning plaintiffs away. They presume that deceit is widespread in courtship, sexual relationships, and marriage and take it as common sense that the judiciary should be fiercely committed to defending that status quo. Judges are much less likely to provide remedies when they think the intimate deception is typical and more likely to provide redress when they think the deceit is deviant and unusual. Judges also tend to be expansive in identifying what counts as commonplace deception within intimacy, treating some life-altering deceit as unexceptional. When judges presume that many examples of harmful deception are ordinary and expected aspects of romance, sex, and marriage, they help make that so—normalizing the deceit by protecting it from legal condemnation and redress. Moreover, judges sometimes protect admittedly extraordinary intimate deception out of concern that providing remedies might create a slippery slope that could eventually threaten more ordinary deceivers.

The same impulse to shield intimate deceivers and withhold remedies for the damage they cause appears when courts consider parents who have deceived their children, including their adult children. Indeed, judges sometimes write as if parents have a legal prerogative to dupe their children, whether the children are minors or adults. Courts are eager to uphold parents' authority and decisionmaking—even when it takes the form of harmful deceit—and quick to blame children for having been fooled.

The law can and should reorient its approach to deception within intimate relationships, extending more help to people injured by deceitful intimates and offering less protection to their deceivers. Courts should begin with a rebuttable presumption that deceived intimates will have access to the same causes of action as people equivalently deceived outside of intimacy. Legislatures and courts should also transform how they regulate intimate deception before litigation begins, countering the incentives to deceive, making it more difficult for deceivers to accomplish their plans, and limiting the damage that duplicitous intimates can inflict.

Deceit within intimate relationships is a persistent part of life and a consistent issue for the law. The legal rules, practices, and presumptions governing intimate deception have attracted little attention, remaining overlooked in the shadows rather than studied in the light. But this far-reaching body of law shapes both the everyday details and the overarching course of many lives, structuring people's decisionmaking, struggles, and opportunities. Intimate deception and the law governing it require much more critical scrutiny. The law of intimate deception is too important and needs too much reform to remain hidden in plain sight.

ACKNOWLEDGMENTS

It gives me great pleasure to thank the many people who helped me as I wrote this book. Jamie Abrams, Brian Bix, June Carbone, Maxine Eichner, Allan Erbsen, Carol Hasday, Clare Huntington, Serena Mayeri, and Barbara Welke did me the tremendous favor of reading the entire manuscript. I am grateful for their insightful comments.

Many more colleagues and friends read individual chapters and offered valuable feedback. I would like to thank Susanna Blumenthal, Jessica Clarke, Bella DePaulo, Deborah Dinner, Elizabeth Emens, Kristin Hickman, Craig Konnoth, Jason Mazzone, Tamara Piety, Robert Pollak, Rachel Rebouché, Jane Stoever, Kathryn Swanson, and the participants in workshops at Columbia Law School, Duke Law School, Harvard Law School, SMU Dedman School of Law, the University of Illinois College of Law, the University of Minnesota, UNLV William S. Boyd School of Law, and Washington University. I also benefited from presenting and discussing portions of the manuscript at many conferences on family law, feminist legal theory, and interdisciplinary approaches to law.

The University of Minnesota provided a wonderfully supportive environment in which to write this book. I began working on the book during a fellowship at Minnesota's Institute for Advanced Study. The Institute's collegial interdisciplinary environment and the semester off from teaching were both extraordinarily helpful as I outlined the book's arguments and dove into research. After I was immersed in writing the book, the grant I received when I became a Distinguished McKnight University Professor allowed me to take a year's leave that I used to complete multiple chapters.

The University of Minnesota Law Library is superb. The library's unparalleled commitment to supporting faculty scholarship enabled me to research this project without hiring research assistants. I have been fortunate to have the help of many fantastic librarians, including Scott Dewey, Connie Lenz, Suzanne Thorpe, and David Zopfi-Jordan.

David McBride, my editor at Oxford University Press, skillfully guided this book to publication. I appreciate his support and enthusiasm. I am also grateful for the thoughtful and constructive reviews that I received from Oxford's reviewers.

Most importantly, I would like to thank my family members for their love and support. My husband, Allan Erbsen, and my parents, Carol and Robert Hasday, have read my work for years and always encourage me to pursue my intellectual interests and personal goals. My children, Sarah, Daniel, and David, are the joy of my life. I dedicate *Intimate Lies and the Law* to my loved ones. They did not inspire me to write this book.

NOTES

Introduction

1. *See* Whelan v. Whelan, 56 Va. Cir. 362, 362–65 (2001).
2. *See* Smith v. Smith, 438 S.E.2d 457, 458–60 (N.C. Ct. App. 1994).
3. *See* Conley v. Romeri, 806 N.E.2d 933, 935–39 (Mass. App. Ct. 2004).
4. *See* Starr v. Woolf, No. C047594, 2005 WL 1532369, at *1–13 (Cal. Ct. App. June 30, 2005).
5. *See* Smith v. Nat'l R.R. Passenger Corp. (Amtrak), 25 F. Supp. 2d 574, 575–78 (E.D. Pa. 1998).
6. *See* Collins v. Huculak, 783 N.E.2d 834, 836–41 (Mass. App. Ct. 2003).
7. *See, e.g.,* Terry Teachout, *Looking for Your 15 Minutes? All You Need Is Infidelity,* N.Y. TIMES, July 21, 2002, § 2, at 28.
8. DORY HOLLANDER, 101 LIES MEN TELL WOMEN: AND WHY WOMEN BELIEVE THEM (1995).
9. PHILIP B. STORM, WHY MEN MUST LIE (2010).
10. SALLY CALDWELL, ROMANTIC DECEPTION: THE SIX SIGNS HE'S LYING (2000).
11. *Should the Law Punish Lovers Who Lie? 84 Percent Say Yes,* GLAMOUR, June 1994, at 133, 133.
12. Lisa Lombardi, *Fake Your Way into Her Bed,* MAXIM, May 2001, at 74; Brett Forrest, *Perfect Your Poker Face: Card Champs Mike Caro and Chris Ferguson Show How Bluffing Can Help You Get Lucky,* MAXIM, May 2001, at 76.
13. *See* Susan D. Cochran & Vickie M. Mays, *Sex, Lies, and HIV,* 322 NEW ENG. J. MED. 774, 774 & tbl.1 (1990).
14. *See* Michael J. Stebleton & James H. Rothenberger, *Truth or Consequences: Dishonesty in Dating and HIV/AIDS-Related Issues in a College-Age Population,* 42 J. AM. C. HEALTH 51, 51–52, 53 tbl.2 (1993).
15. *See* Stephen L. Eyre et al., *Adolescent Sexual Strategies,* 20 J. ADOLESCENT HEALTH 286, 287–88, 291 & tbl.3 (1997); *see also* William Tooke & Lori Camire, *Patterns of Deception in Intersexual and Intrasexual Mating Strategies,* 12 ETHOLOGY & SOCIOBIOLOGY 345, 348, 351, 354 (1991).
16. *See* Martie G. Haselton et al., *Sex, Lies, and Strategic Interference: The Psychology of Deception Between the Sexes,* 31 PERSONALITY & SOC. PSYCHOL. BULL. 3, 9, 14–16 (2005).
17. *See, e.g.,* DAVID NYBERG, THE VARNISHED TRUTH: TRUTH TELLING AND DECEIVING IN ORDINARY LIFE 66–75 (1993); ALDERT VRIJ, DETECTING LIES AND DECEIT: PITFALLS AND OPPORTUNITIES 14–15 (2d ed. 2008); Nobuhito Abe, *How the Brain Shapes Deception: An Integrated Review of the Literature,* 17 NEUROSCIENTIST 560, 560 (2011); Roderick M. Chisholm & Thomas D. Feehan, *The Intent to Deceive,* 74 J. PHIL. 143, 143–45 (1977); Robert Hopper & Robert A. Bell, *Broadening the Deception Construct,* 70 Q.J. SPEECH 288, 300 (1984); Steven A. McCornack & Timothy R. Levine, *When Lies Are Uncovered: Emotional and Relational Outcomes of Discovered Deception,* 57 COMM. MONOGRAPHS 119, 120 (1990); H. Dan O'Hair & Michael J. Cody, *Deception, in* THE DARK SIDE OF INTERPERSONAL

COMMUNICATION 181, 182–83 (William R. Cupach & Brian H. Spitzberg eds., 1994); Miron Zuckerman et al., *Verbal and Nonverbal Communication of Deception, in* 14 ADVANCES IN EXPERIMENTAL SOCIAL PSYCHOLOGY 1, 3–4 (Leonard Berkowitz ed., 1981).

18. Mark Twain, *My First Lie and How I Got Out of It*, WORLD (N.Y.), Dec. 10, 1899, at Supp. 1.

19. 2 T. WEMYSS REID, LIFE OF THE RIGHT HONOURABLE WILLIAM EDWARD FORSTER 167 (London, Chapman & Hall 3d ed. 1888) (quoting William Edward Forster) (internal quotation marks omitted).

20. MARK TWAIN, *On the Decay of the Art of Lying, in* THE STOLEN WHITE ELEPHANT ETC. 217, 219 (Boston, James R. Osgood & Co. 1882).

21. Christine Reinhardt, *Exclusive Survey: The Surprising Ethics of Today's Wives*, MCCALL'S, Nov. 1992, at 160, 160.

22. *See* Mary E. Kaplar & Anne K. Gordon, *The Enigma of Altruistic Lying: Perspective Differences in What Motivates and Justifies Lie Telling Within Romantic Relationships*, 11 PERS. RELATIONSHIPS 489, 489, 496–99, 502 (2004); *infra* Chapter 1.

23. *See* David C. Atkins et al., *Understanding Infidelity: Correlates in a National Random Sample*, 15 J. FAM. PSYCHOL. 735, 736, 738 (2001).

24. *See* Michael W. Wiederman, *Extramarital Sex: Prevalence and Correlates in a National Survey*, 34 J. SEX RES. 167, 168–69, 171 (1997).

25. *See* EDWARD O. LAUMANN ET AL., THE SOCIAL ORGANIZATION OF SEXUALITY: SEXUAL PRACTICES IN THE UNITED STATES 43, 215–16, 553 (1994).

26. *See* JAMES PATTERSON & PETER KIM, THE DAY AMERICA TOLD THE TRUTH: WHAT PEOPLE REALLY BELIEVE ABOUT EVERYTHING THAT REALLY MATTERS 94, 248, 251 (1991).

27. *See, e.g.*, Ruprecht v. Ruprecht, 599 A.2d 604, 605, 607–08 (N.J. Super. Ct. Ch. Div. 1991); Alexander v. Inman, 825 S.W.2d 102, 103–05 (Tenn. Ct. App. 1991); RICHARD ALAN, FIRST AID FOR THE BETRAYED: RECOVERING FROM THE DEVASTATION OF AN AFFAIR; A PERSONAL GUIDE TO HEALING 19–20 (2006); BRETT FLETCHER LAUER, FAKE MISSED CONNECTIONS: DIVORCE, ONLINE DATING, AND OTHER FAILURES 7, 15, 17–18 (2016).

28. Bella M. DePaulo et al., *Serious Lies*, 26 BASIC & APPLIED SOC. PSYCHOL. 147, 150, 162 (2004).

29. *See, e.g.*, DiMichele v. Perrella, 120 A.3d 551, 552–53 (Conn. App. Ct. 2015); Parker v. Parker, 950 So. 2d 388, 389–90 (Fla. 2007); Koelle v. Zwiren, 672 N.E.2d 868, 870–71 (Ill. App. Ct. 1996); Denzik v. Denzik, 197 S.W.3d 108, 109–12 (Ky. 2006); Eck v. Eck, 793 S.W.2d 858, 858–59 (Ky. Ct. App. 1990); Doe v. Doe, 747 A.2d 617, 618 (Md. 2000); G.A.W., III v. D.M.W., 596 N.W.2d 284, 286 (Minn. Ct. App. 1999); Day v. Heller, 653 N.W.2d 475, 476–77 (Neb. 2002); Howard S. v. Lillian S., 876 N.Y.S.2d 351, 352 (App. Div. 2009); Miller v. Miller, 956 P.2d 887, 891 (Okla. 1998); Hodge v. Craig, 382 S.W.3d 325, 329–32 (Tenn. 2012); Wise v. Fryar, 49 S.W.3d 450, 453–55 (Tex. Ct. App. 2001); St. Hilaire v. DeBlois, 721 A.2d 133, 134–35 (Vt. 1998); *Should I Tell My Estranged Husband that My Son Is Not His Child?*, EBONY, June 1998, at 34, 34; Alex Tresniowski et al., *Dads by Default*, PEOPLE, Nov. 25, 2002, at 78, 78–80.

30. Kermyt G. Anderson, *How Well Does Paternity Confidence Match Actual Paternity? Evidence from Worldwide Nonpaternity Rates*, 47 CURRENT ANTHROPOLOGY 513, 513, 516 (2006). This review noted that "[t]he relative frequencies of men with high and low paternity confidence are unknown, which makes it difficult to estimate true nonpaternity rates for human societies." *Id.* at 513.

31. *See* Kim Severson, *Edwards Jury Is Told How Wife Was Torn*, N.Y. TIMES, May 10, 2012, at A16.

32. *See* Roby v. Roby, 11 Conn. L. Rptr. 509, 509–10 (Super. Ct. 1994); Tobon v. Sanchez, 517 A.2d 885, 886 (N.J. Super. Ct. Ch. Div. 1986); BRUCE BUFFER, IT'S TIME! MY 360° VIEW OF THE UFC 45–49 (2013); MIKE O'CONNOR, CRISIS, PURSUED BY DISASTER, FOLLOWED CLOSELY BY CATASTROPHE: A MEMOIR OF LIFE ON THE RUN 200 (2007); WENDY PLUMP, VOW: A MEMOIR OF MARRIAGE (AND OTHER AFFAIRS) 21–25, 108 (2013); BRANDO SKYHORSE, TAKE THIS MAN: A MEMOIR 228–29 (2014); GREGORY HOWARD WILLIAMS, LIFE ON THE COLOR LINE: THE TRUE STORY OF A WHITE BOY WHO DISCOVERED HE WAS BLACK 49 (1995).

33. *See* Ebron v. Gonzales, 180 F. App'x 722, 723 (9th Cir. 2006); *In re* Adoption of a Child by L.C., 425 A.2d 686, 689–90 (N.J. 1981); Kwame Anthony Appiah, *Should I Tell My Sister She's*

Adopted?, N.Y. TIMES, Mar. 6, 2016, Magazine, at 22; Akiko Matsuda, *Woman Seeking Adopted Half-Sister*, J. NEWS (Lower Hudson Valley), Jan. 25, 2009, at 1B; Linnet Myers, *40 Years After Adoption, Sister Finds Her Family*, CHI. TRIB., May 25, 1990, § 2, at 3; Christine Show, *Finally, Reunited*, NEWSDAY (Long Island), July 29, 2006, at A5; Paul Vitello, *Richard H. Poff, Who Withdrew Court Bid, Dies at 87*, N.Y. TIMES, July 2, 2011, at D8.

34. *See* ANNETTE BARAN & REUBEN PANNOR, LETHAL SECRETS: THE SHOCKING CONSEQUENCES AND UNSOLVED PROBLEMS OF ARTIFICIAL INSEMINATION 5, 58–59, 62–63 (1989); R. SNOWDEN ET AL., ARTIFICIAL REPRODUCTION: A SOCIAL INVESTIGATION 75–76, 89, 93–96, 109–10, 113–14, 116–17 (1983); Kwame Anthony Appiah, *Can I Tell My Brother the Truth About Our Paternity?*, N.Y. TIMES, Sept. 9, 2018, Magazine, at 24; Sylvia Rubin, *Family Secrets*, S.F. CHRON., Jan. 15, 1995, at 1.

35. *See In re* Will of Young, 592 N.Y.S.2d 905, 906 (Sur. Ct. 1992), *aff'd mem.*, 619 N.Y.S.2d 678 (App. Div. 1994); Steve Almond & Cheryl Strayed, *Mom's Affair Led to a Long Secret*, N.Y. TIMES, June 21, 2018, at D2; Rachel Dodes, *A Family Detective Story*, WALL ST. J., May 3, 2013, at D5; Justin Rocket Silverman, *Mistaken Identity*, N.Y. DAILY NEWS, Nov. 30, 2014, at 6.

36. *See* SKYHORSE, *supra* note 32, at 1, 3, 30, 99.

37. *See* Mills v. Atl. City Dep't of Vital Statistics, 372 A.2d 646, 651, 655 (N.J. Super. Ct. Ch. Div. 1977); Clare Ansberry, *Siblings Find a Brother They Never Knew They Had*, WALL ST. J., Aug. 3, 2016, at D1; Virginia Hick, *'Lost' Siblings: Found Families*, ST. LOUIS POST-DISPATCH, Mar. 8, 1993, at 1W; Kirk Johnson, *'Gertie's Babies,' Sold at Birth, Use DNA to Unlock Secret Past*, N.Y. TIMES, Apr. 5, 2015, at 1; Elizabeth Moore, *Split by Adoption, Two Are Reunited*, SUNDAY STAR-LEDGER (N.J.), Nov. 17, 2002, § 1, at 27; Mick Walsh, *Ohio Couple Looking for a Long-Lost Brother*, COLUMBUS LEDGER-ENQUIRER, July 22, 2006, at A1; Christopher Woytko, *Family Finds Long-Lost Brother*, READING EAGLE, Aug. 31, 2007, at C2.

38. *See* Barbara A. v. John G., 193 Cal. Rptr. 422, 426 (Ct. App. 1983); Murphy v. Myers, 560 N.W.2d 752, 753 (Minn. Ct. App. 1997); C.A.M. v. R.A.W., 568 A.2d 556, 556–57 (N.J. Super. Ct. App. Div. 1990); *Should the Law Punish Lovers Who Lie? 84 Percent Say Yes*, *supra* note 11, at 133.

39. *See* Erwin L.D. v. Myla Jean L., 847 S.W.2d 45, 47 (Ark. Ct. App. 1993); Stephen K. v. Roni L., 164 Cal. Rptr. 618, 619 (Ct. App. 1980); Beard v. Skipper, 451 N.W.2d 614, 614 (Mich. Ct. App. 1990); Faske v. Bonanno, 357 N.W.2d 860, 861 (Mich. Ct. App. 1984) (per curiam); Wallis v. Smith, 22 P.3d 682, 682–83 (N.M. Ct. App. 2001); Jose F. v. Pat M., 586 N.Y.S.2d 734, 735 (Sup. Ct. 1992); Hughes v. Hutt, 455 A.2d 623, 624 (Pa. 1983).

40. *See* MARK SEAL, THE MAN IN THE ROCKEFELLER SUIT: THE ASTONISHING RISE AND SPECTACULAR FALL OF A SERIAL IMPOSTER 208–09 (2011); Elizabeth Miller et al., *Male Partner Pregnancy-Promoting Behaviors and Adolescent Partner Violence: Findings from a Qualitative Study with Adolescent Females*, 7 AMBULATORY PEDIATRICS 360, 362–63 (2007).

41. *See* Desta v. Anyaoha, 371 S.W.3d 596, 598–99 (Tex. Ct. App. 2012); Miller et al., *supra* note 40, at 362–64.

42. *See* Starr v. Woolf, No. C047594, 2005 WL 1532369, at *1 (Cal. Ct. App. June 30, 2005); RA v. OA-H, No. CN08-05726, 2009 WL 5697871, at *3 (Del. Fam. Ct. Dec. 31, 2009); Hill v. Hill, 398 N.E.2d 1048, 1052–53 (Ill. App. Ct. 1979); *In re* Adoption of S.K.N., No. COA10-1515, 2011 WL 2848751, at *1 (N.C. Ct. App. July 19, 2011); Miller et al., *supra* note 40, at 362.

43. *See* V.J.S. v. M.J.B., 592 A.2d 328, 328–30 (N.J. Super. Ct. Ch. Div. 1991); Sabbagh v. Copti, 674 N.Y.S.2d 329, 330–31 (App. Div. 1998).

44. *See* Heike Thiel de Bocanegra et al., *Birth Control Sabotage and Forced Sex: Experiences Reported by Women in Domestic Violence Shelters*, 16 VIOLENCE AGAINST WOMEN 601, 602, 605 (2010); *infra* Chapter 1.

45. *See* JAMES E. MCGREEVEY WITH DAVID FRANCE, THE CONFESSION 4, 6, 109, 149 (2006); David Amsden, *Married Man Seeks Same for Discreet Play*, N.Y., July 30–Aug. 6, 2007, at 26, 28; Philip Galanes, *Coming Out in Time*, N.Y. TIMES, Aug. 21, 2016, at ST6.

46. *See* Yang v. Lee, 163 F. Supp. 2d 554, 557 (D. Md. 2001); McMillan v. Plummer, Nos. A120258, A120260, 2009 WL 1020653, at *7–8 (Cal. Ct. App. Apr. 16, 2009); Woy v. Woy, 737 S.W.2d 769, 770–74 (Mo. Ct. App. 1987); S.K. v. F.K., No. XXXXX, 2010 WL 979701,

at *1, *5–6, *8 (N.Y. Sup. Ct. Mar. 10, 2010); Doe v. Doe, 519 N.Y.S.2d 595, 597, 599 (Sup. Ct. 1987).

47. See CAROL GREVER, MY HUSBAND IS GAY: A WOMAN'S GUIDE TO SURVIVING THE CRISIS 55–56 (2001); DINA MATOS MCGREEVEY, SILENT PARTNER: A MEMOIR OF MY MARRIAGE 237 (2007); SALLY LOWE WHITEHEAD, THE TRUTH SHALL SET YOU FREE: A FAMILY'S PASSAGE FROM FUNDAMENTALISM TO A NEW UNDERSTANDING OF FAITH, LOVE, AND SEXUAL IDENTITY 42, 212 (1997).

48. See Seth Stephens-Davidowitz, How Many American Men Are Gay?, N.Y. TIMES, Dec. 8, 2013, at SR5 (internal quotation marks omitted).

49. See Anne E. Lucchetti, Deception in Disclosing One's Sexual History: Safe-Sex Avoidance or Ignorance?, 47 COMM. Q. 300, 303, 307 tbl.3 (1999).

50. See Michele G. Alexander & Terri D. Fisher, Truth and Consequences: Using the Bogus Pipeline to Examine Sex Differences in Self-Reported Sexuality, 40 J. SEX RES. 27, 28–29, 31 (2003).

51. See Terri D. Fisher, Gender Roles and Pressure to Be Truthful: The Bogus Pipeline Modifies Gender Differences in Sexual but Not Non-Sexual Behavior, 68 SEX ROLES 401, 405, 409 tbl.4 (2013).

52. See Gorman v. Fedor, No. FA 990067446S, 2000 WL 256108, at *2 (Conn. Super. Ct. Feb. 23, 2000); Wolfe v. Wolfe, 378 N.E.2d 1181, 1182–84 (Ill. App. Ct. 1978); Charley v. Fant, 892 S.W.2d 811, 811–13 (Mo. Ct. App. 1995); Jordan v. Jordan, 345 A.2d 168, 168 (N.H. 1975) (per curiam).

53. See CAROL ROSS JOYNT, INNOCENT SPOUSE: A MEMOIR 174 (2011).

54. See Mayo v. Mayo, 617 S.E.2d 672, 673 (N.C. Ct. App. 2005).

55. See Leax v. Leax, 305 S.W.3d 22, 30 (Tex. Ct. App. 2009); see also Adler v. Adler, 805 So. 2d 952, 953 (Fla. Dist. Ct. App. 2001); Sanderson v. Sanderson, 186 S.E.2d 84, 85 (Va. 1972) (per curiam); Ranney v. Ranney, 608 S.E.2d 485, 488 (Va. Ct. App. 2005).

56. See, e.g., Norton v. McOsker, 407 F.3d 501, 503 (1st Cir. 2005); Brown v. Strum, 350 F. Supp. 2d 346, 347 (D. Conn. 2004); Manko v. Volynsky, No. 95 CIV. 2585 (MBM), 1996 WL 243238, at *1–2 (S.D.N.Y. May 10, 1996); Jackson v. Brown, 904 P.2d 685, 686 (Utah 1995); Walter v. Stewart, 67 P.3d 1042, 1044–46 (Utah Ct. App. 2003); Slawek v. Stroh, 215 N.W.2d 9, 17 (Wis. 1974); J.M. SHORT, CARNAL ABUSE BY DECEIT: HOW A PREDATOR'S LIES BECAME RAPE 31–32, 39 (2013); Bonnie Miller Rubin, When Tall and Handsome Turns Out Short and Pudgy, CHI. TRIB., July 30, 2006, at 1.

57. See, e.g., Anna Jane Grossman, Honestly Online, CHI. SUN-TIMES, July 4, 2005, at 32.

58. ROBERT J. BRYM & RHONDA L. LENTON, LOVE ONLINE: A REPORT ON DIGITAL DATING IN CANADA 42, 50 (2001).

59. See Katherine Davidson, Safety? A Nice Photo? Help's Out There, for a Fee, N.H. SUNDAY NEWS, Oct. 23, 2005, at A1; Sara Kehaulani Goo, Dinner, Movie — and a Background Check — for Online Daters, WASH. POST, Jan. 28, 2007, at A1. True.com apparently did not release its data for outside verification, however, so the accuracy of its reports cannot be confirmed.

60. See DIANE WOOD MIDDLEBROOK, SUITS ME: THE DOUBLE LIFE OF BILLY TIPTON 229–30 (1998); Jim Adams, Boyfriend's Trail of Lies Ends with Charge of Killing Boy, 3, STAR TRIB. (Minneapolis), Nov. 11, 2003, at A1.

61. See Koshel v. Koshel, No. CIV.A.3:01-CV-2006-M, 2002 WL 1544681, at *1–2 (N.D. Tex. July 11, 2002); In re Marriage of Jones, 241 Cal. Rptr. 231, 232–34 (Ct. App. 1987); Moe v. Moe, No. A04-953, 2005 WL 354028, at *1–2 (Minn. Ct. App. Feb. 15, 2005); Kathianne Boniello, Weddy or Not, N.Y. POST, Jan. 24, 2016, at 14.

62. See Hill v. Bert Bell/Pete Rozelle NFL Player Ret. Plan, No. 09-4051, 2010 WL 4452523, at *1–4 (E.D. Pa. Nov. 4, 2010), aff'd, 548 F. App'x 55 (3d Cir. 2013); Estate of Hafner, 229 Cal. Rptr. 676, 677–79 (Ct. App. 1986); In re Estate of Vargas, 111 Cal. Rptr. 779, 779–80 (Ct. App. 1974); Feldman v. Feldman, 480 A.2d 34, 34–36 (N.H. 1984); Paul Bradley, Bigamy Suspect Seen on 'Dr. Phil,' RICHMOND TIMES-DISPATCH, Dec. 14, 2005, at A1; Kevin Deutsch, Man Who Married Two Women in Less Than Year Sought by Police, PALM BEACH POST, Feb. 15, 2006, at 3B; Inmate with Two Wives Faces Sentence for Bigamy, BUFFALO NEWS, Feb. 21, 2002, at B2; Man with Three Wives Pleads Guilty to Bigamy, BEACON J. (Akron), Sept. 19, 1996, at A15; Tim McGlone, Bigamist Put on Probation, Must Pay Fine, VIRGINIA-PILOT, Apr. 7, 2001, at B5; Richard C. Paddock, Doctor Led Three Lives with Three Wives, L.A. TIMES, Oct. 14,

1991, at A3; Christopher Quinn, *Call Leads to Bigamy Charge*, PLAIN DEALER (Cleveland), Mar. 19, 1998, at 1-A.

63. Bill Muller, *Wives Catch Restless Romeo*, ATLANTA J./ATLANTA CONST., Dec. 29, 1994, at B4 (internal quotation marks omitted); *see also Man with Four Wives Is Told to Repent in Jail*, PLAIN DEALER (Cleveland), Apr. 4, 1995, at 11A.

64. *See* Aetna Cas. & Sur. Co. v. Sheft, 989 F.2d 1105, 1105–06 (9th Cir. 1993); Kathleen K. v. Robert B., 198 Cal. Rptr. 273, 274 (Ct. App. 1984); AMITY PIERCE BUXTON, THE OTHER SIDE OF THE CLOSET: THE COMING-OUT CRISIS FOR STRAIGHT SPOUSES AND FAMILIES 242 (rev. ed. 1994); *Should the Law Punish Lovers Who Lie? 84 Percent Say Yes, supra* note 11, at 133.

65. *See* Daniel H. Ciccarone et al., *Sex Without Disclosure of Positive HIV Serostatus in a US Probability Sample of Persons Receiving Medical Care for HIV Infection*, 93 AM. J. PUB. HEALTH 949, 953 (2003).

66. *See id.* at 949–51, 953.

67. *See* Kathleen M. Sullivan, *Male Self-Disclosure of HIV-Positive Serostatus to Sex Partners: A Review of the Literature*, 16 J. ASS'N NURSES AIDS CARE 33, 42 (2005); *see also* Allison G. Dempsey et al., *Patterns of Disclosure Among Youth Who Are HIV-Positive: A Multisite Study*, 50 J. ADOLESCENT HEALTH 315, 315–16 (2012); Tara McKay & Matt G. Mutchler, *The Effect of Partner Sex: Nondisclosure of HIV Status to Male and Female Partners Among Men Who Have Sex with Men and Women (MSMW)*, 15 AIDS BEHAV. 1140, 1141, 1145, 1147–48 (2011); Sarahmona M. Przybyla et al., *Serostatus Disclosure to Sexual Partners Among People Living with HIV: Examining the Roles of Partner Characteristics and Stigma*, 25 AIDS CARE 566, 566 (2013).

68. *See* Yuzo Arima et al., *Disclosure of Genital Human Papillomavirus Infection to Female Sex Partners by Young Men*, 39 SEXUALLY TRANSMITTED DISEASES 583, 583–85 (2012); Mary L. Keller et al., *Self-Disclosure of HPV Infection to Sexual Partners*, 22 W.J. NURSING RES. 285, 288–94 (2000); Jaime L. Myers et al., *Associations Between Individual and Relationship Characteristics and Genital Herpes Disclosure*, 21 J. HEALTH PSYCHOL. 2283, 2285–88 (2016).

69. *See* Anonymous, *A Sober Look Back*, UTAH B.J., Jan./Feb. 2008, at 22, 22.

70. *See* Costello v. Porzelt, 282 A.2d 432, 433–34 (N.J. Super. Ct. Ch. Div. 1971).

71. *See* Friedman v. Comm'r, 53 F.3d 523, 527 (2d Cir. 1995); THEO PAULINE NESTOR, HOW TO SLEEP ALONE IN A KING-SIZE BED: A MEMOIR 8–9 (2008).

72. *See* Nicole B. Ellison et al., *Profile as Promise: A Framework for Conceptualizing Veracity in Online Dating Self-Presentations*, 14 NEW MEDIA & SOC'Y 45, 53–54 (2012).

73. *See* RONI RABIN, SIX PARTS LOVE: ONE FAMILY'S BATTLE WITH LOU GEHRIG'S DISEASE 9, 13–15, 26, 34–35, 57 (1985).

74. *See* Joseph Fletcher, *The Case of the Untold Secret*, HARD CHOICES: MAG. ON ETHICS SICKNESS & HEALTH, 1980, at 9, 9.

75. *See In re* Marriage of Farr, 228 P.3d 267, 268–70 (Colo. App. 2010).

76. *See id.*

77. *In re* Marriage of McNeill, 206 Cal. Rptr. 641, 643–44 (Ct. App. 1984); *see also* Whelan v. Whelan, 588 A.2d 251, 252 (Conn. Super. Ct. 1991).

78. *See* Sherri A. Groveman, *The Hanukkah Bush: Ethical Implications in the Clinical Management of Intersex*, 9 J. CLINICAL ETHICS 356, 357–59 (1998); J. David Hester, *Intersex and the Rhetorics of Healing, in* ETHICS AND INTERSEX 47, 53 (Sharon E. Sytsma ed., 2006).

79. ALLIANZ LIFE INS. CO. OF N.Y., ALLIANZ LIFE INS. CO. OF N. AM., THE ALLIANZ WOMEN, MONEY, AND POWER STUDY: EMPOWERED AND UNDERSERVED 2, 6 (2013) (internal quotation marks omitted).

80. *See* Russ Wiles, *'Financial Infidelity' Often Destroys Relationships*, ARIZ. REPUBLIC, Feb. 20, 2014, at B6.

81. *See* JOYNT, *supra* note 53, at 40–41.

82. *See* Borowski v. Firstar Bank Milwaukee, N.A., 579 N.W.2d 247, 248–49 (Wis. Ct. App. 1998).

83. *See* Adams, *supra* note 60, at A1.

84. *See* NESTOR, *supra* note 71, at 8–9, 71.

85. *See In re* Marriage of Rossi, 108 Cal. Rptr. 2d 270, 272–75 (Ct. App. 2001).

86. *See* United States v. Okoye, 731 F.3d 46, 47–48 (1st Cir. 2013); *see also* United States v. Torres, 251 F.3d 138, 143 (3d Cir. 2001).

87. *See* HIRERIGHT, EMPLOYMENT SCREENING BENCHMARKING REPORT 5, 13 (2013); Jeffrey Kluger, *Pumping Up Your Past*, TIME, June 10, 2002, at 45; David Koeppel, *Fudging the Facts on a Résumé Is Common, and Also a Big Risk*, N.Y. TIMES, Apr. 23, 2006, § 10, at 1; *see also* EDWARD C. ANDLER WITH DARA HERBST, THE COMPLETE REFERENCE CHECKING HANDBOOK: THE PROVEN (AND LEGAL) WAY TO PREVENT HIRING MISTAKES 17 (2d ed. 2003); Elizabeth Stanton, *If a Résumé Lies, Truth Can Loom Large*, N.Y. TIMES, Dec. 29, 2002, at BU8; Keith J. Winstein, *Inflated Credentials Surface in Executive Suite*, WALL ST. J., Nov. 13, 2008, at B1.

88. *See Tracy and Jeff: A Love Story*, *in* STRAIGHT WIVES: SHATTERED LIVES: STORIES OF WOMEN WITH GAY HUSBAND[s] 53, 54 (Bonnie Kaye ed., 2006).

89. *See* Sareen v. Sareen, 858 N.Y.S.2d 285, 286 (App. Div. 2008).

90. *See* GEOFFREY WOLFF, THE DUKE OF DECEPTION: MEMORIES OF MY FATHER 8–9, 61, 65–66 (1979).

91. *See* FRANK W. ABAGNALE WITH STAN REDDING, CATCH ME IF YOU CAN: THE AMAZING TRUE STORY OF THE YOUNGEST AND MOST DARING CON MAN IN THE HISTORY OF FUN AND PROFIT! 133–39 (1980).

92. *See id.* at 82; Dan P. Lee, *He Said, They Said*, PHILA., Oct. 2007, at 102, 104, 200, 202; Robert Moran, *His Life Is a Lie, Woman Testifies*, PHILA. INQUIRER, May 26, 2007, at B1.

93. *See* Lee, *supra* note 92, at 104, 200, 202; Moran, *supra* note 92, at B1; Michael Neill & William Sonzski, *Posing as an Astronaut Was Just One Small Step for Flimflam Man Robert Hunt*, PEOPLE WKLY., Mar. 6. 1989, at 271, 271–72, 274.

94. *See* Lee, *supra* note 92, at 104–05, 200, 202; Moran, *supra* note 92, at B1; Manuel Roig-Franzia & Michelle Boorstein, *Cheaters, Done in by Digital*, WASH. POST, Nov. 14, 2012, at C1.

95. *See* John Crewdson, *False Courage*, CHI. TRIB., Oct. 26, 2008, at 1.

96. *See* Summers v. Renz, No. H024460, 2004 WL 2384845, at *2, *4 (Cal. Ct. App. Oct. 26, 2004).

97. *See* Marion Callahan, *Vet Service, Probation for Medal Faker*, MIAMI HERALD, Dec. 4, 1996, at 1A.

98. *See* Don Bosley, *Navy Discredits Sailor's Story of Being a SEAL in Afghanistan*, SACRAMENTO BEE, Feb. 7, 2002, at E1.

99. *See* Glenna Whitley, *G.I. Jerk*, DALL. OBSERVER, Sept. 1–7, 2005, at 20; *see also* Annys Shin, *Boast-Busters Stay Busy Exposing Fake SEALs*, WASH. POST, June 14, 2011, at A3.

100. *See* B.G. BURKETT & GLENNA WHITLEY, STOLEN VALOR: HOW THE VIETNAM GENERATION WAS ROBBED OF ITS HEROES AND ITS HISTORY 489–93 (1998).

101. *See* Elliott v. James, 977 P.2d 727, 729, 731 n.12 (Alaska 1999) (per curiam).

102. *See* Joseph Goldstein, *The Pickpocket's Tale*, N.Y. TIMES, July 20, 2014, at 22.

103. *See* Jonathan J. Cooper, *First Lady Admits to Sham Marriage*, E. OREGONIAN, Oct. 10, 2014, at 1A.

104. *See* Haacke v. Glenn, 814 P.2d 1157, 1157 (Utah Ct. App. 1991).

105. *See* Goo, *supra* note 59, at A1.

106. *See* Nora Koch, *Man Gets 3 Years for DWI Deaths*, PHILA. INQUIRER, Apr. 12, 2003, at B1.

107. *See* Strat Douthat, *The Fugitive*, L.A. TIMES, June 18, 1989, pt. I, at 2.

108. *See* Davidson, *supra* note 59, at A1; Goo, *supra* note 59, at A1.

109. *See* Doe v. SexSearch.com, 551 F.3d 412, 415 (6th Cir. 2008); Murray v. Murray, 706 N.Y.S.2d 164, 164 (App. Div. 2000); S.H. v. C.C., No. CA2006-12-051, 2007 WL 2410716, at *3 (Ohio Ct. App. Aug. 27, 2007); BRYM & LENTON, *supra* note 58, at 42; Nicole Ellison et al., *Managing Impressions Online: Self-Presentation Processes in the Online Dating Environment*, 11 J. COMPUTER-MEDIATED COMM. 415, 427 (2006); Jeffrey T. Hancock et al., *The Truth About Lying in Online Dating Profiles*, CHI 2007 PROCEEDINGS 449, 450–52 (2007).

110. *See* SHORT, *supra* note 56, at 48; WOLFF, *supra* note 90, at 9, 64–65, 144, 258.

111. *See* BLISS BROYARD, ONE DROP: MY FATHER'S HIDDEN LIFE — A STORY OF RACE AND FAMILY SECRETS 16–17, 181 (2007); GAIL LUKASIK, WHITE LIKE HER: MY FAMILY'S STORY OF RACE AND RACIAL PASSING 22–23 (2017); WILLIAMS, *supra* note 32, at 32–34, 54.

112. *See* FRANK C. GIRARDOT JR., NAME DROPPER: INVESTIGATING THE CLARK ROCKEFELLER MYSTERY 28, 31–32, 45, 221–22 (2013); WALTER KIRN, BLOOD WILL OUT: THE TRUE STORY OF A MURDER, A MYSTERY, AND A MASQUERADE 51, 53, 55, 132, 168–69 (2014); SEAL, *supra* note 40, at 9, 151–52, 154–58, 160–61, 200; Abby Goodnough, *Man Who Called Himself a Rockefeller Is Set for Trial in Daughter's Kidnapping*, N.Y. TIMES, May 26, 2009, at A10.
113. Bonhomme v. St. James, 970 N.E.2d 1, 2–4, 10–11 (Ill. 2012).

Chapter 1

1. *See, e.g.*, DINA MATOS MCGREEVEY, SILENT PARTNER: A MEMOIR OF MY MARRIAGE 195 (2007); MARY TURNER THOMSON, THE BIGAMIST: THE TRUE STORY OF A HUSBAND'S ULTIMATE BETRAYAL 234 (2008); *infra* Chapter 2.
2. *See, e.g.*, ROBERT FELDMAN, THE LIAR IN YOUR LIFE: THE WAY TO TRUTHFUL RELATIONSHIPS 21 (2009); CHARLES V. FORD, LIES! LIES!! LIES!!! THE PSYCHOLOGY OF DECEIT 99–100 (1996).
3. *See* Anne K. Gordon & Arthur G. Miller, *Perspective Differences in the Construal of Lies: Is Deception in the Eye of the Beholder?*, 26 PERSONALITY & SOC. PSYCHOL. BULL. 46, 48–51 (2000); Robin M. Kowalski et al., *Lying, Cheating, Complaining, and Other Aversive Interpersonal Behaviors: A Narrative Examination of the Darker Side of Relationships*, 20 J. SOC. & PERS. RELATIONSHIPS 471, 484–85 (2003).
4. JAMES E. MCGREEVEY WITH DAVID FRANCE, THE CONFESSION 197 (2006) (emphasis omitted).
5. *See* Brad J. Sagarin et al., *Deceiver's Distrust: Denigration as a Consequence of Undiscovered Deception*, 24 PERSONALITY & SOC. PSYCHOL. BULL. 1167, 1167, 1169, 1172–74 (1998); *see also* Sunyna S. Williams, *Sexual Lying Among College Students in Close and Casual Relationships*, 31 J. APPLIED SOC. PSYCHOL. 2322, 2322, 2336 (2001).
6. *See* Susan D. Boon & Beverly A. McLeod, *Deception in Romantic Relationships: Subjective Estimates of Success at Deceiving and Attitudes Toward Deception*, 18 J. SOC. & PERS. RELATIONSHIPS 463, 463, 467, 469, 471–72 (2001).
7. *See In re* Marriage of Meagher & Maleki, 31 Cal. Rptr. 3d 663, 664–69 (Ct. App. 2005); Dunlap v. Current, 57 Conn. L. Rptr. 783, 783–85 (Super. Ct. 2014); Rice v. Monteleone, No. FA020563144S, 2004 WL 503689, at *2 (Conn. Super. Ct. Feb. 25, 2004); Stepp v. Stepp, No. 03CA0052-M, 2004 WL 626116, at *1–2 (Ohio Ct. App. Mar. 31, 2004); Francis v. Francis, 21 V.I. 263, 264–66 (Terr. Ct. 1985).
8. *See In re* Marriage of Johnston, 22 Cal. Rptr. 2d 253, 254–55 (Ct. App. 1993).
9. *See* Elliott v. James, 977 P.2d 727, 729–31 (Alaska 1999) (per curiam); *Dunlap*, 57 Conn. L. Rptr. at 783–85; McKee v. McKee, 262 So. 2d 111, 112–14 (La. Ct. App. 1972).
10. *See Elliott*, 977 P.2d at 729–31; Fattibene v. Fattibene, 441 A.2d 3, 5–7 (Conn. 1981); Adler v. Adler, 805 So. 2d 952, 953–54 (Fla. Dist. Ct. App. 2001); *In re* Marriage of Igene, 35 N.E.3d 1125, 1126–29 (Ill. App. Ct. 2015); Charley v. Fant, 892 S.W.2d 811, 811–13 (Mo. Ct. App. 1995); Sanderson v. Sanderson, 186 S.E.2d 84, 85 (Va. 1972) (per curiam).
11. *See* Roby v. Roby, 11 Conn. L. Rptr. 509, 509–10 (Super. Ct. 1994); Tobon v. Sanchez, 517 A.2d 885, 885–86 (N.J. Super. Ct. Ch. Div. 1986).
12. *See, e.g.*, *In re* Marriage of Schmidt & Green, No. A102104, 2004 WL 745696, at *1–4 (Cal. Ct. App. Apr. 8, 2004); Radochonski v. Radochonski, No. 21050-9-II, 1998 WL 267062, at *1–2 (Wash. Ct. App. May 22, 1998).
13. *See* Bilowit v. Dolitsky, 304 A.2d 774, 775–76 (N.J. Super. Ct. Ch. Div. 1973).
14. *See* V.J.S. v. M.J.B., 592 A.2d 328, 328–30 (N.J. Super. Ct. Ch. Div. 1991).
15. *Cf.* Yang v. Lee, 163 F. Supp. 2d 554, 557 (D. Md. 2001); McMillan v. Plummer, Nos. A120258, A120260, 2009 WL 1020653, at *7–8 (Cal. Ct. App. Apr. 16, 2009); Woy v. Woy, 737 S.W.2d 769, 770–74 (Mo. Ct. App. 1987); S.K. v. F.K., No. XXXXX, 2010 WL 979701, at *1, *5–6, *8 (N.Y. Sup. Ct. Mar. 10, 2010); Doe v. Doe, 519 N.Y.S.2d 595, 597, 599 (Sup. Ct. 1987).
16. *Cf.* Frances B. v. Mark B., 355 N.Y.S.2d 712, 713–14 (Sup. Ct. 1974); Anonymous v. Anonymous, 325 N.Y.S.2d 499, 499 (Sup. Ct. 1971); Morin v. Morin, No. 2006-418, 2007

WL 5313306, at *2 (Vt. May 2007); Louise Rafkin, *A Husband's Secret Takes Its Toll*, N.Y. TIMES, Apr. 3, 2016, at ST17; *The Ebony Advisor*, EBONY, Oct. 1987, at 124, 124.

17. PAUL OYER, EVERYTHING I EVER NEEDED TO KNOW ABOUT ECONOMICS I LEARNED FROM ONLINE DATING 188 (2014).

18. Rosemary Counter, *The Lure of Kismet*, N.Y. TIMES, Jan. 4, 2015, at ST5 (internal quotation marks omitted).

19. *See* Dahl v. McNutt, No. C3-97-601906, slip op. at 1–3, 12–13 (Minn. Dist. Ct. Jan. 21, 1998).

20. *See id.* at 3.

21. *See* Amy Goldstein, *Woman Alleges Fiance Stole Her Heart, Brother's Kidney*, WASH. POST, Oct. 21, 1997, at A1.

22. *See* Wolfe v. Wolfe, 378 N.E.2d 1181, 1182–84 (Ill. App. Ct. 1978); Jordan v. Jordan, 345 A.2d 168, 168 (N.H. 1975) (per curiam).

23. *See Wolfe*, 378 N.E.2d at 1183.

24. *See, e.g.,* J.M. SHORT, CARNAL ABUSE BY DECEIT: HOW A PREDATOR'S LIES BECAME RAPE 49–50 (2013).

25. Frederick Burger, *For the Expert Witness, a Few Tough Questions*, WASH. POST, Apr. 10, 2005, at D1 (quoting Selina Volz) (internal quotation marks omitted).

26. *See* Frederick Burger, *Perjury Lands Ex-SLC Radio Host in Prison*, SALT LAKE TRIB., May 5, 2006, at B2.

27. OYER, *supra* note 17, at 25–27.

28. *See id.* at 112–13.

29. *Id.* at 27.

30. *See* 8 U.S.C. § 1151(b)(2)(A)(i) (2012).

31. *See id.* § 1154(a).

32. *See id.* § 1186a(a)(1), (h)(1).

33. *See id.* § 1186a(c)–(d).

34. *See* KATHERINE WITSMAN, U.S. DEP'T OF HOMELAND SEC., ANNUAL FLOW REPORT: LAWFUL PERMANENT RESIDENTS 5 tbl.2 (2018).

35. 8 U.S.C. § 1154(c).

36. *See, e.g.,* Jonathan J. Cooper, *First Lady Admits to Sham Marriage*, E. OREGONIAN, Oct. 10, 2014, at 1A; Andy Newman, *Officials Say Woman Admitted She Wed for Cash and to Aid with Citizenship*, N.Y. TIMES, Apr. 11, 2015, at A15.

37. *See* 8 U.S.C. §§ 1154(c), 1186a(b)(1)(A)(i), (d)(1)(A)(i)(III), 1227(a)(1)(G), 1325(c).

38. *See id.*

39. *See, e.g.,* Nakamoto v. Ashcroft, 363 F.3d 874, 876–77, 882–83 (9th Cir. 2004); Rodriguez v. INS, 204 F.3d 25, 26–28 (1st Cir. 2000); United States v. Dedhia, 134 F.3d 802, 803–05 (6th Cir. 1998).

40. *See, e.g., In re* Marriage of Khalsa & Singh, No. A128518, 2011 WL 940850, at *5–6 (Cal. Ct. App. Mar. 18, 2011); *In re* Marriage of Butler & Mayas, No. B192837, 2008 WL 3906796, at *2–3 (Cal. Ct. App. Aug. 26, 2008); *In re* Marriage of Liu, 242 Cal. Rptr. 649, 651 (Ct. App. 1987); *In re* Marriage of Joel & Roohi, 404 P.3d 1251, 1252–53 (Colo. App. 2012); Gubin v. Lodisev, 494 N.W.2d 782, 783–85 (Mich. Ct. App. 1992); Ur-Rehman v. Qamar, No. FM-10-151-08, 2012 WL 3889129, at *1–6 (N.J. Super. Ct. App. Div. Sept. 10, 2012) (per curiam); S.K. v. F.K., No. XXXXX, 2010 WL 979701, at *8 (N.Y. Sup. Ct. Mar. 10, 2010); Manjlai v. Manjlai, 447 S.W.3d 376, 377–82 (Tex. Ct. App. 2014); Montenegro v. Avila, 365 S.W.3d 822, 823–28 (Tex. Ct. App. 2012).

41. *See Ur-Rehman*, 2012 WL 3889129, at *1.

42. *See id.* at *1–3.

43. *See id.* at *2–3.

44. *See* 8 U.S.C. § 1186a(c)–(d) (2012).

45. *See Montenegro*, 365 S.W.3d at 823–26.

46. *See* 42 U.S.C. § 402(a), (b), (c), (e), (f) (2012).

47. *See id.* § 415(a).

48. *See id.* § 402(b)(2), (c)(2).

49. *See id.* § 402(e)(2)(A), (f)(2)(A).

50. *See* OFFICE OF RET. & DISABILITY POLICY, OFFICE OF RESEARCH, EVALUATION, & STATISTICS, SOC. SEC. ADMIN., ANNUAL STATISTICAL SUPPLEMENT TO THE SOCIAL SECURITY BULLETIN, 2017, at 5.22 tbl.5.A14, G.5 (2018).

51. *See infra* notes 55–56 and accompanying text.

52. *See supra* notes 49–50 and accompanying text.

53. *See* 42 U.S.C. § 416(b), (f).

54. *See id.* §§ 402(e)(1)(A), (e)(3), (f)(1)(A), (f)(3), 416(c), (g).

55. *See id.* §§ 402(b)(1)(C), (b)(1)(G), (b)(3), (c)(1)(C), (c)(1)(G), (c)(3), 416(d)(1), (d)(4).

56. *See* Weinberger v. Salfi, 422 U.S. 749, 753–56 (1975).

57. *See id.* at 781.

58. *Id.* at 780.

59. *Id.* at 777.

60. *See* David Rosenzweig, *Woman Accused of Sham Marriage, Defrauding U.S.*, L.A. TIMES, Oct. 9, 1998, at B3.

61. *See infra* Chapter 6.

62. *See, e.g.*, Tonya Alanez, *Promise of Romance Ends with Deceit*, S. FLA. SUN SENTINEL, Nov. 22, 2014, at 1B; Robin Gaby Fisher, *Web of Deceit Unravels Around Con Artist*, SUNDAY STAR-LEDGER (N.J.), Feb. 24, 2002, § 1, at 1; Angel Hernandez, *'Sweetheart Swindler' Sentenced*, ROCKY MTN. NEWS, Feb. 12, 1994, at 38A; Richard Jerome et al., *7 Wives in 10 Years*, PEOPLE, May 30, 2005, at 97; Ginny McKibben, *Scam Artist Sentenced to 16 Years*, DENVER POST, Feb. 12, 1994, at 1B; James C. McKinley Jr. & Rick Rojas, *An Impostor's Lives and Lies*, N.Y. TIMES, Feb. 7, 2016, at 22; Matt O'Connor, *Con Man Preyed on the Lonely*, CHI. TRIB., Feb. 16, 1999, § 2, at 1; Elizabeth Olson, *Swept off Her Feet, Then Bilked Out of Thousands*, N.Y. TIMES, July 18, 2015, at B4; Edgar Sanchez, *Man Says 'Sweetheart Swindler' Stole His Heart — and His Cash*, SACRAMENTO BEE, June 10, 2003, at B2; Renee Winkler, *Charmer Pleads Guilty to Fraud*, COURIER-POST (N.J.), Jan. 26, 1999, at 1B.

63. *See* Bill Swayze, *Accused Con Man Faces New Charges*, STAR-LEDGER (N.J.), June 30, 2005, at 25.

64. *See* Margaret McHugh, *Judge Annuls Con Man's Latest Marriage*, STAR-LEDGER (N.J.), Oct. 20, 2005, at 20.

65. *See* Bridget Harrison & Jeane MacIntosh, *A 'Sick' Trick*, N.Y. POST, June 21, 2005, at 17.

66. *See* McHugh, *supra* note 65, at 20.

67. *See* Margaret McHugh & Bill Swayze, *To the Wives He Deceived, 3 Years in Jail Is Far Too Kind*, STAR-LEDGER (N.J.), Sept. 23, 2005, at 1.

68. *See* Shawn Hubler, *Man Given 3 Years for Stealing Stocks*, L.A. TIMES, July 6, 1990, at B3; Shawn Hubler, *'Sweetheart Swindler' Captured, Police Say*, L.A. TIMES, May 18, 1990, at B1; Jane Meinhardt, *Man Accused of Bilking Women*, ST. PETERSBURG TIMES, May 19, 1990, at 1B.

69. Shawn Hubler, *'I Made Them Very Happy,' Sweetheart Swindler Declares*, L.A. TIMES, June 22, 1990, at B1 (quoting Leslie Gall) (internal quotation marks omitted).

70. Dale Brazao, *'Sweetheart Swindler' Took Love — and Money*, SUNDAY STAR (Toronto), Apr. 19, 1992, at A1 (quoting Leslie Gall) (internal quotation marks omitted).

71. Brad Hamilton, *Bigamist Con Back in Slam*, N.Y. POST, Dec. 17, 2006, at 7; *see also* Marsha Kranes & Jeane MacIntosh, *He Led 2 Lives & Had 12 Wives*, N.Y. POST, June 17, 2005, at 5.

72. Brazao, *supra* note 71, at A1.

73. KATHA POLLITT, LEARNING TO DRIVE: AND OTHER LIFE STORIES 31 (2007); *see also id.* at 4, 23.

74. *See* PAUL EKMAN, TELLING LIES: CLUES TO DECEIT IN THE MARKETPLACE, POLITICS, AND MARRIAGE 76–79 (1992).

75. *See* Nicole E. Ruedy et al., *The Cheater's High: The Unexpected Affective Benefits of Unethical Behavior*, 105 J. PERSONALITY & SOC. PSYCHOL. 531, 531–32, 534–45 (2013).

76. *See* GINNY NiCARTHY, GETTING FREE: YOU CAN END ABUSE AND TAKE BACK YOUR LIFE 261–62 (4th ed. 2004).

77. *I Married a Monster: The Horrors of Domestic Violence*, R.I.B.J., Jan./Feb. 2003, at 29, 29 (citation omitted).

78. *See* Winborne v. Winborne, 255 S.E.2d 640, 642–43 (N.C. Ct. App. 1979); Dvorak v. Dvorak, 329 N.W.2d 868, 870–72 (N.D. 1983); Brown v. Brown, No. W2013-00263-COA-R3-CV, 2013 WL 12180656, at *1–2 (Tenn. Ct. App. Sept. 12, 2013); Barnes v. Barnes, 340 S.E.2d 803, 803–05 (Va. 1986).

79. *See* Ball v. Von Hoffman, No. 3:11-CV-621, 2013 WL 4046317, at *1 (E.D. Tenn. Aug. 8, 2013).

80. *See, e.g.*, Barbara A. v. John G., 193 Cal. Rptr. 422, 426 (Ct. App. 1983).

81. *See id.*

82. Arthur D. Sorosky et al., The Adoption Triangle: The Effects of the Sealed Record on Adoptees, Birth Parents, and Adoptive Parents 89 (1978) (paraphrasing adoptive parents) (internal quotation marks omitted).

83. R. Snowden et al., Artificial Reproduction: A Social Investigation 118 (1983) (quoting "One husband") (internal quotation marks omitted).

84. *Id.* at 119 (quoting "Husband 1030") (internal quotation marks omitted).

85. Sylvia Rubin, *Family Secrets*, S.F. Chron., Jan. 15, 1995, at 1 (quoting Suzanne Ariel) (internal quotation marks omitted).

86. Annette Baran & Reuben Pannor, Lethal Secrets: The Shocking Consequences and Unsolved Problems of Artificial Insemination 62 (1989) (quoting Judith).

87. *See* Mary E. Kaplar & Anne K. Gordon, *The Enigma of Altruistic Lying: Perspective Differences in What Motivates and Justifies Lie Telling Within Romantic Relationships*, 11 Pers. Relationships 489, 489, 496–99, 502 (2004); *see also* Sissela Bok, Lying: Moral Choice in Public and Private Life 212 (1978).

88. Baran & Pannor, *supra* note 87, at 68 (quoting Judith).

89. *See* Jill Elaine Hasday, Family Law Reimagined 111–14, 116–18 (2014).

90. For a remarkable story from the 1930s about intimate deception from subordination, see Norma Rosen, *Hers*, N.Y. Times, Jan. 20, 1983, at C2.

91. For examples from the late nineteenth and early twentieth centuries, see Viviana A. Zelizer, The Social Meaning of Money 45–47, 56 (1994).

92. *See, e.g.*, Bonnie Eaker Weil, Financial Infidelity: Seven Steps to Conquering the #1 Relationship Wrecker 92 (2008); Ellyn Spragins, *The Case Against Joint Checking*, N.Y. Times, Apr. 6, 2003, at BU12; *see also* Ryland v. Ryland, 12 So. 3d 1223, 1232 (Ala. Civ. App. 2009); Nelson v. Nelson, 66 S.W.3d 896, 899–900 (Tenn. Ct. App. 2001).

93. Heidi Evans, How to Hide Money from Your Husband . . . and Other Time-Honored Ways to Build a Nest Egg: The Best-Kept Secret of a Good Marriage 26 (1999).

94. *See id.* at 59–61.

95. *Id.* at 33.

96. *Id.* at 76–78 (quoting Holly) (emphasis and internal quotation marks omitted).

97. *Id.* at 43–44.

98. *See, e.g.*, Dep't of Research & Analysis, State Bar of Tex., The Gender Bias Task Force of Texas Final Report 66–78 (1994); Gender and Justice in the Courts: A Report to the Supreme Court of Georgia by the Commission on Gender Bias in the Judicial System 1–50 (1991); Neil Websdale, Rural Woman Battering and the Justice System: An Ethnography 91–158 (1998).

99. Planned Parenthood of Se. Pa. v. Casey, 505 U.S. 833, 889 (1992) (quoting the district court's findings of fact) (internal quotation marks omitted).

100. *In re* Adoption of S.K.N., No. COA10-1515, 2011 WL 2848751, at *1–2 (N.C. Ct. App. July 19, 2011) (internal quotation marks omitted).

101. *See In re* Adoption of S.K.N., 735 S.E.2d 382, 384–89 (N.C. Ct. App. 2012).

102. *See* Heike Thiel de Bocanegra et al., *Birth Control Sabotage and Forced Sex: Experiences Reported by Women in Domestic Violence Shelters*, 16 Violence Against Women 601, 601–02, 605 (2010).

103. *See id.* at 606.

104. *See* Elizabeth Miller et al., *Male Partner Pregnancy-Promoting Behaviors and Adolescent Partner Violence: Findings from a Qualitative Study with Adolescent Females*, 7 Ambulatory Pediatrics 360, 360, 362–64 (2007). For an example from the 1960s of an abused woman

deceiving her husband to conceal her use of birth control, see JOHANNA SCHOEN, CHOICE & COERCION: BIRTH CONTROL, STERILIZATION, AND ABORTION IN PUBLIC HEALTH AND WELFARE 1–2 (2005).

105. *See* HASDAY, *supra* note 90, at 142–55.

106. *See* Laura W. Morgan, *When Will It Ever End? The Duty to Support Adult Children*, *in* 2001 FAMILY LAW UPDATE 155, 157–59 (Eric Pierson ed., 2001).

107. Lene Arnett Jensen et al., *The Right to Do Wrong: Lying to Parents Among Adolescents and Emerging Adults*, 33 J. YOUTH & ADOLESCENCE 101, 101, 105, 106 fig.1, 108 tbl.II (2004).

108. *See* Nancy Darling et al., *Predictors of Adolescents' Disclosure to Parents and Perceived Parental Knowledge: Between- and Within-Person Differences*, 35 J. YOUTH & ADOLESCENCE 667, 669–70, 674 (2006).

109. *Id.* at 675.

110. *See* GEOFFREY WOLFF, THE DUKE OF DECEPTION: MEMORIES OF MY FATHER 9, 64–65, 144, 258 (1979); Francine Prose, *The Brothers Wolff*, N.Y. TIMES, Feb. 5, 1989, § 6 (Magazine), at 22.

111. WOLFF, *supra* note 111, at 258 (quoting Rosemary Wolff) (internal quotation marks omitted).

112. *See* BRANDO SKYHORSE, TAKE THIS MAN: A MEMOIR 1, 3, 26, 100 (2014).

113. *See id.* at 3.

114. *Id.* at 141–42.

115. *See* WOLFF, *supra* note 111, at 8–9, 60–61, 65–66, 150.

116. *See supra* Introduction.

117. JACK DEVINE WITH VERNON LOEB, GOOD HUNTING: AN AMERICAN SPYMASTER'S STORY 223–24 (2014). For striking examples of British undercover police officers practicing intimate deception to maintain a preexisting facade, see ROB EVANS & PAUL LEWIS, UNDERCOVER: THE TRUE STORY OF BRITAIN'S SECRET POLICE 27–29, 45–50, 54, 59–60, 62–64, 142–43, 176–82, 184–89, 193–94, 196–97, 322–25 (2013).

118. James Risen, *Spy's Wife Speaks, After Taking a Lie Test*, N.Y. TIMES, May 16, 2002, at A18 (quoting Bonnie Hanssen) (internal quotation marks omitted).

119. *See* Letter from Lan Nguyen, Assistant U.S. Attorney, to Judge Allyne R. Ross at 1–3, United States v. Dickman, No. 14-610 (ARR) (E.D.N.Y. Sept. 7, 2015); Stephanie Clifford, *Legal Clients Called Him Shlomo; U.S. Calls Him a Fraud*, N.Y. TIMES, Aug. 8, 2014, at A18.

120. *See* Clifford, *supra* note 120, at A18.

121. *See* Letter from Lan Nguyen, Assistant U.S. Attorney, to Judge Allyne R. Ross, *supra* note 120, at 1.

122. *See* Clifford, *supra* note 120, at A18.

123. John Marzulli, *'Lawyer' Arrest Stalls Settlement*, N.Y. DAILY NEWS, Aug. 9, 2014, at 24 (quoting fiancée) (internal quotation marks omitted).

124. *See* Clifford, *supra* note 120, at A18.

125. *See* Letter from Lan Nguyen, Assistant U.S. Attorney, to Judge Allyne R. Ross, *supra* note 120, at 1.

Chapter 2

1. *See, e.g.*, Doe v. Dilling, 888 N.E.2d 24, 40–45 (Ill. 2008); *In re* Marriage of Broday, 628 N.E.2d 790, 794–97 (Ill. App. Ct. 1993); *In re* Adoption of A.A.T., 196 P.3d 1180, 1188–89 (Kan. 2008); Schoen v. Walling, 728 So. 2d 982, 986–87 (La. Ct. App. 1999); Lasater v. Guttmann, 5 A.3d 79, 104 (Md. Ct. Spec. App. 2010); Collins v. Huculak, 783 N.E.2d 834, 839–40 (Mass. App. Ct. 2003); Patel v. Navitlal, 627 A.2d 683, 688 (N.J. Super. Ct. Ch. Div. 1992); Fixler v. Fixler, 736 N.Y.S.2d 111, 112 (App. Div. 2002); Pacchiana v. Pacchiana, 462 N.Y.S.2d 256, 257–58 (App. Div. 1983); Avnery v. Avnery, 375 N.Y.S.2d 888, 890–92 (App. Div. 1975); Dubovsky v. Dubovsky, 725 N.Y.S.2d 832, 837 (Sup. Ct. 2001); Freiman v. Freiman, 680 N.Y.S.2d 797, 799 (Sup. Ct. 1998); Porreco v. Porreco, 811 A.2d 566, 571–72 (Pa. 2002); Hanna v. Sheflin, 275 S.W.3d 423, 425–28 (Tenn. Ct. App. 2008); Millan v. Dean Witter Reynolds, Inc., 90 S.W.3d 760, 763–66 (Tex. Ct. App. 2002).

2. *See, e.g.,* Betty Deramus, *Adults Have Choices: Taking Responsibility for Children Isn't One,* DETROIT NEWS, Mar. 13, 2006, at 1B; Tony Dokoupil, *What Should Have Tipped Anne Hathaway that Her Ex-Boyfriend Was Big Trouble?,* NEWSWEEK, July 7/July 14, 2008, at 69; Elizabeth Olson, *Swept off Her Feet, Then Bilked Out of Thousands,* N.Y. TIMES, July 18, 2015, at B4.

3. For discussion of hindsight bias, see DANIEL KAHNEMAN, THINKING, FAST AND SLOW 202–03 (2011); Neal J. Roese & Kathleen D. Vohs, *Hindsight Bias,* 7 PERSP. ON PSYCHOL. SCI. 411, 411–12, 417 (2012).

4. *See, e.g.,* United States v. Brown, 147 F.3d 477, 480–82, 487 (6th Cir. 1998); United States v. Jackson, 95 F.3d 500, 507–08 (7th Cir. 1996); 139 CONG. REC. 18,057–59 (1993) (statement of Sen. Orrin Hatch); *id.* at 27,645 (statement of Sen. Orrin Hatch).

5. *See* A. CONAN DOYLE, A STUDY IN SCARLET 26–29 (London, Ward, Lock, Bowden, & Co. 1892) (1887); ROBERT GALBRAITH, THE CUCKOO'S CALLING 156–57 (2013); ROBERT GALBRAITH, THE SILKWORM 80, 313 (2014).

6. FRIEDRICH NIETZSCHE, BEYOND GOOD AND EVIL: PRELUDE TO A PHILOSOPHY OF THE FUTURE 72 (Rolf-Peter Horstmann & Judith Norman eds., Judith Norman trans., Cambridge Univ. Press 2002) (1886).

7. 3 SIGMUND FREUD, *Fragment of an Analysis of a Case of Hysteria* (1905), *in* COLLECTED PAPERS 13, 94 (Alix & James Strachey trans., 1959).

8. TYLER COHEN WOOD, CATCHING THE CATFISHERS: DISARM THE ONLINE PRETENDERS, PREDATORS, AND PERPETRATORS WHO ARE OUT TO RUIN YOUR LIFE 188 (2014) (capitalization and emphasis omitted).

9. GREGORY HARTLEY & MARYANN KARINCH, HOW TO SPOT A LIAR: WHY PEOPLE DON'T TELL THE TRUTH . . . AND HOW YOU CAN CATCH THEM (rev. ed. 2012) (capitalization omitted).

10. PHILIP HOUSTON ET AL., SPY THE LIE: FORMER CIA OFFICERS TEACH YOU HOW TO DETECT DECEPTION (2012) (capitalization omitted).

11. DAVID LAMBERT, BODY LANGUAGE 101: THE ULTIMATE GUIDE TO KNOWING WHEN PEOPLE ARE LYING, HOW THEY ARE FEELING, WHAT THEY ARE THINKING, AND MORE (2008) (capitalization omitted).

12. DAVID J. LIEBERMAN, NEVER BE LIED TO AGAIN: HOW TO GET THE TRUTH IN 5 MINUTES OR LESS IN ANY CONVERSATION OR SITUATION (1998) (capitalization omitted).

13. *See* Charles F. Bond, Jr. & Bella M. DePaulo, *Accuracy of Deception Judgments,* 10 PERSONALITY & SOC. PSYCHOL. REV. 214, 214–15, 217, 219, 230–31 (2006); *see also* ALDERT VRIJ, DETECTING LIES AND DECEIT: PITFALLS AND OPPORTUNITIES 146–48 (2d ed. 2008); Timothy R. Levine et al., *Accuracy in Detecting Truths and Lies: Documenting the "Veracity Effect,"* 66 COMM. MONOGRAPHS 125, 125, 139, 141–42 (1999).

14. *See* MARK L. KNAPP, SOCIAL INTERCOURSE: FROM GREETING TO GOODBYE 222–23 (1978); Charles F. Bond Jr. & Bella M. DePaulo, *Individual Differences in Judging Deception: Accuracy and Bias,* 134 PSYCHOL. BULL. 477, 487–88 (2008); Mark L. Knapp & Mark E. Comadena, *Telling It Like It Isn't: A Review of Theory and Research on Deceptive Communications,* 5 HUM. COMM. RES. 270, 273 (1979).

15. Bond & DePaulo, *supra* note 14, at 477; *see also id.* at 485–86.

16. Maureen O'Sullivan & Paul Ekman, *The Wizards of Deception Detection, in* THE DETECTION OF DECEPTION IN FORENSIC CONTEXTS 269, 271, 274–76 (Pär Anders Granhag & Leif A. Strömwall eds., 2004); *see also* Paul Ekman et al., *A Few Can Catch a Liar,* 10 PSYCHOL. SCI. 263, 263–65 (1999); Paul Ekman & Maureen O'Sullivan, *Who Can Catch a Liar?,* 46 AM. PSYCHOLOGIST 913, 913–16, 920 (1991).

17. *See* KAHNEMAN, *supra* note 3, at 8, 12, 97–98; Amos Tversky & Daniel Kahneman, *Judgment Under Uncertainty: Heuristics and Biases,* 185 SCI. 1124, 1124 (1974).

18. *See* VRIJ, *supra* note 13, at 148–49; D. Eric Anderson et al., *Love's Best Habit: Deception in the Context of Relationships, in* THE SOCIAL CONTEXT OF NONVERBAL BEHAVIOR 372, 394 (Pierre Philippot et al. eds., 1999).

19. *See* Raymond S. Nickerson, *Confirmation Bias: A Ubiquitous Phenomenon in Many Guises,* 2 REV. GEN. PSYCHOL. 175, 175–78, 180 (1998).

20. *See* KNAPP, *supra* note 14, at 223.

21. *See* Anderson et al., *supra* note 18, at 385.
22. *See id.* at 391–92, 397; Steven A. McCornack & Malcolm R. Parks, *What Women Know That Men Don't: Sex Differences in Determining the Truth Behind Deceptive Messages*, 7 J. Soc. & Pers. Relationships 107, 107, 110, 112, 116–17 (1990); James B. Stiff et al., *Truth Biases and Aroused Suspicion in Relational Deception*, 19 Comm. Res. 326, 326, 328, 330, 332, 340–41 (1992).
23. Sandra L. Murray et al., *The Benefits of Positive Illusions: Idealization and the Construction of Satisfaction in Close Relationships*, 70 J. Personality & Soc. Psychol. 79, 79–80, 92 (1996); Sandra L. Murray & John G. Holmes, *A Leap of Faith? Positive Illusions in Romantic Relationships*, 23 Personality & Soc. Psychol. Bull. 586, 586–87, 589, 596–98 (1997).
24. *See* Tim Cole, *Deception Confidence in Romantic Relationships: Confidently Lying to the One You Love*, *in* 34 Advances in Psychology Research 127, 136 (Serge P. Shohov ed., 2005); Timothy R. Levine & Steven A. McCornack, *Linking Love and Lies: A Formal Test of the McCornack and Parks Model of Deception Detection*, 9 J. Soc. & Pers. Relationships 143, 148, 152–53 (1992); Steven A. McCornack & Malcolm R. Parks, *Deception Detection and Relationship Development: The Other Side of Trust*, *in* 9 Communication Yearbook 377, 381, 385–86, 388 (Margaret L. McLaughlin ed., 1986); *see also* William B. Swann, Jr. et al., *On "Knowing Your Partner": Dangerous Illusions in the Age of AIDS?*, 2 Pers. Relationships 173, 173–78, 181–82 (1995).
25. *See* Murray et al., *supra* note 23, at 79, 92; Murray & Holmes, *supra* note 23, at 586, 597–98, 600.
26. *See* Anderson et al., *supra* note 18, at 382; Roos Vonk, *Self-Serving Interpretations of Flattery: Why Ingratiation Works*, 82 J. Personality & Soc. Psychol. 515, 515 (2002).
27. *See, e.g.,* Kathryn Edin & Maria Kefalas, Promises I Can Keep: Why Poor Women Put Motherhood Before Marriage 92 (2005).
28. Vrij, *supra* note 13, at 149.
29. Aldert Vrij, Detecting Lies and Deceit: The Psychology of Lying and the Implications for Professional Practice 222 (2000) (internal quotation marks omitted).
30. Vrij, *supra* note 13, at 149 (internal quotation marks omitted).
31. Vrij, *supra* note 29, at 222.
32. Paul Oyer, Everything I Ever Needed to Know About Economics I Learned from Online Dating 82–83 (2014).
33. Erik Eckholm, *Private Snoops Find GPS Trail Legal to Follow*, N.Y. Times, Jan. 29, 2012, at 1 (quoting Jonathan Zittrain) (internal quotation marks omitted).
34. Tan Vinh, *Dating Detectives*, Seattle Times & Seattle Post-Intelligencer, Nov. 18, 2007, at K1 (quoting Aaron Silverberg) (internal quotation marks omitted).
35. *Id.* (quoting Pamela Robinson) (internal quotation marks omitted).
36. Joanna Pearson, *So, Tell Me Everything I Know About You*, N.Y. Times, Sept. 14, 2008, at 6ST.
37. Carolyn Hax, *A Few Fun Dates, a Dark Google Revelation, and a Dilemma*, Wash. Post, Nov. 25, 2013, at C4 (emphasis omitted).
38. Carolyn Hax, *Googling the Person You're Dating: Readers Weigh in*, Wash. Post, Nov. 26, 2013, at C5 (emphasis omitted).
39. Randy Cohen, *Is Googling O.K.?*, N.Y. Times, Dec. 15, 2002, Magazine, at 50 (capitalization and emphasis omitted).
40. Hax, *supra* note 38, at C5.
41. Samantha Henig, *Stop* Googling *Your Dates!*, Glamour, Apr. 2013, at 154, 156 (quoting Jessica Bennett) (emphasis and internal quotation marks omitted).
42. Susan Forward with Donna Frazier, When Your Lover Is a Liar: Healing the Wounds of Deception and Betrayal 10–11 (1999).
43. Dory Hollander, 101 Lies Men Tell Women: And Why Women Believe Them 325 (1995).
44. *Id.* at 84, 325.
45. *Id.* at 325; *see also* Sally Caldwell, Romantic Deception: The Six Signs He's Lying 207–08 (2000); Robert Feldman, The Liar in Your Life: The Way to Truthful Relationships 253–54 (2009); Forward with Frazier, *supra* note 42, at 227–28.

46. Dina Matos McGreevey, Silent Partner: A Memoir of My Marriage 30 (2007).

47. *See* Wood, *supra* note 8, at 34.

48. *See* Charles Seife, Virtual Unreality: Just Because the Internet Told You, How Do You Know It's True? 60, 202 (2014); Wood, *supra* note 8, at 87.

49. *See* Susan Nash, Skip Tracing Basics & Beyond: A Complete Step-by-Step Guide for Locating Hidden Assets 99, 106 (2d ed. 2012); Robert Scott, The Investigator's Little Black Book 3, at 222–23 (2002); Seife, *supra* note 48, at 60; Wood, *supra* note 8, at 213; Tom W. Smith & Jibum Kim, *An Assessment of the Multi-Level Integrated Database Approach*, 645 Annals Am. Acad. Pol. & Soc. Sci. 185, 201 (2013).

50. *See* Seife, *supra* note 48, at 57–58, 202.

51. *See* Wood, *supra* note 8, at 84–85.

52. *See id.* at 213.

53. *See* Edward C. Andler with Dara Herbst, The Complete Reference Checking Handbook: The Proven (and Legal) Way to Prevent Hiring Mistakes 3–4 (2d ed. 2003); Nash, *supra* note 49, at x–xii; Scott, *supra* note 49, at introduction; The Guide to Background Investigations: A Comprehensive Source Directory for Employee Screening and Background Investigations 5–6, 10, 15 (9th ed. 2000); The Sourcebook to Public Record Information: The Comprehensive Guide to County, State, & Federal Public Records Sources 5 (11th ed. 2015).

54. *See* Gannett Co. v. City Clerk's Office, Rochester, 596 N.Y.S.2d 968, 969–70 (Sup. Ct. 1993); Nash, *supra* note 49, at 107, 212–13.

55. *See In re* Marriage of Purcell, 879 P.2d 468, 469 (Colo. App. 1994); Barron v. Fla. Freedom Newspapers, Inc., 531 So. 2d 113, 114, 116–19 (Fla. 1988); *In re* Marriage of Johnson, 598 N.E.2d 406, 407, 409–11 (Ill. App. Ct. 1992); *In re* Keene Sentinel, 612 A.2d 911, 915–17 (N.H. 1992); Providence Journal Co. v. Clerk of the Family Court, 643 A.2d 210, 211 (R.I. 1994) (per curiam); Nash, *supra* note 49, at 104, 107, 212–13, 232; Wood, *supra* note 8, at 54.

56. *See* Nash, *supra* note 49, at 213, 272.

57. *See id.* at 213; Scott, *supra* note 49, at 87–88.

58. *See* Nash, *supra* note 49, at 123–24, 217–21; Scott, *supra* note 49, at 4, 7, 182, 189–91; The Guide to Background Investigations, *supra* note 53, at 12.

59. *See, e.g.,* Fla. Stat. Ann. § 943.053(3) (West Supp. 2019); Minn. Stat. §§ 13.82(2), 13.87(1)(b) (2018); Okla. Stat. Ann. tit. 51, § 24A.8 (West 2017); Paul v. Davis, 424 U.S. 693, 712–13 (1976); State v. Benoit, 311 P.3d 874, 881–82 (Or. 2013) (en banc); Andler with Herbst, *supra* note 53, at 132–34, 146; Nash, *supra* note 49, at 215–17; Scott, *supra* note 49, at 62, 215, 233–34; The Guide to Background Investigations, *supra* note 53, at 23–25.

60. *See* Nash, *supra* note 49, at 213.

61. *See* 11 U.S.C. § 107 (2012); The Sourcebook to Public Record Information, *supra* note 53, at 1947.

62. *See* Rowley v. United States, 76 F.3d 796, 797–98, 801–02 (6th Cir. 1996); The Guide to Background Investigations, *supra* note 53, at 30.

63. *See* Nash, *supra* note 49, at 251–52; Wood, *supra* note 8, at 53–54; Tom Zeller Jr., *Personal Data for the Taking*, N.Y. Times, May 18, 2005, at C1.

64. *See* Nash, *supra* note 49, at 107.

65. *See* Andler with Herbst, *supra* note 53, at 138; Nash, *supra* note 49, at 100–02, 108, 121, 214; Scott, *supra* note 49, at 263; Seife, *supra* note 48, at 59.

66. *See* Andler with Herbst, *supra* note 53, at 138; Nash, *supra* note 49, at 214.

67. *See* Nash, *supra* note 49, at 104, 209–10; Scott, *supra* note 49, at 49, 209.

68. *See* Nash, *supra* note 49, at 104, 208, 222; Scott, *supra* note 49, at 35–36, 115–16, 231–32.

69. *See* The Sourcebook to Public Record Information, *supra* note 53, at 1923.

70. *See* Nash, *supra* note 49, at 115; The Sourcebook to Public Record Information, *supra* note 53, at 1952.

71. *See* The Guide to Background Investigations, *supra* note 53, at 10; The Sourcebook to Public Record Information, *supra* note 53, at 1923–31.

72. *See* THE SOURCEBOOK TO PUBLIC RECORD INFORMATION, *supra* note 53, at 1923–24, 1930, 1943, 1945.

73. *See id.* at 1924–25.

74. *See* ANDLER WITH HERBST, *supra* note 53, at 134, 138; THE GUIDE TO BACKGROUND INVESTIGATIONS, *supra* note 53, at 13–14.

75. Sara Kehaulani Goo, *Dinner, Movie — and a Background Check — for Online Daters*, WASH. POST, Jan. 28, 2007, at A1 (quoting Kimberly Hall) (internal quotation marks omitted).

76. Bonnie Miller Rubin, *When Tall and Handsome Turns Out Short and Pudgy*, CHI. TRIB., July 30, 2006, at 1 (quoting Roberta Beier) (internal quotation marks omitted).

77. GINI GRAHAM SCOTT, PLAYING THE LYING GAME: DETECTING AND DEALING WITH LIES AND LIARS, FROM OCCASIONAL FIBBERS TO FREQUENT FABRICATORS 145 (2010) (quoting Blanche).

78. *Id.* at 144 (quoting Dee).

79. *See* California v. Greenwood, 486 U.S. 35, 37–41 (1988); NASH, *supra* note 49, at 128; SCOTT, *supra* note 49, at 341, 454–55.

80. *See* Marlys Duran, *Ex-Husband of Psychic Claims Fraud*, ROCKY MTN. NEWS, Apr. 7, 1990, at 24.

81. *See* Xin Guo et al., Letter to the Editor, *A Noninvasive Test to Determine Paternity in Pregnancy*, 366 NEW ENG. J. MED. 1743, 1744–45 (2012); Andrew Pollack, *Before Birth, Dad's ID*, N.Y. TIMES, June 20, 2012, at B1.

82. *See* Delawese Fulton, *A Home Paternity Test? Yep, It's True*, ORLANDO SENTINEL, Apr. 8, 2008, at E1.

83. *See* Hodge v. Craig, 382 S.W.3d 325, 330–31 (Tenn. 2012).

84. *See* D.W. v. R.W., 52 A.3d 1043, 1045–46, 1058 (N.J. 2012).

85. *See* Shirley L. Shih et al., *Screening for Sexually Transmitted Infections at Home or in the Clinic?*, 24 CURRENT OPINION INFECTIOUS DISEASES 78, 78, 81 (2011); Joseph D. Tucker et al., *Point-of-Care Testing for Sexually Transmitted Infections: Recent Advances and Implications for Disease Control*, 26 CURRENT OPINION INFECTIOUS DISEASES 73, 73, 75–77 (2013).

86. C. Willig, *'I Wouldn't Have Married the Guy If I'd Have to Do That': Heterosexual Adults' Constructions of Condom Use and Their Implications for Sexual Practice*, 5 J. COMMUNITY & APPLIED SOC. PSYCHOL. 75, 81–82 (1995) (quoting Sam) (internal quotation marks omitted); *see also id.* at 76–77, 79, 83; Janet Holland et al., *Between Embarrassment and Trust: Young Women and the Diversity of Condom Use*, *in* AIDS: RESPONSES, INTERVENTIONS AND CARE 127, 139–40 (Peter Aggleton et al. eds., 1991); Lisbeth G. Lane & Linda L.L. Viney, *Toward Better Prevention: Constructions of Trust in the Sexual Relationships of Young Women*, 32 J. APPLIED SOC. PSYCHOL. 700, 714 (2002); Carla Willig, *The Limitations of Trust in Intimate Relationships: Constructions of Trust and Sexual Risk Taking*, 36 BRIT. J. SOC. PSYCHOL. 211, 214, 218, 220 (1997).

87. *See infra* text accompanying notes 125–97.

88. *See infra* text accompanying notes 89–96, 169–71, 192–95.

89. *See* Omnibus Crime Control and Safe Streets Act of 1968, Pub. L. No. 90-351, § 802, 82 Stat. 197, 212–23.

90. *Invasions of Privacy: Hearings Before the Subcomm. on Admin. Practice & Procedure of the S. Comm. on the Judiciary*, 89th Cong., pt. 5, at 2261 (1967) (statement of Sen. Edward Long).

91. United States v. Hall, 488 F.2d 193, 197 n.7 (9th Cir. 1973); *see also* United States v. Giordano, 416 U.S. 505, 517 n.7 (1974); United States v. Murdock, 63 F.3d 1391, 1397 (6th Cir. 1995); Thompson v. Dulaney, 970 F.2d 744, 748 (10th Cir. 1992); Heggy v. Heggy, 944 F.2d 1537, 1541 (10th Cir. 1991); Pritchard v. Pritchard, 732 F.2d 372, 374 (4th Cir. 1984); United States v. Jones, 542 F.2d 661, 668–69 (6th Cir. 1976); Nations v. Nations, 670 F. Supp. 1432, 1434 (W.D. Ark. 1987); Heyman v. Heyman, 548 F. Supp. 1041, 1047 (N.D. Ill. 1982); Kratz v. Kratz, 477 F. Supp. 463, 471 (E.D. Pa. 1979).

92. *Right of Privacy Act of 1967: Hearings on S. 928 Before the Subcomm. on Admin. Practice & Procedure of the S. Comm. on the Judiciary*, 90th Cong., pt. 2, at 413 (1967) (testimony of G. Robert Blakey, Professor of Law, Notre Dame Law School); *see also Anti-Crime Program: Hearings on H.R. 5037, H.R. 5038, H.R. 5384, H.R. 5385, & H.R. 5386 Before*

Subcomm. No. 5 of the H. Comm. on the Judiciary, 90th Cong. 1045 (1967) (testimony of G. Robert Blakey, Professor of Law, Notre Dame Law School).

93. 114 CONG. REC. 14,747 (1968) (statement of Sen. Karl Mundt).

94. *Id.* at 14,480 (statement of Sen. Joseph Tydings).

95. S. REP. No. 90-1097, at 67 (1968).

96. *Id.* at 224, 225 ("INDIVIDUAL VIEWS MESSRS. DIRKSEN, HRUSKA, SCOTT, AND THURMOND ON TITLES I, II, AND III").

97. *See, e.g.,* People v. Otto, 831 P.2d 1178, 1195 (Cal. 1992) (in bank).

98. Fischer v. Hooper, 732 A.2d 396, 398, 402 (N.H. 1999).

99. Steve Eder & Jennifer Valentino-DeVries, *A Spy-Gear Arms Race Transforms Modern Divorce*, WALL ST. J., Oct. 6–7, 2012, at A1 (quoting Michele Mathias) (internal quotation marks omitted).

100. *See infra* text accompanying notes 186–95.

101. United States v. Thomas, ACM 37660, 2011 WL 6010242, at *1 (A.F. Ct. Crim. App. July 6, 2011) (per curiam).

102. *See* United States v. Carroll, No. 97-4012, 1997 WL 279754, at *1 (4th Cir. May 28, 1997) (per curiam).

103. *See* Tom Farmer, *Sources: E-Mails Sent Mayor's Hubby into a Jealous Rage*, BOS. HERALD, Aug. 3, 2004, at 2.

104. *See* Caroline Louise Cole, *Faced with Tough Campaign, Clancy Decides to Skip Race*, BOS. SUNDAY GLOBE, July 31, 2005, at N6.

105. *See* Nancy Keates, *One Tough Day for Two-Timers*, WALL ST. J., Feb. 10, 2006, at W1; Stefanie Scarlett, *It's Payback Time*, J. GAZETTE (Fort Wayne), Mar. 16, 2002, at 1D.

106. CHRISTINE GALLAGHER, THE WOMAN'S BOOK OF REVENGE: TIPS ON GETTING EVEN WHEN "MR. RIGHT" TURNS OUT TO BE ALL WRONG 101–02 (1998).

107. *See id.* at 15–16.

108. *See id.* at 90.

109. *See id.* at 19–20.

110. *Id.* at 151–52 (emphasis omitted); *see also* REGINA BARRECA, SWEET REVENGE: THE WICKED DELIGHTS OF GETTING EVEN 43–44, 80–82 (1995).

111. *See, e.g.,* Libby Copeland, *Cyber-Snooping into a Cheating Heart*, WASH. POST, Aug. 8, 2000, at C1; Eder & Valentino-DeVries, *supra* note 99, at A1; *Tracy and Jeff: A Love Story, in* STRAIGHT WIVES: SHATTERED LIVES: STORIES OF WOMEN WITH GAY HUSBAND[s] 53, 58 (Bonnie Kaye ed., 2006).

112. *See* Chris Seper, *Net Adds Wrinkle to Fabric of Marriage*, PLAIN DEALER (Cleveland), Jan. 7, 2002, at C1.

113. Copeland, *supra* note 111, at C1 (quoting Spectorsoft advertisement) (internal quotation marks omitted); *see also* Adam Cohen, *Internet Insecurity*, TIME, July 2, 2001, at 44, 49; Eder & Valentino-DeVries, *supra* note 99, at A1.

114. *See* Copeland, *supra* note 111, at C1; Eder & Valentino-DeVries, *supra* note 99, at A1; *see also* Joyce Wadler, *The 'Other Woman' Gets to Play Sleuth*, N.Y. TIMES, June 1, 2014, at ST11.

115. Electronic Communications Privacy Act of 1986, Pub. L. No. 99-508, 100 Stat. 1848.

116. *See* 18 U.S.C. § 2511(1), (2)(d) (2012).

117. *See id.* § 2511(4).

118. *See id.* § 2520.

119. *See id.* § 2520(b).

120. *See id.* § 2520(c)(2).

121. *See id.* § 2701(a).

122. *See id.* § 2701(b).

123. *See id.* § 2707.

124. *See id.* § 2707(c).

125. *See, e.g.,* LaRocca v. LaRocca, 86 F. Supp. 3d 540, 541–44 (E.D. La. 2015); Mahoney v. DeNuzzio, No. 13-11501-FDS, 2014 WL 347624, at *1–6 (D. Mass. Jan. 29, 2014); Miller v. Meyers, 766 F. Supp. 2d 919, 921–25 (W.D. Ark. 2011); Glob. Policy Partners, LLC v. Yessin, 686 F. Supp. 2d 642, 644–46 (E.D. Va. 2010); Becker v. Toca, No. 07-7202, 2008 WL 4443050, at *1–6 (E.D. La. Sept. 26, 2008); Bailey v. Bailey, No. 07-11672, 2008

WL 324156, at *1–12 (E.D. Mich. Feb. 6, 2008); Crain v. Limbaugh (*In re* Limbaugh), 155 B.R. 952, 954–55, 960–61 (Bankr. N.D. Tex. 1993); People v. Walker, 813 N.W.2d 750, 750 (Mich. 2012); *id.* at 751 (Kelly, J., dissenting); Teeter v. Teeter, 759 S.E.2d 144, 146–48 (S.C. Ct. App. 2014); Kathleen Brady Shea, *Husband Faces Trial in E-Mail Dispute*, PHILA. INQUIRER, Aug. 28, 2003, at B10; Mike Wendland, *State Targets Cyber Spies*, DETROIT FREE PRESS, Sept. 6, 2001, at 1B; *infra* text accompanying notes 126–60.

126. *See* State v. Hormann, 805 N.W.2d 883, 886–87, 892, 894–95 (Minn. Ct. App. 2011); Eder & Valentino-DeVries, *supra* note 99, at A1; *see also* People v. Sullivan, 53 P.3d 1181, 1182–85 (Colo. App. 2002); Nicole Brodeur, *Stalking Victim Uncovers Dark Use of Technology*, SEATTLE TIMES, Sept. 3, 2006, at B1; Matt Gryta, *Man Convicted of Stalking Wife with Technology*, BUFFALO NEWS, Feb. 5, 2004, at B1; Meg Jones, *Kenosha Man Sentenced for Stalking*, MILWAUKEE J. SENTINEL, June 6, 2003, at 3B; Regina B. Schofield, *Waging a Battle on Electronic Crime*, SEATTLE POST-INTELLIGENCER, Jan. 18, 2007, at B7; John Schwartz, *This Car Can Talk. What It Says May Cause Concern.*, N.Y. TIMES, Dec. 29, 2003, at C1.

127. *See* Klumb v. Goan, 884 F. Supp. 2d 644, 645–48 (E.D. Tenn. 2012).

128. *See id.* at 646, 663.

129. *See id.* at 646–48.

130. *See id.* at 653–54, 661–62.

131. *See id.* at 666.

132. *See id.* at 650–51, 653–54.

133. *See id.* at 645.

134. *See id.* at 645–46, 665–67.

135. *Id.* at 666.

136. *See* Ken Little, *State Supreme Court Censures Attorney Goan*, GREENEVILLE SUN, Nov. 7, 2014, at A-11.

137. *See* Lewton v. Divingnzzo, 772 F. Supp. 2d 1046, 1048–50 (D. Neb. 2011).

138. *See id.* at 1049.

139. *See id.* at 1048, 1050, 1053, 1057.

140. *See id.* at 1048.

141. *See id.* at 1048, 1050–51.

142. *See id.* at 1048, 1059.

143. *See id.* at 1061.

144. *See* SEX, LIES, AND VIDEOTAPE (Miramax Films 1989).

145. *See* H.E.S. v. J.C.S., 815 A.2d 405, 408–10, 414–18 (N.J. 2003); Miller v. Brooks, 472 S.E.2d 350, 352–57 (N.C. Ct. App. 1996); *see also* Clayton v. Richards, 47 S.W.3d 149, 151, 153–56 (Tex. Ct. App. 2001). For an unsuccessful suit, see Colon v. Colon, 2006 WL 2318250, at *1–5 (N.J. Super. Ct. App. Div. Aug. 11, 2006) (per curiam).

146. *In re* Marriage of Tigges, 758 N.W.2d 824, 825 (Iowa 2008).

147. *See id.* at 827.

148. *See id.* at 825–26.

149. *See* Glazner v. Glazner, 347 F.3d 1212, 1213–16 (11th Cir. 2003) (en banc); Heggy v. Heggy, 944 F.2d 1537, 1538–41 (10th Cir. 1991); Fultz v. Gilliam, 942 F.2d 396, 400 (6th Cir. 1991); Kempf v. Kempf, 868 F.2d 970, 971–73 (8th Cir. 1989); Pritchard v. Pritchard, 732 F.2d 372, 372–74 (4th Cir. 1984); United States v. Jones, 542 F.2d 661, 666–73 (6th Cir. 1976); Heyman v. Heyman, 548 F. Supp. 1041, 1045 (N.D. Ill. 1982); Gill v. Willer, 482 F. Supp. 776, 777–78 (W.D.N.Y. 1980); Kratz v. Kratz, 477 F. Supp. 463, 476 (E.D. Pa. 1979); *Ex parte* O'Daniel, 515 So. 2d 1250, 1252–53 (Ala. 1987); People v. Otto, 831 P.2d 1178, 1179–80, 1184–85 (Cal. 1992) (in bank); Dommer v. Dommer, 829 N.E.2d 125, 138 (Ind. Ct. App. 2005); Young v. Young, 536 N.W.2d 254, 254–55, 257 (Mich. Ct. App. 1995); Stamme v. Stamme, 589 S.W.2d 50, 53 (Mo. Ct. App. 1979); Rickenbaker v. Rickenbaker, 226 S.E.2d 347, 348–49, 352–53 (N.C. 1976); Pulawski v. Blais, 506 A.2d 76, 77 n.2 (R.I. 1986). *But see* Anonymous v. Anonymous, 558 F.2d 677, 677–79 (2d Cir. 1977); Simpson v. Simpson, 490 F.2d 803, 804–10 (5th Cir. 1974); Lizza v. Lizza, 631 F. Supp. 529, 533 (E.D.N.Y. 1986); Stewart v. Stewart, 645 So. 2d 1319, 1321 (Miss. 1994); Baumrind v. Ewing, 279 S.E.2d 359, 360 (S.C. 1981).

150. *See Heggy*, 944 F.2d at 1538.

The

151. *See* Ed Godfrey, *Trial Turns to Heggy's Wiretap*, DAILY OKLAHOMAN, Feb. 27, 1990, at 1.
152. *See Former Narcotics Director Files for Bankruptcy*, TULSA WORLD, Sept. 22, 1990, at A-10.
153. *See, e.g.*, State v. Shaw, 404 S.E.2d 887, 887–89 (N.C. Ct. App. 1991).
154. *See* United States v. Schrimsher, 493 F.2d 848, 849–50, 853 (5th Cir. 1974).
155. *Id.* at 850.
156. *See* State v. Jock, 404 A.2d 518, 519–24 (Del. Super. Ct. 1979); Burgess v. Burgess, 447 So. 2d 220, 221–23 (Fla. 1984); State v. Lombardo, 738 N.E.2d 653, 654–55, 657–60 (Ind. 2000); Scott v. Scott, 649 A.2d 1372, 1373–75, 1379 (N.J. Super. Ct. Ch. Div. 1994).
157. Duffy v. State, 33 S.W.3d 17, 19–20 (Tex. Ct. App. 2000) (internal quotation marks omitted).
158. *See* Standiford v. Standiford, 598 A.2d 495, 497–98 (Md. Ct. Spec. App. 1991).
159. *See* 18 U.S.C. §§ 1702, 1708 (2012).
160. *See* Miller v. Brooks, 472 S.E.2d 350, 352–53 (N.C. Ct. App. 1996).
161. *See* 15 U.S.C. § 1681b (2012).
162. *See id.* § 1681n(a).
163. *See id.* § 1681q.
164. *See* Cole v. Am. Family Mut. Ins. Co., 410 F. Supp. 2d 1020, 1021–25 (D. Kan. 2006); Thibodeaux v. Rupers, 196 F. Supp. 2d 585, 586–87, 591–93 (S.D. Ohio 2001); *see also* Jones v. Federated Fin. Reserve Corp., 144 F.3d 961, 962–63 (6th Cir. 1998); Rodgers v. McCullough, 296 F. Supp. 2d 895, 898–902 (W.D. Tenn. 2003); Northrup v. Hoffman of Simsbury, Inc., Nos. 3:96CV00097 AVC, 3:98CV01219 AVC, 2000 WL 436612, at *1–2, *4–5 (D. Conn. Mar. 15, 2000); Bils v. Nixon, Hargrave, Devans & Doyle, 880 P.2d 743, 745 (Ariz. Ct. App. 1994).
165. *See* Yohay v. City of Alexandria Emps. Credit Union, Inc., 827 F.2d 967, 969 (4th Cir. 1987).
166. *See id.* at 969–74.
167. *See* Telephone Records and Privacy Protection Act of 2006, Pub. L. No. 109-476, § 3(a), 120 Stat. 3568, 3569 (2007) (codified at 18 U.S.C. § 1039(a) (2012)).
168. Telephone Records and Privacy Protection Act § 2(4)(B) (internal quotation marks omitted).
169. *See Internet Data Brokers: Who Has Access to Your Private Records? Hearings Before the Subcomm. on Oversight & Investigations of the H. Comm. on Energy & Commerce*, 109th Cong. 6, 929 (2006) (statement of Rep. Diana DeGette); *id.* at 13, 1176 (statement of Rep. Greg Walden); *id.* at 1177 (statement of Rep. Janice Schakowsky); *see also id.* at 1225 (testimony of Gregory Schaffer, Chief Security Officer, Alltel).
170. *See* 18 U.S.C. § 2725(3).
171. *See* Driver's Privacy Protection Act of 1994, Pub. L. No. 103-322, 108 Stat. 2099.
172. *See* 18 U.S.C. § 2722(a).
173. *See id.* § 2723(a).
174. *See id.* § 2724.
175. *See* Schierts v. City of Brookfield, 868 F. Supp. 2d 818, 819–20 (E.D. Wis. 2012) (quoting Bart Engelking) (internal quotation marks omitted).
176. *See id.* at 821.
177. *See id.* at 819.
178. Health Insurance Portability and Accountability Act of 1996, Pub. L. No. 104-191, 110 Stat. 1936.
179. *See* 45 C.F.R. § 164.510(b) (2017).
180. *See* Jane Gross, *Under Law, Keeping Patients' Details Private, Even from Their Kin*, N.Y. TIMES, July 3, 2007, at A12.
181. *See* Somogye v. Toledo Clinic, Inc., No. 3:11 CV 496, 2012 WL 2191279, at *1–3, 6–7 (N.D. Ohio June 14, 2012).
182. *See* Koch v. Koch, 961 So. 2d 1134, 1134–35 (Fla. Dist. Ct. App. 2007).
183. *See* McKenzie v. Pierce, 403 S.W.3d 565, 568, 570–72 (Ark. 2012); *see also* M.M. v. L.M., 55 A.3d 1167, 1168, 1174–75, 1177 (Pa. Super. Ct. 2012).
184. *See* Katherine Reynolds Lewis, *Return Has Wealth of Infidelity Clues*, HOUS. CHRON., May 7, 2007, at D4.
185. *See* 26 U.S.C. § 6103(e)(1)(B) (2012).
186. *See id.* § 6103(a).

187. *See id.* § 7213A.

188. *See id.* § 7213.

189. *See id.* § 7431.

190. *See* U.S. GEN. ACCOUNTING OFFICE, GAO/T-AIMD-97-82, IRS SYSTEMS SECURITY AND FUNDING: EMPLOYEE BROWSING NOT BEING ADDRESSED EFFECTIVELY AND BUDGET REQUESTS FOR NEW SYSTEMS DEVELOPMENT NOT JUSTIFIED 1–2 (1997); U.S. GEN. ACCOUNTING OFFICE, GAO/AIMD-97-49, IRS SYSTEMS SECURITY: TAX PROCESSING OPERATIONS AND DATA STILL AT RISK DUE TO SERIOUS WEAKNESSES 2, 4, 8–11 (1997).

191. United States v. Czubinski, 106 F.3d 1069, 1071–78 (1st Cir. 1997).

192. *See* H.R. REP. NO. 105-220, at 704 & n.15 (1997) (Conf. Rep.); 143 CONG. REC. 4817 (1997) (statement of Sen. Paul Coverdell); *id.* at 5473 (statement of Rep. William Coyne); *id.* at 5476 (statement of Rep. Gerald Kleczka).

193. *See* Taxpayer Browsing Protection Act, Pub. L. No. 105-35, § 2, 111 Stat. 1104, 1104–05 (1997).

194. Letter from George Ellard, Inspector Gen., Nat'l Sec. Agency, to Charles E. Grassley, Ranking Member, Senate Judiciary Comm. 1–5 (Sept. 11, 2013) (on file with author) (internal quotation and alteration marks omitted).

195. *Examining Recommendations to Reform FISA Authorities: Hearing Before the H. Comm. on the Judiciary*, 113th Cong. 82 (2014) (statement of Rep. Robert Scott).

Chapter 3

1. *See supra* Chapter 1.

2. *See* MARY TURNER THOMSON, THE BIGAMIST: THE TRUE STORY OF A HUSBAND'S ULTIMATE BETRAYAL 14, 96, 124, 151, 161–62, 173, 201, 203–08 (2008).

3. *See* Jeannie O'Sullivan, *Romance Fraud Suspect Admits to Theft*, BURLINGTON COUNTY TIMES, Nov. 11, 2014, at A1.

4. *See* Government's Sentencing Memorandum at 2–3, United States v. Vandemore, No. 3:14-cr-75 (S.D. Iowa Mar. 23, 2015); Barb Ickes, *Woman Gets Prison for Scheme*, QUAD-CITY TIMES, Mar. 28, 2015, at B1; Barb Ickes & Brian Wellner, *Feds: Woman Fakes Birth to Collect Money*, QUAD-CITY TIMES, Dec. 19, 2014, at B1; Grant Rodgers, *Iowa Woman to Spend 18 Months in Prison for Fake Pregnancy Swindle of over $95,000*, DES MOINES REG., Mar. 28, 2015, at 4A.

5. *See* Elizabeth Olson, *Swept Off Her Feet, Then Bilked Out of Thousands*, N.Y. TIMES, July 18, 2015, at B4.

6. INTERNET CRIME COMPLAINT CTR., FED. BUREAU OF INVESTIGATION, 2017 INTERNET CRIME REPORT 4 (2018).

7. *Id.* at 20.

8. *Id.* at 26.

9. *See id.* at 21.

10. *See, e.g.*, Dale v. Dale, 78 Cal. Rptr. 2d 513, 514–15 (Ct. App. 1998); Rocca v. Rocca, 760 N.E.2d 677, 679–81 (Ind. Ct. App. 2002); Burris v. Burris, 904 S.W.2d 564, 566–67 (Mo. Ct. App. 1995); Dussart v. Dussart, 546 N.W.2d 109, 112–13 (S.D. 1996); Buck v. Rogers, 709 S.W.2d 283, 284–86 (Tex. Ct. App. 1986).

11. Ridgway v. Ridgway, 497 N.E.2d 126, 127 (Ill. App. Ct. 1986).

12. *See In re* Marriage of Conrad, 81 P.3d 749, 750–51 (Or. Ct. App. 2003).

13. *See* Sargent v. Sargent, 622 A.2d 721, 721–22 (Me. 1993).

14. *See In re* Marriage of Palacios, 656 N.E.2d 107, 109–11 (Ill. App. Ct. 1995); Phillip J. O'Connor, *Ex-Wife Wins Big in Court's Lotto Ruling*, CHI. SUN-TIMES, Sept. 27, 1995, at 8; *see also In re* Marriage of Rossi, 108 Cal. Rptr. 2d 270, 271–76 (Ct. App. 2001); Questel v. Questel, 960 N.Y.S.2d 860, 863, 867 (Sup. Ct. 2013); Mayes v. Stewart, 11 S.W.3d 440, 446–47 (Tex. Ct. App. 2000).

15. *See* Kahn v. Kahn, 21 F.3d 859, 860 (8th Cir. 1994).

16. Wallace v. Wallace, 736 F.3d 764, 765 (8th Cir. 2013) (internal quotation marks omitted).

17. *See In re* Marriage of O'Neill, 563 N.E.2d 494, 495 (Ill. 1990).

18. *See* Church v. Church, 630 P.2d 1243, 1245–46 (N.M. Ct. App. 1981).

19. *See id.* at 1245.

20. *See id.* at 1245–46.

21. *See id.* at 1245.

22. *See* Smith v. Nat'l R.R. Passenger Corp. (Amtrak), 25 F. Supp. 2d 574, 575, 577 (E.D. Pa. 1998); Pettid v. Comm'r, 77 T.C.M. (CCH) 1816, 1817 (1999); Lee v. Yang, 3 Cal. Rptr. 3d 819, 821–22 (Ct. App. 2003); Thorpe v. Collins, 263 S.E.2d 115, 117 (Ga. 1980); Beaton v. LaFord, 261 N.W.2d 327, 328 (Mich. Ct. App. 1977) (per curiam); Turner v. Shavers, 645 N.E.2d 1324, 1325 (Ohio Ct. App. 1994).

23. *See Pettid,* 77 T.C.M. (CCH) at 1817; *Turner,* 645 N.E.2d at 1325.

24. *See Lee,* 3 Cal. Rptr. 3d at 821–22; Anna Jane Grossman, *Honestly Online,* Chi. Sun-Times, July 4, 2005, at 32.

25. *See* Koelle v. Zwiren, 672 N.E.2d 868, 870–71 (Ill. App. Ct. 1996).

26. *See* Gubin v. Lodisev, 494 N.W.2d 782, 784 (Mich. Ct. App. 1992).

27. *See* 131 Cong. Rec. 30,710 (1985) (statement of Sen. Carl Levin).

28. *See id.; Gubin,* 494 N.W.2d at 786.

29. *See Gubin,* 494 N.W.2d at 785–86.

30. *See American Wins Divorce from Soviet Husband,* L.A. Times, Mar. 10, 1988, pt. I, at 2.

31. *See Gubin,* 494 N.W.2d at 784.

32. *See* Michael Neill & William Sonzski, *Posing as an Astronaut Was Just One Small Step for Flimflam Man Robert Hunt,* People Wkly., Mar. 6. 1989, at 271, 271–72, 274; Laurel J. Sweet, *Boston's Other Mystery Man . . .,* Bos. Herald, Aug. 12, 2008, at 4.

33. *See* Haacke v. Glenn, 814 P.2d 1157, 1157–59 (Utah Ct. App. 1991).

34. *See* Doe v. Roe, 841 F. Supp. 444, 445 (D.D.C. 1994); Behr v. Redmond, 123 Cal. Rptr. 3d 97, 103 (Ct. App. 2011); Kathleen K. v. Robert B., 198 Cal. Rptr. 273, 274 (Ct. App. 1984); Beller v. Tilbrook, 571 S.E.2d 735, 735–36 (Ga. 2002); R.A.P. v. B.J.P., 428 N.W.2d 103, 104, 108 (Minn. Ct. App. 1988); Maharam v. Maharam, 510 N.Y.S.2d 104, 105, 107 (App. Div. 1986).

35. *See Doe,* 841 F. Supp. at 445.

36. *See* Martinez v. Brazen, No. 91 Civ. 7769 (RPP), 1992 WL 93245, at *1 (S.D.N.Y. Apr. 22, 1992); John B. v. Superior Court, 137 P.3d 153, 155–56, 162–63 (Cal. 2006); Plaza v. Estate of Wisser, 626 N.Y.S.2d 446, 449–50 (App. Div. 1995).

37. *See* H. Hunter Handsfield, Color Atlas & Synopsis of Sexually Transmitted Diseases 109–10, 112, 119, 133, 135, 157, 159 (3d ed. 2011); The Merck Manual of Diagnosis and Therapy 1401, 1438–39, 1449, 1454, 1457–58, 1470–71 (Robert S. Porter & Justin L. Kaplan eds., 19th ed. 2011).

38. *See John B.,* 137 P.3d at 156; *Kathleen K.,* 198 Cal. Rptr. at 274.

39. *See* Mussivand v. David, 544 N.E.2d 265, 266–67 (Ohio 1989); Hamblen v. Davidson, 50 S.W.3d 433, 434–36 (Tenn. Ct. App. 2000); Endres v. Endres, 968 A.2d 336, 338, 342 (Vt. 2008).

40. *See* J.B. v. Bohonovsky, 835 F. Supp. 796, 797–98, 800–01 (D.N.J. 1993); *In re* Louie, 213 B.R. 754, 757 & n.3, 758–61 (Bankr. N.D. Cal. 1997).

41. Sally Lowe Whitehead, The Truth Shall Set You Free: A Family's Passage from Fundamentalism to a New Understanding of Faith, Love, and Sexual Identity 212, 215–16 (1997); *see also* Carol Grever & Deborah Bowman, When Your Spouse Comes Out: A Straight Mate's Recovery Manual 69 (2008).

42. *See* Barbara A. v. John G., 193 Cal. Rptr. 422, 426 (Ct. App. 1983); Amanda Spake, *Trial and Eros,* Mother Jones, July 1985, at 25, 25–26.

43. *See In re* Hansen, 473 B.R. 240, 244, 246–48 (Bankr. E.D. Tenn. 2012).

44. *See, e.g.,* People v. James, 74 Cal. Rptr. 2d 7, 9–10 (Ct. App. 1998); John W. Martyny et al., *Chemical Concentrations and Contamination Associated with Clandestine Methamphetamine Laboratories,* 14 J. Chemical Health & Safety 40, 40, 47–48 (2007).

45. *See In re* Hansen, 473 B.R. at 248–49.

46. For discussion of Bradway's sentencing, see *Sickness Schemer Receives Sentence,* Berkshire Eagle, Apr. 3, 2008, at A1.

47. *See* Bradway v. Whitmont, No. 112356/07, slip op. at 1–2 (N.Y. Sup. Ct. June 17, 2011).

48. *See* John Christoffersen, *Police Say Father Put Boy on Diet to Fake Cystic Fibrosis*, SPOKESMAN-REVIEW (Spokane), Sept. 22, 2006, at A5; Fernanda Santos, *Abuse Charge Filed Against Father Who Claimed His Son Had Cystic Fibrosis*, N.Y. TIMES, Sept. 22, 2006, at B5.

49. Christoffersen, *supra* note 48, at A5 (quoting J. Michael Sconyers, Hollander's attorney) (internal quotation marks omitted).

50. *See* Mark Bowes, *No Contest Is Plea in Sex DVD Case*, RICHMOND TIMES-DISPATCH, Apr. 17, 2007, at B1; *Former Boyfriend Pleads No Contest over Sex DVDs*, CHESTERFIELD OBSERVER, Apr. 25, 2007, at 5.

51. *See supra* Chapter 1.

52. *See In re* Neal, 179 B.R. 234, 235, 237 (Bankr. D. Idaho 1995); Neal v. Neal, 873 P.2d 871, 873, 876 (Idaho 1994).

53. *In re Neal*, 179 B.R. at 237; *Neal*, 873 P.2d at 876–77 (quoting Mary Neal) (internal quotation marks omitted).

54. *See Neal*, 873 P.2d at 873; *see also* Endres v. Endres, 968 A.2d 336, 342 (Vt. 2008).

55. Manko v. Volynsky, No. 95 CIV. 2585 (MBM), 1996 WL 243238, at *1–2 (S.D.N.Y. May 10, 1996) (quoting Manko's amended complaint) (internal quotation marks omitted).

56. *See id.* at *1.

57. *Id.* (quoting Manko's amended complaint) (internal quotation and alteration marks omitted); *see also* Brown v. Strum, 350 F. Supp. 2d 346, 347–48 (D. Conn. 2004).

58. *See* J.M. SHORT, CARNAL ABUSE BY DECEIT: HOW A PREDATOR'S LIES BECAME RAPE 31–33, 39, 47–48 (2013).

59. *Id.* at 49.

60. *See* Hardesty v. Dulin, No. 91-5151, 1992 WL 189106, at *1 (10th Cir. Aug. 6, 1992).

61. *See Robbery Suspect Held*, PITTSBURGH POST-GAZETTE, June 13, 2001, at B-3.

62. *See* Jason Meisner, *Judge Gives 40-Year Term for 'Beyond Reckless' Arson*, CHI. TRIB., Jan. 9, 2015, § 1, at 9; Annie Sweeney, *Federal Arson Charges Filed in Fatal City Blaze*, CHI. TRIB., Mar. 23, 2012, § 1, at 4.

63. *See* Virginia Black, *Wiley Open to New Sentence*, S. BEND TRIB., Aug. 6, 2015, at A1.

64. *See* Virginia Black, *A Bad Choice, Tough Sentence*, S. BEND TRIB., May 17, 2015, at A1.

65. *See* Black, *supra* note 63, at A1.

66. Madeline Buckley, *Teen Fighting Sex Offender Status*, INDIANAPOLIS STAR, Aug. 7, 2015, at 1A (quoting Berrien County Prosecutor Michael J. Sepic) (internal quotation marks omitted).

67. *See* Black, *supra* note 64, at A1.

68. *See* Julie Bosman, *Teenager's Jailing Brings a Call to Fix Sex Offender Registries*, N.Y. TIMES, July 5, 2015, at 1.

69. *See* Virginia Black, *Sentence for Elkhart Teen Tossed*, S. BEND TRIB., Sept. 9, 2015, at A1.

70. *See* Virginia Black, *Anderson Might Avoid Indiana Sex Registry*, S. BEND TRIB., Oct. 25, 2015, at A2; Virginia Black, *Leniency from Judge in Sex Case*, S. BEND TRIB., Oct. 20, 2015, at A1; Julie Bosman, *Sex Registry Challenge Cuts Penalty for Man, 19*, N.Y. TIMES, Oct. 20, 2015, at A13.

71. *See* Virginia Black, *Tough Probation Rules for Elkhart Man*, S. BEND TRIB., Nov. 9, 2015, at A1.

72. *See* Debra Haight, *Probation Ends in High-Profile Teen Sex Case*, HERALD-PALLADIUM (St. Joseph), Mar. 8, 2018, at B1; Mary Beth Spalding, *Probation Release Is Denied*, S. BEND TRIB., Dec. 9, 2017, at A1. For other examples, see Doe v. SexSearch.com, 551 F.3d 412, 415–16 (6th Cir. 2008); Owens v. State, 724 A.2d 43, 45 (Md. 1999).

73. *See* SARA SAEDI, AMERICANIZED: REBEL WITHOUT A GREEN CARD 1–5 (2018); JOSE ANTONIO VARGAS, DEAR AMERICA: NOTES OF AN UNDOCUMENTED CITIZEN 31–37 (2018); Cindy Carcamo, *Caught off Guard*, L.A. TIMES, Dec. 14, 2013, at A11.

74. *See* Rhina Guidos, *Utahn Finds Herself Without a Country*, SALT LAKE TRIB., Jan. 31, 2005, at A1.

75. *See id.*; Thomas Burr, *Student Watches Reform Measure*, SALT LAKE TRIB., Mar. 29, 2006, at A6.

76. *See* S. 2999, 108th Cong. (2004); 151 CONG. REC. 7681–82 (2005) (statement of Sen. Orrin Hatch).

77. *See* Thorpe v. Collins, 263 S.E.2d 115, 117 (Ga. 1980).

78. DINA MATOS MCGREEVEY, SILENT PARTNER: A MEMOIR OF MY MARRIAGE 234 (2007).

79. McCann v. McCann, 593 N.Y.S.2d 917, 918–19, 923 (Sup. Ct. 1993) (internal quotation marks omitted).

80. *Id.* at 919, 922.

81. *See* Conley v. Romeri, 806 N.E.2d 933, 935–37 (Mass. App. Ct. 2004).

82. *Id.* at 935.

83. *See id.* at 935, 937.

84. *Id.* at 937, 939.

85. *See* Perry v. Atkinson, 240 Cal. Rptr. 402, 403 (Ct. App. 1987).

86. *See* M.N. v. D.S., 616 N.W.2d 284, 285–88 (Minn. Ct. App. 2000).

87. *See* SHORT, *supra* note 58, at 13, 30.

88. *See id.* at 37–39.

89. *See* Hodge v. Craig, 382 S.W.3d 325, 330–32 (Tenn. 2012); *see also Deceived Doctor Sues His Sons' Real Father*, BEACON J., Dec. 16, 1994, at A13.

90. *See In re* Baby A, 363 P.3d 193, 196–97 (Colo. 2015) (en banc); *In re* Adoption of S.D.W., 758 S.E.2d 374, 380–81 (N.C. 2014); A Child's Hope, LLC v. Doe, 630 S.E.2d 673, 673–79 (N.C. Ct. App. 2006); *In re* Baby Boy K., 546 N.W.2d 86, 87–89, 101 (S.D. 1996); *In re* Adoption of B.Y., 356 P.3d 1215, 1219–30 (Utah 2015).

91. *See In re* Adoption of A.A.T., 196 P.3d 1180, 1185 (Kan. 2008).

92. *See id.* at 1186.

93. *See id.* at 1185.

94. *See id.* at 1186.

95. *See id.* at 1184–85.

96. RICHARD ALAN, FIRST AID FOR THE BETRAYED: RECOVERING FROM THE DEVASTATION OF AN AFFAIR; A PERSONAL GUIDE TO HEALING 19 (2006); *see also id.* at 20, 25.

97. GREVER & BOWMAN, *supra* note 41, at 54 (quoting Claire) (emphasis omitted); *see also* Cindy B., *Broken Promises and Shattered Dreams, in* STRAIGHT WIVES: SHATTERED LIVES: STORIES OF WOMEN WITH GAY HUSBAND[s] 9, 13–14 (Bonnie Kaye ed., 2006).

98. *Dud Affair Finally Explodes*, TUSCALOOSA NEWS, Sept. 13, 1982, at 10 (quoting Letter from "ABOUT TO CRACK UP" to "DEAR ABBY").

99. *See* Graham Allan, *Being Unfaithful: His and Her Affairs, in* THE STATE OF AFFAIRS: EXPLORATIONS IN INFIDELITY AND COMMITMENT 121, 136 (Jean Duncombe et al. eds., 2004) (quoting "H2805; female, 31").

100. BONNIE EAKER WEIL, FINANCIAL INFIDELITY: SEVEN STEPS TO CONQUERING THE #1 RELATIONSHIP WRECKER 148 (2008); *see also* Ellyn Spragins, *The Case Against Joint Checking*, N.Y. TIMES, Apr. 6, 2003, at BU12.

101. *See* Stephanie Stewart et al., *Sex Differences in Desired Characteristics of Short-Term and Long-Term Relationship Partners*, 17 J. SOC. & PERS. RELATIONSHIPS 843, 846–48 (2000).

102. *See* Bella M. DePaulo et al., *Serious Lies*, 26 BASIC & APPLIED SOC. PSYCHOL. 147, 150, 162 (2004); H. Dan O'Hair & Michael J. Cody, *Deception, in* THE DARK SIDE OF INTERPERSONAL COMMUNICATION 181, 203 (William R. Cupach & Brian H. Spitzberg eds., 1994).

103. *See, e.g.*, ANNETTE BARAN & REUBEN PANNOR, LETHAL SECRETS: THE SHOCKING CONSEQUENCES AND UNSOLVED PROBLEMS OF ARTIFICIAL INSEMINATION 62, 67–68 (1989) (quoting Judith); JOHN COLAPINTO, AS NATURE MADE HIM: THE BOY WHO WAS RAISED AS A GIRL 260–61, 267–68 (2000) (quoting David Reimer); Martha Coventry, *Finding the Words*, CHRYSALIS: J. TRANSGRESSIVE GENDER IDENTITIES, Fall 1997/Winter 1998, at 27, 27–29; Mary E. Kaplar & Anne K. Gordon, *The Enigma of Altruistic Lying: Perspective Differences in What Motivates and Justifies Lie Telling Within Romantic Relationships*, 11 PERS. RELATIONSHIPS 489, 489, 496–99, 502 (2004); Sylvia Rubin, *Family Secrets*, S.F. CHRON., Jan. 15, 1995, at 1 (quoting Suzanne Ariel).

104. *See* Sherri A. Groveman, *The Hanukkah Bush: Ethical Implications in the Clinical Management of Intersex*, 9 J. CLINICAL ETHICS 356, 357–58 (1998).

105. *See* Sherri A. Groveman, Letter to the Editor, *Sex, Lies and Androgen Insensitivity Syndrome*, 154 CAN. MED. ASS'N J. 1829, 1829 (1996).

106. Groveman, *supra* note 104, at 358.

107. Groveman, *supra* note 105, at 1829.

108. MCGREEVEY, *supra* note 78, at 58.

109. *Id.* at 192.
110. *Id.* at 283.
111. *See supra* Chapter 2.
112. GINI GRAHAM SCOTT, PLAYING THE LYING GAME: DETECTING AND DEALING WITH LIES AND LIARS, FROM OCCASIONAL FIBBERS TO FREQUENT FABRICATORS 126 (2010) (quoting Frances); *see also* GREVER & BOWMAN, *supra* note 41, at 5 (quoting Kim); WHITEHEAD, *supra* note 41, at 242–43; *Should the Law Punish Lovers Who Lie? 84 Percent Say Yes*, GLAMOUR, June 1994, at 133, 133 (quoting survey respondent).
113. ALAN, *supra* note 96, at 43.
114. Nora Donoher as told to Melba Newsome, *Sweet Revenge*, GOOD HOUSEKEEPING, June 2005, at 110, 112; *see also* CAROL GREVER, MY HUSBAND IS GAY: A WOMAN'S GUIDE TO SURVIVING THE CRISIS 51, 67–68 (2001); Rachel Monroe, *The Perfect Man*, ATLANTIC, Apr. 2018, at 54, 60.
115. GREVER & BOWMAN, *supra* note 41, at 29 (quoting Zhi) (emphasis omitted).
116. McMillan v. Plummer, Nos. A120258, A120260, 2009 WL 1020653, at *16 (Cal. Ct. App. Apr. 16, 2009) (quoting Terry McMillan) (emphasis and internal quotation and alteration marks omitted).
117. Michael Catalini, *Fraud Could Result in Rape Charge Under Bill*, TIMES (Trenton), Nov. 29, 2014, at A5 (quoting Mischele Lewis) (internal quotation marks omitted).
118. *See supra* Chapter 2.
119. *See* THOMSON, *supra* note 2, at 203–08.
120. *Id.* at 234; *see also id.* at 221; MCGREEVEY, *supra* note 78, at 195.
121. *See* Vance v. Vance, 408 A.2d 728, 729 (Md. 1979).
122. *See id.* at 729–30.
123. *Id.* at 734.
124. *See* Lee v. Yang, 3 Cal. Rptr. 3d 819, 822 (Ct. App. 2003); GREVER, *supra* note 114, at 68 (quoting Alice); *id.* at 107; SHORT, *supra* note 58, at 40.
125. Martin Kasindorf, *Men Wage Battle on 'Paternity Fraud,'* USA TODAY, Dec. 3, 2002, at 3A (quoting Damon Adams) (internal quotation marks omitted).
126. Doran v. Doran, 820 A.2d 1279, 1281 (Pa. Super. Ct. 2003) (quoting trial court); *see also* Hughes v. Hughes, No. 684, 2009, 2011 WL 579242, at *1–2 (Del. Feb. 18, 2011); Fontenot v. Fontenot, 774 So. 2d 330, 331 (La. Ct. App. 2000); Williams v. Williams, 843 So. 2d 720, 721–23 (Miss. 2003); Day v. Heller, 653 N.W.2d 475, 477 (Neb. 2002); M.L. v. J.G.M., 132 A.3d 1005, 1007 (Pa. Super. Ct. 2016); Gebler v. Gatti, 895 A.2d 1, 2 (Pa. Super. Ct. 2006); Miscovich v. Miscovich, 688 A.2d 726, 727–28 (Pa. Super. Ct. 1997); *In re* T.S.S., 61 S.W.3d 481, 482–83 (Tex. Ct. App. 2001); Betty L.W. v. William E.W., 569 S.E.2d 77, 80–81 (W. Va. 2002) (per curiam).
127. Cain v. Cain, 777 S.W.2d 238, 239 (Ky. Ct. App. 1989).
128. *See* Hodge v. Craig, 382 S.W.3d 325, 330–31 (Tenn. 2012).
129. *Id.* at 331 (quoting Kyle Chandler Craig) (internal quotation marks omitted).
130. *Id.* at 332 (quoting Kyle Chandler Craig) (internal quotation marks omitted).
131. *See* Julie Bosman, *Edwards Admits He Fathered Girl with Mistress*, N.Y. TIMES, Jan. 22, 2010, at A12; Kim Severson, *Edwards Jury Is Told How Wife Was Torn*, N.Y. TIMES, May 10, 2012, at A16; Kim Severson & John Schwartz, *Edwards Acquitted on One Count; Mistrial on 5 Others*, N.Y. TIMES, June 1, 2012, at A1.
132. *See* GREGORY HOWARD WILLIAMS, LIFE ON THE COLOR LINE: THE TRUE STORY OF A WHITE BOY WHO DISCOVERED HE WAS BLACK 2, 21, 32–34, 37–42, 49 (1995); *see also* GAIL LUKASIK, WHITE LIKE HER: MY FAMILY'S STORY OF RACE AND RACIAL PASSING 9, 21–23 (2017).

Chapter 4

1. *See* 1 JOEL PRENTISS BISHOP, NEW COMMENTARIES ON MARRIAGE, DIVORCE, AND SEPARATION 80–102 (Chicago, T.H. Flood & Co. 1891); 2 JAMES SCHOULER & ARTHUR W. BLAKEMORE, A TREATISE ON THE LAW OF MARRIAGE, DIVORCE, SEPARATION AND DOMESTIC RELATIONS 1544–45 (6th ed. 1921).

2. *See* BISHOP, *supra* note 1, at 570–73; TAPPING REEVE & JAMES W. EATON, JR., THE LAW OF HUSBAND AND WIFE, OF PARENT AND CHILD, GUARDIAN AND WARD, MASTER AND SERVANT 90–91 (Albany, William Gould, Jr., & Co. 4th ed. 1888).

3. *See* Robert C. Brown, *The Action for Alienation of Affections*, 82 U. PA. L. REV. 472, 472–74, 476–78 (1934).

4. *See* BISHOP, *supra* note 1, at 80–102; SCHOULER & BLAKEMORE, *supra* note 1, at 1510–45.

5. *See* BISHOP, *supra* note 1, at 98–100; SCHOULER & BLAKEMORE, *supra* note 1, at 1536–39; Kurtz v. Frank, 76 Ind. 594, 597–98 (1881).

6. Carter v. Rinker, 174 F. 882, 883 (D. Kan. 1909).

7. *Id.* at 883, 886; *see also* Kelley v. Riley, 106 Mass. 339, 339–43 (1871); Ashley v. Dalton, 81 So. 488, 488 (Miss. 1919); Blattmacher v. Saal, 7 Abb. Pr. 409, 410–11 (N.Y. Sup. Ct. 1858); Waddell v. Wallace, 121 P. 245, 245–47 (Okla. 1911) (per curiam); Coover v. Davenport, 48 Tenn. (1 Heisk.) 368, 370–82 (1870); Robinson v. Shockley, 266 S.W. 420, 420–21 (Tex. Civ. App. 1924).

8. *See, e.g.*, Emery v. Gowen, 4 Me. 33, 34, 39–41 (1826); Martin v. Payne, 9 Johns. 387, 387, 389–91 (N.Y. Sup. Ct. 1812).

9. *See* ALA. CODE pt. 3, tit. 1, ch. 1, § 2133 (1852); ALASKA COMP. LAWS ch. 3, § 865 (1913); CAL. CIV. PROC. CODE § 374 (1872); IDAHO REV. STAT. tit. 3, § 4097 (1887); Act of June 18, 1852, pt. 2, ch. 1, § 24, 2 IND. REV. STAT. 27, 33 (1852); IOWA CODE tit. 19, ch. 100, § 1696 (1851); MISS. REV. CODE ch. 58, § 1508 (1880); An Act to provide a code of civil procedure in the territory of Montana, § 11, 1877 Mont. Laws 40, 41; NEV. REV. LAWS ch. 6, § 4994 (1912); OKLA. STAT. ch. 70, art. 2, § 13 (1890); OR. CODES tit. 3, ch. 1, § 36 (1892); Act of Feb. 25, 1903, ch. 212, § 2, 1903 S.D. Laws 277, 277; TENN. CODE § 2801 (1858); UTAH COMP. LAWS tit. 3, § 3176 (1888); An Act to regulate the practice and proceedings in civil actions, ch. 1, § 11, WASH. CODE 35, 36 (1881); Watson v. Watson, 14 N.W. 489, 490–91 (Mich. 1883); Hood v. Sudderth, 16 S.E. 397, 399 (N.C. 1892).

10. Swett v. Gray, 74 P. 551, 551 (Cal. 1903) (quoting Nellie Swett's complaint) (internal quotation marks omitted).

11. *See id.* at 551–52; *see also* Shadix v. Brown, 113 So. 581, 583 (Ala. 1927); *Hood*, 16 S.E. at 398–99.

12. Savage v. Embrey, 184 N.W. 503, 504 (Mich. 1921).

13. *Id.* at 504–06.

14. *See id.* at 504.

15. *See id.* at 506.

16. *See* Simons v. Busby, 21 N.E. 451, 451–52 (Ind. 1889).

17. *Id.* at 452.

18. *See id.* at 453.

19. *See* Verwers v. Carpenter, 166 Iowa 273, 275–77 (1914).

20. *See id.* at 278.

21. *Id.* at 275, 277.

22. *See id.* at 274.

23. *See, e.g.*, People v. Dohring, 59 N.Y. 374, 382–84 (1874); Brown v. State, 106 N.W. 536, 538–39 (Wis. 1906).

24. *See Verwers*, 166 Iowa at 283.

25. *Id.* at 275.

26. *See id.* at 277.

27. *Id.* at 279.

28. *See id.* at 284.

29. *See, e.g.*, MICHAEL GROSSBERG, GOVERNING THE HEARTH: LAW AND THE FAMILY IN NINETEENTH-CENTURY AMERICA 51–63 (1985).

30. *See Aching Hearts Are Itching Palms, Says Woman Legislator as Men Gallantly Pass "Love Bill,"* INDIANAPOLIS NEWS, Feb. 1, 1935, pt. 1, at 1.

31. *See* Laura S. Gaus, *Roberta West Nicholson, in* THE ENCYCLOPEDIA OF INDIANAPOLIS 1053, 1053 (David J. Bodenhamer & Robert G. Barrows eds., 1994).

32. *See* Mary E. Bostwick, *Only Woman Member of Legislature Says Being Lawmaker "Simply Swell,"* INDIANAPOLIS STAR, Jan. 16, 1935, at 5.

33. *Love v. Extortion,* TIME, Feb. 18, 1935, at 16 (quoting Roberta West Nicholson) (internal quotation marks omitted).

34. *Aching Hearts Are Itching Palms, Says Woman Legislator as Men Gallantly Pass "Love Bill," supra* note 30, at 1 (quoting Roberta West Nicholson) (internal quotation marks omitted).

35. *Id.*

36. *More Women for Assembly Asked,* INDIANAPOLIS NEWS, Feb. 13, 1935, at 2.

37. *Aching Hearts Are Itching Palms, Says Woman Legislator as Men Gallantly Pass "Love Bill," supra* note 30, at 1 (quoting Roberta West Nicholson) (internal quotation marks omitted).

38. Jack Cejnar, *Victor Against Heart Balm to Conduct National Battle,* SUNDAY SPARTANBURG HERALD-J., Mar. 31, 1935, at 4 (quoting Leo Smith) (internal quotation marks omitted).

39. *"Heart Balm" Bill Passed by Senate,* INDIANAPOLIS STAR, Mar. 8, 1935, at 11 (quoting Leo Smith) (internal quotation marks omitted).

40. Cejnar, *supra* note 38, at 4 (quoting Leo Smith) (internal quotation marks omitted).

41. *Id.* (quoting Jesse Wade) (internal quotation marks omitted).

42. *"Heart Balm" Bill Passed by Senate, supra* note 39, at 11 (quoting William Dennigan) (internal quotation marks omitted).

43. *See* Act of Mar. 11, 1935, ch. 208, § 1, 1935 Ind. Laws 1009, 1009.

44. *See Aching Hearts Are Itching Palms, Says Woman Legislator as Men Gallantly Pass "Love Bill," supra* note 30, at 1; *"Heart Balm" Bill Passed by Senate, supra* note 39, at 11.

45. *See Heart Balm Bill Introduced in Ohio,* INDIANAPOLIS STAR, Feb. 6, 1935, at 1; *Love v. Extortion, supra* note 33, at 16; *Woman Legislator Will Appear in Behalf of 'Heart Balm' Bill,* INDIANAPOLIS NEWS, Feb. 7, 1935, at 5; *see also The Outlawry of Heart-Balm Suits,* LITERARY DIG., Apr. 13, 1935, at 22, 22.

46. *"Safe for Men,"* TIME, Apr. 1, 1935, at 15 (quoting Roberta West Nicholson) (internal quotation marks omitted).

47. *See* Act of Mar. 29, 1935, ch. 263, § 1, 1935 N.Y. Laws 732, 733.

48. *See* Act of June 27, 1935, ch. 279, 1935 N.J. Acts 896, 896.

49. *See* Act of Apr. 27, 1937, ch. 111, § 4, 1937 Colo. Laws 403, 404.

50. *See* Act of Feb. 10, 1941, ch. 36, § 1, 1941 Wyo. Sess. Laws 32, 32.

51. *See* Act of Mar. 5, 1943, ch. 53, § 1, 1943 Nev. Stat. 75, 75.

52. *See* Act of May 4, 1945, ch. 1010, § 1, 1945 Md. Laws 1759, 1760.

53. *See* Act of June 11, 1945, ch. 23,138, 1945 Fla. Acts 1342, 1342.

54. Act of Mar. 29, 1935, ch. 263, § 1, 1935 N.Y. Laws 732, 733.

55. *Ban on Heart Balm Is Made State Law,* N.Y. TIMES, Mar. 30, 1935, at 3 (quoting Herbert Lehman) (internal quotation marks omitted).

56. *See id.; 'Balm' Ban Is Voted by Albany Senate,* N.Y. TIMES, Mar. 20, 1935, at 1.

57. *Move Planned in 8 Other States,* N.Y. TIMES, Mar. 30, 1935, at 3 (quoting John McNaboe) (internal quotation marks omitted).

58. *The Outlawry of Heart-Balm Suits, supra* note 45, at 22 (quoting John McNaboe) (internal quotation marks omitted).

59. In addition to Indiana and New York, see Act of Sept. 7, 1935, No. 356, § 1, 1935 Ala. Laws 780, 780; Act of June 3, 1935, No. 127, § 1, 1935 Mich. Pub. Acts 201, 201; Act of June 27, 1935, ch. 279, § 1, 1935 N.J. Acts 896, 896. For anti-heart balm statutes that left seduction actions untouched, see Act of May 4, 1935, § 1, 1935 Ill. Laws 716, 716; Act of June 22, 1935, No. 189, § 2, 1935 Pa. Laws 450, 451.

60. *See* Act of May 10, 1939, ch. 128, § 2, 1939 Cal. Stat. 1245, 1245; Act of Apr. 27, 1937, ch. 111, § 1, 1937 Colo. Laws 403, 403; Act of June 11, 1945, ch. 23,138, § 1, 1945 Fla. Acts 1342, 1342; Act of Feb. 10, 1941, ch. 36, § 2, 1941 Wyo. Sess. Laws 32, 32. For anti-heart balm statutes that left seduction actions untouched, see Act of Mar. 25, 1941, ch. 104, § 1, 1941 Me. Acts 140, 140; Act of May 4, 1945, ch. 1010, § 2, 1945 Md. Laws 1759, 1760; Act of May 24, 1938, ch. 350, § 1, 1938 Mass. Acts 326, 326; Act of Mar. 5, 1943, ch. 53, § 2, 1943 Nev. Stat. 75, 75; Act of June 5, 1941, ch. 150, § 1, 1941 N.H. Laws 223, 224.

61. For post-1945 statutes, see An Act Abolishing Breach of Promise and Alienation of Affections Suits, No. 275, § 1, 1967 Conn. Pub. Acts 324, 324; Act of July 5, 1972, ch. 489, § 1, 58 Del. Laws 1601, 1601 (1972); Act of Jan. 4, 1977, No. 1-193, § 111(a), 23 D.C. Reg. 5869, 5881–82 (Feb. 11, 1977); Act of Mar. 23, 1978, ch. 515, § 2, 1978 Minn. Laws 141, 141; Act of Mar.

7, 1963, ch. 200, § 2, 1963 Mont. Laws 598, 599; Act of Apr. 14, 1983, ch. 172, § 9, 1983 N.D. Laws 441, 446; Act of Mar. 8, 1978, No. 248, § 1, 1978 Ohio Laws 2225, 2225; Act of May 31, 1976, ch. 164, § 2, 1976 Okla. Sess. Laws 230, 230; Act of June 14, 1985, ch. 123, § 2, 1985 R.I. Pub. Laws 182, 183; Act of May 1, 1990, ch. 1056, § 1, 1990 Tenn. Pub. Acts 773, 773–74; Act of Apr. 2, 1974, No. 198, § 1, 1974 Vt. Acts & Resolves 208, 208; Act of Apr. 8, 1974, ch. 606, § 1, 1974 Va. Acts 1163, 1163; Act of Apr. 5, 1968, ch. 716, § 1, 1968 Va. Acts 1259, 1259; Act of Mar. 6, 1969, ch. 101, 1969 W. Va. Acts 1036, 1036; Act of Oct. 28, 1959, ch. 595, § 73, 1959 Wis. Sess. Laws 740, 765.

62. Dorothy Dunbar Bromley, *Breach of Promise—Why?*, WOMAN CITIZEN, Sept. 1927, at 8, 9; *see also Ending a Vicious Racket*, PITTSBURGH PRESS, Apr. 8, 1935, at 10.

63. Harter F. Wright, *The Action for Breach of the Marriage Promise*, 10 VA. L. REV. 361, 378 (1924).

64. Robert C. Brown, *Breach of Promise Suits*, 77 U. PA. L. REV. 474, 494 (1929).

65. Delancey Knox, *The High Cost of Loving: What Is a Breach of Promise?—Cupid's Indemnity*, 61 FORUM 736, 747–48 (1919).

66. Bromley, *supra* note 62, at 9.

67. Brown, *supra* note 64, at 493.

68. *See* HARRIET SPILLER DAGGETT, *The Action for Breach of the Marriage Promise, in* LEGAL ESSAYS ON FAMILY LAW 39, 91–92 (1935).

69. Talcott Powell, *A Merit System*, INDIANAPOLIS TIMES, Feb. 18, 1935, at 6.

70. 4 CHESTER G. VERNIER, AMERICAN FAMILY LAWS 268 (1936); *see also* R.M.J., Legislation Note, *Abolition of Actions for Breach of Promise, Enticement, Criminal Conversation, and Seduction*, 22 VA. L. REV. 205, 211 (1935).

71. Nathan P. Feinsinger, *Legislative Attack on "Heart Balm,"* 33 MICH. L. REV. 979, 988 (1935).

72. *Law Banning Heart-Balm Suits Wins Approval of First Lady*, WASH. POST, Mar. 26, 1935, at 2 (quoting Eleanor Roosevelt) (internal quotation marks omitted).

73. VERNIER, *supra* note 70, at 268; *see also* Feinsinger, *supra* note 71, at 979.

74. Bromley, *supra* note 62, at 40.

75. THEODORE E. APSTEIN, THE PARTING OF THE WAYS: AN EXPOSÉ OF AMERICA'S DIVORCE TANGLE 18 (1935).

76. Bromley, *supra* note 62, at 8.

77. Editorial, *No Balm for Blackmail*, CHRISTIAN SCI. MONITOR, Apr. 2, 1935, at 16.

78. *See* U.S. CONST. amend. XIX.

79. Doris Blake, *Suit for Heart Balm Is Tawdry Label for Love*, CHI. DAILY TRIB., May 9, 1934, at 19.

80. *See* LINDA GORDON, PITIED BUT NOT ENTITLED: SINGLE MOTHERS AND THE HISTORY OF WELFARE, 1890–1935, at 192–98 (1994); ALICE KESSLER-HARRIS, OUT TO WORK: A HISTORY OF WAGE-EARNING WOMEN IN THE UNITED STATES 218–19, 230, 232–37, 249, 258–63 (1982).

81. *See* LESLIE J. REAGAN, WHEN ABORTION WAS A CRIME: WOMEN, MEDICINE, AND LAW IN THE UNITED STATES, 1867–1973, at 5, 14–15, 29, 133 (1997).

82. *See* Civil Rights Act of 1964, Pub. L. No. 88-352, tit. VII, 78 Stat. 241, 253–66; Equal Pay Act of 1963, Pub. L. No. 88-38, 77 Stat. 56.

83. *See* Reed v. Reed, 404 U.S. 71, 74–77 (1971).

84. *See* Roe v. Wade, 410 U.S. 113, 164–65 (1973).

85. Brown, *supra* note 64, at 491.

86. Bromley, *supra* note 62, at 8.

87. For (arguably) narrower interpretations of anti-heart balm statutes, see Piccininni v. Hajus, 429 A.2d 886, 887–89 (Conn. 1980); Turner v. Shavers, 645 N.E.2d 1324, 1324–25 (Ohio Ct. App. 1994); Bryan v. Lincoln, 285 S.E.2d 152, 152–55 (W. Va. 1981).

88. *See* Sulkowski v. Szewczyk, 6 N.Y.S.2d 97, 97, 99 (App. Div. 1938).

89. *Id.* at 97.

90. *Id.* at 99 (citation and internal quotation marks omitted).

91. A.B. v. C.D., 36 F. Supp. 85, 85–87 (E.D. Pa. 1940), *aff'd per curiam*, 123 F.2d 1017 (3d Cir. 1941).

92. *See id.* at 85.

93. *Id.* at 85–86.

94. *Id.* at 87 (citation and internal quotation marks omitted).

95. Boyd v. Boyd, 39 Cal. Rptr. 400, 401–02 (Dist. Ct. App. 1964) (citation and internal quotation marks omitted).
96. *See id.* at 401.
97. *Id.* at 404, 402.
98. *Id.* at 402.
99. *Id.* at 404; *see also* Bressler v. Bressler, 133 N.Y.S.2d 38, 39–42 (N.Y.C. Mun. Ct. 1954); Grunberg v. Grunberg, 99 N.Y.S.2d 771, 771–74 (Sup. Ct. 1950).
100. *See* Manko v. Volynsky, No. 95 CIV. 2585 (MBM), 1996 WL 243238, at *1–2 (S.D.N.Y. May 10, 1996); Askew v. Askew, 28 Cal. Rptr. 2d 284, 285–86, 293–94 (Ct. App. 1994); *In re* Marriage of Buckley, 184 Cal. Rptr. 290, 291–94 (Ct. App. 1982); Dahl v. McNutt, No. C3-97-601906, slip op. at 13–15, 19–22 (Minn. Dist. Ct. Jan. 21, 1998); Vrabel v. Vrabel, 459 N.E.2d 1298, 1299–303 (Ohio Ct. App. 1983); Koestler v. Pollard, 471 N.W.2d 7, 8–12 (Wis. 1991); Slawek v. Stroh, 215 N.W.2d 9, 17–18 (Wis. 1974).
101. 350 F. Supp. 2d 346 (D. Conn. 2004).
102. *See id.* at 347–48.
103. *Id.* at 347 (quoting Cleveland Brown's complaint) (internal quotation and alteration marks omitted).
104. *Id.* at 350.
105. *See id.* at 347–52.
106. 616 N.W.2d 284 (Minn. Ct. App. 2000).
107. *See id.* at 285–87.
108. *See id.* at 287–88.
109. *Id.* at 286.
110. *See id.* at 287–88.
111. *See id.* at 286–87.
112. *Id.* at 288.
113. 25 F. Supp. 2d 574 (E.D. Pa. 1998).
114. *Id.* at 575 (quoting Susan Smith's complaint) (internal quotation marks omitted).
115. *Id.* at 578.
116. *See Questions Raised as Top Amtrak Inspector Resigns*, BOS. GLOBE, June 20, 2009, at A2.
117. 163 F. Supp. 2d 554 (D. Md. 2001), *aff'd per curiam*, 32 F. App'x 112 (4th Cir. 2002).
118. *See id.* at 556–57.
119. *See id.* at 557–58.
120. *See id.* at 557.
121. Lee v. Yang, 3 Cal. Rptr. 3d 819, 821–22 (Ct. App. 2003).
122. *Id.* at 822 (quoting Janet Yang) (internal quotation marks omitted).
123. *See Yang*, 163 F. Supp. 2d at 557.
124. *Id.* at 560 (quoting questionnaire from Helen and Edward Yang) (internal quotation marks omitted).
125. *Id.* at 557.
126. *See id.* at 556–57.
127. *See id.* at 558–59, 564.
128. *See id.* at 557.
129. *See id.* at 558.
130. *See id.* at 564.
131. *See id.* at 559 & n.5.
132. *Id.* at 558–59, 564.
133. *Id.* at 559.
134. *See* Shea v. Cameron, 93 N.E.3d 870, 876–77 (Mass. App. Ct. 2018).
135. No. H024460, 2004 WL 2384845 (Cal. Ct. App. Oct. 26, 2004).
136. *See id.* at *1–2.
137. *See id.* at *3–4.
138. *See id.* at *3.
139. *See id.* at *1, *4.
140. *Id.* at *10.
141. *Id.* at *11 (citations and internal quotation marks omitted).
142. Singh v. Singh, 611 N.E.2d 347, 350 (Ohio Ct. App. 1992).

143. *See* Plessy v. Ferguson, 163 U.S. 537, 552 (1896); CHARLES S. MANGUM, JR., THE LEGAL
     STATUS OF THE NEGRO 1–13 (1940).

144. For excellent historical studies examining trials that pivoted on determining a person's racial
     status, see ARIELA J. GROSS, WHAT BLOOD WON'T TELL: A HISTORY OF RACE ON TRIAL
     IN AMERICA (2008); PEGGY PASCOE, WHAT COMES NATURALLY: MISCEGENATION LAW
     AND THE MAKING OF RACE IN AMERICA 109–30 (2009).

145. *See* REBA LEE AS TOLD TO MARY HASTINGS BRADLEY, I PASSED FOR WHITE 157, 258–62
     (1955).

146. *See* WILLIAM M. ASHBY, REDDER BLOOD 108, 159–70, 188 (1915); CHARLES
     W. CHESNUTT, THE HOUSE BEHIND THE CEDARS 71–76, 86–87, 143–46, 152–53, 292–94
     (1900); JESSIE REDMON FAUSET, PLUM BUN: A NOVEL WITHOUT A MORAL 160, 163, 167
     (1929); FANNIE HURST, IMITATION OF LIFE 295–304 (1933); NELLA LARSEN, PASSING
     41–42, 122, 129, 208–09 (1929); CID RICKETTS SUMNER, QUALITY 19, 126–35 (1946);
     WALTER WHITE, FLIGHT 253, 260, 300 (1926); I PASSED FOR WHITE (Allied Artists 1960);
     PINKY (Twentieth Century-Fox 1949).

147. For engagements, see Van Houten v. Morse, 38 N.E. 705, 705–07 (Mass. 1894); *Nurse Sues
     Colored Man*, WASH. POST, Apr. 12, 1914, at 1. For marriages, see Taylor v. Taylor, 181 N.Y.S.
     894, 895 (Sup. Ct. 1920); *Calls Husband a Negro*, WASH. POST, Oct. 12, 1918, at 16; *Can't
     Tell Wives from Negro Women!*, TOPEKA PLAINDEALER, Feb. 12, 1915, at 1; *Color Question
     Starts Divorce*, CHI. DEFENDER, July 12, 1919, at 1; *Husband a Negro, Says Wife in Suit*, N.Y.
     TIMES, Feb. 16, 1922, at 17; *Married Negro; White Girl Seeks Annulment*, N.Y. AMSTERDAM
     NEWS, Aug. 22, 1923, at 1; *Married 10 Years; Says Wife Is Colored*, N.Y. AMSTERDAM NEWS,
     May 6, 1925, at 2; *Mate Charges Wife Went with Negroes*, S.F. EXAMINER, Dec. 30, 1924, at
     6; *New Orleans Has Rhinelander Case*, AFRO-AM. (Balt.), Dec. 26, 1925, at 3; *Rhinelander
     Case Echoes Rock New England*, PITTSBURGH COURIER, Sept. 18, 1937, at 3; *Says Husband
     Is Colored*, WASH. POST, Nov. 11, 1915, at 16; *Says Wife Not White, Asks Divorce*, CHI.
     DEFENDER, June 1, 1940, at 1; *She Deceived Me!*, PITTSBURGH COURIER, June 1, 1940, at 1;
     Vagaries of Prejudice, 2 CRISIS 144, 144 (1911); *White Wife Sues "Inca Prince,"* PITTSBURGH
     COURIER, Oct. 17, 1925, at 1; *Wife Charges Racial Fraud in Divorce*, MILWAUKEE SENTINEL,
     Aug. 30, 1926, at 2; *Wife Is Colored, He Says in Suit*, N.Y. AMSTERDAM NEWS, Dec. 6, 1922, at
     1; *Wife Must Show She Isn't Negro*, N.Y. AMSTERDAM NEWS, July 6, 1935, at 4.

148. *See A Young Wife's Discovery*, WASH. POST, Dec. 14, 1888, at 1; *Annul Marriage for Race
     Deception*, CHI. DEFENDER, June 7, 1947, at 4; *Learns Wife Is Negro After Year*, N.Y.
     AMSTERDAM NEWS, Dec. 15, 1945, at 1. For a divorce, see *Nurse Given Divorce from Hubby
     Who Posed as Nordic*, PITTSBURGH COURIER, Sept. 13, 1930, at 8.

149. *See* Sunseri v. Cassagne, 185 So. 1, 1–2 (La. 1938).

150. *Id.* at 2.

151. *Id.* at 4.

152. *Id.* at 5.

153. *See* Sunseri v. Cassagne, 196 So. 7, 7, 9 (La. 1940).

154. *See id.* at 8–9.

155. *Id.* at 7–8.

156. *See id.* at 9.

157. *Sunseri*, 185 So. at 2.

158. *See* Loving v. Virginia, 388 U.S. 1, 6 n.5, 12 (1967).

159. *See* People v. Godines, 62 P.2d 787, 788, 790 (Cal. Dist. Ct. App. 1936).

160. *Id.* at 788.

161. *See id.* at 790.

162. *See id.* at 788, 790.

163. *See id.* at 789–90.

164. *See id.* at 788–90.

165. *See* Theophanis v. Theophanis, 51 S.W.2d 957, 958 (Ky. Ct. App. 1932); Neuberger
     v. Gueldner, 72 So. 220, 220 (La. 1916); Ferrall v. Ferrall, 69 S.E. 60, 60–62 (N.C. 1910);
     Court Says J. Bornn Is Pure White, CHI. DEFENDER, May 6, 1922, at 1; *Refuse to Annul Dwyer's
     Marriage*, MORNING WORLD-HERALD (Omaha), July 3, 1919, at 14.

166. *Ferrall*, 69 S.E. at 62 (Clark, C.J., concurring).

167. *Id.* at 60–61 (majority opinion) (citation and internal quotation marks omitted).

168. *Id.* at 60 (internal quotation marks omitted).

169. *Id.* at 62 (Clark, C.J., concurring).

170. *Theophanis*, 51 S.W.2d at 960.

171. *Id.* at 957–58.

172. *Id.* at 960.

173. *See id.* at 957–58.

174. *See id.* at 958–59. For another possible example, see *Race of Bride Ruled Out Divorce Court*, Chi. Defender, Jan. 31, 1925, pt. 1, at 8.

175. *Rhinelander Loses; No Fraud Is Found; Wife Will Sue Now*, N.Y. Times, Dec. 6, 1925, § 1, at 1.

176. *See* Earl Lewis & Heidi Ardizzone, Love on Trial: An American Scandal in Black and White (2001); Angela Onwuachi-Willig, According to Our Hearts: Rhinelander v. Rhinelander and the Law of the Multiracial Family (2013); Elizabeth M. Smith-Pryor, Property Rites: The Rhinelander Trial, Passing, and the Protection of Whiteness (2009); A. Cheree Carlson, *"You Know It When You See It:" The Rhetorical Hierarchy of Race and Gender in* Rhinelander V. Rhinelander, 85 Q.J. Speech 111 (1999); Mark J. Madigan, *Miscegenation and "the Dicta of Race and Class": The Rhinelander Case and Nella Larsen's Passing*, 36 Mod. Fiction Stud. 523 (1990); Charlene Regester, *Headline to Headlights: Oscar Micheaux's Exploitation of the Rhinelander Case*, 22 W.J. Black Stud. 195 (1998); Jamie L. Wacks, *Reading Race, Rhetoric, and the Female Body in the* Rhinelander *Case*, *in* Interracialism: Black-White Intermarriage in American History, Literature, and Law 162 (Werner Sollors ed., 2000); Night of the Quarter Moon (Metro-Goldwyn-Mayer 1959).

177. *See Society Youth Weds Cabman's Daughter*, N.Y. Times, Nov. 14, 1924, at 1.

178. *Rhinelander's Wife Admits Negro Blood*, N.Y. Times, Nov. 11, 1925, at 1.

179. *See Rhinelanders Flee Glare of Publicity*, N.Y. Times, Nov. 15, 1924, at 6; *Sire Unaware Rhinelander Wed Poor Girl*, Chi. Daily Trib., Nov. 15, 1924, at 2; *Society Youth Weds Cabman's Daughter*, *supra* note 177, at 1.

180. *Society Youth Weds Cabman's Daughter*, *supra* note 177, at 1 (capitalization omitted); *see also Daughter of Taxi Man Wed to Rhinelander*, Chi. Daily Trib., Nov. 14, 1924, at 1; *Leonard Rhinelander Weds Taxicab Driver's Daughter*, Wash. Post, Nov. 14, 1924, at 1; *Millionaire's Marriage to Poor Girl Startles World*, Chi. Defender, Nov. 22, 1924, at 1; *Rich Youth Weds Daughter of Cab Driver*, N.Y.J., Nov. 14, 1924, at 1.

181. *Leonard Rhinelander Weds Taxicab Driver's Daughter*, *supra* note 180, at 1.

182. *Negro Taint of Bride Is in Records*, L.A. Sunday Times, Nov. 16, 1924, pt. I, at 14 (internal quotation marks omitted); *see also Rhinelander Bride Not of White Race, Record Discloses*, Wash. Post, Nov. 16, 1924, at 3; *Rhinelanders Drop from Public Sight*, N.Y. Times, Nov. 16, 1924, at 13; *Search Records to Show Race of Rich Man's Bride*, Chi. Sunday Trib., Nov. 16, 1924, pt. 1, at 3.

183. *See Young Rhinelander Leaves His Bride's Home and Neighbors Debate Possible Separation*, N.Y. Times, Nov. 22, 1924, at 1.

184. *Negro Taint of Bride Is in Records*, *supra* note 182, at 14 (capitalization omitted).

185. *See Rhinelander Bride Fears He Is Captive*, N.Y. Times, Nov. 30, 1924, at 14.

186. *See Philip Rhinelander Sued by Son's Wife*, N.Y. Times, July 14, 1929, at 10.

187. *See Rhinelander Bride Fears He Is Captive*, *supra* note 185, at 14.

188. *Rhinelander Sues to Annul Marriage; Alleges Race Deceit*, N.Y. Times, Nov. 27, 1924, at 1 (quoting Leonard Kip Rhinelander's complaint) (internal quotation marks omitted).

189. *See id.*; *Rhinelander's Wife Denies She Is Negro*, N.Y. Times, Nov. 29, 1924, at 15.

190. *See Rhinelander's Wife Admits Negro Blood*, *supra* note 178, at 1.

191. *Id.* (quoting Lee Parsons Davis) (internal quotation marks omitted); *see also Admit Wife of Rhinelander Is of Negro Blood*, Chi. Daily Trib., Nov. 11, 1925, at 3.

192. *Says Rhinelander Knew of Girl's Race*, N.Y. Times, Nov. 26, 1925, at 3 (quoting testimony of Ross Chidester) (internal quotation marks omitted); *see also Told Rhinelander Truth About Girl, Witness Asserts*, Wash. Post, Nov. 26, 1925, at 5.

193. *See Rhinelander Loses; No Fraud Is Found; Wife Will Sue Now, supra* note 175, at 1.

194. *See* Rhinelander v. Rhinelander, 219 N.Y.S. 548, 548–50 (App. Div.) (per curiam), *aff'd per curiam*, 157 N.E. 838 (N.Y. 1927).

195. *See Divorce Given to Rhinelander,* L.A. Times, Dec. 28, 1929, pt. I, at 3; *Kip Rhinelander Gets Divorce in Nevada from His Negro Wife,* Chi. Daily Trib., Dec. 28, 1929, at 13; *Rhinelander Divorces His Octoroon Wife,* N.Y. Times, Dec. 28, 1929, at 3.

196. *See In re* Rhinelander's Estate, 47 N.E.2d 681, 682–83 (N.Y. 1943); *L. Kip Rhinelander Dead of Pneumonia,* N.Y. Times, Feb. 21, 1936, at 17; *Rhinelander Case Closed,* N.Y. Times, Sept. 6, 1930, at 17; *Rhinelander Makes $31,500 Settlement,* N.Y. Times, July 18, 1930, at 21.

197. 627 A.2d 683, 685 (N.J. Super. Ct. Ch. Div. 1992).

198. *See* Louis Dumont, Homo Hierarchicus: The Caste System and Its Implications 21, 66–68 (Mark Sainsbury et al. trans., Univ. of Chi. Press rev. ed. 1980) (1966); Marc Galanter, Competing Equalities: Law and the Backward Classes in India 9–10, 13–16 (1984); Oliver Mendelsohn & Marika Vicziany, The Untouchables: Subordination, Poverty and the State in Modern India 6–7, 11 (1998); Brian K. Smith, Classifying the Universe: The Ancient Indian *Varna* System and the Origins of Caste 3, 28–29 (1994).

199. *See* Dumont, *supra* note 198, at 21; Galanter, *supra* note 198, at 8–9; Mendelsohn & Vicziany, *supra* note 198, at 7.

200. *See* Dumont, *supra* note 198, at 21, 61–62, 109, 112–13; Galanter, *supra* note 198, at 8; Mendelsohn & Vicziany, *supra* note 198, at 6.

201. *See Patel,* 627 A.2d at 685.

202. *See id.* at 685–86.

203. *Id.* at 686 (emphasis omitted).

204. *See id.* at 688.

205. *Id.* at 687.

206. *Id.* at 688.

207. *Id.* at 687.

208. *Id.* at 688.

209. *See supra* Chapter 2.

210. *Patel,* 627 A.2d at 688.

211. 466 U.S. 429 (1984).

212. *See id.* at 430–31.

213. *See id.* at 430.

214. *Id.* at 431 (quoting Florida court) (emphasis and internal quotation marks omitted).

215. *Id.* at 432.

216. *Id.* at 430.

217. *See* Jill Elaine Hasday, Family Law Reimagined 133–42 (2014).

218. *Palmore,* 466 U.S. at 432.

219. *Id.* at 433.

220. 112 Pa. 244 (1886).

221. *See id.* at 244–45.

222. *Id.* at 245; *see also id.* at 248–49.

223. *Id.* at 245.

224. *Id.* at 249.

225. *Id.* at 250.

226. *Id.* at 249.

227. 157 N.Y.S. 819 (Sup. Ct. 1916).

228. *See id.* at 819.

229. *Id.* at 820–21.

230. *Id.* at 820 (citations omitted).

231. 115 Ill. App. 27 (1904).

232. *See id.* at 29.

233. *Id.* at 28.

234. *Id.* at 30.

235. 611 N.E.2d 347 (Ohio Ct. App. 1992).

236. Patel v. Navitlal, 627 A.2d 683, 685 (N.J. Super. Ct. Ch. Div. 1992).
237. *Singh*, 611 N.E.2d at 350.
238. *Id.* at 348 (internal quotation marks omitted).
239. *Id.* at 351 (internal quotation marks omitted).
240. *See id.* at 349.
241. *Id.* at 350 (citation omitted).
242. *See* J.D. Sumner, Jr., *The South Carolina Divorce Act of 1949*, 3 S.C. L.Q. 253, 257–59 (1951).
243. *See* Act of Apr. 27, 1966, ch. 254, 1966 N.Y. Laws 833.
244. *See* NELSON MANFRED BLAKE, THE ROAD TO RENO: A HISTORY OF DIVORCE IN THE UNITED STATES 7–8 (1962); ISABEL DRUMMOND, GETTING A DIVORCE 71 (1931); GROSSBERG, *supra* note 29, at 251.
245. Act of Feb. 16, 1931, ch. 228, § 1, 1931 Kan. Sess. Laws 336, 336 (capitalization omitted).
246. Act of Apr. 1, 1872, ch. 272, § 1, 1872 Md. Laws 444, 444–45.
247. Act of Apr. 1, 1853, ch. 50, § 1, 1853 Cal. Stat. 70, 70.
248. Caton v. Caton, 17 D.C. (6 Mackey) 309, 310 (1888) (citation and internal quotation marks omitted).
249. *See id.* at 309.
250. *Id.* at 310; *see also* Ritter v. Ritter, 5 Blackf. 81, 81–84 (Ind. 1839).
251. *See* Note, *The Void and Voidable Marriage: A Study in Judicial Method*, 7 STAN. L. REV. 529, 530–31 (1955).
252. *See* Smith v. Smith, 44 N.Y.S.2d 826, 827 (Sup. Ct. 1943).
253. *See* BISHOP, *supra* note 1, at 194–97; 2 WILLIAM T. NELSON, A TREATISE ON THE LAW OF DIVORCE AND ANNULMENT OF MARRIAGE 563–68 (Chicago, Callaghan & Co. 1895); Leonard J. Emmerglick, *Nullity of Marriage for Fraud*, 19 KY. L.J. 295, 306, 310–11 (1931).
254. Bielby v. Bielby, 165 N.E. 231, 233 (Ill. 1929).
255. Hyslop v. Hyslop, 2 So. 2d 443, 445 (Ala. 1941).
256. Marshall v. Marshall, 300 P. 816, 818 (Cal. 1931) (in bank) (per curiam) (citation and internal quotation marks omitted).
257. *See* Millar v. Millar, 167 P. 394, 395–97 (Cal. 1917) (in bank); Bernstein v. Bernstein, 201 A.2d 660, 661–62 (Conn. Super. Ct. 1964); Jett v. Jett, 221 A.2d 925, 926–27 (D.C. 1966); Louis v. Louis, 260 N.E.2d 469, 470–72 (Ill. App. Ct. 1970); Anders v. Anders, 113 N.E. 203, 203–04 (Mass. 1916); Steerman v. Snow, 118 A. 696, 696–98 (N.J. Ch. 1922); Pretlow v. Pretlow, 14 S.E.2d 381, 383, 388 (Va. 1941); Zerk v. Zerk, 44 N.W.2d 568, 569–71 (Wis. 1950).
258. *See* Vileta v. Vileta, 128 P.2d 376, 376–77 (Cal. Dist. Ct. App. 1942); Aufort v. Aufort, 49 P.2d 620, 620–21 (Cal. Dist. Ct. App. 1935); Zoglio v. Zoglio, 157 A.2d 627, 628–29 (D.C. 1960); Stegienko v. Stegienko, 295 N.W. 252, 253–54 (Mich. 1940); Turney v. Avery, 113 A. 710, 710–11 (N.J. Ch. 1921).
259. *See Marshall*, 300 P. at 816–18; Mayer v. Mayer, 279 P. 783, 784, 787–88 (Cal. 1929) (in bank); Williams v. Williams, 118 A. 638, 639 (Del. Super. Ct. 1922); Woodward v. Heichelbech, 128 A. 169, 170–72 (N.J. Ch. 1925).
260. *See* Reynolds v. Reynolds, 85 Mass. (3 Allen) 605, 609–11 (1862); Harrison v. Harrison, 54 N.W. 275, 276 (Mich. 1893); Sinclair v. Sinclair, 40 A. 679, 679–81 (N.J. Ch. 1898).
261. For decisions granting annulments, see Parks v. Parks, 418 S.W.2d 726, 726–28 (Ky. Ct. App. 1967); Masters v. Masters, 108 N.W.2d 674, 675–79 (Wis. 1961).
262. For decisions denying annulments, see Mobley v. Mobley, 16 So. 2d 5, 7 (Ala. 1943); Husband v. Wife, 262 A.2d 656, 656–58 (Del. Super. Ct. 1970); Brandt v. Brandt, 167 So. 524, 525–26 (Fla. 1936).
263. For decisions granting annulments, see Douglass v. Douglass, 307 P.2d 674, 675–76 (Cal. Dist. Ct. App. 1957); Brown v. Scott, 117 A. 114, 114–19 (Md. 1922); Jandro v. Jandro, 246 S.W. 609, 610 (Mo. Ct. App. 1923); Dooley v. Dooley, 115 A. 268, 269–70 (N.J. Ch. 1921). For decisions denying annulments, see Wier v. Still, 31 Iowa 107, 107–11 (1871); Heath v. Heath, 159 A. 418, 418, 425 (N.H. 1932); Brown v. Brown, 112 A.2d 1, 2–3 (N.J. Super. Ct. Ch. Div. 1954).
264. *See* NAT'L CTR. FOR HEALTH STATISTICS, U.S. DEP'T OF HEALTH, EDUC., & WELFARE, 100 YEARS OF MARRIAGE AND DIVORCE STATISTICS UNITED STATES, 1867–1967, at 23 tbl.2 (1973).

NOTES

265. *See* Domschke v. Domschke, 122 N.Y.S. 892, 892–96 (App. Div. 1910); Baiter v. Baiter, 194 N.Y.S.2d 189, 190–94 (Sup. Ct. 1959); Gambacorta v. Gambacorta, 136 N.Y.S.2d 258, 258–59 (Sup. Ct. 1954); Costello v. Costello, 279 N.Y.S. 303, 304–08, 311 (Sup. Ct. 1934).
266. *See* Yucabezky v. Yucabezky, 111 N.Y.S.2d 441, 441–42, 444–46 (Sup. Ct. 1952).
267. *See* Shonfeld v. Shonfeld, 184 N.E. 60, 61–62 (N.Y. 1933); *see also* Siek v. Siek, 95 N.Y.S.2d 234, 234–35 (App. Div. 1950) (per curiam); Tuchsher v. Tuchsher, 184 N.Y.S.2d 131, 132–33 (Sup. Ct. 1959).
268. *See* Family Law Act, ch. 1608, 1969 Cal. Stat. 3314.
269. *See, e.g.*, Herma Hill Kay, *Equality and Difference: A Perspective on No-Fault Divorce and Its Aftermath*, 56 U. CIN. L. REV. 1, 5–14 (1987).
270. *See, e.g.*, CAL. FAM. CODE § 2254 (West 2004); CONN. GEN. STAT. ANN. § 46b-60 (West 2018); MD. CODE ANN., FAM. LAW § 11-102 (LexisNexis 2012); MINN. STAT. § 518.03 (2018); N.Y. DOM. REL. LAW § 236 (McKinney Supp. 2019); WIS. STAT. ANN. § 767.61 (West 2009); Kindle v. Kindle, 629 So. 2d 176, 176–77 (Fla. Dist. Ct. App. 1993); Splawn v. Splawn, 429 S.E.2d 805, 806–07 (S.C. 1993).
271. *See, e.g.*, Janda v. Janda, 984 So. 2d 434, 435–39 (Ala. Civ. App. 2007); Eck v. Eck, 793 S.W.2d 858, 858–59 (Ky. Ct. App. 1990); Seirafi-Pour v. Bagherinassab, 197 P.3d 1097, 1098–101 (Okla. Civ. App. 2008).
272. *See In re* Marriage of Farr, 228 P.3d 267, 268–70 (Colo. App. 2010).
273. *See* V.J.S. v. M.J.B., 592 A.2d 328, 328–30 (N.J. Super. Ct. Ch. Div. 1991).
274. *See* Doe v. Doe, 519 N.Y.S.2d 595, 597–98 (Sup. Ct. 1987).
275. Mims v. Mims, 305 So. 2d 787, 788 (Fla. Dist. Ct. App. 1974) (internal quotation marks omitted).
276. *Id.* at 789–90 (citation omitted).
277. *See* Askew v. Askew, 28 Cal. Rptr. 2d 284, 299 (Ct. App. 1994).
278. *See id.* at 286–88.
279. *Id.* at 295 (emphasis omitted).

Chapter 5

1. *See* Conley v. Romeri, 806 N.E.2d 933, 936–37 (Mass. App. Ct. 2004).
2. *See id.* at 935.
3. *Id.* at 935, 937.
4. *See id.* at 937.
5. *See id.* at 935, 937–38.
6. *Id.* at 935 (internal quotation and alteration marks omitted).
7. *Id.* at 935–36.
8. *See id.* at 935.
9. *Id.* at 936.
10. *Id.* at 937 (citation and internal quotation and alteration marks omitted).
11. *See* Jonathan Saltzman, *Court Opts Not to Delve into an Affair of the Heart*, BOS. GLOBE, Apr. 16, 2004, at B1.
12. *Conley*, 806 N.E.2d at 936 (citation and internal quotation marks omitted).
13. *Id.* at 938 (citation and internal quotation marks omitted).
14. *Id.* (citation and internal quotation and alteration marks omitted).
15. *Id.* at 939.
16. *See id.* at 935, 937.
17. Perry v. Atkinson, 240 Cal. Rptr. 402, 403 (Ct. App. 1987).
18. *See id.* at 403 n.2.
19. *Id.* at 403.
20. *Id.* at 406.
21. *Id.* at 405.
22. Philip Hager & Jane Fritsch, *Bid to Sue Atkinson Thrown Out*, L.A. TIMES, Jan. 9, 1988, pt. II, at 1 (quoting Lee Perry) (internal quotation marks omitted).
23. Jonathan Kaufman, *Harvard Professor Files Fraud Suit*, BOS. GLOBE, Sept. 15, 1982, at 29 (quoting Richard Atkinson) (internal quotation marks omitted).
24. *Perry*, 240 Cal. Rptr. at 405.

25. *Id.*
26. Smith v. Smith, 438 S.E.2d 457, 458 (N.C. Ct. App. 1994).
27. *Id.* at 459.
28. Beers v. Beers, 724 So. 2d 109, 112 & n.2 (Fla. Dist. Ct. App. 1998).
29. *Id.* at 116.
30. *Id.* at 117 n.5.
31. *Id.* at 117.
32. *Id.* at 117 n.5.
33. *Id.* at 116 (emphasis omitted).
34. *See In re* Marriage of O'Neill, 563 N.E.2d 494, 495 (Ill. 1990).
35. *See id.* at 496.
36. *Id.* at 497 (citation and internal quotation marks omitted).
37. *See id.* at 496.
38. *Id.* at 498.
39. *See id.* at 499–504 (Stamos, J., dissenting).
40. *Id.* at 497 (majority opinion) (citation and internal quotation marks omitted).
41. *See id.* at 497–99.
42. *See* Whelan v. Whelan, 56 Va. Cir. 362, 364–65 (2001).
43. *See id.* at 363.
44. *See id.* at 362.
45. *Id.* at 363.
46. *See id.* at 365.
47. *Id.* at 364 (emphasis, citation, and internal quotation marks omitted).
48. *Id.* at 364–65 (internal quotation marks omitted). For another decision refusing to count financial deception as dissipation because it occurred during an ongoing marriage, see Smith v. Smith, 444 S.E.2d 269, 271–72 (Va. Ct. App. 1994).
49. 1 JOEL PRENTISS BISHOP, NEW COMMENTARIES ON MARRIAGE, DIVORCE, AND SEPARATION 194 (Chicago, T.H. Flood & Co. 1891).
50. Reynolds v. Reynolds, 85 Mass. (3 Allen) 605, 607 (1862).
51. BISHOP, *supra* note 49, at 194 (footnote omitted).
52. Leonard J. Emmerglick, *Nullity of Marriage for Fraud*, 19 KY. L.J. 295, 306 (1931).
53. *See* Chipman v. Johnston, 130 N.E. 65, 66 (Mass. 1921).
54. BISHOP, *supra* note 49, at 194.
55. *Reynolds*, 85 Mass. (3 Allen) at 607.
56. *See, e.g.,* IOWA CODE ANN. § 598.31 (West 2001); N.J. STAT. ANN. § 2A:34-20 (West 2010); N.C. GEN. STAT. § 50-11.1 (2017).
57. *See, e.g.,* Sinaei v. Avakian, No. B153242, 2002 WL 31727268, at *1–3 (Cal. Ct. App. Dec. 5, 2002); Hanes v. Giambrone, 471 N.E.2d 801, 807–09 (Ohio Ct. App. 1984).
58. *See* Dunlap v. Current, 57 Conn. L. Rptr. 783, 783–85 (Super. Ct. 2014); Rice v. Monteleone, No. FA020563144S, 2004 WL 503689, at *1–2 (Conn. Super. Ct. Feb. 25, 2004); Stepp v. Stepp, No. 03CA0052-M, 2004 WL 626116, at *1–2 (Ohio Ct. App. Mar. 31, 2004).
59. *In re* Marriage of Meagher & Maleki, 31 Cal. Rptr. 3d 663, 664 (Ct. App. 2005).
60. *Id.* at 665.
61. *Id.* at 664.
62. *See id.* at 665.
63. *Id.* at 666 (internal quotation and alteration marks omitted).
64. *See id.* at 665–66.
65. *Id.* at 666.
66. *Id.* at 666–67.
67. *Id.* at 666 (internal quotation and alteration marks omitted).
68. *See id.* at 664 n.1, 666–67.
69. *Id.* at 664 (citation and internal quotation marks omitted).
70. *Id.* at 667 (emphasis, citation, and internal quotation marks omitted).
71. *Id.* at 669.
72. *See* Francis v. Francis, 21 V.I. 263, 264 & n.1 (Terr. Ct. 1985).
73. *See id.* at 264 n.1.
74. *See id.* at 264 & n.1.

75. *Id.* at 264.
76. *Id.* at 266.
77. *Id.* at 264.
78. *Id.* at 266 (citation and internal quotation marks omitted).
79. *Id.* at 264–65 (footnote and citation omitted).
80. *Id.* at 266.
81. *Id.*
82. 970 N.E.2d 1 (Ill. 2012).
83. *See id.* at 2–3.
84. *See, e.g.,* Erik Brady & Rachel George, *Te'o's 'Catfish' Story Common*, USA TODAY, Jan. 18, 2013, at 1C.
85. *See Bonhomme*, 970 N.E.2d at 2.
86. *See id.* at 2–3.
87. *Id.* at 3 (internal quotation marks omitted).
88. *Id.* at 3–4 (internal quotation and alteration marks omitted).
89. *Id.* at 4 (internal quotation marks omitted).
90. *See id.* at 2, 9–10.
91. *Id.* at 10.
92. *See id.* at 11.
93. *Id.* at 10 (citation and internal quotation marks omitted).
94. *Id.* at 11.
95. For another Illinois Supreme Court decision holding that a person reportedly deceived within a personal relationship could not bring a tort suit for fraudulent misrepresentation, see Doe v. Dilling, 888 N.E.2d 24, 36–40 (Ill. 2008).
96. 198 Cal. Rptr. 273 (Ct. App. 1984).
97. *See id.* at 274.
98. *Id.* at 276.
99. *Id.* at 276 n.3.
100. *Id.* at 276.
101. Perry v. Atkinson, 240 Cal. Rptr. 402, 406 (Ct. App. 1987).
102. 267 Cal. Rptr. 564 (Ct. App. 1990).
103. *See id.* at 565.
104. *See id.* at 568.
105. *See id.* at 565.
106. *Id.* at 564; *see also id.* at 568.
107. *Id.* at 568.
108. R.A.P. v. B.J.P., 428 N.W.2d 103, 104 (Minn. Ct. App. 1988).
109. *Id.* at 108.
110. *Id.* at 107 (footnotes omitted).
111. *Id.* at 108.
112. Doe v. Johnson, 817 F. Supp. 1382, 1385 (W.D. Mich. 1993).
113. *See Magic Johnson Settles AIDS Infection Lawsuit*, COM. APPEAL (Memphis), Dec. 11, 1993, at D3.
114. *See Doe*, 817 F. Supp. at 1384–85.
115. *See id.* at 1387.
116. *See id.* at 1385.
117. *See id.* at 1391–93.
118. *Id.* at 1391.
119. *Id.* at 1393.
120. *Id.* at 1392.
121. *See, e.g.,* JOHN D'EMILIO & ESTELLE B. FREEDMAN, INTIMATE MATTERS: A HISTORY OF SEXUALITY IN AMERICA 354–60 (3d ed. 2012); Allan M. Brandt, *AIDS in Historical Perspective: Four Lessons from the History of Sexually Transmitted Diseases*, 78 AM. J. PUB. HEALTH 367, 367–69 (1988).
122. *Doe*, 817 F. Supp. at 1392 (citation omitted).
123. *See Magic Johnson Settles AIDS Infection Lawsuit, supra* note 113, at D3.

Chapter 6

1. Goodridge v. Dep't of Pub. Health, 798 N.E.2d 941, 948 (Mass. 2003).
2. *Id.* at 955.
3. *Id.* at 954.
4. Obergefell v. Hodges, 135 S. Ct. 2584, 2602 (2015).
5. *Id.* at 2601.
6. *Id.* at 2594.
7. Art Hoppe, *Free Sex*, S.F. CHRON., June 20, 1993, Sunday Punch, at 1.
8. Shulamith Gold, *Don Juan in Court*, CHI. TRIB., Jan. 5, 1993, § 5, at 1 (quoting Camille Paglia) (internal quotation marks omitted).
9. Editorial, *You Can't Criminalize a Person's Caddishness*, STAR-LEDGER (N.J.), Nov. 25, 2014, at 16.
10. *See* Starr v. Woolf, No. C047594, 2005 WL 1532369, at *1 (Cal. Ct. App. June 30, 2005).
11. *See id.* at *1–2, *7.
12. *See id.* at *1, *7.
13. *See id.* at *1.
14. *Id.* at *2.
15. *See id.* at *1.
16. *See id.* at *3, *11.
17. *See id.* at *2.
18. *See id.* at *1.
19. *See id.* at *2.
20. *See id.* at *1, *7.
21. *See id.* at *1.
22. *See id.*
23. *Id.* at *6 (emphasis added).
24. *Id.* at *10 (emphasis added) (citation and internal quotation marks omitted).
25. *See id.* at *1–2.
26. *See id.* at *1, *3, *7, *11.
27. *Id.* at *6.
28. *Id.* at *10.
29. *Id.*
30. *See* Tobon v. Sanchez, 517 A.2d 885, 885–86 (N.J. Super. Ct. Ch. Div. 1986).
31. *Id.* at 885.
32. *Id.* at 886.
33. *Id.*
34. *Id.*
35. *Id.*
36. *See* 8 U.S.C. § 1409 (2012).
37. *See* Nguyen v. INS, 533 U.S. 53, 58–59, 65 (2001).
38. *See Tobon*, 517 A.2d at 886.
39. *See* LaBranche v. LaBranche, 41 Conn. L. Rptr. 171, 173 (Super. Ct. 2006).
40. *Id.* at 172 (citation and internal quotation marks omitted).
41. *See id.*
42. Nerini v. Nerini, 11 Conn. Supp. 361, 365 (Super. Ct. 1943).
43. *See LaBranche*, 41 Conn. L. Rptr. at 172.
44. Woodward v. Heichelbech, 128 A. 169, 170 (N.J. Ch. 1925).
45. *Id.* at 171.
46. Jones v. Jones, 69 N.Y.S.2d 223, 225 (Sup. Ct. 1947) (internal quotation marks omitted).
47. *Id.* at 226.
48. *Id.* at 227.
49. *See, e.g.,* Norton v. McOsker, 407 F.3d 501, 503 (1st Cir. 2005); Brown v. Strum, 350 F. Supp. 2d 346, 347 (D. Conn. 2004); Manko v. Volynsky, No. 95 CIV. 2585 (MBM), 1996 WL 243238, at *1–2 (S.D.N.Y. May 10, 1996); S.H. v. C.C., No. CA2006-12-051, 2007 WL 2410716, at *3 (Ohio Ct. App. Aug. 27, 2007); Walter v. Stewart, 67 P.3d 1042, 1044–46

(Utah Ct. App. 2003); Slawek v. Stroh, 215 N.W.2d 9, 17 (Wis. 1974); J.M. SHORT, CARNAL ABUSE BY DECEIT: HOW A PREDATOR'S LIES BECAME RAPE 31–32, 39 (2013); Bonnie Miller Rubin, *When Tall and Handsome Turns Out Short and Pudgy*, CHI. TRIB., July 30, 2006, at 1.

50. *See, e.g.*, State v. Fitzgerald, 726 P.2d 1344, 1345–47 (Kan. 1986); Ledvinka v. Ledvinka, 840 A.2d 173, 181–82 (Md. Ct. Spec. App. 2003); Butt v. State, 986 So. 2d 981, 982–84 (Miss. Ct. App. 2007); David v. Pillai, 757 N.Y.S.2d 326, 327 (App. Div. 2003); Liming v. Liming, 691 N.E.2d 299, 300–02 (Ohio Ct. App. 1996). For female bigamists, see Estate of Sacchetti v. Sacchetti, 128 A.3d 273, 276–77, 279–81, 283–86 (Pa. Super. Ct. 2015); Jeffco v. Jeffco, No. 402 WDA 2013, 2014 WL 10988175, at *1–5 (Pa. Super. Ct. Jan. 14, 2014).

51. Commonwealth v. Erb, 428 A.2d 574, 574–75 (Pa. Super. Ct. 1981).

52. *See id.* at 575–76.

53. *Id.* at 576 (quoting Emma Welsh).

54. Brown v. Buhman, 947 F. Supp. 2d 1170, 1196 (D. Utah 2013) (citation and internal quotation marks omitted), *vacated as moot*, 822 F.3d 1151 (10th Cir. 2016).

55. *See* Bradley v. Bradley, 56 A.3d 541, 544 (Md. Ct. Spec. App. 2012).

56. *See id.* at 544–45.

57. *Id.* at 545 (internal quotation marks omitted).

58. *See id.*

59. *See id.* at 544–45.

60. *See id.* at 546.

61. *Id.* at 547 (quoting trial judge).

62. *Id.* at 547–48 (quoting trial judge).

63. *Id.* at 549–50; *see also* Lampus v. Lampus, 660 A.2d 1308, 1311–12 (Pa. 1995).

64. *See* Jackson v. Brown, 904 P.2d 685, 687–88 (Utah 1995).

65. *See id.* at 686.

66. *Id.* at 688 (citation and internal quotation marks omitted).

67. *See, e.g.*, Linne v. State, 674 P.2d 1345, 1348–57 (Alaska Ct. App. 1983); People v. Collins, 710 N.Y.S.2d 216, 217–18 (App. Div. 2000).

68. *See* United States v. Jennings, No. 99-2056, 2000 WL 32005, at *1–5 (7th Cir. Jan. 12, 2000).

69. *Id.* at *1.

70. *See id.* at *1–2.

71. *Id.* at *3.

72. *See id.* at *1, *5.

73. *See* Lambert v. State, 243 N.W.2d 524, 526–34 (Wis. 1976), *superseded by statute on other grounds as recognized in* State v. Shah, 397 N.W.2d 492, 495 n.4 (Wis. 1986).

74. *See* Lambert, 243 N.W.2d at 526–28.

75. *See id.* at 531.

76. *See id.* at 526–27.

77. *Id.* at 533.

78. *Id.* at 534.

79. *Id.* at 531.

80. *Id.* at 533–34 (quoting trial judge) (internal quotation marks omitted).

81. *See id.*

82. For criminal cases, see United States v. Booker, 25 M.J. 114, 116 (C.M.A. 1987); Boro v. Superior Court, 210 Cal. Rptr. 122, 126 n.5 (Ct. App. 1985); People v. Evans, 379 N.Y.S.2d 912, 914, 922 (Sup. Ct. 1975), *aff'd mem.*, 390 N.Y.S.2d 768 (App. Div. 1976).

83. *See* Boyles v. Kerr, 855 S.W.2d 593, 594 (Tex. 1993).

84. *Id.* (internal quotation marks omitted).

85. *Id.*

86. *See id.* at 611 (Doggett, J., dissenting).

87. *See id.* at 594 (majority opinion).

88. *See id.* at 595.

89. *Id.* at 601–02.

90. *Id.* at 602 (internal quotation and alteration marks omitted).

91. *See* 567 U.S. 709, 715, 730 (2012) (plurality opinion); *id.* at 730 (Breyer, J., concurring in the judgment).

92. *Id.* at 715–16 (plurality opinion) (citation and internal quotation marks omitted).
93. *See id.* at 713–14.
94. *Id.* at 724.
95. *See id.* at 714.
96. *See id.* at 713–14.
97. *See* 617 F.3d 1198, 1200 (9th Cir. 2010), *reh'g and reh'g en banc denied*, 638 F.3d 666, 673–75 (9th Cir. 2011) (Kozinski, C.J., concurring in the denial of rehearing en banc).
98. 567 U.S. at 722 (plurality opinion).
99. *Id.* at 736 (Breyer, J., concurring in the judgment) (emphasis added).
100. *See* Summers v. Renz, No. H024460, 2004 WL 2384845, at *1–4 (Cal. Ct. App. Oct. 26, 2004).
101. Brad Hamilton, *Bigamist Con Back in Slam*, N.Y. POST, Dec. 17, 2006, at 7; *see also* Marsha Kranes & Jeane MacIntosh, *He Led 2 Lives & Had 12 Wives*, N.Y. POST, June 17, 2005, at 5.
102. *See* Margaret McHugh, *Judge Annuls Con Man's Latest Marriage*, STAR-LEDGER (N.J.), Oct. 20, 2005, at 20; Margaret McHugh & Bill Swayze, *To the Wives He Deceived, 3 Years in Jail Is Far Too Kind*, STAR-LEDGER (N.J.), Sept. 23, 2005, at 1.
103. 676 F.3d 854, 856 (9th Cir. 2012) (en banc).
104. 18 U.S.C. § 1030(a)(4) (2012).
105. *See* 676 F.3d at 856.
106. *See id.* at 856 & n.1.
107. *Id.* at 857 (internal quotation marks omitted).
108. *See id.* at 858.
109. *See id.* at 864.
110. *Id.* at 863–64 (internal quotation marks omitted).
111. *Id.* at 859 (citations and internal quotation marks omitted).
112. *See id.* at 859, 861–62.
113. *Id.* at 861.
114. *Id.* at 862.
115. *Id.; see also* United States v. Drew, 259 F.R.D. 449, 466 (C.D. Cal. 2009).
116. *Nosal*, 676 F.3d at 864 (Silverman, J., dissenting) (emphasis added).

Chapter 7

1. *See* JILL ELAINE HASDAY, FAMILY LAW REIMAGINED 142–55 (2014).
2. Miller v. Pelzer, 199 N.W. 97, 97–98 (Minn. 1924). For Susanna Pelzer's first name, see Miller v. Pelzer, No. 12476, slip op. at 1 (Minn. Dist. Ct. Sept. 14, 1923).
3. *See Miller*, 199 N.W. at 97.
4. *See id.* at 97–98.
5. *See id.* at 97; *Miller*, slip op. at 3.
6. *Miller*, 199 N.W. at 98.
7. *Id.*
8. *Id.* at 97.
9. *Id.* at 97–98.
10. *See* HASDAY, *supra* note 1, at 154–55.
11. *Miller*, 199 N.W. at 97.
12. *Id.* at 98.
13. *See* Harkness v. Fitzgerald, 701 A.2d 370, 371 (Me. 1997).
14. *Id.* at 371–72.
15. *Id.* at 371.
16. *See id.* at 371–73.
17. *Id.* at 371–72.
18. *See id.* at 371–73.
19. *Id.* at 372–73.
20. *Id.* at 373; *see also* Doe v. Roe No. 1, 52 F.3d 151, 152–56 (7th Cir. 1995); Hardesty v. Dulin, No. 91-5151, 1992 WL 189106, at *1 (10th Cir. Aug. 6, 1992); Glaze v. Deffenbaugh, 172 P.3d 1104, 1106–08 (Idaho 2007).

21. Mills v. Atl. City Dep't of Vital Statistics, 372 A.2d 646, 648 (N.J. Super. Ct. Ch. Div. 1977).
22. *Id.* at 652.
23. *Id.* at 648–50.
24. *See id.* at 652–54.
25. *See id.* at 650–52.
26. *Id.* at 651.
27. *See* FLORENCE FISHER, THE SEARCH FOR ANNA FISHER 195–207, 223–24 (1973).
28. Enid Nemy, *Adopted Children Who Wonder, 'What Was Mother Like?,'* N.Y. TIMES, July 25, 1972, at 22 (quoting Florence Fisher) (internal quotation marks omitted).
29. *See* FISHER, *supra* note 28, at 24–27, 31, 34–35, 51–54, 78–79.
30. *See id.* at 53–55, 82–91.
31. *See id.* at 154–55, 166–72, 185.
32. *See id.* at 148, 155–56, 174, 181, 190–91, 207.
33. Mills v. Atl. City Dep't of Vital Statistics, 372 A.2d 646, 655 (N.J. Super. Ct. Ch. Div. 1977).
34. *See id.*
35. *Id.* at 650.
36. *See In re* Adoption of a Child by L.C., 425 A.2d 686, 688 n.1 (N.J. 1981).
37. *Id.* at 687 (emphasis, citation, and internal quotation marks omitted).
38. *Id.* at 689.
39. *Id.* at 690 (citation omitted).
40. *Id.* at 693.
41. *See, e.g.,* Schoen v. Walling, 728 So. 2d 982, 986–87 (La. Ct. App. 1999).
42. *See* Collins v. Huculak, 783 N.E.2d 834, 836–37 (Mass. App. Ct. 2003).
43. *See id.* at 837.
44. *Id.* at 836 (internal quotation marks omitted).
45. *Id.* at 836–38.
46. *See id.* at 837–38.
47. *Id.* at 837 (internal quotation and alteration marks omitted).
48. *See id.* at 836.
49. *Id.* at 838 (internal quotation marks omitted).
50. *Id.* at 841 (internal quotation marks omitted).
51. *Id.* at 837–38 (internal quotation marks omitted).
52. *Id.* at 838 (internal quotation marks omitted).
53. *Id.*
54. *See id.* at 836.
55. *See id.* at 836, 840.
56. Hanna v. Sheflin, 275 S.W.3d 423, 425 (Tenn. Ct. App. 2008).
57. *Id.* at 427.
58. *See id.* at 425.
59. *Id.* at 425, 428 n.5.
60. *Id.* at 425.
61. *See id.* at 426.
62. *Id.* at 425–26.
63. *See id.* at 426.
64. *See id.* at 425, 428.
65. *See id.* at 427–28.
66. *See id.* at 428.
67. *Id.* at 427–28.
68. *Id.* at 425.
69. *Cf.* First State Bank of Miami v. Fatheree, 847 S.W.2d 391, 392–97 (Tex. Ct. App. 1993).
70. *See* Tucek v. Mueller, 511 N.W.2d 832, 833 (S.D. 1994).
71. *See id.* at 833–34.
72. *See id.* at 833.
73. *Id.* at 833, 835.
74. *See id.* at 835–36.
75. *See id.* at 833–34.

76. *See id.* at 837.
77. *See id.* at 834.
78. *Id.* at 836–37.
79. *See id.* at 834, 837.
80. *See id.* at 834.
81. *See id.* at 834–35.
82. *See id.* at 834, 836.
83. *Id.* at 836.
84. *See id.* at 834.
85. *Id.* at 835.
86. *See id.* at 833–34.
87. *See id.* at 833–34 (majority opinion), 840–41 (Amundson, J., dissenting).
88. *Id.* at 834, 836–37 (majority opinion).
89. *See id.* at 834–37.
90. *Id.* at 837 (internal quotation marks omitted).
91. *See id.* at 834.
92. *See id.* at 833–34.
93. *Id.* at 840 (Amundson, J., dissenting).
94. *See, e.g.,* People v. Leonard, 970 N.E.2d 856, 859–60 (N.Y. 2012).
95. *See, e.g.,* Wisconsin v. Yoder, 406 U.S. 205, 231–34 (1972).
96. *See, e.g.,* Solomon v. Solomon, 13 Pa. D. & C.4th 395, 396–99 (Ct. Com. Pl. 1991).
97. *See In re* Doe 4, 19 S.W.3d 322, 326 (Tex. 2000); Philip Galanes, *Coming Out in Time*, N.Y. Times, Aug. 21, 2016, at ST6.
98. *See* State v. Matavale, 166 P.3d 322, 324–27, 341 (Haw. 2007).
99. *See id.* at 324.
100. *See id.* at 324–25.
101. *See id.* at 325.
102. *See id.* at 325–26.
103. *Id.* at 326 (internal quotation marks omitted).
104. *See id.* at 327.
105. *See id.* at 324.
106. *See id.*
107. *See id.* at 331–32, 341.
108. *Id.* at 340.
109. *Id.* at 338.
110. *See id.* at 345 (Nakayama, J., dissenting).
111. *Id.* at 353.
112. *See* W.S. v. Dep't of Pub. Welfare, 882 A.2d 541, 542–48 (Pa. Commw. Ct. 2005).
113. *See id.* at 546.
114. *See id.* at 543, 546.
115. *See id.* at 543.
116. *See id.* at 546.
117. *See id.* at 543, 546.
118. *See id.* at 542–43, 546.
119. *See id.* at 542.
120. *See id.* at 542–43.
121. *Id.* at 543.
122. *Id.* at 546.
123. *See id.* at 543.
124. *Id.* at 546 n.5.
125. *See id.* at 543.
126. *Id.* at 542.
127. *See id.* at 542, 548.
128. *See id.* at 548.
129. *Id.* at 544.
130. *Id.* at 547–48.

131. *Id.* at 546.
132. *Id.* at 543.
133. Gonzalez v. Gonzalez, 887 P.2d 562, 563–65 (Ariz. Ct. App. 1994).
134. Pulchny v. Pulchny, 555 S.W.2d 543, 544–47 (Tex. Civ. App. 1977).
135. Townsend v. Morton, 36 So. 3d 865, 866–69 (Fla. Dist. Ct. App. 2010); *see also* White v. White, 519 S.W.2d 689, 691–94 (Tex. Civ. App. 1975). For a successful criminal prosecution, see State v. Mora, 43 P.3d 38, 39–43 (Wash. Ct. App. 2002).
136. *See* Ligotti v. Ligotti, No. 07-P-500, 2008 WL 2019730, at *1–3 (Mass. App. Ct. May 13, 2008); Compton v. Sesso, No. 03-04-00625-CV, 2006 WL 2032394, at *1–5 (Tex. Ct. App. July 21, 2006). For a successful criminal prosecution, see United States v. Scripps, 599 F. App'x 443, 444–46 (3d Cir. 2015).
137. *See* Lopez v. Taylor, 195 S.W.3d 627, 629–31 (Tenn. Ct. App. 2005).
138. *See id.* at 630, 633–34.
139. *See id.* at 631.
140. *See id.* at 629, 631.
141. *See id.* at 636.
142. *See id.* at 631.
143. *See id.* at 631, 634.
144. *See id.* at 631.
145. *See id.* at 629–31.
146. *See id.* at 632 n.3.
147. *See id.* at 636.
148. *See id.* at 632, 636.
149. *Id.* at 632.
150. *Id.* at 636.
151. *See* Wagner v. Wagner (*In re* Wagner), 492 B.R. 43, 46–60 (Bankr. D. Colo. 2013).
152. *See id.* at 47.
153. *See id.* at 47, 51.
154. *See id.* at 47, 50–51.
155. *See id.* at 48.
156. *See id.* at 54, 56.
157. *See id.* at 48–49, 57.
158. *See id.* at 50.
159. *See id.* at 46.
160. *Id.* at 48.
161. *Id.* at 49.
162. *See id.* at 48, 51–52.
163. *See id.* at 52.
164. *Id.* at 54.
165. *See id.* at 59–60.
166. *Id.* at 54.
167. *See* Sykes v. Sykes, No. B164215, 2004 WL 803279, at *1 (Cal. Ct. App. Apr. 15, 2004).
168. *See id.* at *1, *3.
169. *See id.* at *3.
170. *Id.* at *1.
171. *See id.*
172. *See id.* at *2.
173. *See id.* at *2–3.
174. *Id.* at *2.
175. *Id.* at *4.
176. *See* HASDAY, *supra* note 1, at 161–94.
177. *See* Michaels v. Michaels, 767 F.2d 1185, 1191–206 (7th Cir. 1985); Valle v. Wash. Mut. Bank, No. E045930, 2009 WL 1919392, at *1–4 (Cal. Ct. App. July 6, 2009). For successful criminal prosecutions, see United States v. Okoye, 731 F.3d 46, 47–50 (1st Cir. 2013); United States v. Torres, 251 F.3d 138, 142–52 (3d Cir. 2001); Masterson v. State, No. 49A02-1206-CR-485, 2013 WL 485197, at *1–4 (Ind. Ct. App. Feb. 7, 2013); State v. Stahosky, 836 N.W.2d 769, 770–73 (Minn. Ct. App. 2013).

178. *See* Lee v. Ly, No. G026555, 2002 WL 307902, at *1–8 (Cal. Ct. App. Feb. 27, 2002).
179. *See id.* at *1, *7.
180. *Id.* at *7.
181. *See id.* at *1, *3.
182. *See id.* at *1–2, *7.
183. *See id.* at *8.
184. *See id.* at *1, *3–4, *7–8.
185. *Id.* at *1, *3.
186. *Id.* at *7. For another case in which norms of male supremacy may have helped motivate brothers to deceive their sisters, see Osborn v. Griffin, 865 F.3d 417, 427–32 (6th Cir. 2017).
187. *See* Conway v. Conway, 487 N.W.2d 21, 22–25 (S.D. 1992).
188. *See id.* at 22.
189. *See id.* at 24.
190. *See id.* at 22.
191. *See id.* at 22–24.
192. *See id.* at 22.
193. *Id.* at 24.
194. *See id.* at 23.
195. *See id.* at 22–23.
196. *See id.* at 23, 25.
197. *Id.* at 24 (emphasis and citation omitted).
198. *See id.* at 25.
199. *See* Rimscha v. Suprenant, No. 07-P-509, 2008 WL 756216, at *1–3 (Mass. App. Ct. Mar. 21, 2008).
200. *See id.* at *1–2. For Edward's name, see Brief and Appendix of the Plaintiff-Appellant Adam Rimscha at 2, Rimscha v. Suprenant, No. 07-P-509, 2008 WL 756216 (Mass. App. Ct. Mar. 21, 2008).
201. *See Rimscha*, 2008 WL 756216, at *2.
202. *See* Goodridge v. Dep't of Pub. Health, 798 N.E.2d 941, 948, 969–70 (Mass. 2003); Pam Belluck, *Hundreds of Same-Sex Couples Wed in Massachusetts*, N.Y. TIMES, May 18, 2004, at A1.
203. *Rimscha*, 2008 WL 756216, at *1–2.
204. *Id.* at *2.
205. *See id.* at *1.
206. *See* Conley v. Romeri, 806 N.E.2d 933, 935–39 (Mass. App. Ct. 2004).
207. *See id.* at 935–36.
208. *See id.* at 935–39.
209. *Id.* at 937–39 (citation and internal quotation marks omitted).
210. *Rimscha*, 2008 WL 756216, at *3 (citation and internal quotation marks omitted).
211. *See* Maeberry v. Gayle, 955 S.W.2d 875, 877–82 (Tex. Ct. App. 1997).
212. *See id.* at 877–78.
213. *See id.* at 877.
214. *Id.* at 880–81 (internal quotation marks omitted).
215. *See id.* at 877, 881.
216. *See id.* at 880.
217. *See id.* at 878–79.
218. *Id.* at 880.
219. *Id.* at 880–81.
220. *See id.* at 882.

Chapter 8

1. *See supra* Chapter 3.
2. *See supra* Chapter 5.
3. *See supra* Chapter 7.
4. *See, e.g.*, Martha Chamallas, *The Architecture of Bias: Deep Structures in Tort Law*, 146 U. PA. L. REV. 463, 490–92, 499–500 (1998).

5. 970 N.E.2d 1 (Ill. 2012).

6. *Id.* at 2–3.

7. *Id.* at 10–11.

8. *See supra* Chapter 4.

9. 25 F. Supp. 2d 574 (E.D. Pa. 1998).

10. *Id.* at 575 (quoting Susan Smith's complaint) (internal quotation marks omitted).

11. *See id.* at 578.

12. *See id.* at 575.

13. *See supra* Chapter 5.

14. *See supra* Chapter 4.

15. 31 Cal. Rptr. 3d 663 (Ct. App. 2005).

16. *Id.* at 664.

17. *Id.* at 666 (internal quotation and alteration marks omitted).

18. *See id.* at 667–69.

19. *See supra* Chapter 5.

20. *See supra* Chapter 6.

21. 873 P.2d 871 (Idaho 1994).

22. *See id.* at 873, 876.

23. *See id.* at 873–76.

24. *Id.* at 876.

25. *Id.*

26. *Id.* at 877.

27. *See supra* Chapter 7.

28. *See* JILL ELAINE HASDAY, FAMILY LAW REIMAGINED 148–52, 154 (2014).

29. *See, e.g.,* Troxel v. Granville, 530 U.S. 57, 65–73 (2000) (plurality opinion); Wisconsin v. Yoder, 406 U.S. 205, 232–34 (1972); Pierce v. Soc'y of Sisters, 268 U.S. 510, 534–35 (1925); Meyer v. Nebraska, 262 U.S. 390, 399–403 (1923).

30. *See* DAVID M. ENGEL, THE MYTH OF THE LITIGIOUS SOCIETY: WHY WE DON'T SUE 1–2, 22–30, 172–77 (2016).

31. *See, e.g.,* Gerald B. Hickson et al., *Factors that Prompted Families to File Medical Malpractice Claims Following Perinatal Injuries,* 267 JAMA 1359, 1361–63 (1992); Wendy Levinson et al., *Physician-Patient Communication: The Relationship with Malpractice Claims Among Primary Care Physicians and Surgeons,* 277 JAMA 553, 553–54, 557–59 (1997).

32. *See supra* Chapter 2.

33. *See* HASDAY, *supra* note 28, at 109–10, 115.

34. *See* BRUNO S. FREY, NOT JUST FOR THE MONEY: AN ECONOMIC THEORY OF PERSONAL MOTIVATION, at ix–x, 9–10 (1997); Samuel Bowles, *Policies Designed for Self-Interested Citizens May Undermine "the Moral Sentiments": Evidence from Economic Experiments,* 320 SCIENCE 1605, 1605 (2008); Yuval Feldman & Orly Lobel, *The Incentives Matrix: The Comparative Effectiveness of Rewards, Liabilities, Duties, and Protections for Reporting Illegality,* 88 TEX. L. REV. 1151, 1151–52, 1178–81 (2010); Bruno S. Frey & Reto Jegen, *Motivation Crowding Theory,* 15 J. ECON. SURVS. 589, 589–90 (2001).

35. *See* Nagy v. Nagy, 258 Cal. Rptr. 787, 788–89 (Ct. App. 1989); Koelle v. Zwiren, 672 N.E.2d 868, 870 (Ill. App. Ct. 1996); Dier v. Peters, 815 N.W.2d 1, 3–4 (Iowa 2012); Denzik v. Denzik, 197 S.W.3d 108, 109 (Ky. 2006); Doe v. Doe, 747 A.2d 617, 618 (Md. 2000); Mansfield v. Neff, 31 Mass. L. Rptr. 616, 616–17 (Super. Ct. 2014); G.A.W., III v. D.M.W., 596 N.W.2d 284, 286 (Minn. Ct. App. 1999); Day v. Heller, 653 N.W.2d 475, 476–77 (Neb. 2002); Miller v. Miller, 956 P.2d 887, 891 (Okla. 1998); Pickering v. Pickering, 434 N.W.2d 758, 759–60 (S.D. 1989); Hodge v. Craig, 382 S.W.3d 325, 329 (Tenn. 2012); St. Hilaire v. DeBlois, 721 A.2d 133, 134–35 (Vt. 1998). For suits against biological fathers for deception about paternity, see Richard P. v. Superior Court, 249 Cal. Rptr. 246, 247–48 (Ct. App. 1988); Koestler v. Pollard, 471 N.W.2d 7, 8 (Wis. 1991).

36. *Day,* 653 N.W.2d at 479; *see also Nagy,* 258 Cal. Rptr. at 789; *Dier,* 815 N.W.2d at 8–9; *Miller,* 956 P.2d at 892.

37. *See Nagy,* 258 Cal. Rptr. at 789; *Mansfield,* 31 Mass. L. Rptr. at 617; *Day,* 653 N.W.2d at 477–80; *Miller,* 956 P.2d at 893; *Pickering,* 434 N.W.2d at 761.

38. *See* Tharp v. Black, No. C036767, 2001 WL 1380406, at *1–2 (Cal. Ct. App. Nov. 7, 2001); Stephen K. v. Roni L., 164 Cal. Rptr. 618, 619 (Ct. App. 1980); Welzenbach v. Powers, 660 A.2d 1133, 1134 (N.H. 1995); C.A.M. v. R.A.W., 568 A.2d 556, 556–57 (N.J. Super. Ct. App. Div. 1990); Wallis v. Smith, 22 P.3d 682, 682–83 (N.M. Ct. App. 2001); Jose F. v. Pat M., 586 N.Y.S.2d 734, 735 (Sup. Ct. 1992); Douglas R. v. Suzanne M., 487 N.Y.S.2d 244, 244 (Sup. Ct. 1985); Henson v. Sorrell, No. 02A01-9711-CV-00291, 1999 WL 5630, at *1–2 (Tenn. Ct. App. Jan. 8, 1999); Moorman v. Walker, 773 P.2d 887, 888 (Wash. Ct. App. 1989).
39. *See Tharp*, 2001 WL 1380406, at *3; *Stephen K.*, 164 Cal. Rptr. at 619, 621; *C.A.M.*, 568 A.2d at 562; *Wallis*, 22 P.3d at 683, 686; *Douglas R.*, 487 N.Y.S.2d at 245; *Henson*, 1999 WL 5630, at *2–3; *Moorman*, 773 P.2d at 888.
40. *See Stephen K.*, 164 Cal. Rptr. at 619; *Welzenbach*, 660 A.2d at 1134; *Wallis*, 22 P.3d at 683–84; *Douglas R.*, 487 N.Y.S.2d at 244; *Henson*, 1999 WL 5630, at *2; *Moorman*, 773 P.2d at 888.
41. *See Tharp*, 2001 WL 1380406, at *3; *C.A.M.*, 568 A.2d at 557, 561–62; *id.* at 564 (Stern, J., dissenting).
42. *See Tharp*, 2001 WL 1380406, at *2–3; *Stephen K.*, 164 Cal. Rptr. at 619; *Welzenbach*, 660 A.2d at 1134; *C.A.M.*, 568 A.2d at 557; *Jose F.*, 586 N.Y.S.2d at 735.
43. *See* Nagy v. Nagy, 258 Cal. Rptr. 787, 789–92 (Ct. App. 1989); Richard P. v. Superior Court, 249 Cal. Rptr. 246, 248–50 (Ct. App. 1988); Doe v. Doe, 747 A.2d 617, 618, 621–24 (Md. 2000); Day v. Heller, 653 N.W.2d 475, 478–82 (Neb. 2002); Pickering v. Pickering, 434 N.W.2d 758, 761–62 (S.D. 1989); St. Hilaire v. DeBlois, 721 A.2d 133, 134–36 (Vt. 1998); Koestler v. Pollard, 471 N.W.2d 7, 8–12 (Wis. 1991).
44. *See* Koelle v. Zwiren, 672 N.E.2d 868, 870–71, 873–75 (Ill. App. Ct. 1996); Dier v. Peters, 815 N.W.2d 1, 3, 11–14 (Iowa 2012); Denzik v. Denzik, 197 S.W.3d 108, 109–13 (Ky. 2006); Mansfield v. Neff, 31 Mass. L. Rptr. 616, 616–18 (Super. Ct. 2014); G.A.W., III v. D.M.W., 596 N.W.2d 284, 286–90 (Minn. Ct. App. 1999); Miller v. Miller, 956 P.2d 887, 891–92, 899–905 (Okla. 1998); Hodge v. Craig, 382 S.W.3d 325, 329, 341–44, 346–48 (Tenn. 2012).
45. *See Tharp*, 2001 WL 1380406, at *1–5; *Stephen K.*, 164 Cal. Rptr. at 619–21; *Welzenbach*, 660 A.2d at 1134–36; *C.A.M.*, 568 A.2d at 556–63; *Wallis*, 22 P.3d at 682–86; *Jose F.*, 586 N.Y.S.2d at 735–36; *Douglas R.*, 487 N.Y.S.2d at 244–46; *Henson*, 1999 WL 5630, at *1–7; *Moorman*, 773 P.2d at 888–89.
46. *See Tharp*, 2001 WL 1380406, at *2–5; *Welzenbach*, 660 A.2d at 1134–36; *C.A.M.*, 568 A.2d at 557–59, 563; *Wallis*, 22 P.3d at 685; *Jose F.*, 586 N.Y.S.2d at 736; *Douglas R.*, 487 N.Y.S.2d at 245; *Moorman*, 773 P.2d at 889.
47. *Stephen K.*, 164 Cal. Rptr. at 619 (internal quotation marks omitted).
48. *See id.* at 618–21.
49. *Id.* at 620.
50. *Id.* at 619.
51. *Id.* at 620.
52. *Id.* at 621.
53. *Id.*
54. Wallis v. Smith, 22 P.3d 682, 685 (N.M. Ct. App. 2001).
55. Douglas R. v. Suzanne M., 487 N.Y.S.2d 244, 245 (Sup. Ct. 1985); *see also* Jose F. v. Pat M., 586 N.Y.S.2d 734, 736 (Sup. Ct. 1992).
56. *See Jose F.*, 586 N.Y.S.2d at 735–36; *Douglas R.*, 487 N.Y.S.2d at 244–46.
57. *See* Henson v. Sorrell, No. 02A01-9711-CV-00291, 1999 WL 5630, at *2–3 (Tenn. Ct. App. Jan. 8, 1999).
58. For other examples, *see Jose F.*, 586 N.Y.S.2d at 735–36; Koestler v. Pollard, 471 N.W.2d 7, 9–12 (Wis. 1991).
59. Doe v. Doe, 747 A.2d 617, 618 (Md. 2000).
60. *See id.* at 621–25.
61. *See id.* at 621–22.
62. *Id.* at 621; *see also id.* at 624.
63. *See id.* at 618.
64. *See id.* at 621–22.
65. *Id.* at 624.
66. *See id.* at 618.

67. *See* Nagy v. Nagy, 258 Cal. Rptr. 787, 788 (Ct. App. 1989).

68. *See id.* at 788–89.

69. *Id.* at 789 (internal quotation marks omitted).

70. *Id.* at 791; *see also id.* at 788–89.

71. *Id.* at 791.

72. *See* Richard P. v. Superior Court, 249 Cal. Rptr. 246, 249–50 (Ct. App. 1988); Pickering v. Pickering, 434 N.W.2d 758, 761–62 (S.D. 1989).

73. *See* Day v. Heller, 653 N.W.2d 475, 476–82 (Neb. 2002).

74. *See id.* at 477.

75. *See id.* at 476–77.

76. *Id.* at 479.

77. *See* Moorman v. Walker, 773 P.2d 887, 888–89 (Wash. Ct. App. 1989).

78. *See id.* at 888.

79. *Id.* at 889 (citations and internal quotation marks omitted).

80. *See* Conley v. Romeri, 806 N.E.2d 933, 935–39 (Mass. App. Ct. 2004).

81. *See* Barbara A. v. John G., 193 Cal. Rptr. 422, 425 (Ct. App. 1983). For last names, see Amanda Spake, *Trial and Eros*, MOTHER JONES, July 1985, at 25, 25.

82. *See Barbara A.*, 193 Cal. Rptr. at 426.

83. *See id.* at 425–26.

84. *See id.* at 426.

85. *See id.* at 426–27, 433.

86. *Id.* at 426.

87. *See id.* at 429.

88. *See* 42 U.S.C. § 666(a)(5) (2012).

89. *See id.* § 666(a)(5)(D)–(E); 45 C.F.R. § 302.70(a)(5)(vii) (2017).

90. *See* Martin Kasindorf, *Men Wage Battle on 'Paternity Fraud,'* USA TODAY, Dec. 3, 2002, at 3A.

91. *See* McBride v. Boughton, 20 Cal. Rptr. 3d 115, 118 & n.3 (Ct. App. 2004); Day v. Heller, 653 N.W.2d 475, 477 (Neb. 2002); M.L. v. J.G.M., 132 A.3d 1005, 1007 (Pa. Super. Ct. 2016); Doran v. Doran, 820 A.2d 1279, 1281 (Pa. Super. Ct. 2003).

92. Miscovich v. Miscovich, 688 A.2d 726, 727–28 (Pa. Super. Ct. 1997).

93. *In re* T.S.S., 61 S.W.3d 481, 482–83 (Tex. Ct. App. 2001).

94. Ruth Padawer, *Losing Fatherhood*, N.Y. TIMES, Nov. 22, 2009, Magazine, at 38 (quoting Chandria) (internal quotation marks omitted).

95. *See* Sutton *ex rel.* Minor J. v. Diane J., No. 273519, 2007 WL 840900, at *1 (Mich. Ct. App. Mar. 20, 2007) (per curiam); Mills v. Atl. City Dep't of Vital Statistics, 372 A.2d 646, 650, 655–56 (N.J. Super. Ct. Ch. Div. 1977).

96. *See* Hooper v. Moser, No. M2001-02702-COA-R3-CV, 2003 WL 22401283, at *1 (Tenn. Ct. App. Oct. 22, 2003).

97. *See* Tedford v. Gregory, 959 P.2d 540, 543–44 (N.M. Ct. App. 1998).

98. *See Sutton*, 2007 WL 840900, at *1.

99. *See supra* Chapter 1.

100. *See supra* Chapter 1.

101. *Cf.* Gubin v. Lodisev, 494 N.W.2d 782, 783–87 (Mich. Ct. App. 1992).

102. *See* 26 U.S.C. § 1 (2012).

103. *See* Mapes v. United States, 576 F.2d 896, 898 (Ct. Cl. 1978).

104. *See* Johnson v. United States, 422 F. Supp. 958, 965 (N.D. Ind. 1976).

105. *See* 26 U.S.C. § 1.

106. *See* HASDAY, *supra* note 28, at 53–55.

107. For a similar proposal, see H.R. 9325, 93d Cong. (1973).

108. *See supra* Chapter 2.

109. *See In re* Marriage of Wolhaupter-Heinzel & Heinzel, 816 P.2d 672, 674 (Or. Ct. App. 1991); Miller v. Miller, No. 11-08-00255-CV, 2010 WL 4679884, at *2 (Tex. Ct. App. Nov. 18, 2010).

110. *See In re* Marriage of Ramsey, No. B212724, 2010 WL 1951056, at *3 (Cal. Ct. App. May 17, 2010).

111. *See* Webb v. Pioneer Bank & Tr. Co., 530 So. 2d 115, 116–18 (La. Ct. App. 1988); Coraccio v. Lowell Five Cents Sav. Bank, 612 N.E.2d 650, 652 & n.2 (Mass. 1993); Smith v. Smith, 90 So. 3d 1259, 1264–65 (Miss. Ct. App. 2011).

112. *See In re* Hadad, No. 06-14774 (JKF), 2008 WL 2156354, at *4 n.5, *7 (Bankr. E.D. Pa. May 21, 2008); *In re* Marriage of Fossum, 121 Cal. Rptr. 3d 195, 198, 200 (Ct. App. 2011); Hilger v. Hilger, No. MMXFA104012425S, 2011 WL 6117916, at *4 (Conn. Super. Ct. Nov. 14, 2011).

113. *See* Lezine v. Sec. Pac. Fin. Servs., Inc., 925 P.2d 1002, 1003–14 (Cal. 1996); Ledet v. Ledet, 496 So. 2d 381, 382–84 (La. Ct. App. 1986); Wilson v. Wilson, No. E2002-01636-COA-R3-CV, 2003 WL 21673961, at *2 (Tenn. Ct. App. May 19, 2003).

114. *See* Columbus Bar Ass'n v. Garrison, 628 N.E.2d 1341, 1341–42 (Ohio 1994) (per curiam); *see also In re* Andrion, 929 N.Y.S.2d 113, 113–16 (App. Div. 2011) (per curiam).

115. *See Lezine*, 925 P.2d at 1004; *In re Andrion*, 929 N.Y.S.2d at 114.

116. *See* ARIZ. REV. STAT. ANN. § 25-214 (2017); CAL. FAM. CODE § 1100 (West 2004); *id.* § 1102 (West Supp. 2019); IDAHO CODE § 32-912 (2006); LA. CIV. CODE ANN. arts. 2345–2349 (2009); NEV. REV. STAT. ANN. § 123.230 (LexisNexis 2018); N.M. STAT. ANN. §§ 40-3-13, 40-3-14 (West 2013); TEX. FAM. CODE ANN. §§ 3.102, 5.001 (West 2006); WASH. REV. CODE ANN. § 26.16.030 (West 2016); WIS. STAT. ANN. §§ 766.51, 766.53 (West 2009).

117. *See* CAL. FAM. CODE § 721 (West Supp. 2019); *id.* §§ 1100–1101 (West 2004); LA. CIV. CODE ANN. art. 2354; WIS. STAT. ANN. § 766.15; *id.* § 766.70 (West Supp. 2018).

INDEX

For the benefit of digital users, indexed terms that span two pages (e.g., 52–53) may, on occasion, appear on only one of those pages.